Property of
PERTH COUNTY BOARD OF EDUCATION
School No. 83

# Elements
# of Writing

W9-BMH-517

87. 012

# Elements of Writing

**A Process Rhetoric for Canadian Students**

## William E. Messenger
*University of British Columbia*

## Peter A. Taylor
*University of British Columbia*

Prentice-Hall Canada Inc., Scarborough, Ontario

*For Ann and Sue*

**Canadian Cataloguing in Publication Data**
Messenger, William E., 1931-.
    Elements of writing: a process rhetoric for
    Canadian students

Includes index.
ISBN 0-13-273590-3

1. Exposition (Rhetoric).    2. English language—
Rhetoric.    3. Report writing.    I. Taylor, Peter A.
(Peter Alan), 1936-      II. Title.

LB2369.M47 1984      808'.042      C83-099075-5

©1984 by Prentice-Hall Canada Inc.,
Scarborough, Ontario

ALL RIGHTS RESERVED

No part of this book may be reproduced in any form
without permission in writing from the publishers.

Prentice-Hall Inc., Englewood Cliffs, *New Jersey*
Prentice-Hall International Inc., *London*
Prentice-Hall of Australia, Pty. Ltd., *Sydney*
Prentice-Hall of India Pvt., Ltd., *New Delhi*
Prentice-Hall of Japan, Inc., *Tokyo*
Prentice-Hall of Southeast Asia (PTE.) Ltd., *Singapore*
Editora Prentice-Hall do Brasil Ltda., *Rio de Janeiro*

ISBN 0-13-273590-3

Production Editor: Elynor Kagan
Design: Joe Chin
Production: Alan Terakawa

    2    3    4    5    JD    88    87    86

Typesetting by ART-U Graphics Ltd.
Printed and bound in Canada by John Deyell Company

# Contents

## STAGE FOUR: PRESENTING   313

# Preface

If you are like many people, you think of "writing" as something you find printed in a book. As a student, you probably also think of "writing" as a few pages of prose produced because a teacher asked you for it. It will have an introduction, some sort of middle, and a stiff "In conclusion." And there may be no more to it. If you think of writing solely in this way—as a product—you may not be thinking fully enough about what you want to say and how best to say it; you will likely produce formulaic, mechanical, and therefore predictable essays, designed only to fulfill requirements and earn passing grades. Such an approach to writing, however, may be standing in the way of your getting the grades you really want. More important, it will have been depriving you of the pleasures of writing, which come from using language imaginatively and creatively. Changing the way you think about writing, and working to improve the way you write, will enable you to produce work that is less artificial and more individual, and that has purposes other than merely earning a safe grade. For these reasons we emphasize in this book that writing should also be viewed as a *process,* especially by those who are learning about it and developing their writing skills.

Yet obviously the process of writing is one that does culminate in a finished product—a letter, a book, a memo, a lampoon, an ad, a story, a report, a poem, an article, an essay—though this product is often simply the piece of writing as it exists when the process stops. Although the process could be almost never-ending, the exigencies of life—principally the lack of time—force most of us to stop it at some point; but students often let themselves arrive at that point far too soon.

It is true that for many writers, particularly for long-practised and skilled ones, the process of writing, the process that we outline in Chapter I and that governs the organization of this book, is not always one they follow consciously: much will have become automatic, or be determined by the circumstances surrounding a particular writing task. Nevertheless, as a student you will benefit from careful study of this process and practice in following it. And don't think that becoming a more practised writer is the same as becoming a "safe" or formulaic one; on the contrary, you will become a freer, more individual writer. As you become increasingly familiar with the process, you will better understand not only its demands but also—and more important—the opportunities it offers you at each stage. And though the process will increasingly become almost second nature to you, you must begin by understanding it consciously. You can make intelligent choices among available alternatives only if you know what those alternatives are.

The twofold intent of this book is to introduce, or restore, some of the sense of pleasure in working with words, sentences, paragraphs, and whole essays, and at the same time to demonstrate that writing isn't some mysterious sorcery but a craft that you can learn. This second aim, we hope, will also bring you the pleasures of accomplishment, of overcoming difficulties and embracing opportunities. Further, most of us who teach writing and language and literature enjoy words enough to have some fun with them; we think students should as well. What you will find in this book, then, are practical suggestions for improving your writing, including some ways of having fun in the process.

## Preliminaries

Before you begin a systematic study of this book, browse through it, see the kinds of things it contains. You might even want to read through some sections of it on your own, just for interest. And before you hand in any assignments, you should study Chapter XII (Preparing the Final Draft) and Chapter XIII (Proofreading) so that you will know about manuscript conventions and how to check for such matters as spelling errors.

## Using This Book

You can probably best study *Elements of Writing* from start to finish, following the order of the steps in the writing process. But since this process is recursive, often doubling back on itself, there is nothing sacred about that order; you will not violate it if you choose to start elsewhere than at the beginning and work back and forth as you see fit or as your needs direct. (Do read Chapter I first, however.) The chapters interrelate and overlap, like the parts of the writing process itself. But if nothing dictates a different approach, work through the chapters consecutively.

Because of the nature of the different steps they treat, the chapters vary in length and complexity. Chapters IV and XIV, for example, are the longest and most complex: you will want to spend much more time on them than on one as short as Chapter VI.

In addition to discussions and illustrations, each chapter contains several writing projects. These consist mainly of three kinds: exercises, explorations, and essays. With few exceptions, *exercises* call for short answers, a few words or sentences, or at most brief factual reports; *explorations* call for pieces of writing one or two paragraphs long; and *essays* call for extended pieces of writing. In addition, each of the first ten chapters includes a special exercise dealing with *idioms,* and the first twelve chapters all offer *sentence-combining* exercises as well.

Further, each chapter includes assignments that we call "Playing with Language." Some of these amount to exercises, some to explorations, and some to essays, and they also vary a great deal in their degrees of playfulness; a few, for example, are simply letter or word games, whereas others could serve as topics for explorations or essays. But they all approach language and writing with some sense of play. They should not only prove enjoyable in themselves but also increase your pleasure in working with words and sharpen your sense of language and style.

We hope that most of the projects—particularly the exercises, explorations, and "Playing with Language"—are interesting enough to be tackled on their own, even if they haven't been formally assigned. And many of them can lead to interesting discussions as well as to projects for writing.

Almost all the examples we provide are written by students, people like yourselves; you should feel at home with them, as you might not if confronted solely with pieces by seasoned professionals. Yet, as you will see, many of the student-written examples are excellent; their quality is not beyond your reach.

\* \* \*

For advice and encouragement, we are grateful to many people—colleagues, friends, editors, and others. We are of course grateful for the experience we have gained from our many students over the years. And we extend our special thanks to those students who let us use pieces of their work: Mel-Lynda Andersen, Wendy Armstrong, Allen Bain, Effie Balomenos, Kathleen Bogas, R. J. Butler, Justin Campbell, Wendy Clifford, Elaine Del Medico, Mark Driediger, Yvette Hancock, Sue Inglis, Doug Jeffers, Kevin Kennedy, P. Rauri Lindsay, Susan Lowe, Robin Lowenstein, Sherry Lynn, Bruna Martinuzzi, Debbie Michels, Eithne Moore-Stevens, Mary Oud, Gerald Rowse, Trish Scott, Greg Skwarok, Daniel A. Small, Jim Sparks, George Sranko, Liz Wall, David Williams, Kathy Williams, Tim Wyman, Paul Yokoyama. For permission to quote published material, we are grateful to the following: Alfred A. Knopf, Inc., for an excerpt from Peter Farb, *Word Play: What Happens When People Talk,* copyright 1973 by Peter Farb; Hugh MacLennan, for an excerpt from "By Their Foods…" from *Scotchman's Return* (Macmillan, 1960); Collins Publishers, for an excerpt from Roderick Haig-Brown's "Estuaries," in *Fisherman's Fall;* Grove Press, Inc., for an excerpt from Cecil J. Schneer, *Mind and Matter,* copyright ©1969 by Cecil J. Schneer.

*Writing for me is exclusively process.*
*It becomes a product when the book*
*is finished.*     (Graeme Gibson)

CHAPTER I
# Introduction:
# The Elements of Writing
# and the Process of Writing

Before you examine the writing process in detail, look at the whole rhetorical context in which it occurs. And don't be frightened by the word *rhetorical*: it simply means *having to do with the effective use of language.* Although the word *rhetoric* has acquired a negative secondary meaning—as in the phrase "mere rhetoric," meaning fancy or inflated style with little or no substance—it primarily refers to the study of the elements and principles of effective writing—which is precisely what this book is about. The phrase "rhetorical context," then, simply refers to the overall set of circumstances in which the elements of writing come together and interact to bring about a particular piece of writing.

*It is not enough to know what we*
*ought to say; we must also say it as*
*we ought.*     (Aristotle)

## THE RHETORICAL CONTEXT: THE OCCASION

Any writing project has its origin in a specific context. You are writing on or for a specific occasion, which means that you are writing about a specific subject, to an identifiable reader or group of readers, with a specific purpose in mind, and using language that you have chosen for that occasion. For example, when you write a letter to apply for a job, you present yourself in a way that will give you the best chance of getting an interview with the prospective employer. You write to a reader whose objective is to hire the best applicant, and you try to select and order words in a way that will be most effective for the occasion. In the process, you think about yourself as *writer*, about yourself and your qualifications for the job

1

*(subject)*, about the prospective employer *(audience, reader)*, about your reason for writing the letter—namely to persuade your reader to grant you an interview *(purpose)*, and about the words and style that will best get your message across *(language)*. And you think about the relations between these elements.

The rhetorical context for any writing project can be diagrammed this way:

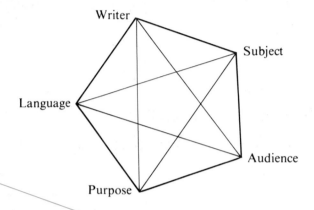

From this diagram you can see that the elements that make up the rhetorical context are all related to one another. Everything connects with everything else. Look at any writing project from each of the points of view: paying close attention to how the elements interact will help you make decisions about how best to proceed at every stage of the process.

Since the occasion of a given piece of writing is its rhetorical context—that is, the whole set of physical and mental circumstances that cause it to come into being—it follows that all the parts of that context will affect the way you compose that piece of writing. To return to our example: Any letter you write applying for a job is first of all occasioned by your need of or desire for that job. But the nature of the specific letter will also depend on your view of yourself in relation to the occasion (how desperately do I need the job?) and in relation to each of the other elements. It will also depend on your view of your subject in relation to the other elements. (How well can you do the job? What special skills or energy could you bring to it?) It will also depend on your awareness of your reader's needs and purposes (he wants to hire the best applicant—but how badly does he need to hire anyone at all?) and also on your view of your reader in relation to the other elements. And so on.

Even time and place can constitute part of the set of circumstances, the occasion, surrounding the writing of the letter and influencing its nature. If the school year is just ending, you may have a lot of competition for the job from other students; if the summer is coming to an end, you'll have less such competition. Either of these conditions could affect the way you write the letter. The kind and amount of your competition could also depend on such circumstances as the rate of unemployment in the region, or even on social and cultural conditions; for example a shortage of particularly skilled or educated people in your town would not only make your task easier but also give you a point to draw to your reader's attention.

Consider each element by itself and in relation to each of the other elements:

***Writer*** You are the writer. On different occasions you will deal with different subjects, purposes, audiences, and linguistic demands, all affecting the way you present yourself and your ideas. In writing, as in conversation, you can't present all of yourself all the time. On some occasions, for example when presenting a lab report, your personality or your taste in music will not enter into it at all; on others, for example when writing a note to a close friend, you already share a good deal of personal experience with your reader and can feel free to express a wide range of your thoughts and feelings.

Here are some questions you can ask about yourself as the writer in different rhetorical contexts:

| | |
|---|---|
| Writer-Subject: | What do I know, think, and feel about my subject? |
| | Did I choose it, or has the occasion determined it for me? |
| Writer-Audience: | What do I know, think, and feel about my audience? |
| | Did I choose it, or does the occasion determine it for me? |
| | What role do I want my readers to play as they read what I am writing? |
| Writer-Purpose: | What is my overall or primary purpose? |
| | Do I have any secondary purposes? |
| Writer-Language: | How can I develop an individual style on this occasion? |

***Subject*** Your subject, put simply, is what you are writing about. But the matter is seldom as simple as that, for different subjects make different demands on you as writer and on your readers; the subject can influence your purpose and your use of language. Further, some subjects are appropriate only for certain kinds of occasions.

Here are some questions to ask about your subject in different rhetorical contexts:

| | |
|---|---|
| Subject-Audience: | Does my subject to any degree determine who my audience is? |
| | Will my subject make any special intellectual or emotional demands on my audience? |
| Subject-Purpose: | To what extent does my subject determine or affect my purpose? |
| Subject-Language: | Does my subject require or discourage any particular linguistic or stylistic choices? |
| Subject-Writer: | What resources of knowledge and experience does this subject invite me to exploit? |

***Audience*** To write effectively, you need constantly to imagine yourself in the role of your readers, for the way you proceed is largely determined by what you perceive as their needs and expectations in relation to the other elements.

Here are some questions to ask about your audience in different rhetorical contexts:

| | |
|---|---|
| Audience-Purpose: | For what purpose will my audience be reading what I write? |
| | To what extent does my audience determine or affect my purpose? |

|                    |                                                                                                    |
|--------------------|----------------------------------------------------------------------------------------------------|
| Audience-Language: | What kind of language is my audience attuned to? What style do they expect on this occasion?        |
| Audience-Writer:   | What does my audience know, think, or feel about me? How can I acceptably establish myself as an individual in the face of their expectations? |
| Audience-Subject:  | What does my audience know, think, or feel about this subject? To what degree does my audience determine my subject? |

***Purpose***   In every piece of writing you have a purpose—sometimes more than one. For example, you may choose to write something in order to argue about some controversial issue, or to describe something beautiful that you saw, or to inform or explain or amuse. Think about the relation of your purpose to the other elements and about the effect purpose can have on those other elements.

Here are some questions to ask about your purpose in different rhetorical contexts:

|                    |                                                                                                    |
|--------------------|----------------------------------------------------------------------------------------------------|
| Purpose-Language:  | To what extent does my purpose determine or affect the language and style I can use on this occasion? |
| Purpose-Writer:    | How does my purpose affect the role I play as writer on this occasion?                               |
| Purpose-Subject:   | Does my purpose to any extent determine my subject?                                                  |
| Purpose-Audience:  | Does my purpose to any extent determine who my audience is?                                          |

***Language***   An unabridged dictionary offers you about half a million words, but not even professional writers, university professors, or top business executives have vocabularies of more than about forty thousand words. The English language, however, is a good deal more than a long list of words: the resources of the language include what we mean by the word *style*, the ways those words can be put together to make statements and ask questions about the world and about the human experience of it, and to influence the way people think and act. Anything you or anyone else writes can use only a limited selection of those resources. How effective that selection is largely depends on how you see the other elements of the rhetorical context.

Here are some questions to begin asking about language and the ways you can use it in different rhetorical contexts:

|                    |                                                                                                    |
|--------------------|----------------------------------------------------------------------------------------------------|
| Language-Writer:   | What constraints does language put on me as a writer? What opportunities does language offer me on this occasion? |
| Language-Subject:  | How will the language and tone I use affect the subject? To what extent does language determine what I know or can find out about the subject or what can be said about it? |
| Language-Audience: | How best can I use language to affect the audience the way I want to? What terms, if any, will I have to define for this audience? |
| Language-Purpose:  | What words will best serve my purpose?                                                               |

These questions about the rhetorical context are not meant to be exhaustive, nor are they all equally important; you can generate still others by continuing to think about the relations between the elements as illustrated in the diagram.

Such questions are not altogether abstract. The kinds of interrelatedness they suggest can affect much of what we do and say. For example, we all know about the bore who can turn a pleasant social luncheon or dinner into an occasion for a formal lecture; he annoys because he misjudges the occasion: that is, he mistakes his audience, his role as speaker, the kind of subject that is appropriate, and the kind of language he should use. If you were to agree to give a talk to a group from your church, the nature of your prospective audience would influence not only your choice of subject but also the language you could use. If you're applying for a job as a child's nurse, you want your language to show sensitivity and lovingness. If you're applying for a job as a computer analyst, you want your language to show that you know the technical terms of the trade. If you attend a certain public lecture, it is probably because of the subject being discussed, and probably also because of the speaker's being an authority on that subject. The language of some northern peoples has dozens of words for snow; we have only one: that is, our language constrains how much we can know and how we can know it. If you keep these questions in mind as you go through the book or as you write, you will soon discover how useful they can be.

## Rhetorical Stance

The position or point of view that you occupy in relation to all these interconnected elements determines your *rhetorical stance* on any given occasion. Your rhetorical stance in turn determines or affects nearly every feature of the style you use for a particular piece of writing. And all these elements of style, working together, constitute your *tone*, which is usually defined as your attitude toward your subject and your audience. But you can just as easily think of *tone* as the quality inherent in a piece of writing that determines how your reader will "hear" it, just as a listener hears your tone of voice when you speak. If your audience is to interpret your writing correctly, you need to be as clear as possible in your own mind about the rhetorical stance or posture you adopt toward them and toward your subject matter on a given occasion. You want to make sure that the attitude you imply is the one you want them to infer.

Your sense of rhetorical stance will naturally influence much of what you do during the planning and drafting stages, but you will usually not need to consider it in self-conscious detail until you begin revising. For that reason we discuss *rhetorical stance* more specifically in Chapter VII.

## THE STEPS IN THE PROCESS OF WRITING

The process of writing consists of four major stages:

Stage One:    Planning
Stage Two:    Writing
Stage Three:  Revising
Stage Four:   Presenting

These stages comprise nine steps:

ONE: PLANNING

Step 1: *Finding a Subject*
Find, choose, or be given a subject.

Step 2: *Narrowing to a Topic*
As much as necessary, limit that subject to a workable topic.

Step 3: *Determining Audience and Purpose*
As precisely as possible, determine and define your audience and your purpose. *Note:* Steps 1, 2, and 3 will often occur together. That is, you will decide or be asked to
   a. inform a certain audience about a particular subject or topic, to explain something to them, or to instruct them;
   b. persuade a certain audience to think or act in a certain way about a particular subject or topic;
   c. amuse or entertain a certain audience with a particular subject or topic, or just interest them in it.

Step 4: *Inventing*
Find things to say about your subject or topic: generate material, discover data, think up ideas. (This step will already have begun during steps 1, 2, and 3.)

Step 5: *Organizing*
Arrange your material, focus on the main idea, and decide how to develop that idea effectively. At this point, if not before, you will need to construct a plan or outline. *Note:* Steps 4 and 5 will often occur together. That is, while you are exploring your subject, searching out ideas, generating material, you will also be determining ways to present it. And during these two steps you will also be circling back to steps 1, 2, and 3 from time to time.

TWO: WRITING

Step 6: *Writing a First Draft*
Write your first draft, following your plan or outline. This is often the easiest part of the process.

THREE: REVISING

Step 7: *Revising: The Several Sweeps*
   a. Go back over steps 1-5, checking the large matters (for example unity and proportion) and looking for ways to improve them.
   b. Examine and reconsider your paragraph structures and strategies: the middle matters.
   c. Examine and reconsider the smaller matters, one by one: sentences, diction, punctuation. Though these are smaller, don't think of them as unimportant: they are the first things your readers will notice.

FOUR: PRESENTING

Step 8: *Preparing a Final Draft*

Prepare the final draft, making sure that the form fits the occasion.

Step 9: *Proofreading*

Check carefully for typographical errors, misspellings, and anything else that may be mechanically wrong.

(*Note:* For handy reference, this outline is reproduced, with relevant page numbers, on the inside front cover of the book.)

Look back over this outline. You can see that the major effort occurs at steps 4, 5, and 7: Inventing, Organizing, and Revising. Steps 1, 2, and 3 are crucial for setting up the project; and steps 8 and 9 are vital for assuring that it looks right. Step 6—writing the first draft—is all too often thought of as the most important, the be-all and end-all of the job of writing. But looked at from the perspective of the larger process as set out here, it can be seen as one of the shortest and most straightforward of the steps—a more-or-less simple step that gets done between the other steps. And a good deal of the process, as you can see, goes on in your head; only parts of it entail putting words, sentences, and paragraphs on paper.

The flow chart on the following page illustrates the nine steps in the process of writing. Note that the straight arrows show how each step leads directly to the next. But the process is usually more flexible than any such rigid diagram can show. For example, during step 4 you could easily be doing some preliminary revising as you generate material and write down words, sentences, maybe even some short paragraphs. And you could even be proofreading while engaged in step 1—for example if you were considering a literary subject and wrote down "Edgar Allen Poe" or "Margaret Lawrence," and then caught the spelling error and corrected it.

Note also that the curved arrows indicate the principal ways in which the process continually circles back on itself. For example, if you change a word or two to sharpen your diction, you might throw the emphasis or rhythm of a sentence out of kilter; rewriting and repunctuating the sentence could mean having to change the whole paragraph to accommodate the revised sentence, perhaps by inserting a new sentence to get a balanced structure, which could mean going back to steps 4 and 5 to generate some new idea of comparison or contrast to put into the new sentence, which in turn could even suggest a whole new perspective on the topic and thus set you to revising all the way from step 2 onwards in order to incorporate the dazzling new idea.

The point is that the basic process is always the same, though different rhetorical contexts will inevitably determine how you emphasize and order the different steps. Most of the nine steps are going on most of the time. Whatever step they are engaged upon at any given moment, writers are constantly cycling and recycling their thoughts, ranging from step 1 to step 9 and back again. But in order to be able to do that comfortably, efficiently, and effectively, you have to understand the nature and requirements of each step; hence you need to study them separately.

And if you don't always take the steps in the same order, neither do you necessarily take all nine of them every time you go through the writing process. It

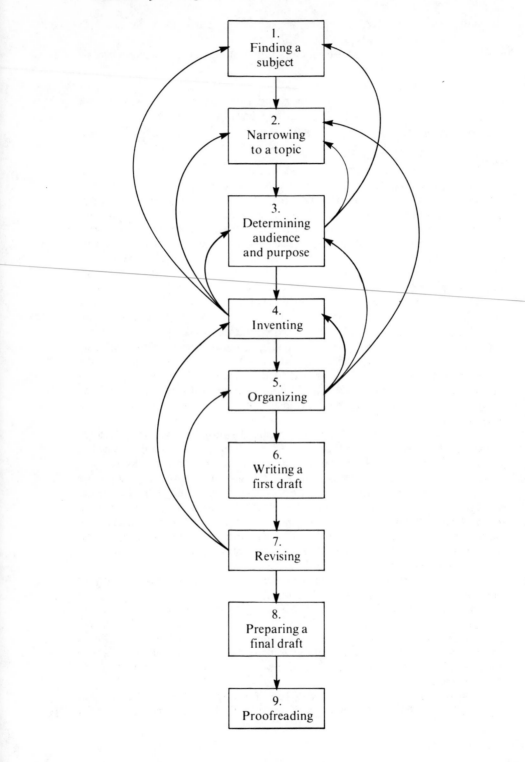

all depends on the occasion. For example, imagine yourself taking an examination in a literature course. The examination question reads, "Discuss the major reasons for the assassination as Shakespeare presents them in *Julius Caesar*." There's your *subject*, all narrowed down to a *topic*, and even partly suggesting a thesis statement—something like "In Shakespeare's *Julius Caesar*, there are both public and private reasons for the assassination." Your *audience*, obviously, is your instructor, and your purpose is similarly clear: the reason you are writing is to demonstrate to your instructor that you understand this part of the motivation of the plot of Shakespeare's play and that you can express yourself reasonably well on the subject. You will carry out this purpose by presenting evidence from the play to support your thesis. Steps 1, 2, and 3, then, would be already taken care of; steps 4 and 5—*inventing* and *organizing*—would require only the mar- shalling of your remembered knowledge of the play into some order that would adequately support the thesis. After only a few minutes of jotting, including sketching a plan, you'd start right in on the *rough draft*. You would try to leave yourself time to do some *revising*—although when you write in class or for an examination most of the little revising you have time for takes place during the writing, so that the first draft is in effect the *final draft* as well. But you would make sure to leave yourself some time for the important final step of *proofreading*.

But if you were assigned a home essay on the reasons for the assassination in *Julius Caesar*, you'd take time to plan more carefully, especially for steps 4 and 5; and you'd have time for much more careful revising than during an examination.

## The Final Steps

In order to illustrate an important principle about the later steps, here is a draft of a student's essay. A simple, unpretentious piece of descriptive writing, it has no particular thesis, its purpose being simply to convey a mood, or the feelings of the writer during the event she describes. Invention, the gathering of material, was no problem: she simply called on her memory of the memorable event and selected the details she wanted to use. Organization was no problem: simple chronological order best suited her purpose. As a plan for so short and straightforward a piece of description, she needed only a list to remind her of the few specific details she wanted to mention: the setting; the wind; the water; the lightning and thunder; the aftermath—and a reminder to herself about pacing the material effectively. The first draft went smoothly, almost without a hitch. And a couple of revising sweeps later, everything seemed pretty well settled. Here is how it reads:

### The Sudden Storm

One day last summer during a peaceful evening, we were relaxing, reading the mail, when a storm came. The sun suddenly disappeared as if it's switch had been pulled. A roll of thunder superseded the laughter of children outside. At first we didn't pay much attention, for thunder storms are a common occurence during Ontario summers. This one had its own ideas, however.

Now, by the window, I am suprised by the velocity of the wind; evident by the helpless flailing of the Lombardi Poplars next door. These trees were at the mercy of the wind. I was certain they'd be snapped in half or totally uprooted at any second. My next realization was that the lawn was under an inch and a half of water. A muddy torrent was rushing down the slope of the lawn past our window. Where was it coming from; how deep would it get? Could it get in the house?

The river kept coming and the rain continued to pelt. At that moment the sky was lit up by lightening and the building shook from the resonating claps of thunder! They were now right over head. This display was repeated several times in rapid succession. I felt exposed near the window, as if the lightening was looking for someone to strike. As I retreated back to the saftey of the room, the next blow struck and the lights went out.

As we sat listening, afraid of what might occur next, the thunder became slowly more distant untill it was inaudible. Then the sun burst forth, and the children returned to their games. The birds sung a thankful tune and hopped about the lawn looking for worms. That peaceful calm of a summer evening had returned. The storm was over. The only reminder was the debris scattered about the lawn where the water had left it as it disappeared back into the earth.

Some students would leave it at that. Others would at least proofread it and catch the spelling errors (all ten) and the awkward present tense at the beginning of the second paragraph (that attempt at greater immediacy just didn't work) and maybe a punctuation error. And they would probably thus save the paper from getting a low grade simply because of its carelessness. If they were careful about their proofreading, they would notice that *poplars* shouldn't be capitalized, and they might even straighten out the awkward handling of the three parallel questions at the end of the second paragraph.

But this student cared about her writing. Since she wrote her drafts soon after the assignment was given, she still had a few days before it was due. She put it away for a couple of days and put it out of her mind. Then she went through it several more times, looking not only for any error or awkwardness she might have missed, but looking also for any ways she could improve it. She found several such opportunities, and at the end of the process submitted this final version:

### A Summer Storm

It happened last summer on a peaceful evening, which began like any other in July. We were relaxing, reading the day's mail, when the storm hit. The sun went out like a turned-off light, and the rolling thunder took over from the laughing taunts of the neighbourhood children. At first we paid little attention; thunderstorms are a common enough occurrence in Ontario summers. But this was something different.

Now at the living room window, I was surprised by the wind's velocity: the towering Lombardy poplars next door flailed helplessly. I was sure that any second they'd be snapped in half or uprooted.

I suddenly realized that the lawn had disappeared under an inch and a half of water. A muddy river was torrenting down the slope of the lawn past the window. Where was it coming from? How deep would it get? Could it get in the house?

The rain kept pelting and the river kept coming. Then for a moment the sky whitened with lightning and the house shook from the resonating claps of thunder, now right overhead. This display was repeated several times in quick succession, like a string of firecrackers. I felt exposed at the window, as if the lightning were seeking someone to spear. And just as I retreated into the safety of the room, the next blow struck and the lights went out.

We sat listening, fearing what might happen next; the thunder became slowly more distant, until it was no longer audible. The sun burst forth as quickly as it had vanished, the children returned to their games, the birds sang a thankful tune while reaping the harvest of worms: the calm of a summer evening had returned. The only reminders of the storm were a styrofoam cup and a few bits of paper strewn about the lawn where the departing water had abandoned them.

Go through the two versions carefully, noting all the changes: each one is an improvement. Here are some of them:

1. The new title is better. (Why?)
2. The beginning is less abrupt; it better suggests the calm before the storm. The punctuation provides a better rhythm. (Why is "*the* storm" better than "*a* storm"?)
3. In the third sentence she tightened the simile. Combining the details of the sun and the thunder in one sentence increases the sense of it all happening at once, suddenly.
4. Changing the last sentence of the first paragraph, she both got rid of *had its own ideas*, a personification that didn't follow logically from the preceding sentence, and avoided letting the paragraph end weakly with the word *however*.
5. She decided, even at this late stage, to change her paragraphing. She decided to risk having two short paragraphs, one dealing with wind and one dealing with water.
6. She tightened the description of the wind, dropping one redundant sentence (with its trite *at the mercy of*) altogether. She substituted an active colon for the incorrectly used semicolon, changed the adjective-noun *helpless flailing* to the more active verb-adverb *flailed helplessly*, changed *certain* to the less formal *sure*, and deleted the redundant and empty intensifier *totally*.
7. In the paragraph about the water, the weak *was* became the more vivid and dramatic *had disappeared*. Since by definition a torrent rushes, she got rid of the redundancy by making the noun *torrent* into a verb, for the nonce.
8. In the next paragraph, she made the two clauses of the first sentence parallel and also put them in the more logical order. She replaced the weak passive voice of *was lit up* with the vivid and active *whitened*, and condensed the third sentence into an adverb modifier at the end of the second sentence. She changed *rapid* to *quick*, which not only sounds quicker but even suggests the sharp cracking of this kind of thunder—and the added simile of the firecrackers further enforces the image. She tightened the personification of the lightning, dropping the usual word for what lightning does, *strike*, in favour of the fresh *spear*, evoking a visual image of the sharp lightning-bolts as they are often seen and drawn. (What is the effect of changing *looking for* to *seeking*? Does the triple alliteration of *s* add anything?) Finally, she tightened the connection between the last two sentences by adding *And just* at the beginning of the last sentence.
9. In the last paragraph, dropping the *As* sharpens the opening, makes it more tautly dramatic. (And why is *happen* better than *occur*?) She decided to handle the next details as a series of three independent clauses leading up to a colon which introduces the climactic clause. And she much improved the final image by changing the general *debris* into specific and concrete details. And notice how she got rid of the too-obvious concluding statement, *The storm was over*, by simply inserting the prepositional phrase *of the storm* near the beginning of the last sentence.

## Exercise 1A

As we said, the writer made several other changes which we have not itemized and discussed above. List them and try to account for each one (include those we ask about in parentheses). We think each change is an improvement; if you disagree, explain why.

Most instructors would probably have been fairly pleased with the earlier version of this paper—assuming, that is, that proofreading had eliminated the errors. But few would have felt pleased enough to do much more than pass it, with some comments and suggestions about improving style. But instructors reading the second version would be delighted. Even without analyzing it in detail, they would sense its quality, its class, and would recognize it as the work of someone who cares about writing. The work put into it shows through.

Students who stop at the earlier stage, who are evidently content to turn in work that is inadequate, or barely adequate, simply aren't finishing the job; they aren't carrying the process of writing to its end. For an assignment like this one ("Write a brief description—250-350 words—of a scene vivid enough that you remember it in some detail. It can be a simple scene or event; it needn't be something cataclysmic or monumental. Avoid melodrama. Try to evoke in the reader the kind of feelings about the scene that you had at the time. Use some narrative if necessary.")—for such an assignment, once you've decided on your subject scene, little or no invention and planning are necessary. Hence the bulk of the time you spend on the assignment should be devoted to revising. We'd guess that the student who wrote "A Summer Storm" spent at least two hours on it, but probably no more than four. But we'd also guess that she spent at least 75% of her time revising. That is, finishing the first draft took from a half-hour to an hour; the rest of the time, one-and-a-half to three hours, was devoted to careful revising.

The result was a piece of writing that she could hand in with confidence. And she could be pretty sure she'd get a much better grade for it than if she'd stopped with the earlier version.

But important as grades may be, at least to some, they aren't the important point here. Getting good grades will probably make you feel good, but a more important good feeling is the pleasure you get from doing a good job. And this final, overall satisfaction isn't the only pleasure: often the principal pleasure is in the process itself. The instructor doesn't need to ask this student if she enjoyed coming up with the word *quick* to replace *rapid*, or if she enjoyed setting up that culminating series in the last paragraph, or if she got a kick out of creating that highly appropriate metaphor about the birds and the worms. He can be pretty sure she did. If he has seen the early draft, or has it for direct comparison, he will be quite sure.

## Essay 1A

Write a description according to the assignment quoted three paragraphs above.

## Exploration 1A

Write a one- or two-paragraph description of something or someone you saw yesterday, or a one- or two-paragraph narrative about something that happened to you or that you witnessed yesterday. Before you begin the actual writing, jot down as many details as you can remember about your topic and select the ones you want to use, or decide which ones you want to emphasize in order to convey a dominant impression. (See p. 82.)

## Essay 1B

Write a narrative of personal experience: tell about something that happened to you when you were much younger. If you remember at all vividly something that happened to you when you were a child, it must be because the incident was in some way striking; try to convey that quality in your narrative so that your readers will feel as you do about it. Aim for between 500 and 750 words (two to three typed pages).

## Essay 1C

*Expressive* writing is personal, sometimes emotional; it is less concerned with audience than other kinds of writing, for its purpose is mainly to *express* something the writer feels or thinks. (If you keep a diary, you probably do more expressive writing in it than other kinds.) Write a short expressive piece to convey your feelings about one of the following:

> being a Canadian
> being an Easterner, or a Westerner, or a Maritimer, or…
> being recently arrived in Canada
> being young
> being male, or female

Since this is not for your diary, however, but for someone else to read, exercise some care with your writing; don't just gush it out. (The sample essay describing the summer storm is essentially expressive writing, and you've seen how careful the author of that was.) Also, with the above topics you should be on guard against another possible danger: try not to fall into patterns of easy cliché.

## Idioms 1

When people make a mistake with an idiom, it usually takes the form of using the wrong or *unidiomatic* preposition after a particular verb, adjective, or noun. For example, it is idiomatic to say "the enemy encroached *on* (or *upon*) our territory"; but to say "the enemy encroached *against* (or *into*) our territory," however logical it may sound, is not idiomatic. (Nor would it be correct to omit the preposition and simply say "the enemy encroached our territory.") People whose native language is not English often have difficulty with idioms simply because they haven't grown up hearing and seeing these customary phrases; but some native speakers evidently grow up hearing but not listening to them and thus have similar problems. In any event, starting with this first chapter and continuing through

Chapter IX, we provide a series of short exercises that will give you a chance to find out how well you know idioms and also to practise with some idioms that sometimes cause writers trouble. Keep a list of any of these idioms that you're not sure about, and any others you come across, and study it periodically until you become familiar with them.

These exercises do not ask you simply to fill in a blank with the idiomatic preposition or to circle or underline the correct one of a pair. Rather, in order to give you a surer feel for these idioms and perhaps also to strengthen your vocabulary, each exercise asks you to write sentences using the idioms. This will also give you useful practice in inventing material and composing good sentences. Therefore don't write dull, flat, vague sentences; try to make them interesting to yourself and to anyone else who might read them. For extra practice, you can also compose sentences using the words *without* any accompanying prepositions; most of them—but not all—can be used that way. The exercises in the first three chapters give you the prepositions; after that, you will have to supply them yourself.

Here are some words that can be followed idiomatically by more than just one particular preposition, yielding different meanings or being appropriate to different contexts. Compose at least one sentence using each verb + preposition. Use whatever number (singular or plural) or tense you need to fit your sentences. If you can't figure out how to use a particular word, get help. And when you've finished each exercise, check your results with other people and with a good dictionary that gives information about idioms and usage.

*Examples:*

| | |
|---|---|
| plunge in: | Eric just sat there, silent, motionless, plunged in despair. |
| plunge into: | When Fat Albert plunged into the pool he created a minor tidal wave. |
| confide in: | He pretended to confide in her, but he related only a heavily edited version of his past. |
| confide to: | She confided her deepest secrets to her diary, and kept it under lock and key. |

(Note that the word and the preposition do not always have to occur side by side.)

| | | |
|---|---|---|
| adapt to | compare to | intervene in |
| adapt for | compare with | intervene between |
| adapt from | consist of | mastery of |
| agree with | consist in | mastery over |
| agree to | differ from | treat of |
| agree on | differ with | treat with |

## Sentence-Combining Exercises

Each of the first twelve chapters includes sentence-combining exercises. Doing them will help you gain greater strength and flexibility in your writing by enabling you to acquire more conscious control over a number of sentence patterns. The increased strength will come in part from the confidence you will feel as you learn how to control your sentences; the flexibility will come as you grow more familiar with the variety of ways to express your meaning.

The exercises begin with simple, familiar patterns and build up to more complicated and unusual patterns. By the end you should be able to make informed choices among alternatives and to find the most suitable form for a particular sentence. But the point is not just to learn how to write longer and more complicated sentences. Many sentences need to be short and simple. Indeed, learning to combine sentences will help you see ways to save words by shortening two sentences into one. And you should, as a result of these exercises, be able to write more effectively as you learn to fold your meanings into neater, more efficient packages.

Most of the sentence-combining exercises consist of three steps. First you neatly and accurately copy a model or pattern sentence. This is not a silly or simple-minded step; don't omit it, for writing a sentence out will help you feel its structure and help imprint the pattern on your mind. Next you practise the pattern by combining pairs of sentences into single sentences. Then you compose sentences modelled on the pattern.

Each exercise ends with a brief explanation of its grammatical and syntactical principles. You may or may not find these notes interesting or useful. Some people find that understanding how sentences work helps them control their writing. Others do better just practising with the sentences themselves, just as some people are content to drive a car by simply stepping on the gas and shifting gears, not concerning themselves with what's going on in the engine and the transmission. Drive whichever way is most comfortable and satisfying for you. (You will find at the end of the book a *Glossary* defining most of the common grammatical and syntactical terms.)

Whether or not you concern yourself with grammar and syntax, practising sentence-combining is almost sure to have a positive effect on your writing. The patterns that follow here and in other chapters don't exhaust the possibilities; rather they illustrate most of the main kinds. Therefore practise them, and make up as many sentences as you like for each one. Experiment with variations, and play around with other patterns you think of or come across. In Chapter XII the exercises are less rigid and controlled, giving you a chance to explore a variety of forms all at once, or several different ways to say the same thing. But start now to explore variations and possibilities on your own. Note for example that different patterns lead to different meanings or emphases, and that different words can sometimes fit into the same patterns (*because* or *though* instead of *and*, for example).

---

## Sentence-Combining 1: Coordination

### Pattern 1A

Base sentence *a*: The train pulled into the station.
Base sentence *b*: We were there to meet it.

Result of combining *a* and *b*:
  The train pulled into the station, and we were there to meet it.

First, COPY the pattern sentence carefully. Be sure to put a comma before the inserted word *and*.

Second, COMBINE each of the following pairs of sentences into a single sentence

modelled on the pattern sentence:
a. I was delighted to get your invitation.
b. I'm sure the party will be a great success.
a. The main switch must be in the "off" position.
b. The back-up generator must be on "standby."

Third, COMPOSE two sentences of your own modelled on Pattern 1A.

In this exercise you are making two simple sentences into a compound sentence by joining them with the coordinating conjunction *and*. (The comma before the *and* is not necessary in all such sentences; see p. 295.)

## *Pattern 1B*

a. Gloria volunteered to finish the report.
b. She doesn't mind working late.

RESULT: Gloria volunteered to finish the report; she doesn't mind working late.

Copy the pattern sentence. Be sure to insert the semicolon.

Combine each of the following pairs into a sentence modelled on the pattern sentence:
a. Summer is nearly over.
b. Classes are about to begin again.
a. Colleen O'Brien will be promoted to manager.
b. Paul Stansky will assume her present job.

Compose two sentences modelled on Pattern 1B.

In this exercise you are making two simple sentences into a compound sentence by joining them with a semicolon. The semicolon indicates a closer relation between the two independent clauses than does a period, which leaves them as two separate sentences.

## *Pattern 1C*

a. I applied for the position immediately.
b. It was three weeks before I received a reply.

RESULT: I applied for the position immediately, but it was three weeks before I received a reply.

Copy the pattern sentence. Be sure to put a comma before the inserted word *but*.

Combine each of the following pairs into a sentence modelled on the pattern sentence:
a. We expected her to return on Thursday.
b. She was apparently delayed by the storm.
a. Most of the players are in good shape.
b. They are having trouble with the new tactics.

Compose two sentences modelled on Pattern 1C.

In this exercise you are making two simple sentences into a compound sentence by joining them with the coordinating conjunction *but*.

## Pattern 1D

a. I intend to buy a home computer.
b. It will help me manage my everyday affairs.

RESULT: I intend to buy a home computer, for it will help me manage my everyday affairs.

Copy the pattern sentence. Be sure to put a comma before the inserted word *for*.

Combine each of the following pairs into a sentence modelled on the pattern sentence:

a. Gloria volunteered to finish the report.
b. She doesn't mind working late.

a. I was delighted to get your invitation.
b. I'm sure the party will be a great success.

Compose two sentences modelled on Pattern 1D.

In this exercise you are making two simple sentences into a compound sentence by joining them with the coordinating conjunction *for*. Always put a comma before *for* as a conjunction, for it prevents its being misread as the preposition *for*.

## Pattern 1E

a. Marie's parents ignored my letter.
b. They refused to return my telephone calls.

RESULT: Marie's parents not only ignored my letter, but they also refused to return my telephone calls.

Copy the pattern sentence, inserting *not only* and *but also*. Note that in sentence *b* the word *they* interrupts *but also*. Be sure to put a comma before *but*.

Combine each of the following pairs into a sentence modelled on the pattern sentence:

a. Acid rain kills lakes.
b. It rots away statues and other stonework.

a. The economy continued to fluctuate wildly.
b. It showed no signs of settling down.

Compose two sentences modelled on Pattern 1E.

In this exercise you are compounding two simple sentences by using the correlative conjunctions *not only* and *but also*.

## Pattern 1F

a. The popularity of the Beatles was highest in the sixties.
b. It lasted well into the seventies.

RESULT: The popularity of the Beatles was highest in the sixties and lasted well into the seventies.

Copy the pattern sentence, noting that you delete the *it* of sentence *b* and that no comma precedes the inserted *and*.

Combine each of the following pairs into a sentence modelled on the pattern sentence:

a.  The president of the club wants new members.
b.  She has asked us to drum up interest among our friends.

a.  The computer revolution is changing the lives of many ordinary people.
b.  It is making a lot of money for manufacturers.

Compose two sentences modelled on Pattern 1F.

In this exercise you are making two simple sentences into one by eliminating the pronoun that repeats the subject. Base sentence *b* then becomes the second half of a compound predicate. You join it to the first half with the coordinating conjunction *and*. (You might wish to use a comma or a dash before the *and* especially if you want emphasis or an ironic tone; see pp. 290-291 and Sentence-Combining 11B.)

## *Pattern 1G*

a.  Marilyn is showing some signs of improvement.
b.  She is still being kept in the intensive-care unit.

RESULT: Marilyn is showing some signs of improvement but is still being kept in the intensive-care unit.

Copy the pattern sentence, noting that you delete the pronoun *she* and that no comma precedes *but*.

Combine each of the following pairs into a sentence modelled on the pattern sentence:

a.  The Zipzap 27B computer has only a 32K memory.
b.  It consistently outperforms its closest competitors.

a.  Bruce writes slowly.
b.  He always gets his work in on time.

Compose two sentences modelled on Pattern 1G.

In this exercise you are again making two simple sentences into one by eliminating the pronoun that repeats the subject. Base sentence *b* then becomes the second half of a compound predicate, as in Pattern 1F; but this time you join the two parts with the coordinating conjunction *but*. (In some instances of this pattern, you might want to use a comma before *but* for a slight pause.)

## *Pattern 1H*

a.  Sam is a good sport.
b.  He is a pleasant companion.

RESULT: Sam is a good sport and a pleasant companion.

Copy the pattern sentence, noting that you delete both *He* and *is* from sentence *b* and that no comma precedes *and*.

Combine each of the following pairs into a sentence modelled on the pattern sentence:

a.  Ottawa is the national capital.
b.  It is a pleasant place to visit.

a.  China is a huge country.
b.  It is increasingly a force to be reckoned with.

Compose two sentences modelled on Pattern 1H.

In this exercise you are making two simple sentences into a single simple sentence by turning the second into the second half of a compound complement after the linking verb *is* and joining it to the first with the coordinating conjunction *and*.

## Pattern 1I

a.  All of his novels contain interesting characters.
b.  They also contain rousing action.
RESULT:  All of his novels contain interesting characters and rousing action.

Copy the pattern sentence. Note that you delete the words *they also contain* and that no comma precedes the inserted *and*.

Combine each of the following pairs into a sentence modelled on the pattern sentence:
a.  The cafeteria offers a salad bar.
b.  It also offers a do-it-yourself sandwich counter.
a.  The union's negotiators insisted on a job-security clause.
b.  They also insisted on a cost-of-living clause.

Compose two sentences modelled on Pattern 1I.

In this exercise you are changing two simple sentences into a single simple sentence by eliminating the subject of the second sentence and turning it into the second half of a compound direct object after a transitive verb. If you want more emphasis on the second part, you can retain the word *also*: All of his novels contain interesting characters and also rousing action.

---

## Playing with Language 1A

A rebus is a puzzle that uses numerals, letters, and pictures to represent a word or phrase or sentence, like

U R 2 good 2 B 4-got-10.

But you can also make word-rebuses, using mainly words and letters (and maybe an occasional diagram to help it along), sometimes using puns and other sound-alikes and anagrams. For example:

| | | |
|---|---|---|
| D     E | S      W | (scattered |
| (square deal) | O      E | showers) |
| A     L | R          S | |
| | H | |

MAN (big man on campus)         ABICAUGHTND (caught in a bind)
campus

WEAR
    (dirty underwear)
DIRTY

GEFLSNEI (mixed feelings)

EN  DS (split ends)

GOGOGOGO (forgo)

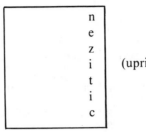

(upright citizen)

Now you see how the game works. Here are a few more for you to figure out:

R
A
O
R

THEATRE

S
E
C
I
R
P

HAND

HAND

KNIHT

ᴄ ᴴ ᴀ ᴵ ᴿ

Make up some of your own. Try them out on friends, or maybe contribute them to a class pool for a puzzling period.

### Playing with Language 1B

Anagrams can be fun. Take for example a simple word like TRACE. At least the following twenty-six words can be made from its letters: ACE, ACT, ACRE, ARC, ARE, ART, ATE, CAR, CARE, CARET, CART, CAT, CATER, CRATE, EAR, EAT, ERA, ETA, RACE, RAT, RATE, REACT, TAR, TARE, TEA, TEAR. We've probably missed one or two, at that. Take a common word like ENGLISH and see how many words you can make out of some or all of its letters. You should be able to make more than fifty without much trouble. Vie with some of your friends or classmates to see who can make the most. Try it out with other words—maybe the name of your home town or your school, or even your own name.

# STAGE ONE:
# Planning

*True ease in writing comes from art, not chance,*
*As those move easiest who have learned to dance.*
(Alexander Pope)

CHAPTER II

# Steps 1, 2, and 3:  Subject; Topic; Audience and Purpose

No one questions how important *planning* is for many of the things people do. You plan a trip in order to use the time to advantage and to avoid confusion and discomfort, but you also plan so that you leave time open to make discoveries along the way. You plan a course of study in order to get the most out of it and to make sure you meet all the requirements. You even plan something as simple as a picnic in order to make sure you bring everything you will need. Yet inexperienced writers too often ignore planning; they simply set down whatever comes to mind and then give it a quick once-over to correct spelling and maybe change a word here and there. But as with most activities that matter, in writing, too, careful planning pays off; it's essential if your writing is to do what you want it to do.

The process of writing consists largely of a series of *choices*. If you plan carefully, you will have a firm ground on which to make subsequent choices. At each step in the writing process you will be choosing among alternatives: you will choose among different views of the subject and different approaches to it; you will decide what to include and what to leave out; you will choose among different methods of presentation; you will even choose among such smaller matters as different kinds of sentences, different words, and different punctuation marks. If you have planned carefully, you will be able to choose consciously, to work by design rather than by accident. And if you make your choices consciously, you can make sure they are consistent: they will support one another and fulfill your objective; your prose will move along logically and smoothly. If your choices are not consistent, if you let chance reign, the result will likely be awkwardness, confusion, even contradiction. Careful planning will enable you to keep your eyes firmly on your objective and therefore to choose consistently.

> *I should not talk so much about
> myself if there were anybody else
> whom I knew so well.*
>
> (Henry David Thoreau)

## STEP 1:  FINDING A SUBJECT

Just as few people have any difficulty finding something to talk about with their
close friends, experienced writers have little difficulty finding subjects to write
about. Subjects come with the territory—not just of being a writer, but of being
alive and human. Subjects are all around us, everywhere, all the time.

Inexperienced writers often think, "What can I write about?" "I can't think
of anything to write about." "I don't know enough about anything to write
about it." Well, there's one subject upon which you are the world's foremost
expert—namely yourself. But of course you can't always write about yourself—at
least not directly. Besides, as a student you will often be assigned a subject to
write about, so the problem doesn't arise.

But suppose you are given an "open" or "free" assignment: Choose any
subject you want, and deal with it any way you want. Don't panic. Rather, start
thinking. Think about yourself, your interests and hobbies, your experiences,
your hopes and fears, your beliefs, your biases; about your friends, their interests,
their experiences; about your family; about your pets; about your town or city,
your school or college or university. Or look around you: chances are there are
dozens of things in view that could be subjects for essays, or could suggest some.
Or read around: in newspapers, magazines, books, even posters and billboards.
Or listen around: to radio, television, what people are talking about. If you
think, look, read, and listen with a piece of paper in front of you and a moving
pencil in your hand, you should soon have a long list of possible subjects.

### Keeping a Journal

One sure-fire way to find subjects to write about is to keep a journal or diary. If
you do so regularly and conscientiously, you will have always at your physical
and mental finger tips a large crop of subjects and ideas just waiting to be
harvested. A good journal is a record of the adventures of your own mind from
day to day; it will be full of things you can and will want to write about—in fact
you will already have begun writing about them in the journal itself. Steps 2 and
4 (topic and invention) will already be under way.

Here is a list of potential subjects generated by about a dozen students after
only a short period of thinking and remembering:

| | | |
|---|---|---|
| cable television | baking | losing weight |
| have-not provinces | relatives | scuba diving |
| dormitory life | traffic | time |
| education | getting a job | books |
| hate | Ottawa | bricks |
| space shuttles | pet control | the Battle of |
| garbage | parents | Trafalgar |
| woman | happiness | Picasso |

| | | |
|---|---|---|
| violence on TV | discipline in | Antarctica |
| violence in sport | elementary schools | neighbours |
| pollution | spoiled kids | comedians |
| hospitals | ballet | student government |
| horses | video games | tennis balls |
| food | music | chess |
| the armed services | old people | blood |
| finding a place | the moon | exercise |
| to live | Canada | the human voice |
| swimming | dogs | contradictions |
| colours | travel | night |
| teachers | interest rates | Beethoven |
| generation gap | fear | small towns |
| kite-flying | weather | Newfoundland |
| spring | the energy crisis | cosmetics |

## Exercise 2A

Take a pencil and a sheet of paper and spend *exactly 15 minutes* jotting down subjects you could or might want to write about. Look around you; close your eyes and think about what you've read or heard in the way of news in the last day or two; think about yourself and other people you know. Let your mind wander; give free association full play. Time yourself exactly—and write fast: you're racing the clock. Chances are you'll end up with a list longer than the one printed above.

## Exercise 2B

Comment on the following as possible subjects for writing. Which ones would need drastic narrowing? Are any simply impossible? Which ones sound too dull? Why? Could any of those be made interesting? Which ones sound most promising? Why? Would some be suitable, but only for a limited audience? Are any too specialized?

| | |
|---|---|
| puppy-love | heroism in war |
| Shakespeare's *Julius Caesar* | TV programs |
| the French Revolution | Halley's comet |
| baking buttermilk biscuits | our high-school play |
| a mother's love | automobiles |
| last summer | clip-boards |
| how the NDP won the federal election | the Tang dynasty |
| tying flies | my new baby kitten |
| ethics | Solidarity |
| living in a basement apartment | pop music |
| architecture in North America | *a, an,* and *the* |
| fear | why students should run this school |
| insect life in Central America | the politics of feminism |
| fad food | pawn moves in chess |
| bricks | pencils |

| | |
|---|---|
| the pleasures of poverty | lasers |
| the function of commas in a novel by Henry James | the Group of Seven |
| | Hamlet's grandmother |
| the canals of Mars | the standard of living in |
| my life so far | South Africa |

---

# STEP 2:  NARROWING A SUBJECT TO A WORKABLE TOPIC

Any job of writing faces restrictions. The most obvious are those of time and space. Before you begin working on a piece of writing, ask yourself two questions:

1.  How much time will I be able to spend on this essay?
2.  How much space do I have—that is, how long can my essay be?

A moment's thought is usually enough to make you realize that your limits are quite severe—and your time will likely be more limited in practice than it seems in anticipation. Further, experience shows that many subjects in the form in which they first come to you are rather large: they will often need drastic *narrowing* or *limiting* before you have *topics* you can realistically expect to treat adequately in the limited time and space you have at your disposal.

Look again at the foregoing list. Most of those *subjects* could more accurately be described as *subject areas*. To try to deal with a subject like "pollution" in a short essay would force you to stay almost entirely at the level of generalizations; you could scarcely do more than repeat the broadest sorts of common knowledge and common feelings about the subject, thus boring your readers silly instead of interesting them with new facts, new ideas, new slants. Only a few of the listed subjects even approach being limited enough for an essay of, say, 1000 words (about four typed pages): "video games," perhaps; or "getting a job"; "losing weight"; "kite-flying." Many are obviously far too broad—"education," for example—though two other items on the list represent at least some narrowing of it: "discipline in elementary schools," "teachers." But even these would clearly need more narrowing. "Teachers," for example, might be further narrowed to "red-haired teachers" or "History teachers I have known" or even "my accident-prone chemistry teacher." Whole books are written about such subjects as "the energy crisis," "old people," and "ballet." Even a seemingly quite narrow subject like "dormitory life" would almost surely require considerable narrowing. "Relatives" has been narrowed to "parents," but not until you got down to something like "the day my dad lost his job" or "my mother's overprotectiveness" would you have a topic narrow enough for a short essay.

Many of the subjects are not only too broad but also too abstract, too vague and general: for example "hate," "music," "colours," "weather." Sometimes simply moving to a more specific example can narrow such a topic: sonatas, Christmas carols, jazz; climate control, how hurricanes form, the blizzard of '82. The next chapter further discusses techniques for limiting these and other such subjects, along with ways to overcome the common feeling of "I don't know enough about it." That is, although we here discuss "narrowing" as a separate step, remember that the process of writing is partly a circular one, especially during the planning stages. Subject-narrowing, focussing on audience and purpose, inventing, and organizing—they all go on together. For example, the questions about audience and purpose that we provide you with in the next few pages, and—even more—the *invention questions* in the next chapter, are also partly devices to help you narrow a subject to a workable topic.

Note that, among the subjects in any such rapidly generated list, not only will some overlap (education and teachers, relatives and parents, have-not provinces and Newfoundland, violence in TV and in sport), but some will also reveal or presume a perspective, an attitude, an approach: "have-not provinces," for example, or perhaps even "Newfoundland," and certainly "my mother's over-protectiveness." In other words, as you begin looking at subjects, and especially as you begin narrowing them, the process of discovering a purpose, perhaps even an audience and a thesis, will already have begun.

## Exercise 2C

Starting from these five subjects,

sarcasm    marriage    hockey    rock music    clothing fashions

a group of students came up with the following list of narrowed topics for possible essays:

1. The key to a stable and everlasting marriage.
2. The implications of choice of clothing for a university student.
3. Defence play in the NHL has deteriorated in the last few years.
4. One teacher's use of sarcasm to maintain discipline in class.
5. Analysis of sarcasm in a political cartoon.
6. Rock isn't the only kind of music teenagers like.
7. The difficulties of keeping up with fashion today.
8. Violence in hockey.
9. Marriage: This is my Mom and Dad.
10. African rhythms in rock music.
11. Uses and misuses of sarcasm.
12. The latest fashion trends in our gymnasium.
13. Rock's greatest guitar player: Jimi Hendrix.
14. Intermarriage helps break down the barriers of racism.
15. If there is a "language of clothes," what is it saying?

Evaluate these topics; perhaps rate each as *good, fair,* or *poor.* What makes the good ones good? Why are the poor ones poor? Can some of the poor or fair ones be revised to make them good? For those not already formulated as such, suggest possible thesis questions or thesis statements.

## Exercise 2D

Below are sixteen subjects of various breadth and generality. For each, provide (a) a limited topic that you think would suit a 2500-word essay (10 typed pages) and (b) one that would suit a 1000-word essay (4 typed pages).

*Examples:*  pollution      (a) cleaning up Lake Erie
                       (b) enforcing the local anti-noise law

           Canadian
           Literature    (a) the treatment of small towns in two Prairie novels
                       (b) imagery in a story by Alice Munro

           politics      (a) some strengths and weaknesses of a minority government
                       (b) polling my neighbourhood

| | |
|---|---|
| 1. forest fires | 9. Picasso |
| 2. journalism | 10. inflation |
| 3. campus architecture | 11. superstition |
| 4. television advertising | 12. conformity |
| 5. crime | 13. sanitation |
| 6. Newfoundland | 14. communication |
| 7. unions | 15. fiction |
| 8. beauty | 16. doubt |

## Exercise 2E

From the following ten subjects or subject areas, select five, and for each one list five different narrowed topics that would be suitable for a 1000-word essay. Then do the same for a 500-word essay.

| | |
|---|---|
| movies | morals |
| transportation | international relations |
| food | travel |
| books | health |
| education | Canadian history |

---

# STEP 3:  DETERMINING AUDIENCE AND PURPOSE

Two other important elements affect any act of writing: *audience* and *purpose*. All too often even experienced writers forget or ignore these constraints; inexperienced writers should be especially alert to them. Neglect of audience and purpose is the root cause of almost all weaknesses in a given piece of writing.

As with the other steps under "Planning," step 3 may occur at almost any time, or little by little as you go through the steps of subject-narrowing, invention, and organization. Similarly, identifying your audience and determining your purpose may occur together, or one may partly or wholly precede the other; one will inevitably influence the other, whenever they occur, which is why we put them together in step 3. The important thing is that you make sure that they do occur consciously during the planning stage. And once you have defined your audience and your purpose, you should keep them constantly in mind as you plan, write, and revise. This linked pair is your indispensable guide to writing effectively in any given instance, whatever your topic. Think of your decisions about audience and purpose as lenses through which you look to focus your material.

> *When the writer becomes the center*
> *of his attention, he becomes a nudnik.*
> (Isaac Bashevis Singer)

## Audience

It is easy to forget that you're writing for a specific reader or group of readers. When you're talking to someone face to face, your listener can easily let you know how you're doing, whether your message is getting across. A nod of the head or a puzzled look will usually let you know if you're communicating successfully. You can adjust what you're saying according to these and other signals: you can speed up or slow down; you can back up and explain more fully; when your listeners indicate that they've had enough, you can stop. But when you're writing, you don't have the advantages of such feedback. For that reason you need to take special care to keep in mind the needs of your readers.

**Audience and Occasion**   The nature of your audience often depends upon the *occasion* for a given piece of writing. If you write in a diary, you have an audience of one, yourself—unless you decide to share it with someone. If you write a letter, you have an audience of one, or of a few specific people. If you write a job application or a memo or a business report you again have a small audience, perhaps one person, or a committee, or a specific group of employees. If you write for a club newsletter or for a special-interest publication of some kind, your audience will still be fairly small and easily definable—at least for your present *purpose*. But when you write for a larger, more general, more remote audience, and when you have less specifically focussed or designated purposes, your audience is more difficult to define.

The larger your audience, the more diverse will be your readers' backgrounds and motives, their levels of education and experience, their goals and values. The greater these differences, the greater the challenge to you as a writer. Hence the importance of keeping your audience, as well as your purpose, constantly in mind: as far as possible, know your readers, understand your readers, write for your readers.

**Audience and Choice**   If for example you know how strongly your readers feel about a particular issue, you'll have a better idea how strongly you have to argue to persuade them to change their minds. You'll know whether you need only a little evidence or a moderate amount of evidence or a great deal of evidence. You'll know whether you can inject a light touch or whether you should maintain a serious tone. If you're writing an informative piece, consider how much your readers already know about the subject, for then you'll know how much information to supply. Too much background and detail will bore your readers or make them impatient; too little will confuse them or simply lose them.

Knowing your audience can sometimes be crucial to the way you present something, to the choices you make. One writer we know, for example, was faced with writing a highly technical and primarily argumentative piece to be presented to a small group of his superiors. But though the audience was relatively small, it was not uniform. Some of the group were fully informed about the past and present state of the subject; to provide basic information about it would seriously risk boring them and insulting their intelligence. Other members of the group had little or no background in the subject; to fail to provide them with basic information would risk preventing their understanding the argument at all. The writer solved his dilemma quite simply. In the first part of his paper he both introduced his argument to his more informed readers and also included enough background information to enable his less informed readers to catch up and follow the argument; but in order to avoid insulting or boring his knowledgeable readers, he put all of the background detail in subordinate clauses and phrases. The information was there, then, for those who needed it, but the main or independent clauses of the sentences carried the main flow of ideas and set the tone. No one was offended or left out.

The purpose of this and the next section is to provide you with ways to help you define your audience and your purpose for any particular job of writing. And as with the next step, inventing, it helps here to have a battery of specific questions to ask, and to *write down* your answers. Don't just think them; *write* them. Writing *is* thinking—and usually better thinking than what occurs without it. In fact, you should work with the questions in steps 3 and 4 at the same time, for the answers you get to the questions in one step will often influence the answers you get to those in the other, and together they will help determine your later choices.

**Audience Variables**   Here is a list of some possible variables among readers; you will be able to think of others as you confront various rhetorical contexts:

| | |
|---|---|
| age | biases |
| income | affiliations |
| social class | cultural |
| education | assumptions |
| occupation | ethnic origin |
| experience | nationality |
| sex | superstitions |
| values | special interests |

Think about these and other variables as you define your audience; awareness of one or another of them could be crucial not only to the larger strategies you adopt but also to the kind of language you use.

Basically you want to try to answer the following questions as well as you can:

Who is my audience?
What do I know about it?
How do I feel toward it?
How precisely can I identify it?
Can I construct a "profile" of it?

It will be of little use to say, "Oh, my audience consists of anyone who is interested in my topic." If you think of your readers that way, you are unlikely to give them any thought at all as you write, and as a result you will be careless and produce the wrong kinds of effects even on those among your actual readers who do happen to be interested in your topic.

## *Exercise 2F*

Examine two or three recent issues of *two* of the following publications; select two that you expect to produce dissimilar results. From what you can infer from their contents, draw up a profile of the readership of each. As a guide, use the list of possible variables on p. 29—added to as necessary. Don't forget to consider advertisements as well as editorial content: the ads can tell you a lot about the supposed readers of the publication they appear in.

| | | |
|---|---|---|
| *Ms* | *Cosmopolitan* | *US News and World Report* |
| *Maclean's* | *The Nation* | *Fortune* |
| *Saturday Night* | *Chatelaine* | *Consumer Reports* |
| *TV Guide* | *The National Geographic* | *The New Statesman* |
| *The Reader's Digest* | *The Canadian Forum* | *The National Review* |
| *The New Yorker* | *Canadian Wildlife* | *Gourmet* |
| *Outdoor Life* | *The Atlantic* | *Homemaker* |

# Purpose

People write for many different purposes, and on many different kinds of occasions. They write

 to express themselves
 to impress others, show off, or gain recognition
 to confess something
 to inform others about something
 to instruct others about something
 to explain something
 to warn about something
 to explain or justify themselves
 to evaluate, judge
 to mock, parody, ridicule, satirize, or otherwise make fun of something or someone
 to criticize adversely
 to praise, eulogize
 to express gratitude
 to share something (ideas, feelings, knowledge) with others
 to arouse interest in something
 to recommend something
 to sell something
 to correct some mistaken view
 to learn about or discover something (e.g. a literary work)
 to investigate, learn the truth about something
 to meet a challenge, whether from a subject or an opposing view
 to attack something or someone
 to console someone
 to encourage someone
 to create a feeling of fellowship, a bond in a common cause
 to shock or outrage or frighten someone

to charm or seduce someone

to reinforce ideas or beliefs (preaching to the converted)

to "improve" others ("consciousness raising")

to make others feel important or right, or just comfortable and good ("stroking")

And surely you can think of still other reasons. No doubt you've already thought of one: to fulfill an assignment. Many people write just to write, to make something out of words—a poem, an essay, a story. They write for their own pleasure; they enjoy writing. And sometimes, to be sure, people write to con others, to confuse, fool, deceive. And of course there is often another motive lying behind the immediate or ostensive reason for an act of writing, namely professional or economic necessity. "No man but a blockhead," according to Samuel Johnson, "ever wrote, except for money."

This list is not meant to be complete, and obviously there is a good deal of overlap among the purposes listed. Nevertheless, as you work on a particular piece of writing, try to think consciously of yourself as writing with one or more of these or other ends in view.

But most of the reasons for writing can be subsumed under three headings:

1. to inform (explain, instruct)
2. to persuade (convince, argue)
3. to entertain (amuse, interest)

These three purposes are not mutually exclusive: often two or sometimes even all three will be present in a given piece of writing, especially if it is long. But most pieces of writing will have one or another of them as their primary or overall purpose, however many secondary purposes they may have as well.

## Questions to Aid in Focussing on Audience and Purpose

The questions that follow will help you arrive at a clear view of your audience and purpose. And always *write down* your answers to the questions. Writing them down helps clarify and stimulate your thinking; it may even give you words and phrases you can use later.

1. *Writer and Subject*
   Do I know my subject personally? How well? Where can I find out more about it, if I need to?

2. *Audience and Subject*
   Does my audience know my subject personally? How well? What background information do they need? Do I need to simplify the subject for them?
   What does the subject mean to them? What do they think or feel about it? Are they likely to be friendly, hostile, or neutral toward it?

If you have a subject, but no clear idea of any audience, ask these questions:
   To whom is this subject important? Who might be interested in it?

If you have an audience in mind, but as yet no subject, or only a vague or broad one, ask these questions:
   What does my audience care about? What kinds of things are important to them?

3. *Writer and Audience*

Do my readers know me at all? How do they feel about me? Are they likely to be friendly, hostile, or neutral toward me?

How do I want them to feel about me?

How do I feel about them?

What do they expect of me?

What *role* do I want them to play?

4. *Purpose and Audience*

Is my audience aware of my purpose before they begin to read—perhaps because of the nature of the occasion, or the medium?

What do I want this particular piece of writing to do for my readers?

What do I want or expect my readers to do as a result of this piece of writing?

Are they likely to be receptive to my purpose, or hostile, or neutral?

Some other questions worth asking about your audience:

How do the members of my audience identify or think of *themselves*? (If you know, you may have to decide whether to appeal to that image, ignore it, or challenge it.)

How large is my audience? (You can't expect to please everyone, as irate letters to the editors of large-circulation publications show. The larger and more heterogeneous the audience, the more difficult it is to satisfy all of them.)

There are also a few questions you should ask about your subject or topic in order to clarify your purpose. The answers to these evaluative questions could—but need not—lead to an argumentative component in an essay or to an argumentative essay:

Is my subject a good thing, or a bad thing? Are its effects good, or bad?

Should it be encouraged, or discouraged?

Should it be changed?

Should it be prevented?

These questions should help you get a clear picture of your audience and your purpose for a particular piece of writing. You'll probably be surprised at how well, and in how much detail, you can answer them if you concentrate on them. Once you've answered them to the best of your ability, draw up a profile of your audience and a statement of your purpose. Write them out and keep them literally and figuratively in view as you proceed with your writing project. Similarly, until such things become second nature, it might be a good idea to type up a list of *do*'s and *don't*'s for any particular piece of writing you're engaged upon—things to guard against and things to strive for, based on your detailed knowledge of your audience and purpose as revealed in your answers to these questions and any others you think to ask.

## The Roles of Writer and Reader

When you write an essay you are playing a role. That is, by the way you use words and sentences—language—you project a voice and a tone (see pp. 151-152). You create a particular image of yourself in order to convey a particular message to a particular audience for a particular purpose on a particular occasion. When you write a letter applying for a job you are not the same person as when you write a letter to a schoolmate about your summer trip abroad. The "you" who writes an essay for your history professor is not the same "you" who writes an angry complaint to a mail-order company about some shoddy merchandise. The voices are different, the tones are different, the images are different: you are playing different roles, each appropriate to its occasion.

Just as you create an image of yourself as writer in a given rhetorical context, so do you to a considerable degree create an image of your readers. By the way you write, you assign your readers a role to play, or at least invite them to play a particular role.

Here is the beginning of a student's "how-to" paper. Note how it establishes a role for both the writer and the readers:

## Italian Spaghetti Sauce—Make Your Own!

People often buy their spaghetti sauce ready-made from the grocery store because they feel incapable of making their own. If you are one of these people, here is a recipe which should prove to you that making spaghetti sauce is a lot easier than you think. Just follow these easy instructions and the result of your efforts will be a spaghetti sauce much more delicious than any you could ever get from a can or a jar.

The writer is playing "teacher" and inviting readers to play "student." Even readers who already know how to make spaghetti sauce will feel comfortable, for they will be interested in possibly learning something new, or at least comparing recipes.

Here is the beginning of another student's essay on exactly the same topic:

## Italian Meat Sauce

The secret in making delicious meat sauce, Italian style, is to let the sauce cook slowly over low heat, for 2 hours. The utensils needed are few: 1 medium size saucepan, and 1 wooden spoon. Begin by lightly covering bottom of saucepan with olive oil. Sauté over low heat: 1 small, finely chopped onion and garlic clove, and 1 lb. ground hamburger.

This beginning may seem to have the virtue of directness, and readers might well infer that they are to play learners to the writer's teacher. But unlike the first example, this one doesn't *create* an occasion and a relationship; rather it *assumes* one, which might be all right if the occasion were different, for example if this were only one of a number of recipes in a collection rather than a piece of writing meant to stand on its own. (Note also the difference between the two titles; and note how this second example shifts into recipe style, using numerals and abbreviations and leaving words out.) But even if some readers are willing to imagine they are reading a cookbook, the writer hasn't made it easy for them. Even willing readers might wonder if "secret in" shouldn't be "secret of" or "secret to" and if there shouldn't be a comma after the word *slowly* or none after *heat*. They would be puzzled by "slowly" and "low heat": wouldn't it be rather difficult to cook something slowly over anything *but* low heat? They might feel pleased to learn that so few utensils are needed—only to be disconcerted two sentences later by finding that they'd better have a chopping knife handy, too (and later still a measuring spoon as well). In their role as readers they would probably find the word *size* unnecessary after *medium*; and in their role as learners they might well wonder if a medium saucepan would be big enough if they wanted to make sauce for ten or twelve people. They might even, unlike readers of the other beginning, wonder what this "meat sauce" was to be used for. Their distrust of this "teacher" would probably increase when they read of "ground hamburger" rather than "ground beef" or just "hamburger." The writer has managed these few opening sentences in such a way that it is almost impossible for even willing readers to settle comfortably into their role.

## THE SPECIAL PROBLEMS OF THE STUDENT WRITER

Students have some particular problems with audience and purpose. If you're in a class in history or economics, for example, your occasion is clear, and your subject area is pretty much determined for you. Even your narrowed topic is often set. In one sense this makes your task easier: you don't have to worry about finding a subject and narrowing it; even your purpose is often determined beforehand. But such circumstances deprive you of some of the freedom of choice you might otherwise exercise. Nevertheless, exercise all the freedom you can; whenever there is room for exploration of a subject, take full advantage of it: most instructors will appreciate fresh, original approaches and ideas on a topic, as long as you stay within reason. In any event, remember this important point: however much freedom you have, be sure to exercise it in the direction of finding a subject you will enjoy working with. If you settle for a subject that bores you, you will probably bore your readers.

In a composition class you will probably be less tied to specific subject matter. You will more often have open assignments, and more chance to practise and experiment with different kinds of subjects and styles. The matter of your audience, however, may remain a problem, since there is often a sense of artificiality about the *occasion* for student writing. When you write an academic essay, you are writing it for your instructor; your instructor is your audience (unless, as sometimes happens, it has been arranged that your essay will be reproduced and distributed to the class for discussion and criticism).

In order to try to avoid this problem of the seeming artificiality of the academic context, some instructors will tell you to write for a "general audience"—that is, an entirely undefined and perhaps quite mythical audience— or for an "audience of your peers," which is to say your classmates. In any event, your *instructor* is the person who will read your essay, pronounce upon its quality, and put a grade on it. So what do you do about this ineluctable fact of academic life?

If you take the easy, the clichéd route, you'll ask, "What does my instructor *want?*" and then try to supply it. And in doing so you may not go wrong. Your broad purpose in writing an academic essay, especially for an examination, is to demonstrate that you understand the material you've been studying and can say something intelligent about it. But even if it isn't something your instructor might consciously "want," your *self* as a thinking individual and a writer should come through, even in an examination essay. And practising with the techniques provided in this and other sections of this book can help that to happen.

"But," you say, "I'm still writing for my instructor. I'm still writing for an audience of one. How do I manage?"

Here's how.

## MAKING YOUR READER YOUR ACCOMPLICE

Your rhetorical task in an academic essay or examination is to allow your teacher to assume a reader's role that is comfortable. He does not *want* to become a judge for the purpose of marking up and displaying the errors in your writing, but you can compel him to take on such a role by putting something unpalatable under his nose. It's far better strategy to allow your reader to assume the role you would like him to assume. At best you'd like him to become a companion on a search for truth, for mutual understanding and even illumination. You might have to settle, however, for a neutral reader, since most of the time you can assume that he starts out with at least a neutral attitude, if not a positive one. What you do with your reader after that is largely up to you. You may, for example, want to cast him in the role of a neophyte for the purposes of receiving instructions on how to do something. Your reader will be willing to play such a role, unless you impose too heavy a demand upon his credulity: he *wants* to be allowed to be friendly and willing to learn; he wants to be a general and receptive but normally skeptical reader. Your task is to allow him to be that.

Even if your teacher is a specialist and you are a generalist (here you're the neophyte), he will be interested in how you bring things together. Suppose you've undertaken an essay for a history class on R. B. Bennett (Prime Minister during the Depression) and his attitudes toward the unemployed in the early 1930's. You're aware that your teacher probably knows a good deal more than you do about both Bennett and the plight of the unemployed in those years. But the role he will accept will likely be that of an interested observer: he will remain genuinely interested (if your writing allows him to be) in the facts and ideas you come up with and in how you put them together. But an inadvertent inaccuracy in historical fact or an ungrammatical or awkward sentence will force him to shift his role from that of willing spectator to that of unwilling proofreader and judge.

Remember: you largely *create* your audience; you suggest to your readers what role they are to play. Your teacher will be an adversary only if you make him one, only if you cast him in that role by what and how you write. Try to keep him on your side—or at least neutral.

---

## *Exercise 2G*

Here is how a possible rhetorical context could take shape:

Suppose you wanted to write an essay on children—a subject that presumably everyone knows something about, if only by virtue of having once been a child. In thinking how you might narrow it, you begin recalling your own childhood, and find yourself focussing on the elementary-school years. Asking who might be interested in such a subject, you quickly think of teachers and parents, and these thoughts prompt you to think about children's education. Your subject is getting narrower, and you're beginning to think about audience. A few days later, when you're returning a book to the library, you notice a sign on the counter announcing that National Library Week is coming up in about a month. You try some random association with your still-percolating writing subject, and remember some happy experiences you had in the library as a child, discovering new books with funny and interesting characters in them. And you remember one of your childhood friends, who wasn't interested in reading, only in sports and television. You too enjoyed sports and television, but you remember that you thought your friend was missing something by not being interested in books. Is there an angle there that would help you focus your writing topic? Perhaps something about the joys or the importance of reading, especially for children? It would be a good topic for an English class, and maybe you could send it to your local newspaper, too: they often publish short pieces by local free-lance writers. You could even tie it in with Library Week. But then your audience would be the general public. No, anyone could read it, of course; but you decide you'd be aiming primarily at parents, those with the power to do something. Teachers could help, and they'd probably read your essay with pleasure. But surely teachers are already thoroughly aware of the importance of encouraging children to read. Now you begin to see that your principal audience is parents of elementary-school children, and that your purpose is partly to inform but mainly to persuade.

(a) Given that rhetorical context, look back over this chapter. Which of the questions about audience and purpose have now been answered? Write them out, with the answers. Then write out the as yet unanswered questions and, imagining yourself to be the writer concerned, supply answers for as many of them as you can. Write up a profile of your audience. List as many of the reasons for writing as you think are applicable (see pp. 31-32), adding any others that you think are appropriate. Finally, compile a list of *do*'s and *don't*'s, as recommended on p. 32.

(b) Make the following change in the rhetorical context: You see an item in the newspaper that says the city government, in order to cut costs during a period of financial restraint, is planning to close several facilities of various kinds, among them the branch library in the neighbourhood where you grew up. You decide to write a letter to the city officials, protesting this plan and arguing that the library should be kept in operation. Now write out the answers that would be different, including a new audience profile and a list of reasons for writing and a list of *do*'s and *don't*'s.

---

## Exploration 2A

Choose some incident that occurred to you within the last week or two and write a short letter about it to two distinctly different audiences or readers, and for two different purposes. Here is an example.

A letter to the Director of Traffic and Security:

> Dear Mr. Huckabye:
>     I am writing to you concerning a very frightening and upsetting incident that happened to me on campus because of the carelessness of a university employee. At approximately 10:00 a.m. on Monday, Sept. 14, I was cycling along the main boulevard, heading to my residence, when I was pushed off the road by a Power Plant vehicle. The truck made a right turn after I was in the intersection, on the right side of the vehicle, and forced me over the curb. I ended up on the ground, and the truck kept going. I was not seriously injured, only badly shaken up, and my bicycle was only slightly damaged; but I think something should be done about the driver.

A bystander told me the truck had the number 17 painted on it. I hope you will share my concern and take immediate action. If I have not heard from you in the next week, I will assume nothing has been done and will take this matter to a higher authority.

Yours truly,

Part of a letter to a friend:

Dear Mike,

. . . . . . . . . . . . . . . . . . . . . . . . . . . . . . . . . .

I've got a story to tell you about the unintelligent nitwits the university employs. Last Monday morning I was riding my bike back to the dorm after a stint in the library when a power-plant truck passed me and made a right turn when I was right beside it. Whoever was driving obviously wasn't watching and I had to swerve into the curb to keep from being clobbered. I smacked into the curb and went sprawling. Luckily I landed on the grass and didn't get hurt, but I wasn't much good for anything the rest of the day. Boy was I mad—the guy didn't even stop! It took a chunk out of my front tire, but didn't do much other damage, maybe a few new scratches on the fender. Anyhow, I got the truck's number and wrote to the traffic and security director about it, and I'd better hear from him this week or I'll raise a stink. I hope nothing like that happens again. I don't think my nerves could take it.

. . . . . . . . . . . . . . . . . . . . . . . . . . . . . . . . . .

So long for now,

## Exploration 2B

(a) Write a short letter to your parents expressing how you feel about the new school year.

(b) Write a similarly short letter on the same subject to a friend your own age and sex, perhaps one who isn't going to school this year, or who is going to school elsewhere.

(c) List six specific differences between the two letters.

## Exploration 2C

James Thurber once remarked (in a letter) on his "own surprising ability to write that hardest of all things, a letter to a girl six years old." Why should writing such a letter be so difficult? Write a short letter to someone you know who is about six, perhaps a relative of the opposite sex (Thurber was referring to his daughter). Send the letter. If you do a good job, you could make a child very happy.

## Exploration 2D

Find a magazine advertisement or billboard or poster that depends almost entirely on a picture rather than on words. Choose one that has at least two people in it, or a person and an animal. Write a brief (about 300-word) combination narrative-description, a brief story that accounts for what seems to be going on in the picture. Your purpose: to satirize; criticize the ad by making fun of it. If necessary, incorporate a brief reference or two to the copy accompanying the ad, but focus on the picture itself.

### Essay 2A

(a) Look up some of the better-known stories from classical mythology (for example Daedalus and Icarus, Hercules, Oedipus, Perseus and Medusa, Demeter and Persephone, Philomela). Choose a tale or an episode from a tale and, in your own words, write it up as a narrative of about 500 words for an audience of your classmates.

(b) Then rewrite it, again in about 500 words, but this time for an audience of seven- or eight-year-old children. Perhaps you can try it out on one or more children you happen to know.

(c) Hand them in together, along with a one- or two-paragraph explanation of the kinds of changes you had to make to adjust your account to the needs of the younger audience.

### Essay 2B

(a) Write a 500-word essay on one of the following large and abstract topics. It won't be easy, but do the best you can. Use the single word as your title. Do not try to narrow the subject.

| | |
|---|---|
| romance | Canada |
| beauty | sports |
| hatred | transportation |
| television | politics |
| architecture | science |

(b) When you have finished that short essay, take the same subject and narrow it down to a small, tightly limited topic. For example, had your original choice of subject been music, your narrowed version of it could be something like "My First Piano Lesson," "What to Listen for in Ragtime," "How to Blow into a Flute," "A New Hit Record," "A Rock-Concert Experience," "A Mozart Melody Analyzed," or "What Is a Sackbut?" Then write an essay of 800-1000 words on your narrowed topic.

(c) Hand the two pieces in together, along with one or two paragraphs commenting on your own experience of writing them. Did you find that, paradoxically, you had more to say about the small topic than about the large one?

### Essay 2C

Write a short expressive essay to convey the mood you feel now, or the one you felt at some point earlier in the day and still remember vividly.

### Essay 2D

Write an essay (not more than 300 words) for the purpose of introducing yourself to someone else in the class. Be honest about yourself, but while you are planning and writing this piece, acknowledge—at least to yourself—how reluctant you are to reveal some things about yourself and how eager you are to display certain other things. How much of your feeling about what you can or cannot say depends on your knowledge or lack of knowledge about your reader?

### Essay 2E

You are E.T. him/her/it-self. Write a report about Earth for your rulers on returning home.

### Essay 2F

Someone we know once remarked, looking back on childhood, youth, and adolescence, "It's amazing how much more intelligent my parents became as I grew older." Did your feelings toward and understanding of your parents or other adults in authority change as you grew up? Write an essay contrasting your attitudes as a child with those you hold as a young adult. Don't get bogged down in sweeping generalizations: get specific.

---

### Idioms 2

See the instructions for the first idiom exercise, p. 14. Here are more words that can be followed idiomatically by more than one preposition. Compose sentences using each.

| | |
|---|---|
| accountable to | contrast to |
| accountable for | contrast with |
| afraid of | grateful to |
| afraid for | grateful for |
| assist at | introduce to |
| assist in | introduce into |
| careless with | prevail on (upon, with) |
| careless of (in, about) | prevail against |
| concur with | pronounce on (upon) |
| concur in | pronounce against |

---

### Sentence-Combining 2: Subordination

### Pattern 2A

Base sentence *a*: The navigator did not have an accurate chronometer.
Base sentence *b*: Therefore he could not plot the ship's position.

Result of combining *a* and *b*:

> Because the navigator did not have an accurate chronometer, he could not plot the ship's position.

First, COPY the pattern sentence carefully, noting the opening *Because*, the comma inserted after sentence *a*, and the omission of *Therefore*.

Second, COMBINE each of the following pairs into a single sentence modelled on the pattern sentence:

a. The committee did not have a clear precedent.
b. Therefore they could make only tentative recommendations.

a. The biologist was frustrated by repeated failures.
b. Therefore he considered abandoning the experiment.

Third, COMPOSE two sentences of your own modelled on Pattern 2A.

In this exercise you are making two simple sentences into a complex sentence by using the subordinating word *because* to turn the first independent clause into a subordinate, or dependent, clause. Subordinating the first clause has the effect of emphasizing the second clause. Combining two such sentences also enables you to avoid the heavy-sounding *Therefore* by expressing the cause-and-effect relation with *because*. The resulting sentence flows more smoothly than the two separate and somewhat choppy sentences.

### *Pattern 2B*

a.  I applied for the position immediately.
b.  It was three weeks before I received a reply.

RESULT:  Although I applied for the position immediately, it was three weeks before I received a reply.

Copy the pattern sentence, noting the opening *Although* and the comma inserted after sentence *a*.

Combine each of the following pairs into a sentence modelled on the pattern sentence:
a.  We expected her to return on Thursday.
b.  She was apparently delayed by the storm.

a.  Bruce writes slowly.
b.  He always gets his work in on time.

Compose two sentences modelled on Pattern 2B.

In this exercise you are making two simple sentences into a complex sentence by using the subordinating word *although* to turn the first into a subordinate clause—in this pattern, as in Pattern 2A, an adverbial clause.

Now, compose five more sentences following the same pattern, but instead of using *although*, start each sentence with a different one of the following subordinators: *if, unless, when, since, until, before, after, as long as*.

### *Pattern 2C*

a.  Bruce always gets his work in on time.
b.  He writes slowly.

RESULT:  Bruce always gets his work in on time, even though he writes slowly.

Copy the pattern sentence, noting that you insert a comma and the words *even though* before sentence *b*.

Combine each of the following pairs into a sentence modelled on the pattern sentence. You may use *even though, although,* or *though* as the inserted term. And the comma in this pattern is sometimes optional.
a.  The players are having trouble with the new tactics.
b.  Most of them are in good shape.

a.  The Zipzap 27B computer consistently outperforms its closest competitors.
b.  It has only a 32K memory.

Compose two sentences modelled on Pattern 2C.

In this exercise, as in Pattern 2B, you are forming a complex sentence by inserting a subordinator like *even though* or *although* in front of one of two independent clauses. This time, however, the subordinate clause comes after the main clause instead of before it.

Now compose five more sentences following this pattern, but using the other subordinators listed at the end of 2B. Perhaps you can simply reverse the order of some of the sentences you wrote for 2B, as we did with the sentence about Bruce. Try it.

## Pattern 2D

a. I applied for the position immediately.
b. It was three weeks before I received a reply.

RESULT: I applied for the position immediately, although it was three weeks before I received a reply.

Copy the pattern sentence, noting that you insert a comma and the word *although* before sentence *b*.

Combine each of the following pairs into a sentence modelled on the pattern sentence:
a. We expected her to return on Thursday.
b. She was apparently delayed by the storm.
a. Most of the players are in good shape.
b. They are having trouble with the new tactics.

Note that in this exercise you are doing the same thing as in Patterns 2B and 2C, but that in each of the examples above—all repeated from 2B and 2C—this time the *other* base sentence is subordinated. Try, then, to compose your two sentences for this exercise by simply subordinating the other half of the sentences you wrote for 2A and 2B. Use any of the listed subordinators you want. If that doesn't seem to work, compose a new sentence or two that *will* permit you to subordinate either half—such as in the following examples:

> Although the popularity of the Beatles was highest in the sixties, it lasted well into the seventies.

> The popularity of the Beatles was highest in the sixties, although it lasted well into the seventies.

> Although the quality of most television programs is poor, many of them are highly popular.

> The quality of most television programs is poor, though many of them are highly popular.

The point is that by subordinating one part of such a sentence, you can emphasize the other part. You can choose which of the two clauses to emphasize by leaving it the independent or main clause.

---

## Playing with Language 2A

"What I did last summer" or "How I spent my summer holidays"—the cliché essay topic assigned over and over again by teachers getting students started in a new academic year. For a change try using the topic humorously; write a funny essay on it. Or, to give you a different edge, change the topic slightly: "What I did *not* do last summer," or "What I didn't do last summer, but should have," or "The most boring thing I did last summer" (can you make this interesting?), or "What last summer did to me, not to mention the cat," or "Last summer? That was some laster!"

### Playing with Language 2B

Consider the words used to name a resident of a particular place: Vancouverite, Bostonian, Ottawan (why not Ottawite?), Los Angeleno, New Yorker, Haligonian, Liverpudlian, Glaswegian, and so on. What are the principles, if any, on which derivations of place-names are concocted for the people who live in those places? Are there any rules? What is the word for the inhabitants of your city or town, and others nearby? Why are they called what they are? Could they be labelled differently? Study and compare these and other such terms to see if you can find any patterns. What are the people of Ontario called? What are people from Brandon called? or Yellowknife? or Etobicoke? Do some places simply not have words for their inhabitants? Why? Write up a short report of your findings.

### Playing with Language 2C

Play some "word-golf," a game Vladimir Nabokov was fond of. Four-letter words seem to work best. To play, you start with one word and, by changing one letter at a time (each time making a legitimate word), try to get to another word in as few steps as possible. Thinking of golf, for example, one gets the BALL to the HOLE in just three shots: BALL, HALL, HALE, HOLE. Or one can go from WARM to COOL in five shots: WARM, WORM, WORD, WOOD, WOOL, COOL. Try your hand. You should be able to get from HATE to LOVE in three, from SICK to WELL in four, from SLOW to FAST in six or fewer, from WILD to TAME in five or fewer, from HAIR to BALD in five or fewer, from SOFT to HARD in six or fewer, from HEAT to COLD in four. If you want to play with other than four-letter words, try getting from ONE to TWO. In how few steps can you get the BRIDE to the GROOM? From AYE to NAY shouldn't take you more than seven steps. A DOG becomes a CAT in only three. How about BRICK to STONE? From SLEEP to AWAKE? But four-letter words do work best: How quickly can the LION get to its PREY?

Compete with some of your friends. See who can use the fewest strokes to get from

| | | |
|---|---|---|
| HEAD to FOOT | SOFT to HARD | NOUN to VERB |
| DAWN to DUSK | FARM to CITY | BEER to WINE |
| LORD to LADY | TOWN to CITY | HOME to WORK |

Make up some starting points and destinations of your own. Use a standard dictionary to settle any challenges. (*Note:* It is generally considered unfair to use proper nouns—but you can set your own house rules.)

*You just jot down ideas as they occur to you.*
*The jotting is simplicity itself—it is the occurring*
*which is difficult.* (Stephen Leacock)

CHAPTER III

# Step 4: Inventing, Generating Material

*Inventing*—gathering data and generating ideas—is a step in the process of composition that beginning writers often slight. They seem to think that the necessary material will come of its own accord. And indeed if you do little or no planning, if you just start writing a draft, that is how ideas will come; one idea will call up another until there seem to be enough, and the draft will be done. Essays written that way sometimes turn out all right, but usually they will be shallow, slight, relatively empty—the kind in which one or two simple ideas are spun out repetitiously.

To avoid such chancy writing, take advantage of what this chapter offers you: techniques for generating ideas. The word *invent* comes from the Latin *invenire*, meaning to find, to come upon, to discover. This chapter discusses ways to find more and better material, and find it faster, than you would by accident or by casual thinking.

Ideas, opinions, facts, data—the material that goes into a piece of writing has to come from somewhere. If you're writing a narrative of personal experience, you have all the necessary information in your head. Other kinds of writing—expository or argumentative—will sometimes require you to get material from other sources, such as newspapers, magazines, scholarly journals, books, and discussions with other people. We are thinking here not of the library research paper—the subject of Chapter XIV—but of essays that require two or three outside sources for some statistics to bolster an argument, or a statement to illustrate a point, or an opinion or two to back up your own.

Such data-gathering often takes place as a matter of course; it offers little difficulty. But even more often, students miss the opportunities for finding more material—and more interesting material—from their own experience; if you settle for too little, the quality of your writing will suffer.

> *The road of excess leads to the palace*
> *of wisdom.*            (William Blake)

## THE PRINCIPLE OF SELECTION

Say you're writing a five-page essay and decide that you need ten basic ideas to furnish it; if you simply take the first ten that come to mind, the essay will probably be weak. If you first find twenty ideas and then use only the best ten, the essay will be much stronger. And think how much better still the quality of your material will be if you start with fifty ideas from which to select the best ten. It's unlikely that the ten you choose will be the ten that first came to mind. Always try to operate on this principle when gathering material: the more you can throw away, the stronger will be what you keep.

> *Language starts in the compost heap*
> *of life.*            (Theodore Roethke)

## BRAINSTORMING

One way to generate material is what is often called "brainstorming": you sit down with blank sheets of paper and quickly jot down everything you can about a proposed subject—anything that comes to mind. Don't stop to analyze or evaluate; just get it all out in front of you. Later you can sift and organize, guided by considerations of audience and purpose. In brainstorming you want to get on paper as many ideas, facts, opinions, statistics, or even wild guesses, as you can. Don't worry about spelling, or style, or writing complete sentences: words, phrases, even abbreviations will do. Let your brain run free and fast; even try free-associating. You'll soon have words, phrases, clauses, sentences, perhaps even diagrams and pictures, scrawled all over the page. As items accumulate and as one idea or train of thought calls up another, you'll begin grouping ideas together, making lists, circling and underlining and marking with asterisks and drawing arrows; the process of selecting and organizing will have already begun.

Often a good way to engage in brainstorming is in a group. Your instructor may want to try it with the whole class, or to divide the class into several groups. If not, try it on your own: even just two or three people bouncing ideas off one another can often generate an astonishing amount of material in a short time.

### Exercise 3A

(a) Pick a subject from the list in the preceding chapter (pp. 23-24), or from the list you made for Exercise 2A—one that you think you know something about—and try brainstorming it. Give yourself about 20 or 30 minutes—no more—and work fast.

(b) Pick another subject from the list, this time one that you think you know little or nothing about, and brainstorm it in the same way. See if you don't surprise yourself by coming up with ideas you didn't think you had.

(c) Now try brainstorming the same subjects with one or more other people. Your results should expand.

---

## INVENTING WITH QUESTIONS

The process of inventing is already going on during steps 1, 2, and 3: when you find or are given a subject, you automatically begin thinking about it; when you narrow the subject to a workable topic, you begin the process of selecting and of developing it; and when you define your audience and your purpose, you clearly begin to select ideas and limit your approach. And just as these steps of focussing are aided by asking questions, so is the step of inventing. In fact, the process of inventing is almost entirely one of asking questions.

For at least two reasons, it is essential that you *write down* whatever answers you come up with:

1. Writing them down enables you to hang onto them. An idea not written down can all too easily drift away, or be driven out of your mind by another idea, even just a few seconds after it comes to you. Writing ideas down puts them on record, so that at a later stage you can look and think your way back through them all, evaluating, selecting, discarding, making connections.
2. The act of writing ideas down will itself inspire further thoughts, generate more ideas. Writing something down forces your mind to work on an idea. And seeing an idea in writing will help stimulate you to come up with other ideas.

Rapidly asking as many questions as you can about your subject is similar to brainstorming, but it should prove more effective in the long run: because you work with a prepared arsenal of questions, including some that will invite imaginative responses, the process is more organized and directed, and less likely to leave gaps. Even if you're working alone, you can pretend to be several people—a whole roomful of people—shouting out questions and answers and suggestions, bouncing ideas off one another, with one of your multiple selves appointed recording secretary for the occasion, jotting down every idea that surfaces. And as with brainstorming, do work fast: don't stop to criticize, evaluate, ponder, or follow up ideas—not yet. Don't stop to think about the results until all the results are in, until you're through—or think you're through. Just keep going, piling up the material.

### The Reporter's Standard Questions

A newspaper reporter's standard formula of *Who-What-Where-When-Why*, with a judicious *How* added, serves well enough for some subjects, especially events:

1. What is it? What is happening?
2. Who is doing it, and to whom?

3. Where and when is it? Where and when is it being done?
4. Why is it? Why is it happening? Why is it being done?
5. How is it happening? How is it being done? With what is it being done?

Answering such questions will yield useful information about many subjects:

1. What: nature, identity, appearance, definition
2. Who: human agents or victims (if any)
3. Where and when: setting, or scene
4. Why: motivation, cause
5. How: method, agency, instrument

You can ask such questions about almost any subject. Take for example the subject "Ottawa." "What is it?" is easy; it's a place, a city, a capital. The "who" questions could produce several kinds of answers, including possibly some victims. So could questions about motivation and method. Such questions could easily help you narrow the subject down to, say, the operation of a single government agency or department. But if you tried such questions on "a brick" or "night," you'd have a harder time. By doing a little twisting and judicious combining, you could derive some useful answers, but your frustration level would probably be high.

When your purpose is not, like a reporter's or a detective's, merely fact-finding, but rather the *generation of ideas*, the *discovery or invention* of material for writing about a given subject, then you'll do better if you increase the spectrum of questions, though including these basic ones. You need *more* questions, and more *kinds* of questions, to minimize frustration and maximize excitement and the production of useful ideas. Since the reason for asking questions about a subject is to prompt your mind and your imagination, the more questions the better.

## QUESTIONS ABOUT IDENTITY

If your subject is a thing, an *object*, you can ask such questions as these:

What is it?
Does it exist?
When does it exist? (When did it exist? When will it exist?)
Where does it exist? (Where did it exist? Where will it exist?)
What is its appearance? (shape, size, colour, feel, smell, taste, sound)
Does it move?
How does it work?
Is it unchanging, or can it be changed?
Does it have degrees?
What is it made of?
What are the main kinds of it?
Does it have parts?
Is it a part of something else?
What is it like?
What is it unlike?
Does it have an opposite?
Is it unique? Can it be made plural?

If your subject is an *event*, some questions would be slightly different:

Did (does, will) it happen? What happened?
When did (does, will) it happen?
Where did (does, will) it happen?

And so on. If your subject is a *person*, or other creature, you would again change some questions a little:

Does he (she, it) exist?
Who is it?
When? Where?

And so on. If your subject is a *place*:

Does it exist?
Where is it? When?
What happens there?

And so on. Most of the questions, sometimes in varied form, can be applied to any kind of subject.

## QUESTIONS ABOUT HUMAN CONNECTIONS

Who is associated with it?
Who made it?
Who owns it?
Who uses it?
Who sees it, watches it, listens to it?
Who respects, fears, likes, or dislikes it?

Again, with some variations, such questions can be asked about different kinds of subjects.

## QUESTIONS ABOUT CAUSE AND EFFECT

Why does (did, will) it exist (happen)?
What causes it?
Who causes it?
What does (did, will, can) it do, or cause?
How, or for what, is it used?
Is it part of a process?
What if it *didn't* exist?

## QUESTIONS ABOUT TESTIMONY, AUTHORITY, USAGE

What has been said about it? Any useful quotations?
What information about it is there from statistics, precedents, history, past or present actions on it?
Does it occur loosely or figuratively—in clichés or other common phrases, proverbs, anecdotes, stories?
What can I learn about it from its etymology? Can it be different parts of speech?

If you try to answer these questions conscientiously, along with those directed at identifying your audience and defining your purpose (see the preceding chapter), you can invent, or discover, a great deal about a subject. If you discover that you don't yet know enough about a subject, the questions will help direct you toward the necessary research and even enable you to do that research efficiently. But don't resort too early to external aids, for you will then cut off much of the flow of your own ideas. Exhaust the resources of your own thinking before you begin seeking outside help.

---

### *Exercise 3B*

Such questions, if pursued diligently, can open up an almost endless number of avenues of thought and development. And it often pays to push your mind to what may seem an exaggerated degree. One teacher we know, for example, asks his students to list 101 ways to use a brick (What is it for? What can it do?). A brick is useful in—and primarily designed for—building walls, of course. But go on: A brick makes an effective paperweight for a stack of newspapers. A brick can hold down the corner of a tent, or a tarpaulin covering a compost heap. It is handy for smashing a window, or an unsightly plaster statue. Several bricks along with some boards can make a functional and even attractive bookcase. A properly aimed brick can squash an unwanted insect, or a rat. A brick makes an excellent doorstop. Bricks placed in a row make good garden or sidewalk borders. You can use a brick to practise the shot-put with. A brick can be ground or pounded into brick-dust—if you have any use for brick-dust. Bricks—in large numbers—provide jobs for brick-makers and workers in brickyards. A brick can be sat upon, in the absence of anything bigger or more suitable. A brick.... Take it from there; you need only about 85 more.

---

## INVENTING AND SUBJECT-NARROWING

"Invention" actually begins as soon as you find a subject and begin trying to narrow it. It continues as you define your purpose and identify your audience. And it continues as you work on strategies of development and organization, as the next chapter makes clear. Although it is necessary to consider these steps separately in order to understand them, the process of composition continually doubles back on itself—especially during the planning stage. Subject-narrowing, determining audience and purpose, inventing, planning organization and development—these processes are going on at the same time, each contributing to the others. Together they constitute what some call "pre-writing."

If you have a subject but aren't sure how best to narrow it or how to define your purpose and identify your audience, jump right to step 4 and begin asking questions about it. Even if you do quickly narrow a subject, try going systematically through the questions in step 4 anyway, as if you hadn't yet narrowed it. You may even find that it is more productive to narrow your topic a little and then to expand it once again by asking more of the invention questions, and then to narrow it once more. Work back and forth as much as your subject or topic permits. If for example your subject area is "energy," you can take one of three different paths:

1. limit or narrow the subject first, perhaps by asking questions about it, and then ask some invention questions about the narrowed topic in order to generate ideas about it;
2. first ask questions about the large subject area in order to narrow it and at the same time generate ideas about it;
3. go ahead and narrow it, but ask questions about it as if you hadn't yet narrowed it.

Taking the second or third route rather than the first will usually produce more ideas for writing.

For example, if you have narrowed the subject "energy" to something more manageable, like "rising gasoline prices" or "OPEC's apparent strategy," you can then ask several useful questions about the narrowed topic, such as

> When and where does it happen?
> How does it work?
> Can it be changed?
> Is it part of a process?
> Who is involved with it?
> What and who causes it?
> What does it cause?

And the answers to such questions would likely constitute a solid core of material for an essay on the topic. But if you directed your questions first, or as well, at the larger subject, "energy," you'd be more likely to include among them questions like these:

> Does it have an opposite?
> What can I learn from its etymology?
> What is its appearance?
> What is it like?
> What does it do?
> What has been said about it?

And you'd then probably generate some other ideas, ideas which may not be so obviously and practically useful but which may be interesting and provocative in themselves; they could at least enable you to inject some extra sparkle into your essay through such things as quotations and metaphors; they might provide you with an effective device for beginning or ending the essay; they might even suggest entirely different approaches to the subject or the topic:

> Energy's opposite is lethargy, weakness, impotence, powerlessness. (Just the kind of feeling the poor consumer has in the face of rising costs?)
>
> Etymology: it's from the Greek *energeia*, coined by Aristotle from *energes, energos*, "active, at work," from *en*, "at," and *ergon*, "work." (Aristotle gave us the word *energy*, but his philosophy probably won't help us solve our modern problems with it.)

Metaphorically, its appearance is that of something large, muscular; its colour is probably red (like the figures in many people's budgets these days).

It looks like oil wells and power lines (is hydro our best answer?) and gymnasts (maybe we'll all benefit by walking more) and kids (no energy shortage there!) and hurricanes.

"Energy is Eternal Delight." (William Blake)

"Power when wielded by abnormal energy is the most serious of facts." (Henry Adams)

The point is that if you leave your options open for a while, you will ask a wider range of questions that will generate a greater variety of potentially useful answers—ideas to be going on with. Also, according to Aristotle, what is true for a *genus* is also true for its *species*; so if you discover things to say about a large subject or subject area, you may well be able to apply those same ideas to a small part of that subject.

## Exploration 3A

Select three of the following general and abstract terms and for each compose a short paragraph that wholly or partly defines it by supplying specific and concrete examples:

| | | |
|---|---|---|
| beauty | generosity | hope |
| power | dignity | cruelty |
| speed | ennui | happiness |
| friendship | sloth | worry |
| culture | gratitude | independence |

## Exercise 3C

In one or more dictionaries of quotations, find and copy out at least two quotations using each of the following words. For each quotation, indicate how you might make use of it in an essay.

| | | |
|---|---|---|
| moon | horses | luck |
| hate | education | music |

## Exercise 3D

In a good standard dictionary or in an etymological dictionary, look up the etymology of each of the following words. Copy it out, and indicate whether it would be of possible use in an essay, and how.

| | | |
|---|---|---|
| fear | education | parents |
| harmony | calligraphy | pollution |
| luck | garbage | food |
| nemesis | dormitory | whisky |

## Kinds of Subjects

Most subjects can be thought of as belonging to one or another of about ten categories. The following list is somewhat arbitrary, but it is sufficiently valid to serve as a way of getting started on the process of generating ideas through asking questions:

1. things, objects, artifacts
   (books, tennis balls, bricks, food, the moon, Superman's cape, garbage, blood, the *Challenger*)
2. people and other creatures
   (Picasso, Margaret Laurence, problem children, Achilles, teachers, horses, dogs, gremlins, Donald Duck)
3. places
   (Montreal, bird sanctuaries, Antarctica, small towns, Atlantis, New Zealand)
4. events, occurrences
   (last summer, the Battle of Trafalgar, the Martian invasion, the Great Depression, the Winnipeg General Strike, the Vietnam War)
5. activities, processes
   (dormitory life, chess, kite-flying, swimming, the colonizing of space, picnics, calligraphy)
6. conditions—the natural way things are
   (night, spring, weather, generation gap, contradictions)
7. institutions—human-caused conditions, conventions, systems (e.g. political, social, economic, religious)
   (hospitals, pollution, fashions, education, traffic, energy crisis, language, cable TV)
8. ideas, feelings, beliefs, states of mind
   (puppy-love, hate, morals, fear, happiness, obsession, paganism, nemesis)
9. qualities, abstractions
   (truth, harmony, time, beauty, health)

And perhaps an extra category for subjects that don't seem to belong in any of these:

10. other, miscellaneous
    (luck, variable, green, perhaps)

For a subject that does not easily fall into one of these categories, merely asking some of the questions about it will usually enable you to begin defining it in such a way that it will fit into one or another category—that is, to get a handle on it as a subject.

---

### Exercise 3E

(a) You may feel a bit uneasy about some of our categories. If so, consider changing some of them. You could divide or sub-divide some, or combine some, or add some. Try to justify any changes you make.

(b) You must surely feel uneasy about the way we have classified some of the sample subjects. Reclassify *luck, perhaps,* and at least three others from categories 1-9. Explain your reasons for each change.

## Cross-fertilizing: Shifting Categories

It would seem obvious that the questions you can profitably ask about some subjects would be few. You might even be tempted to think that the fewer questions that are applicable, the easier your task is. But don't give in to that temptation, for part of the reason for going through the inventing step is to discover ideas that you would otherwise be unlikely to come up with—to discover, that is, not only the obvious but also the unexpected.

One way to increase your range of discovery is to look at a subject in unusual ways. Since we all tend to look at things in standard, clichéd ways, we can often discover fresh ideas by adopting unorthodox points of view. This is where the ten subject-categories come in. Thinking of your subject in its most obvious category will enable you to concentrate on logically appropriate questions. But thinking of your subject in a different category will enable you to ask questions that are *not* logically appropriate to it.

For this reason, we can rejoice that many subjects look as though they belong in more than one category. Categories, after all, do not exist in nature; they are human-made. In looking at the list, you no doubt wondered why "education" was put under "institution"; shouldn't it be thought of as a "process," something one goes through? Indeed it should; or rather it should be thought of in *both* ways while inventing is still the main activity. Later in the process one of the ways of looking at it will probably predominate—but even then the other view can be useful, for example to provide a point of contrast for an effective beginning. In fact, "education" could be thought of as belonging elsewhere, as well: it's a "condition," in the sense that it's something that happens to all people as they go through life, not just in formal institutions. It could also be considered an "event"—or at least a particular phase of it could; one might say, for example, "well, that experience taught me a lesson." Can it be moved around any more? Could it also be thought of as an "idea," or maybe even a "place"?

Or take a subject like "Ottawa." Obviously it belongs in the category "place." But once you start asking some of the questions—What caused it? How does it work? Is it a part of something? What does it do? Does it change? Is it part of a process? To whom is it important? What does it mean? and so on—you should before long be thinking of Ottawa not only as a place, a city, but as a part of Canada; as the seat of government; as the place where decisions are made that affect us all; as a sort of "presence," whatever party is in power; as part of the process we call democracy; as, in a way, an *idea* or a state of mind. You could think of it as a person, or agent, as journalists do when it stands for the federal government: Ottawa disagreeing with the provinces, Ottawa upset with Washington. Or you could see it not only as part of a process but as itself an event or activity. What would happen if you considered the word *Ottawa* as a verb? What would it imply to speak of "ottawing" something or someone? What could be the direct object of such a verb, or who could be the agents? As you can see, you can come up with interesting perspectives by using these questions and categories—and your imagination.

By mentally shifting a given subject from category to category and directing at it the questions appropriate to each, you can often discover interesting and useful ideas and fresh ways of looking at things. When we asked about "energy," "What does it look like?"—as if it were an object—we got some potentially useful ideas, including even a colour. When a group of students was asked to think of "hate" as an object, and to say what colour it was, one said it was red, thinking of the fairly obvious connotations of anger, passion, danger. Another, thinking perhaps of an enraged person's face, said it was purple. This made a third think of the punning "ultra-violent." Still another thought it should be yellow, explaining that hate was a kind of disease. Another thought hate was at least sometimes a result of envy, and therefore green; whereupon someone else consulted a dictionary and found that the Old English word *hete* meant both "hate" and "envy." By means of such associations several possibly useful avenues are opened up.

Thinking of "hate" as an *object* could also lead one to think of it as something heavy, a burden that some people carry around with them. Thinking of it as an *activity* could lead you to think of it as something one engages in, and something some people even enjoy—a kind of hobby. Thinking of it as a *condition* might lead one to speculate on whether it's a part of human nature, a potential built into us, part of "the human condition." Could hate also be thought of as an *institution*? Could it even be thought of, metaphorically, as a kind of *place*?

## METAPHORS AND SIMILES

One valuable technique for generating ideas is to invent metaphors. Asking the question "What is it like?" can often produce not only literal comparisons but also useful metaphorical ones. We've already done this by thinking of the abstraction "hate" as something concrete, a kind of physical burden that weighs down some people. Or it could be personified—another kind of metaphor—as a creature, a sort of incubus. We've already noted that it can be thought of as a disease. Some would say that hate was *like* a poison in a person's or a community's system; that would be a simile. Or you could say it *was* a poison; that would be a metaphor. Or hate could be like food: some people seem to thrive on it. Or one might say something like "I ran into a wall of hatred." If you asked whether the word or idea occurred in any common phrases, you'd probably come up with the cliché "blind hatred," again personifying it—which could lead to interesting ironic comparisons with the other common phrases "Love is blind" and "Justice is blind."

It is unlikely that an essay on hate that made use of some of these notions would turn out flat or dull or over-generalized or otherwise weak in content. Further, pursuing such questions can be invaluable in helping you narrow a subject, focus on audience and purpose, and even construct a thesis and an outline.

So don't just rest easy once you've asked the questions obviously appropriate to your subject. Instead, cast about for ideas that wouldn't occur to you in the normal way. With questions from the list and any others you can think of, hammer your square peg of a subject into all the round-holed categories. And even if you get few reasonable-sounding answers, or none, keep on questioning:

something may turn up, something may spark a train of thought, some obviously absurd answer may suggest a useful contrast or a new direction to take.

---

### Exercise 3F

Invent at least two metaphors or similes for each of the following; include at least five examples of personification.

| | | |
|---|---|---|
| garbage | blood | pollution |
| swimming | education | Calgary |
| dormitory life | music | traffic |
| fear | spring | relatives |

---

## RANDOM ASSOCIATION

The reason for asking *in*appropriate questions about a subject or topic is to force yourself out of the ruts of standardized or clichéd thinking about it. Another way to do that is what we call "random association." Whatever your subject, suddenly putting it beside another word or idea and trying to make sense of the association or combination can often stir up potentially useful trains of thought that would not otherwise occur to you. Think of it as grabbing a word out of thin air and throwing it at your subject to see if the collision of the two sends off any sparks. Usually it will.

One way to get a word you can use is to open a dictionary at random and, with your eyes closed or averted, jab your finger at the page: the dictionary-listing your finger hits is the word you will then try to force into some sort of relation with your subject.

Or you can use other books; sometimes a book of nonfictional prose will work better than a dictionary. Say you've got a book 400 pages long, with 40 lines per page, and about 12 words per line. Quickly write down three numbers—one between 1 and 400, one between 1 and 40, and one between 1 and 10 (safer than 12, since some lines will have fewer than the average). We tried for example 288, 21, and 2; opening a handy book to page 288, we found the 2nd word in the 21st line to be *value*—a promising word to set beside almost any subject.

Occasionally, with either method, you'll hit upon a technical or other word that obviously won't do you any good. Then simply try again, or move along the line (or down the dictionary page) until you get to a better word. But don't abandon a word too quickly; even a conjunction or preposition or article could send off a spark or two. But if after a moment's thought with a word nothing comes, find another word, and then another. Try several. You may be surprised at how often you can generate interesting ideas.

You can probably devise other ways of randomly getting something to throw at your subject—maybe looking quickly out of the window and taking the first object your eye lights upon, or grabbing a handful of letters from a word game and seeing what word or words you can arrange them into.

### Exercise 3G

It is true that simple brainstorming is quicker than going through all these questions and writing down all the answers—even the silly ones. But we believe that using such a battery of questions will be not only much more productive of ideas but also, in the long run, more efficient.

Take the same two subjects you used in the exercise on brainstorming (3A), and run each of them through as many invention questions as possible. Don't hesitate to make up other questions that might be useful; don't consider our list sacred, or complete. And be sure to force each of the subjects into as many of the categories as possible, and also to try some random association. See what happens—or rather what else happens.

### ONE QUESTION LEADS TO ANOTHER

Here is how it might work. Ask the questions we suggest—but don't stop there. The answer to one question will lead to another question, and the answer to that will lead to another, and so on. Pile up the answers. Let your material grow—and your subject narrow. And as your subject narrows, you should find it easier and easier to get more ideas about it.

If for example your large subject area is *education*—something we're all interested in—and you've asked enough questions to narrow it down to "methods of teaching and methods of learning," keep making up questions that will enable you to narrow it further, to get more and more specific:

> What are the methods of teaching I've been exposed to?
> What method gets the best work out of me?
> How important is what goes on in the classroom as opposed to what I do when I'm studying on my own?

Such questions as these can lead to further and still more focussed questions:

> What study habits are most effective for me?
> Which of the teachers I've had do I feel most grateful to?
> Does a seemingly disorganized teacher sometimes spark more interest than one who is carefully organized?
> At what time of the day do I study most efficiently?
> How important is taking good notes?
> Do some teachers obviously care more about me and my work than others do?
> Do I get as much out of lectures as I do out of discussions?
> How valuable are these "workshop" sessions?
> How important is humour in the classroom? If I laugh, do I learn?

And so on. Soon you'll be asking even more specific, more focussed questions and producing even more specific answers:

> What is the best way to take notes?
> How many times do I need to read a chapter in the textbook?
> Why did my math teacher glare at me this morning?

Is the word-count of an essay as crucial as some teachers seem to think?
How should I behave in a private conference with a teacher?
Do I contribute enough in the classroom?
What's the best way to prepare for an exam?
Dare I contradict something a teacher says?
Am I using my dictionary properly, or enough?

Eventually you decide that, as a student, you're in a better position to say something about "methods of learning" than "methods of teaching": your focus has gradually narrowed down to you, as an individual student. You decide that your audience, for now, is your fellow students. Perhaps you can do them a service by telling them the results of your thinking on one or two matters that pertain to their best interests as well as yours. You look over the answers that you've been jotting down and see that "How should I use my dictionary?" and "How should I prepare for an exam?" are the questions that have made you think harder than the others, though some of your answers to the many other questions still look interesting, and you may want to use them on another occasion—if in fact you can't use some of them in the essay you're working on.

You decide that "How to use a dictionary" sounds rather dry (though important), and that "How should I prepare for an exam?" promises something more immediately interesting to both you and your readers. Subject-narrowing, audience, purpose, and the first stages of invention have come together. Your purpose, you decide, is to interest, but primarily to inform, even to instruct, your audience of fellow students.

## Formulating a Thesis: The Thesis Question

In the next chapter we discuss the thesis, or thesis statement, as it takes shape along with your decisions about form and development. But you will likely begin to formulate a thesis during the invention stage. At this stage, however, your thesis is more likely to be a question than a statement. That is, you will focus your questions more and more narrowly until you arrive at something like "How should one prepare for an exam?"—a question you hope to be able to answer in your essay. As you begin to think about possible ways of answering your thesis question, you will find that it grows into a statement and that particular methods of development will present themselves as the natural ways to proceed.

But as you set about bombarding your topic with more invention questions, you find yourself taking another look at it: "How should a student prepare for an exam?" (Notice that it keeps changing as you keep thinking about it, and about your prospective audience.) How can you write about how to prepare for *an* exam? Each examination is different—unique. Maybe, in thinking about yourself and one particular course, you've become *too* specific, too narrow. Maybe you should broaden your thoughts a bit again, and think about the phenomenon of "exams," or the "exam period" itself. By thinking about it, and consulting your own experience, perhaps you can actually give your fellow students some useful advice. You rephrase your thesis question once more: "What is the best way for students to prepare themselves for the examination period at the end of each term?"

## Exercise 3H

Construct two possible thesis questions for each of the two subjects you used in Exercise 3G.

## Exercise 3I

List as many uses as you can think of for one or more of the following. Try to reach at least 100.

| | |
|---|---|
| a paper-clip | a tennis ball |
| a wire coat-hanger | a styrofoam cup |
| a wooden match | a potato |
| a clothes-pin | Australia |

## Exploration 3B

In about 200 words, write a description of a natural scene or object in which you move beyond the literal level by means of one of these three devices: metaphor, simile, or analogy. As far as possible, choose a scene or object untouched by human hands and uncontaminated by human presence; then make the secondary level of your description an application to human matters. The subject can be animate or inanimate, or both. Describe from observation rather than from memory. Consider carefully what proportion of your description the secondary level is to occupy, and how soon it is to be introduced.

## Essay 3A

Think of something you witnessed recently and found amusing or even absurd or ironic, such as the spectacle of hundreds of people lined up to see a bad film; a driver roaring past you on the wrong side and then turning off at the next corner; a homeowner watering the garden during a heavy rain; an unusually small man or woman walking two unusually large dogs; someone in a supermarket check-out, basket heaped with empty calories, vehemently protesting allegedly being overcharged two cents. Use one of these if you wish, and have seen it yourself recently. But better yet, keep your eyes and ears open, and your pencil ready, and record the essence of such a scene when it appears before you. Use a vivid description of one or more such episodes as at least the partial focus of a mainly light piece on human behaviour. Make a special effort to use your own behaviour, as well, to help illustrate whatever thesis you formulate.

## Essay 3B

(a) Write a free-wheeling short expressive essay responding to something someone said to you recently but which you couldn't think of a good answer to at the time.

OR

(b) Open a dictionary at random and look for a word that produces some kind of emotional reaction in you. Write a short piece expressing that reaction.

### Essay 3C

In an essay of about 500 words, explain why a particular possible subject (such as *music, horses, Calgary, sports, transportation, darkness, mountain-climbing, love, literature, television*) should be thought of as belonging in more than just one of the ten subject categories listed on p. 51. Feel free to come up with new and different categories if ours don't seem to be satisfactory for the subject you choose.

### Essay 3D

You have been left a small fortune in the will of a distant relative whom you never met. Write an essay of no more than 750 words describing and explaining what you intend to do with it. Or write a letter to the lawyers, accepting or rejecting the inheritance.

---

### Idioms 3

See the instructions for the first idiom exercise, p. 14. Here are more words that can be followed idiomatically by more than one preposition. Compose sentences using each.

| | | |
|---|---|---|
| admit of | concerned in | healed of |
| admit to | concerned for | healed by |
| apprehensive of | concerned with | liable for |
| apprehensive for | decide on (upon) | liable to |
| astonished at | decide for | responsible for |
| astonished by | decide against | responsible to |

---

### Sentence-Combining 3: Prepositional Phrases

### Pattern 3A

Base sentence *a*: Gardens often need help.
Base sentence *b*: They often need weeding and fertilizing.
Result of combining *a* and *b*:
    Gardens often need the help of weeding and fertilizing.

First, COPY the pattern sentence carefully, noting that you delete the words *They often need* from sentence *b* and that in sentence *a* you insert the word *the* before *help* and the word *of* after it.

Second, COMBINE each of the following pairs of sentences into a single sentence modelled on the pattern sentence:
a. Many social programs depend on charity.
b. They depend on a generous public.
a. The transportation system needs support.
b. It needs government subsidies.

Third, COMPOSE two sentences of your own modelled on Pattern 3A.

    In this exercise you are making two simple sentences into one simple sentence by first eliminating the pronoun and verb in *b* that repeat the subject and the verb of *a*, and then using the preposition *of* to lead into the remainder of *b*. You are, then, reducing sentence *b* to a prepositional phrase—in this pattern a phrase (*of weeding and fertilizing*) that functions as an adjective, answering the question Which? or What kind of? about the noun (*help*) it modifies.

## Pattern 3B

a. Some people can count themselves fortunate.
b. They have loyal friends.

RESULT: People with loyal friends can count themselves fortunate.

Copy the pattern sentence, noting that you drop the vague modifier *some* and that *with* replaces *they have*.

Combine each of the following pairs into a sentence modelled on the pattern sentence:
a. Some cars are known as gas-guzzlers.
b. They have huge engines.

a. Many countries are poor.
b. They have high birth-rates.

Compose two sentences modelled on Pattern 3B.

In this exercise you are converting two simple sentences into one by reducing the second to a prepositional phrase and inserting it in the first.

## Pattern 3C

a. The students had a good outline to guide them.
b. They then found that they could continue easily.

RESULT: With a good outline to guide them, the students found that they could continue easily.

Copy the pattern sentence, noting that *The students* moves over to replace *They then* in sentence *b*, that *With* replaces *had*, and that a comma follows the first part of the new sentence.

Combine each of the following pairs into a sentence modelled on the pattern sentence:
a. Janice had the evidence in her hand.
b. She then went straight to see her lawyer.

a. The team has two new players on defence.
b. The team now expects to make the playoffs.

Compose two sentences modelled on Pattern 3C.

In this exercise you are reducing one sentence to a prepositional phrase and using it to open the new sentence. Note that the relation between the two parts is one of cause and effect.

## Pattern 3D

a. The committee did not have a clear precedent.
b. Therefore they could make only tentative recommendations.

RESULT: Without a clear precedent, the committee could make only tentative recommendations.

Copy the pattern sentence, noting that *The committee* moves over to replace *Therefore they*, that *Without* replaces *did not have,* and that a comma follows the first part of the new sentence.

Combine each of the following pairs into a sentence modelled on the pattern sentence:
a.  The navigator did not have an accurate chronometer.
b.  Therefore he could not plot the ship's position.
a.  We do not have enough volunteers.
b.  Therefore we cannot complete the project.

Compose two sentences modelled on Pattern 3D.

In this exercise, as in Pattern 3C, you are reducing one sentence to a prepositional phrase and using it to open the new sentence, in the process avoiding the heavy *Therefore* formerly used to establish the cause-and-effect relation.

### Playing with Language 3A

Write down five numbers: your age, the day of the month on which you were born, the number of the month in which you were born, the last two digits of the year of your birth and of the present year. If your age and birthdate should chance to be the same, double one of them. For example, if you are now 18, were born on April 23, 1967, and the current year is 1985, your five numbers would be 18, 4, 23, 67, 85. Then open any book you happen to have handy and, counting from the beginning or from the top of a randomly selected page, write down the word that occurs at each of your numbers (for the above example that would be the 4th, 18th, 23rd, 67th, and 85th words)—except, if that word is not a *noun*, move along the sentence or line until you come to a noun and write *it* down. You will then have a list of five nouns. However wildly incompatible they may seem, try to make something of them. Combine them, oppose them, string them out—anything that will work. Make some sort of use of them in some sort of an essay at least 300 words long.

### Playing with Language 3B

Trace the etymology of the following words. Choose either three of the individual words or one or two of the groups of words and write a brief report (not over 1000 words) of your findings, including information about any associated words or word-groups that you discover and find interesting. For example, if you look up the word *economy,* you might be surprised to find that it is etymologically related to such words as *ecumenical, parish,* and *parochial.*

Some useful references, in addition to your own dictionary:

W. W. Skeat, *An Etymological Dictionary of the English Language*
Eric Partridge, *Origins*
Wilfred Funk, *Word Origins and Their Romantic Stories*
Edward C. Pinkerton, *Word for Word*

| | | |
|---|---|---|
| rival | companion | savour, savant |
| service | ignoramus | suspect, circumspect |
| charge | chapel | lord, lady |
| focus | curfew | influenza, disaster, auspices |
| opera | credenza | notch, orange, nickname, apron |
| jewel | money | trivial, obvious, envoy |
| vanity | cattle | patriarch, patriotic |
| cosmetic | culprit | serendipity, pandemonium |
| profane | excruciating | titanic, vulcanize, bedlam, bohemian, |
| tawdry | scrupulous | dunce, laconic |
| candidate | cathedral | Sunday, Monday, Tuesday, Wednesday, |
| calculate | trite | Thursday, Friday, Saturday |
| calisthenics | bonfire | January, February, March, April, May, |
| envy | infantry | June, July, August, September, |
| cynic | delirious | October, November, December |

*Good writing, like a good house,*
*is an orderly arrangement of parts.*
(Mortimer Adler)

CHAPTER IV
# Step 5: Organizing —
# Development, Arrangement, Thesis

This chapter suggests ways to find the most effective forms for your ideas, ways of shaping your material to fulfill your purposes.

Form can be seen as a mould into which you fit your ideas. But if you think of writing as a process, you should think of form as something that emerges as you plan and as you write and revise. Since writing is usually a recursive process, you proceed partly by trial and error and take advantage of what you discover as you go along. Forms and ideas are mutually recursive: you discover form as you work with your ideas, and as the form becomes clearer you find more ideas emerging and relations between ideas becoming clearer.

## DEVELOPING YOUR IDEAS

From your work on steps 1 through 4, you have a narrowed subject, or topic, a collection of ideas about that topic, some sense of your audience and your purpose, and perhaps even a thesis question. The next step is to decide how to develop your material and how to arrange it into a single, coherent whole. To do that, you can use many of the same questions you used to begin finding out *what* you wanted to write—but now you will also be concentrating on finding out *how* you want to write it.

In this chapter we discuss the following methods of developing your ideas:

1. Example and Illustration
2. Definition
3. Classification and Division
4. Comparison and Contrast
5. Description
6. Narration
7. Process Analysis
8. Cause and Effect

62

These methods of development reflect some of the principal ways people think. For most pieces you write, you can choose one method to fit your primary purpose. For example, you might think of a particular essay as primarily a narrative or a job of classification. And many pieces of writing are primarily generalizations supported and explained by a series of examples and illustrations.

As a particular writing project begins to acquire a shape, you will begin to see it as consisting of sections, subsections, and even paragraphs. You need to decide on the best method of development, the best *form*, for each of these parts as well as for the essay as a whole. And you need to decide on the best way to arrange these parts. This fifth and last step of the planning stage can be seen as a series of sub-steps; they may not always take place in this order, or they may all be going on at once, but in making your decisions about development and organization, these are the five things you need to do:

a. *Examine the material generated in steps 1-4.* Look for patterns that are beginning to emerge. Some sort of arrangement might even suggest itself right away. If not, go back to steps 3 and 4 and try some more questioning; concentrate on the relations among the ideas you have already generated. If you haven't already done so, try to formulate at least a tentative thesis question about your topic.

For example, consider the student working with the thesis question "What is the best way for students to prepare themselves for the examination period?" In going back over her material and asking and re-asking more questions and thinking about her own experience and talking to other students, she began to see that the heart of the answer to her question was going to be some sort of plan or schedule consisting of several parts, one having to do with study time, and others having to do with other parts of students' day-to-day lives, such as diet and leisure.

b. *Consider which methods of development will be most effective*—both for the overall essay and for its parts. Many of the questions that help you generate material can also help you discover a form for your material. For example the question "What is it?" might lead you to see that you primarily want to describe an object or define a term or a concept. Or the question "What are the main kinds of it?" might lead you to see that you need to provide a classification showing how the various kinds relate to one another and to your topic as a whole.

Suppose for example you have decided to write about the subject of music and have narrowed your topic to Christmas carols. And suppose that the invention questions about origin and kinds generated the most interesting material. You might then decide that your purpose is to inform an audience of fellow students by classifying Christmas carols in one of three ways: historically (pre-1700, 1700-1800, 1800-1900, 1900-present); or by subject (Mary, the Christ child, shepherds, etc.); or by using the parts of the church service from which groups of carols have come.

Or take the student working on the "exam period" essay. Since her material was shaping up in the form of a schedule for students to follow before exams, she decided that essentially she was going to be writing a "how to" paper, explaining and recommending a process, but that rather than a step-by-step procedure, her essay would consist of an analysis of the process into its parts, with some discussion of each, and with a touch of persuasion.

c. *Construct a thesis that reflects your purpose and the form that is emerging.* Again you can use the invention questions to help. During the invention step you may even arrive at a rough thesis question. As you work with the invention questions, you write down answers; and as you gradually pull together the material you are generating, you can start combining some of these into increasingly developed sentences. Or you may find yourself returning again and again to a few provocative ideas. Either way, your focus is becoming narrower. When you see what the central issue of your project is, or could be, try to put that issue into the form of a statement—a thesis—probably using elements from the sentences and points you've been zeroing in on. If you already have a thesis *question*, now is the time to put it in the form of a *statement* that answers the question.

A *thesis* is an assertion or proposition about your topic, one that the material you have generated will explain or support or prove. Your thesis is the controlling or governing idea of your essay, the point that it is all about. One of the best indications that you're on a promising track is that you are able, near the end of the planning stage, to develop a strong tentative thesis statement. Here for example is a tentative thesis statement, for readers interested in the history of films, about a movie popular in 1981:

> *Raiders of the Lost Ark* reminds me of old adventure serials.

As you proceed through the several stages of the writing process, one of your objectives should be to refine your thesis statement by making it more and more specific. Before you write your first draft, you might develop only a tentative thesis statement, like the one above. But as you work through your material and decide more fully on the most effective methods of development, you should be able to formulate a more specific thesis statement, like this one:

> Several similarities suggest that *Raiders of the Lost Ark* is strongly indebted to old adventure serials.

And then, as you continue arranging your evidence while writing the early drafts of your paper, you might end up with a fully formulated thesis statement something like this:

> The pacing, the structure of the episodes, and the dependence on swift and dramatic action rather than on character, all reveal that *Raiders of the Lost Ark* derives basically from old adventure serials.

You can see that this fully formulated thesis statement clearly offers a specific proposition about the topic, while at the same time suggesting how the material will be developed and arranged.

d. *Begin to divide the material into ordered parts.* See how you can arrange it to best serve your purpose and the needs of your readers. Several of the possible methods of development should automatically suggest effective arrangements. For example, if you are describing something, you could use spatial order, following the eye as it moves across or around an object, or following an observer moving through a scene. If you are comparing and contrasting two things, you could alternate between them. And if you are using narrative, of course time order is the most obvious way to arrange the events you are narrating, although you might decide to use a flashback or a flash-forward to make your point more effectively.

A good thesis statement also helps. As it becomes more and more specific, it may suggest an effective order, as does the revised thesis statement about *Raiders of the Lost Ark*. Our student planning the essay on the exam period went from her thesis question:

> What is the best way for students to prepare for the exam period?

to a preliminary thesis statement:

> Students can best prepare for the approaching exam period by carefully planning their daily study schedules, including some self-indulgence.

to a working thesis statement that is more specific:

> In order to feel confident as you approach the exam period, carefully construct and follow a study schedule, making sure you also allow time for enough sleep, proper food and exercise, and a little pampering.

Again, the form of the thesis statement clearly suggests the arrangement of the main points.

*Note:* Try to select and organize your material so that your essay has *at least three* major parts or sections and *not more than about seven*. Having two parts risks producing a split essay; having more than seven parts risks overtaxing your reader's ability to keep track of ideas.

e. *Compose a plan or a working outline to use as a guide for writing.* Seen schematically, the main points of the thesis statement about *Raiders of the Lost Ark* might look like this:

Evidence that *Raiders* derives from old serials—three main parallels:
1. Pacing
2. Structure of the episodes
3. Dependence on action rather than character.

Under each heading you could list some of the specific examples you intend to use. But this arrangement might not be the best one for the thesis. You can't be sure until you try it out. There is some risk in settling on a firm organization too early in the process. Retain enough flexibility to accommodate new ideas and strategies that might occur to you as you are actually writing and revising the drafts. Be prepared to change both thesis and plan, if necessary, to accommodate good ideas that come along later: serendipity is sometimes your best source of inspiration.

Here is the outline that took shape for the paper on preparing for the exam period:

**Essay Plan: How to Prepare for Exams**

> **T.S.:** In order to feel confident as you approach the exam period, carefully construct and follow a study schedule, making sure you also allow time for enough sleep, proper food and exercise, and a little pampering.

> **Beginning:** Here comes that time again, as it does every year, or twice a year. But take heart: you can manage it.

    I. Draw up a study schedule.
        A. Course priorities.
        B. Be flexible, but firm.
    II. Sleep is important—don't leave it out of your considerations.
    III. Food is important—the mind needs fuel too.
    IV. Exercise is important—it helps the mind as well as the body.
    V. Self-indulgence: pamper yourself a bit for psychological stability.
        A. Take breaks.
        B. Meet friends.
        C. Go to a movie.

**Ending:** That's the way to beat the blues—and remember, you're not alone.

The obvious methods of development to be used for the sections and sub-sections appear to be explanation by example and illustration and some cause and effect. (The completed paper is number 5 in Chapter XV.)

## Methods of Development

### 1. EXAMPLE AND ILLUSTRATION

One of the most powerful ways of making your thoughts clear to both yourself and your readers is through examples and illustrations. Because the human mind depends on sense perceptions, it needs specifics. If you can provide examples of a concept, you really understand it—and so will your reader.

If questions like the following have helped generate ideas about a topic, consider developing part or all of your project by using example and illustration:

> What does it do, what is it used for?
> What are its manifestations?
> When and where, in what contexts, does it appear?
> What has been thought, said, or done about it?
> Does it occur in common phrases, proverbs, or anecdotes?

Examples provide a natural and easy way to clarify a point. Consider the following passage from a student paper on meaning in language:

> There is no "natural" name for anything, except as the speakers of a language determine it, and then it seems right and natural to speakers of that language only. For example, the concept "girl" is rendered as *mädel* in German, *fille* in French, *ragazza* in Italian, and *korizzi* in Greek. All five words represent equally a female child.

If you provide well-chosen and representative examples to support a general statement, your readers will read on in confidence that you know what you're talking about. For instance think how you feel about the writer as you read the following passage. Note how the student immediately lets you know what he means by a generalization by providing specific examples:

> In every society, children model their behaviour on that of their elders, particularly their parents. Bushman children in the Kalahari desert play elaborate games to help them develop the agility and stealth they need to become successful hunters later in

life. In Beirut, Lebanon, children constantly play war games which reflect with bizarre accuracy the horrors that they see around them. Clearly, children's games are often rehearsals for future real-life situations. The tragedy, as they almost always discover, is that the reality is a lot less fun than the fantasy.

This passage also illustrates another feature of the way people often think and write: note how the writer begins with a generalization, then provides specific examples to clarify and support it, and then moves on to further generalizations based on those examples. Much effective writing swings back and forth like this from general to specific and back to general again. To live always in a world of specific detail would be to live in a perennial dust-storm of disconnected particles. To live always on the level of generalizations would be to remain on the icy summits where nothing can grow or be nourished. Specific examples give life and nourishment to generalizations; generalizations give order and coherence to disparate facts.

---

## Exploration 4A

Compose a substantial paragraph (at least seven sentences) developing one of the following topics by consciously moving back and forth from general to specific; try to both begin and end with relatively general statements, as does the paragraph about children in Beirut.

| | |
|---|---|
| owning a pet | poetry |
| your current teachers | crossword puzzles |
| the last hockey game you watched | the school paper |
| your brothers and sisters | the library |
| leisure time | popular music |
| where you eat lunch | foreign languages |

---

**The Role of Experience**   The world is full of potential examples for almost any generalization. Much of the material writers use to clarify and support generalizations comes from their own experience—not just from books and other secondhand sources. Much of your knowledge has been built up from your experience with specific people, places, and events. For example you know a good deal about education just from having been a student for several years. You know about soccer or swimming not from reading books or listening to parents and teachers but from playing and watching soccer games or swimming in rivers or lakes or pools. When you write about such things, you can bring them home to yourself and your readers by providing concrete examples drawn from those experiences. Experience is knowledge.

When you are planning a writing project, then, don't overlook the potential usefulness of the questions about yourself and your subject:

Do I know it personally?
What do I know about it?
What experience have I had with it?
What does it mean to me?
How do I feel about it?

Because examples and illustrations drawn from your own experience are close to you, they are also likely to come across to your readers as more immediate than ideas you get elsewhere. Note how Roderick Haig-Brown, in the following paragraph from *Fisherman's Fall*, uses specific and concrete details to support his general opening statement (and note also how after the details he swings back to a level of greater generalization):

> The third type of estuary, where the stream has cut its channel through tidal meadows, is in many ways the most delightful of all. The low flatland gives a strong sense of space and freedom; every breeze over it is full of sound and meaning, changing the greens of weeds and grass in springtime, rattling the seed pods and dry stems of summer and fall. Mallard and pintails jump from sloughs and pot-holes, Wilson snipe flash from the grass knots and plunge down again into new hiding places; fall may bring a flock of snow geese or white fronts in migration. There is always life and movement somewhere on the flats and it has about it a special quality of wildness that belongs with salt spray and sea storms.

Haig-Brown's main purpose here is neither to instruct nor to inform, but to convey his own pleasure in fishing and just being in a particular kind of place. He uses lively and specific examples to convey that pleasure.

Whatever your purpose in a piece of writing, you can, by using examples, help keep yourself close to the concrete particulars of your subject and also help your readers understand what you are trying to say.

---

## Exercise 4A

From your own experience, list at least five concrete examples or illustrations to clarify or support three of the following general statements:

1. Working for a while between high school and university would help many students.
2. Pausing to enjoy small pleasures even when you are busy can help you do a good job of whatever you are doing.
3. Young people often need breathing space from the pressures of their parents.
4. Young people shouldn't have any so-called "breathing space" from their parents.
5. You don't have to be afraid of snow and cold weather.
6. You can usually trust first impressions.
7. You can seldom trust first impressions.

---

## 2. DEFINITION

Definition is a useful and important tool. Without it, communication between writers and readers would often break down. For example, you sometimes need to define one or more key terms or concepts at the beginning of an essay in order to be sure your readers understand you correctly. Or if you find in the course of a piece of writing that you have to use technical terms, you define them. You may even decide that a particular piece of writing has definition as its primary function—an essay for example that answers a thesis question like "Just what is 'responsible government,' anyway?" or one that explores the meanings of a concept like "security" or "privacy" in our everyday lives. Even if such an essay uses a lot of example and illustration as its main method of development, you could still think of its overall function as defining. But most often definition will be at the service of some other method.

If you find such invention questions as these useful in generating material, you will probably want to use definition to develop parts of your writing project, perhaps even to see it as your primary method:

What is it?
Does it exist?
When and where, in what contexts, does it occur?
Of what is it a part?
What is it like or unlike?
Does it have an opposite?
What information is there from etymology?

Obviously these "methods of development" that we are discussing one by one overlap a great deal. For example you can define something by giving examples of it, comparing or contrasting it with something else, or by analyzing it into its parts. Don't let this overlap disturb or confuse you; it actually reflects the richness and complexity of the way people's minds work. But you need to understand the principles of each method in isolation in order to understand and appreciate the way they can work together.

If you decide you need to define something, for example, you will probably think immediately of the kind of definition we're all most familiar with—that in dictionaries. But you're not limited to that mode of definition. Besides, you probably don't want your prose to sound like a dictionary. Here then are brief discussions of some useful ways of defining.

a. *Ostensive definition*   The word *ostensive* is from a Latin word for "showing"; sometimes the simplest way to define something is to point to it:

"What's a carburetor?"
"That thing there"—pointing—"on the engine."

But of course we can't point that way in our prose, unless with careful description. But dictionaries often do what amounts to the same thing when they supply pictures or drawings or diagrams. And so can you, if the need arises—which it may well do if you're writing on a technical or scientific subject.

b. *Defining by analysis*   Sometimes you can define a thing in terms of its parts, their nature, or their function and purpose. For example we can partly define a carburetor by saying that it is a device on an engine, connected to the throttle, that by means of a valve mixes gasoline with air to produce a vapour that explodes in the cylinder.

c. *Defining by listing members of a class*   For example, one way to define the grammatical item known as an article is to point out that the class *article* has only three members: *a, an,* and *the.* But seldom can you be so exhaustive; usually you have to be content to list several *representative* members of a class. For example you could partly define the preposition in English by saying that "Prepositions are words like *into, of, on, among, about, under.*"

   d. ***Defining by context***    Sometimes you can usefully define a term by putting it in a context, a framework or continuum already familiar to your readers. If your readers know (for example if you've already explained) what the Mesozoic era is, you could define the Cretaceous period as "the first of the three periods of the Mesozoic era."

   e. ***Negative definition***    Another way of defining something is to point out what it is not—a great help when you are trying to correct popular misconceptions about your subject. Although negative definition is usually best when combined with one or more of the positive methods, it can sometimes be a simple but efficient method of defining something by sharply distinguishing it from its surroundings. The central part of the following diagram, for example, can be described as a white circle against a black background:

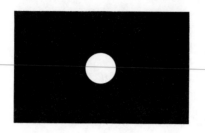

But it can also be described as the area *not* covered by a black screen. A shift of focus or perspective can significantly alter the way you think about something.

   f. ***Defining by appositive***    One of the most common and useful informal methods of defining is to provide an appositive, a word or words equivalent to the term that needs to be defined. Many appositives are enclosed in a pair of commas:

   Nathan, the man in charge of the committee, reported that there was no money left.

But when you define a term this way, you will usually enclose the definition in parentheses:

   In narrative and descriptive writing, it is unwise to depend heavily on adjectives (words that modify nouns) and adverbs (words that modify verbs).

This technique is efficient and smooth; it takes little space and thus helps to prevent distracting your readers. It's a particularly good way to maintain momentum in your writing when you find that you need to define technical terms for your readers: you don't have to stop and take up a whole sentence or two for your definition.

   g. ***Defining by 'genus' and 'differentiae'***    There remains the most familiar kind of definition: the conventional or "formal" definition that we often see in dictionaries. This kind of definition specifies the larger class (*genus*) to which the person or object or concept belongs, and lists those characteristics or features (*differentiae*) which distinguish it from other members of that class. For example, a *filly* is defined as "a young female horse"—the term *horse* specifies the *genus*;

the terms *young* and *female* specify the two *differentiae*. This sort of definition is favoured by philosophers and scientists and lawyers because it is both clear and precise. Here is a passage from a student's paper which uses formal definition:

> Erosion is a geological process wherein natural forces gradually wear away land-forms. For example, wind and waves from the sea gradually wear away the face of a cliff. Or, to take another example, wind, rain, temperature changes, and glaciers cause mountains to erode.

The *genus* in this definition is "geological process"; the *differentiae* include the ideas of "natural forces," "wearing away," and "landforms." The writer then goes on to clarify the definition by providing examples.

## Exercise 4B

Choose ten of the following terms and briefly define each in one or more of the different ways (*a* through *g*) discussed above. Use each of the methods at least once (label your definitions). Keep each definition down to one sentence. Do not simply copy a dictionary's definition; consult more than one dictionary or other source if you wish, but use your own words and phrasing as much as possible.

| | | |
|---|---|---|
| ansate cross | lute | riot |
| comedian | metronome | subordinating |
| evergreen (noun) | mitre (carpentry) | conjunction |
| green | mitre (headdress) | surd (mathematics) |
| heat pump | mountain | twilight |
| *hors-d'oeuvres* | prime number | video game |
| jambalaya | rhombus | winch |

## Exploration 4B

Write a one- or two-paragraph definition of one of the following:

| | | |
|---|---|---|
| frustration | nutrition | representative |
| a student | sportsmanship | government |
| romance | botany | charity |
| entertainment | cybernetics | a sitcom |

Remember that in such an extended definition you will probably want to use more than one of the available techniques, and probably other methods of development as well (perhaps example and illustration, classification, or comparison and contrast).

## Exploration 4C

One dictionary defines the word *irony* this way: "The use of words to convey the opposite of their literal meaning." Write a one- or two-paragraph extended definition of the word *irony* which (a) covers some of the different kinds of irony, (b) includes some examples, and (c) differentiates it from sarcasm.

### Exploration 4D

Write an extended definition (about 200-250 words) of one of the following:

| | |
|---|---|
| taxonomy, in biology | etiquette |
| standard deviation, in statistics | culture, in anthropology |
| harmony, in music | "streaming," in education |
| charisma | balance, in painting |
| designated hitter (baseball) | pedagogue |
| isobars | offside, in hockey |
| laugh-track, in television | parochialism |

---

> *... Classifications both reflect and direct our thinking. The way we order represents the way we think.*
>
> (Stephen Jay Gould)

### 3. CLASSIFICATION AND DIVISION

As you narrow a subject to a topic, two of the ways to look at it are as a member of a class (badminton as one kind of sport) or as a whole made up of a number of parts (the various kinds of racquet sports). Looking at a subject from these two points of view will help you to identify it more precisely and to see both its external and its internal relationships. When you deal with an object or an idea in terms of other things like it, you are working with *classification*; when you deal with the parts or sub-parts of an object or idea, you are using *division*, or analysis. Classification sorts into groups; division separates into parts.

**Classifying**   If you find questions like the following especially productive, consider developing your topic, or part of it, by the method of classification:

What kinds of it are there?
What other things are like it?
What contains it, of what is it a part?
What goes with it?
Does it have an opposite?
In what contexts does it occur?

One of the most powerful abilities of the human mind is its ability to classify, to make and use categories. Much of our thinking about the world is in terms of categories, either those we get from others or those we create for ourselves. One of the continuing dangers to clear thinking and writing, though, is that we may come to believe that such categories are a fixed part of the way things are. We can easily lose sight of the fact that categories are artificial, products of the ability of the human mind to sort out the flux of experience. Too often we accept a given set of categories as the only way to look at things; we think in stereotypes and clichés. (It is partly for this reason that we urge you to try "cross-fertilizing" during step 3, *inventing*; see pp. 52-53.)

When you create new categories or adopt those of others, think of your *purpose* in classifying: what particular problem or problems do you want your categories to help you examine? Suppose for example you've decided to discuss television programs and have narrowed your subject to violence on television. In order to examine violence, you decide to classify television fare into four categories: adventure programs, sports programs, comedy programs, and news programs. But when you set out to examine several different programs in each category, you find significant levels of violence in all of them—including, you suddenly remember, a lot of children's programs. As a result, you might decide to create a different set of categories, one that is more useful for your purpose—for example, programs with different kinds of violence, or different degrees of violence, or accidental as opposed to intentional violence; or you might find that you could classify programs according to how important their violence is to their purpose, as opposed to being simply gratuitous.

Or suppose your subject has to do with the major cities in Canada, and you've decided to focus on Calgary, Edmonton, Halifax, Montreal, Regina, Toronto, Vancouver, and Winnipeg. If your thesis has to do with shipping costs, you'd use a geographical basis for your categories (Maritimes, French Canada, Central Canada, the Prairies, and the West Coast). But if your thesis has to do with public transport, then you would use some entirely different system of classification.

When you have established a principle of classification that suits your purpose and audience, make that principle clear to your readers. In the following passage, for example, the student clearly sets out the basis for the three categories she discovered in her use of language:

> As one who is basically the same on nearly all occasions, I find it difficult to draw real distinctions among my various identities and the way my language presents those roles. However, though my use of language doesn't change much, I have discovered three main areas of difference: 1) in what I say, 2) in how I say it, and 3) in what I don't say. Curiously, the language I *don't* use best reflects the identity I am assuming at that time.

A fully worked-out classification can be quite complicated, with its categories and sub-categories and sub-sub-categories, as you can see if you look in an encyclopedia to find out where whales, for example, fit into the animal kingdom. But not all classifications need to be so complicated or formal. Usually you will need to provide only representative categories. Suppose for instance that you wanted to provide tourists with an idea of the kinds of eating places that were available in and around your town or city. You wouldn't have to list all of them. You could provide a representative sampling classified by kinds (Oriental, French, Italian, seafood, steak, etc.) with a note about price added to each; or, if you felt that your audience would be more concerned about price than cuisine, you could categorize them according to prices and add a word to each designating the kind.

### Exercise 4C

Look around your room or your neighbourhood. Make a list of

| | |
|---|---|
| seven green things | seven small things |
| seven square things | seven broken things |
| seven tasteful things | seven crossed things |
| seven tasty things | |

Write an essay about the things in one of these groups.

OR

Write an essay about those things that turn up in more than one group.

### Exercise 4D

Choose one of the following headings, and list ten to fifteen specific items for it. Then classify those items into at least three categories. Head your classification with a statement explaining the purpose of the scheme you use.

| | |
|---|---|
| winter sports | student housing |
| university courses | musical instruments |
| game fish | automobiles |
| geographical areas of your province | ways to make money |
| local restaurants | movies on television |
| forest products | leisure-time activities |
| religious faiths | dictionaries |

**Division**   When you classify, your development is from individual items to groups of items in categories or classes; when you use division, you move from a whole to its parts. If your notes for some reason list twenty recent movies, you could classify them to see what groups they fall into and what that might lead you to discover about them. But if you began with "movies" as your subject, you could divide it up into its parts—kinds of movies or many individual movies. The two methods are in effect reverses of each other. But if, say, you'd classified movies into adventure, comedy, and drama, and decided you still had too big a topic to handle, you could decide to focus on adventure movies alone—and you then might decide to analyze the adventure movie as a form, to divide it up into its parts to see what makes it tick.

If you find that questions like the following give you some good ideas, consider developing part or all of your topic by the method of division:

Can it be divided?
What are its parts?
Can there be other parts of it?
Does it have degrees?

In a sense, division is fundamental to all writing; every subject must be divided into parts, if only to decide what to write about first and what to write about next. For either a whole essay or a section of an essay, or even just a paragraph, you can decide to develop by dividing a whole into its parts. For instance, in order to explain how an electric motor works, you would probably begin by explaining its separate parts. Or if you're discussing a Shakespearean sonnet, you might begin by looking at its larger parts—the three quatrains and the concluding couplet—and then move on to smaller parts such as individual lines, images, and words.

*A note of caution:* Beware of oversimplifying, both in setting up categories and in breaking up a subject into its parts. There are likely to be several shades of gray between black and white, just as there are degrees of desirability between good and bad.

---

## Essay 4A

Write a short essay (500-700 words) based on a *division* of a typical day in your life. Separate such a day into its constituent parts as well as you can and use each part as the topic of a section of your essay (try to keep the number under seven). From your invention notes decide upon a thesis statement, and use it to guide you in deciding how to order the parts in your plan. Do *not* use straight chronological order.

---

## 4. COMPARISON AND CONTRAST

The human mind delights in perceiving similarities in things that seem different and differences in things that seem similar. As methods of development, comparing and contrasting reveal how one person, object, or idea is like or unlike another. These methods can be prompted by the answers to such questions as these:

> What is it like?
> What is it unlike?
> Is it like or unlike several other things?
> Does it differ in some ways from similar things?

First decide on the main points of comparison. The more points of similarity you reveal, the better the comparison as a means of explanation. To take a simple example, suppose you decide to explain the concept of interest by comparing it to rent. Just as one returns the item one has rented to the rental shop and pays for its use, so one returns the principle of a loan to the lender and pays for its use in interest. Here, since the points of comparison are quite close, the comparison acts as a good explanation.

You can also use contrast to explain how your topic, or part of it, differs from something already familiar to your readers. Of course it would not help much to contrast two things that are obviously different in almost every way. Contrast works best when there are enough similarities to make a difference revealing. In the following passage, for example, a student explains how teachers' and parents' roles in raising children are complementary:

> Parents must provide not only for children's material needs but their social needs as well. These needs can be met at home, where parents and children interact. Then, too, children need friends to play with. Parents can encourage socializing by inviting other children into their homes for birthday parties, overnight stays, and other such occasions. Teachers, on the other hand, are able to help children at school. Social games, recess, and noon-hour play give teachers a chance to watch for problems that can be resolved by guidance and counselling.

Note how the writer here has signalled her contrast explicitly with the phrase "on the other hand."

### Advice for Comparing and Contrasting

a. *Choose a suitable basis* for the things you are comparing or contrasting. Popular wisdom and generations of teachers have assured us that you can't compare apples and oranges. But of course you can if your basis for comparison is their desirability as snacks or their attractiveness for a colourful centrepiece. If you were comparing two used cars in order to point out which one would provide the best utilitarian transportation, then weight, age, model, and economy would be suitable features to consider, whereas colour would be irrelevant. But for the purpose of selecting the best car to use in a film, colour could well be a relevant feature to consider.

b. Generally, *concentrate on the major common or distinguishing features.* Don't waste time on unimportant similarities and differences.

c. *Order the parts of your discussion carefully.* If the overall method of an essay is to compare and contrast two things, you basically have two choices: (1) to discuss the two items one at a time or (2) to discuss them feature by feature. The danger with (1) is that the two discussions tend to establish themselves as separate entities, almost like two separate essays, resulting in a "broken-backed" essay. It is difficult to provide a strong enough transition and conclusion to weld the two parts together; such an essay almost inevitably lacks unity and coherence.

Therefore integrate the parts of your discussion as much as possible—and preferably not just by devoting one paragraph to the first item, then one paragraph to the second item, and so on, alternating between the two, until at the end you try to tie them together in a knot of conclusion. Rather, as much as possible organize your comparison and contrast so that each paragraph discusses both items, so that the two are under consideration simultaneously throughout the essay. Not only does such an organization produce an essay that flows more smoothly, but it also avoids much of the repetition you'd have to use to shift back and forth from one item to the other.

Rather than a structure like that on the left in the sample outlines following, try for one like that on the right; try to organize by *feature* rather than by the two major items themselves. The organizing principle on the left is mechanical; that on the right is analytical, logical, and will likely produce a better essay. Note that it also avoids the problem of the two-part, broken-backed structure—assuming you discuss *at least three* features, as you should.

| **Story A** | **Setting** |
| Setting | Story A |
| Plot | Story B |
| Character | **Plot** |
| **Story B** | Story A |
| Setting | Story B |
| Plot | **Character** |
| Character | Story A |
| | Story B |

On the other hand, some topics are better dealt with mechanically. If for example you're dealing with five or six stories, it will probably be better to deal with them one at a time. Even with just two stories, it may be advantageous to get one of them—especially if it's a minor one—out of the way first so that you can concentrate on the more important one.

d.  To keep your readers oriented, *use linking words or phrases* that explicitly connect the parts of your comparison or contrast; for example:

| **similarity** | **difference** |
| likewise | but |
| the same as | yet |
| also | however |
| too | nevertheless |
| as well as | on the contrary |
| similarly | contrary to |
| parallel to | on the other hand |
| like | unlike |
| in the same way | the opposite |
| just as | in contrast |

---

## Exercise 4E

List five pairs of subjects for possible treatment by comparison and contrast. Draw on your own experience. Some examples: indoor sports and outdoor sports; team sports and individual sports; lecture classes and discussion classes; home essays and in-class essays; home-cooked food and restaurant food; living with your parents and living on your own. You can think of many more examples. For each pair you list, construct a tentative outline. If possible, outline analytically, by feature, rather than mechanically. Do any of your paired topics insist that you construct a mechanical, two-part outline?

## Exercise 4F

Provide a few points of similarity and difference for five of the sets below. Specify for each set the basis of comparison or contrast and the purpose.

> EXAMPLE:  hiking and skiing
> > *Purpose:* To show the superiority of hiking as a pastime.
> > *Basis:* Features of cost, convenience, and pleasure.

> *Similarities:* Both are healthful outdoor activities that get one out into nature.
>
> *Differences:* Hiking is less expensive, can be done in any season and in a much greater variety of locales, and offers better opportunities for companionship and the enjoyment of nature.

| | |
|---|---|
| cabinetmaking and writing a report | sound reproduction by disk and by tape |
| hockey, soccer, and rugby | hunting and fishing |
| Mexican, Chinese, and Greek cuisines | cooking and painting |
| the St. Lawrence and Rhine Rivers | rowboats and canoes |
| country music and rock music | whist and bridge |

---

## Exploration 4E

In a paragraph or two, compare and contrast the items in one of the following pairs; note that you will also be using definition.

| | |
|---|---|
| fear and paranoia | precision and pedantry |
| envy and jealousy | design and scheme |
| pride and vanity | economy and frugality |
| banal and boring | crass and coarse |
| boor and lout | sensibility and sensitivity |

## Exploration 4F

Write a short dialogue (200-300 words) in which you portray a contrast between two speakers or their attitudes. Use only dialogue—no explanatory description or narration—and go no further than "he said" or "she said" (if even that) to indicate who is speaking, or how. Make the speeches themselves reveal the manner of speaking.

---

> *And, Sir, as to metaphorical expression,*
> *that is a great excellence in style, when*
> *it is used with propriety, for it gives you*
> *two ideas for one;—conveys the meaning*
> *more luminously, and generally with a*
> *perception of delight.*
>
> (Samuel Johnson)

## Metaphor and Analogy

### a. *Metaphor*

An extension of the method of comparison is the development of a subject by exploring the similarities between unlike people, objects, events, or ideas. When you express such similarities figuratively rather than literally, you are using metaphor. You use metaphor when you say something like this: "It wasn't a hockey game, it was a street riot." What you would mean by such a statement is not that the Mounties had to be called in to restore order, but that too much fighting and rough play spoiled the game for you. Part of the power of a good metaphor is that although you don't expect your listeners or readers to interpret you literally, you can lend colour and force to your writing.

Like comparison, metaphor brings two things together under a higher, usually abstract, classification. The metaphor in the preceding paragraph asserts, by implication, that undisciplined hockey games and street riots can both be classed as manifestations of the abstract idea of disorder. In an explicit comparison you have to express such a common feature, but using a metaphor allows you to leave it unexpressed. You don't have to ascend to those oxygen-poor heights of abstraction; your thinking and writing can take their nourishment from the rich soil of the concrete and the particular. (See pp. 254-258.)

Exploring the question "What is it like?" then, can often lead to fertile regions of development that you hadn't previously considered. Take advantage of metaphors. And don't think that they're something odd or unusual. People are seldom aware how often they use metaphors when they think and talk and write. In fact, our ordinary conversation is filled with metaphor and potential metaphor—as poets, songwriters, and advertising people know. Consider the metaphoric bases and potentials of these expressions, for example:

> He can't put his material across.
> Her argument goes into considerable depth.
> I couldn't digest the report.
> Let's bring it up for discussion.
> His suggestion bowled me over.
> We're just spinning our wheels.
> They can't face the future.
> Inflation is eating up their profits.

And of course there are hundreds more that we use every day. Whether you choose to pursue any given metaphor of course depends on your purpose and your audience. But remember that it usually helps to appeal to readers' experience of the specific and concrete, and metaphors offer you another way of doing that.

Note how in the following sentence a student uses metaphor to make his point more forcefully and more concretely than he could have without metaphor:

> Many economic and cultural developments have been forged in the automotive foundry of North America.

The metaphor is expressed through the words *forged* and *foundry* and is appropriate to the writer's subject: the effects of the automobile in our culture.

Here is a more elaborate use of metaphor, from Margaret Atwood's *Survival: A Thematic Guide to Canadian Literature:*

> Canadians are forever taking the national pulse like doctors at a sickbed: the aim is not to see whether the patient will live well but simply whether he will live at all.

The virtue of such a metaphor is that it suggests a good deal more than the words say—in this instance, about Canadian doubts and self-consciousness—without having to resort to such abstractions.

b. *Analogy*

If you continue a metaphor through several sentences, you build up an analogy or an "extended" metaphor. In the following implicit comparison between a business organization and the human body, Andrew Weiner keeps his discussion from becoming too abstract by developing an analogy:

> The office is the central nervous system of a business. As in the human body, the main function of this system is to move information from the brain of the organization (management) to the limbs (field operations) and back again.
>
> ("The Computer, the Word Processor, and You")

A word of caution: when you develop a topic by analogy, find as many points of similarity as you can (within reason) between your topic and the thing you're comparing it to. The more points of appropriate comparison, the better the analogy.

And when you use metaphors, be careful not to mix them incongruously. Consider the following mixed metaphor from a student paper:

> The road ahead was studded with pitfalls.

Attentive readers will at first be surprised and then amused as they realize that "studs" stick up out of something whereas "pitfalls" are holes to fall into. Even if your purpose is to amuse your readers, you don't want them laughing *at* you—or distracted by such oddity.

Finally, here's a delightfully self-contradictory mixed metaphor from a Canadian politician:

> If this idea ever catches fire, it will snowball all across the land.

---

## Exercise 4G

Select one of the subjects in column A below and see how many points of comparison you can discover in drawing out an analogy with one or more of the items in column B. Then try it again with a different item from column A.

| A | B |
|---|---|
| applying for a loan | baking bread |
| courtship | a fast-food restaurant |
| diplomacy in the Middle East | a horror movie |
| modern art | portaging a canoe |
| provincial politics | a rock concert |
| psychological testing | snowmobiling |
| writing a letter of apology | a video-game arcade |

---

## Exploration 4G

Write an extended analogy (one or two paragraphs) in which you explain to an audience of ten-year-olds one of the following:

| | |
|---|---|
| inflation | pruning trees |
| how atoms combine | using a telephone |

| | |
|---|---|
| photosynthesis | planting a seed |
| rocket propulsion | osmosis |
| digestion | percussion instruments |

## 5. DESCRIPTION

In your search for what to say about a subject, if you found such questions as these interesting to follow up on, consider developing your topic, or parts of it, by the method of description:

What is its appearance (sound, smell, etc.)?
How does it work?
Does it change, or is it constant?
What are its manifestations?
Does it have parts?
What contains it, of what is it a part?
Is it similar to something else?
Where did it occur?

The two indispensable elements in description are (1) an observer and (2) a person, object, scene, or event observed. These two elements constitute the two ends of a spectrum: the subjective and the objective. Any description can be placed somewhere on this spectrum, according to its focus.

*Objective Description*    If your focus is on the object or scene itself, independent of your feelings and associations, the result will be an objective description—the kind to write when you want simply to impart information. The qualities most important to a good objective description are accuracy and economy. Look for example at the following brief description of the Arctic Loon, from a widely used field guide, *Birds of North America:*

> The Arctic is smaller than the two preceding loons; its light grey crown and white stripes on the side of the throat are diagnostic. In winter the back is grey with pale feather edgings. The bill is thin and straight, more slender than the Common Loon's.

The details are selected in order to enable readers to distinguish the Arctic from other loons, not to convey feelings.

An objective description should include only the details most relevant to your purpose. One of the common uses for objective description is in science or engineering reports, where you might have to describe a piece of equipment in order for your readers to understand a process or an experiment. Here is a student's description of a device for measuring relative vacuum pressure:

> The upper, or vacuum gauge (graduated from 0 to 60 mm) records the vacuum pressure. The lower, or atmospheric pressure gauge (graduated from 500 to 1000 mm) records the air pressure. The dials and needles of both gauges are protected by a clear glass face secured by a circular steel rim.

Most of the details provided here are necessary for readers to understand how data was gathered for the experiment—but the need for including the glass face and the steel rim is questionable.

*Subjective Description*   If your purpose is to convey not only the details of the object or scene but also your feelings about it, then select the details that best convey those feelings. Such description is especially useful if your primary purpose is expressive or persuasive. Here is an example; it's not hard to tell how the student felt about the scene he describes:

> Stumbling around a shipyard for the first time is both exciting and scary. Everything seems to happen in a daze. Through billows of steam and smoke, black and gritty, erupts a terrifying din. Everywhere metal pounding, grinders screaming, welders snarling. Sparks shoot through the air and land hissing on the ground. Men rush here and there shouting goddam. The motion makes you dizzy. The whole place groans and gnashes. Overhead a crane swings its neck a hundred yards and drops its cargo onto the greasy floor. Men cling to scaffolds suspended from the sides of monster ships. You find yourself up against the wall, hands on ears, searching for a way out of this pandemonium.

The writer selected the details in order to convey what is called a "dominant impression," that of the apparent demonic madness of the scene. He chose to ignore other details in order to focus his description on that dominant impression. The result is a description near the subjective end of the spectrum.

> *As to the Adjective: when in doubt,*
> *strike it out.*        (Mark Twain)

### Suggestions for Writing Effective Descriptions

a.  Don't confuse good descriptive writing with an abundance of adjectives. Most of the best descriptive writers prefer to use vivid nouns and verbs to bring their scenes to life. In the last example, to be sure, you will find some adjectives like *scary, gritty*, and *greasy*. But note that several other adjectives are participles, which retain some of the force of the verbs that they are derived from: *exciting, terrifying, pounding, screaming, snarling, hissing, shouting, searching, buzzing.* And a good part of the force of the passage comes from the specific verbs: *erupts, shoot, cling, groans, gnashes.*

Here is a student's paragraph that depends far too heavily on adjectives:

> As the school term drew to a close, the fertile, sandy soil of the strawberry farms south of town filled with thick, long rows of leafy, strawberry-laden plants. Enormous clumps of juicy, sweet red berries hung, ready to be harvested by the hands, big and small, deft and clumsy, of local school-children. In the homes of the nearby city, out came the old ragged jeans, torn T-shirts, and berry-stained straw hats as mothers commenced to equip their energetic offspring to join the ranks destined for the fields.

b.  For an adequate objective description, it shouldn't matter who is seeing the object or scene being described. It should appear the same to all dispassionate viewers. But as description moves toward the subjective end of the spectrum, the details grow more and more to depend upon the eye that is seeing and the ear that is hearing. In any description, however, try to maintain a consistent point of view. You can do that by showing the object or scene from a spatially fixed point of view or by showing how the object or scene looks as the observer moves around or through it.

c. In objective description, begin with a brief overview of the object or scene as a whole; then develop it analytically, using paragraphs (in a long description) or sentences (in a short description) to divide the object into its parts, discussing each in turn in as much detail as your purpose demands.

d. If the overall method of development of a piece of writing is descriptive, you will usually want to order the parts in a way that reflects the arrangement in space of the object or scene you're describing.

Here is a passage from the great pastoral romance by Sir Philip Sidney, *The Countesse of Pembrokes Arcadia* (1590). It describes three men putting off from shore in a small boat to look for a maritime disaster nearby. Note how as they draw closer and closer, the description registers the increasing detail of what they see (we have modernized the spelling):

> [They] were no sooner gone beyond the mouth of the haven, but that some way into the sea they might discern (as it were) a stain of the water's colour, and by times some sparks and smoke mounting thereout.... They steered... as near thitherward as they could: but when they came so near as their eyes were full masters of the object, they saw a sight full of piteous strangeness: a ship, or rather the carcass of the ship, or rather some few bones of the carcass, hulling there, part broken, part burned, part drowned: death having used more than one dart to that destruction. About it floated great store of very rich things, and many chests which might promise no less. And amidst the precious things were a number of dead bodies, which likewise did not only testify both elements' violence, but that the chief violence was grown of human inhumanity: for their bodies were full of grisly wounds, and their blood had (as it were) filled the wrinkles of the sea's visage: which it seemed the sea would not wash away, that it might witness it is not always his fault, when we condemn his cruelty: in sum, a defeat, where the conquered kept both field and spoil: a shipwreck without storm or ill footing: and a waste of fire in the midst of water.

As the nature of what has happened becomes clear, the description backs off once again, generalizing about the event.

---

### Essay 4B

Describe some particular area that you know well—the small town you come from, the campus of your college or university, the section of the city you live or work in, the place where you spend your summer holidays. Try to combine consideration of both its natural and its human-made features, for example as in contrast or in harmony with each other. Work from direct observation as much as possible. Use the point of view of an observer walking through the area, and organize your material accordingly.

---

### Exercise 4H

Read carefully through each of the following descriptive paragraphs, all written by students, and then decide just where you would put each on the spectrum running from 1 (objective) to 10 (subjective).

## The Cafeteria Racket

Entering the residence cafeteria, one is immediately conscious of an incessant hubbub: the erratic symphony of dishes and silverware rattling on the dinner trays—the swoosh of the tray down the metallic runway, where the choice is made between jello or an orange for dessert—the hasty tread of feet jostling their way to the seats—the protesting shriek of chairs scraping against the floor as they are shifted to provide greater comfort for their occupants—the shrill crunch of an apple, piece of celery, wedge of lettuce, or dill pickle when encountering a voracious set of teeth—the chew, chew, chew of other, less brittle, morsels of food—the slurping, and occasional embarrassing gulping, of liquids such as tea, coffee, pop, milk, and juice—the nervous click click of silverware burrowing its way through the food, and too often producing a grating sound when coming in contact with the plate—the rare occurrence of a smug belch—the murmurous tinkling of voices conducting the usual routine of table-talk—the sudden explosion of boisterous male laughter avidly applauding a peer—the eventual hush as many of the diners file out.

---

## The Potential Patch

The cotton remnant is twelve centimetres square; a corner is cut off. The fabric itself is crumpled, worn, and frayed. The blue background is faded and the small white daisies, patterned abstractly over the blue, are lined with dirt.

---

## Clock Time

The sound of the clock's tick, tick, tick and the unending sweep of the slender hands physically announce each moment in the day. Round and round the hands rotate, parading each synthetic hour painted on the clock's face. But the gears, working behind the facial front, are the actual workhorses of this physical time machine. Faithfully, they mesh together to drive the seconds into minutes, minutes into hours, and hours into days. The hands on the clock's front stage are simply marionettes attached to strings: they move at the will of the gears.

---

## The Cheesie

The cheesie is perched perilously on the desk, one end raised like a snake preparing to strike. A distorted cylinder, it resembles a sponge that has been twisted, but hasn't quite sprung back to its original shape. It is a collage of miniature hills and dales. It seems to radiate its orangeness. It is the epitome of artificiality, its plasticity lying in stark contrast against the natural woodgrain of the desktop. Appealing to my sentiment, it conjures up images of childhood birthday parties—the balloons, the jellybeans, the games, the fights. The cheesie is taunting my desire to eat it. Like the forbidden apple, it tempts me to defy my conscience.

---

## The Card-Carrier

A social insurance card is a small white plastic rectangle about the size of a credit card. The front has the owner's name and number permanently stamped into it, a thin strip of white tape for the owner's signature, black printing indicating, in both English and French, what it is, and a thin red border along all four sides. The back of the card also has black printing, in both English and French, telling the owner what to do with it. I never leave home without my social insurance card. It proves that I have a social insurance number, which proves that I exist. With it, I can get a job, a passport, a driver's licence, a university education, or anything else that requires proof of my existence. Unfortunately, it can't buy me dinner.

---

## *Exploration 4H*

Find a simple object among your possessions—a chess piece, a spool of thread, a golf ball, a rose bud, a coffee mug, a paperweight, a pencil, an eraser, a compact, a coin; these are only suggestions: the main thing is that the object should be something *simple* so that you can treat it thoroughly in a short space. First write an *objective* description of it, and then a *subjective* description of it, each in a single paragraph 100-200 words long.

## *Exploration 4I*

(a) Write a one-paragraph physical description of someone you know; write from direct observation if possible (do you have a willing roommate?), or perhaps from a good full-length photograph. Be entirely objective, as if you were writing a police bulletin on a missing person or a wanted criminal. Organize spatially, either top to bottom or bottom to top.

(b) Then write another one-paragraph description of the same person. This time let subjective impressions and knowledge colour your description and guide your selection and ordering of details.

---

## 6. NARRATION

Consider narration as a method of developing an entire paper or a part of one if you have found that questions like these have stimulated your thinking—especially if your subject is in whole or in part an event:

Did it happen?
Where did it happen?
When did it happen?
What happens there?
How did it happen?
What was it like?

Narration recreates in words an action or event as it progresses through time. This should come as no surprise, for most of us have grown up telling, listening to, and reading stories. And we can all appreciate a well-told story, one whose details and proportions are selected to suit its point. The same demands hold for stories that are told for their own sakes—to interest or amuse the reader—as for those that serve to illustrate a more general point or to introduce a paper which is to be developed mainly by some other method.

Chronology is central to narration: first this happened, and then that, and then something else. But you can break free from strict time sequence by using a flashback or flash-forward, as films often do. One reason for doing so is to grab your readers' attention by introducing suspense; another is to reveal a further part of your purpose or focus it more sharply.

Often it's not clear whether you're developing a subject by description or narration, so closely are the two methods bound up with one another. In fact, it's virtually impossible to write narration without at least some description in it. Notice how the student writer of the following paragraph intertwines narrative and description:

> Usually I run down to the beach when the tide's out. Something about the smooth wet sand always makes me run faster: I can feel my feet sink and hear the water spurting out from beneath my sneakers. Sometimes I take along Cyrano, the neighbour's mongrel. He thrashes wildly through the surf and tries to eat the foam. He's a crazy dog at the best of times, but at the beach he goes nuts. Once I reach the gun tower, I turn around to survey our footprints—or pawprints—staring back at me. By this time Cyrano is exhausted from his battle with the breakers, and lies down in the sand for a pant and a slobber. After a five-minute rest, the two of us head home, Cyrano dying of thirst from swallowing too many salt-water waves, and me secure in the knowledge that this beats pumping iron in the gym any day.

**Suggestions for Writing Effective Narration**

a. As in description, select and order details with your purpose in mind. If you are using your narrative as an example, choose details that add up to something genuinely exemplary.

b. Pace your narrative so that it focusses on what is important for your purpose. Especially, make sure that the beginning is not out of proportion with the rest. Inexperienced writers tend to open with too detailed a beginning, sometimes causing their readers to mistake the point of the story.

c. As with description, maintain a consistent point of view.

---

### Exploration 4J

Write a short narrative (about 200 words) using strict chronological order, with the climax in the final sentence. Then write another narrative about the same event which starts in the middle but then flashes back to the beginning; again, save the climax for the end. To make it even more difficult for yourself, try writing it a third time, beginning with the climax; how can you keep the reader interested once you have revealed the end? (You may want to use one of the narratives you wrote for an earlier assignment.)

---

### 7. PROCESS ANALYSIS

Despite our traditional and common-sense belief that things are solid and enduring, scientists and philosophers over the last two hundred years have shown us that everything is constantly undergoing some sort of process. Although a logger may view a cedar tree as an object from which so many cubic metres of lumber can be milled, an ecologist might view it as but one of a number of processes and sub-processes in the environment. One of the fundamental modes of thinking is to consider a topic less as an object than as part of a process that goes on through time.

If questions like the following have stimulated your thinking about a topic, consider developing part or all of it by means of examining one or more of the processes involved in it:

Why does it exist or happen?
How or for what is it used?
How does it work?
Is it part of a larger process or system?
Does it contain any sub-processes?

The purpose of analyzing a process is to explain how something works, how something happens or happened, or how to do something. Processes that lend themselves to this sort of analysis usually consist of a series of events, actions, or steps leading toward a specific result. Such processes can consist of mental actions (how to solve a quadratic equation), mechanical actions (how to repair a pump, how to clean a squid), historical events (how Hitler came to power), or natural occurrences (how a hurricane forms).

Here for example is part of a student's essay about how trees are turned into paper; note that, like narration, explaining a process deals with events that follow one another in time:

> The pulp operators blow the chips into vats, called digesters, which are huge pressure-cookers not much different from the ones used at home, only much larger, sometimes ten to fifteen storeys high. In the digester, the chips are mixed with strong chemicals that break down the chips under pressure and high temperatures, separating the cellulose fibres from the natural turpentines, resins, and other substances that grow together to make a tree in the forest. The cellulose, which is what paper is, is screened out and the rest of the material is burned as fuel in huge boilers that generate the steam for the pulp process and electricity for power. The method used to screen the cellulose reclaims the chemicals so that they can be used again and again, resulting in minimal waste.

The purpose of analyzing the pulp-making process is to explain or report on how something is done. But you also explain a process when you write a set of directions for the purpose of telling somebody how to do something. We are all familiar with the basic characteristics of instructions: the stages in the process are laid out step by step, and the verbs are in the imperative form: "Next, insert Tab A in Slot B," or "Then stir the sauce briskly," or "Be sure to capitalize only the first word in the complimentary closing of a business letter." Much of this book, since it is instructing you in how to follow the steps in the process of composition, uses that kind of language.

Here is a brief passage from a do-it-yourself booklet on building hot tubs. Because it appears near the end of a section on building the tub itself, it uses the word *Finally* to keep its readers informed about where they are in the process:

> Finally, you may still have a few leaks that won't close. If they seem minor, try throwing some very fine sawdust or sander dust into the water. It will tend to be drawn into the leaks where it will lodge and swell and finally close them off.
>
> (Jake Rankin, *The Complete Book of Hot Tubs*)

Note that the instructions explain not only *what* to do but *why* to do it that way. It looks obvious in this passage, but this important principle of written instructions is easy to overlook: because you know perfectly well why you should do something, you might forget that your readers don't.

Consider your readers when you write instructions: consider how much experience they have had, and what special terms you have to define for them, and how much detail you have to go into. The following passage is from a set of instructions written by a student whose purpose was to tell his relatively uninformed readers how to fell a tree. After explaining how to choose the tree and determine where it will fall, he gets down to the business of the first stage of the actual cutting:

> The next step is sawing out the "wedge" or "undercut." With your feet planted firmly on the ground, cut into the side facing the direction you want the tree to fall. After you have cut horizontally about one third of the tree's width, begin a new cut on an angle about ten centimetres below the first cut, up and into the inner edge of the horizontal cut. If you make these two cuts carefully, the wedge should fall out of the trunk. Also, the tree may begin to creak because of the strain on the remaining wood. Before beginning the next cut, which is the most important one, check to see if you are in control of the task: Is the saw running properly? And is the tree going to fall in the right direction?

Basic to developing a topic by process analysis is breaking it down into discrete stages that you can discuss in sequential order, whether your topic is instructing someone how to wax a pair of skis or explaining the events that led up to the Russian Revolution. If a particular process consists of a large number of small steps, find some way to group them into a smaller number of large steps; that is, try to keep the number of main divisions in your plan between three and seven so that your readers can more easily understand the process. Careful planning is important because you want your readers to achieve a specific result, or at least to understand how such a result is or was achieved. For example, if you're writing a set of instructions, follow these steps:

a. Write your introduction, setting out your purpose and including any necessary background information or theory; for example, clarify any necessary equipment or circumstances,

b. List your steps in order.

c. Develop each step; this is the body of your paper.

d. Write your conclusion—perhaps a brief summary, or perhaps an evaluation of the results; or remind your readers of the importance or usefulness of the process.

Your readers will be depending on your accuracy, clarity, and completeness.

## *Exploration 4K*

Write a one- or two-paragraph set of instructions on how to do one of the following things. Be prepared to have your instructions read out to someone who must then try to follow them.

> blowing up a balloon
> putting on a jacket
> using a manual can-opener
> drawing a rhombus on the blackboard
> peeling an onion
> putting on mascara
> playing hop-scotch
> setting up a chess-board to begin a game
> playing a cassette-tape on your portable machine

## *Essay 4C*

Write a short essay (about 1000 words) explaining how to do—and enjoy—something people used to do, but now rarely do, such as churning butter, harnessing a team, making dandelion wine, making root-beer, dancing a waltz, using a washboard, making soap, or winning at hop-scotch or pinball. These are only suggestions. Your topic will have to be something you in fact know how to do.

## *Essay 4D*

For an audience of readers who know nothing about the game (suppose they are from Mars), explain (in an essay of no more than 1500 words) how to play, and do reasonably well at, badminton, racquetball, squash, soccer, tennis, backgammon, hockey, checkers, frisbee, football, pinochle, kite-flying, or some other game or sport.

## 8. CAUSE AND EFFECT

Narration and process depend upon perceiving relationships across time; so does development by cause and effect. Narratives show *what*, process tells *how*, and cause-and-effect tells *why*. If you have found questions like these promising, you might try developing all or part of your topic by looking for causes or results:

> Can it be changed?
> Why does it exist or happen?
> What or who causes it?
> What does it cause?
> For what is it used?
> Is it part of a larger process?
> What if it didn't exist or happen?

Much of people's thinking involves issues of causation: this happened because of that; if we do so and so, the result will be such and such. Business people ask why their profits are declining; a hockey coach ponders why his team lost the last game; cabinet ministers debate the consequences of a proposed hike or cut in taxes. And some of the most valuable things you learn in school or university have to do with answers or hypotheses concerning causation: the causes of the Crimean War; the effects of climate on native cultures; the results of mixing zinc oxide with nitric acid; the effects of different rhyme schemes in poetry; the reasons major cities are declining in population, and what the political and other consequences of that will be. And you devote a good deal of time outside the classroom to questions of causation: Why does the car keep stalling? How will the strike affect our holidays? Why was he so sarcastic on the phone? What caused my headache? Why are so many movies so similar to one another?

Sometimes you're right about causes and sometimes you're wrong. Sometimes what you decide was a cause was only an incidental circumstance, and sometimes it is itself only a result of another more fundamental, underlying cause. In what sense, for example, is it true to say that lightning "causes" thunder? As you begin to look for reasons, then, you need to distinguish between causes and attendant circumstances. To be a true cause, an event must *necessarily* lead to a particular consequence. If A is the cause of B, B never occurs without A's having occurred first.

Further, a number of causes may combine to produce a certain effect, and it may be that all of them must be present for the effect to occur. Consider the following passage from a student paper which tries to sort out causal relations:

> Why is the quality of television programming declining? Is it because people are generally less intelligent and therefore less demanding about the quality of the programs they watch? This seems unlikely, since people are no less intelligent now than they were ten years ago. Could it be that quality is declining because sponsors aren't willing to support a program that won't appeal to a wide range of viewers? This reason probably accounts for many programs never even being shown; a sponsor feels that his product, be it soap flakes or stuffing, would not get enough exposure if a program can cater to only a small group of viewers. Could it be that television programming is becoming more mundane because people don't care what they watch? This certainly could be an answer. Without some sort of negative feedback from the viewers, networks will keep showing and producing programs which insult even a small child's intelligence.

Here, in sorting out competing hypotheses, the student has rejected one possible cause and accepted two others.

### Exercise 4I

Analyze the foregoing paragraph critically. Is it entirely logical? Is it convincing? Are the two causes the writer accepts genuinely different? In a few sentences, evaluate the passage, giving reasons for your judgments.

**Organizing Cause-and-Effect Relations**

Depending on your purpose, and on the nature of your topic and the material you've generated for it, you can

(a) start with an effect and try to explain its cause, or
(b) start with a cause and try to show or predict its effect.

And of course just as one effect can have more than one cause, so can one cause have several effects. You could even find yourself dealing with several interconnected causes that have several interconnected results. Or you might find that the best way to treat your subject is to begin in the present, then explore past causes, and then predict further consequences for the future. You might want to treat it as a kind of chain reaction.

*One caution:* As you are examining several possible causes of a particular event, beware of the *post hoc* fallacy. (See p. 115.) Just because one event follows another in time, the first is not necessarily the cause of the second. You would be right to reject a claim that the amber light somehow caused the red light on a traffic signal. And the hockey fan who always wears a red hat to the games because his team won the first time he wore it is also under the delusion of the *post hoc* fallacy; it is the cause of most superstitions.

---

## Essay 4E

Write a short essay (around 500 words) analyzing one of your own superstitions. For what reasons, logical or illogical, do you persist in it? Or, if you believe you are completely free of superstition, try to explain why. But prepare to be challenged, for few if any of us are without at least one or two small superstitions. (For the purposes of this essay, try not to depend on such well-known and obvious superstitions as those having to with black cats, ladders, and the number 13.)

---

## Exercise 4J

The following proverbs all assert causal relations. They are usually used figuratively. Choose three of them and, for each, first state it in non-metaphorical language and then, in a few sentences, comment on its adequacy as a statement of cause and effect.

1. Where there's smoke, there's fire.
2. Too many cooks spoil the broth.
3. A stitch in time saves nine.
4. A rolling stone gathers no moss.
5. Once bitten, twice shy.
6. Pride goeth before a fall.
7. Still waters run deep.
8. Money is the root of all evil.
9. An apple a day keeps the doctor away.

---

### Essay 4F

Choose one of the topics below and write an essay of about 1000 words that examines the causal relations involved. Apply the principles of cause and effect carefully. For example, distinguish between necessary causes (without A, B would not occur) and incidental causes (A may contribute to B, but something else is the main cause of B). Try to keep your line of reasoning clear for your readers, but remember that this is to be more than a step-by-step lab report: you are examining a circumstance in real life, and you need to make the account lively and interesting, with illustrations and vivid detail. In part your task is to provide a narrative; make it a good one.

1. Why I failed to _____.
2. Why jazz (rock, punk, classical music) is increasing (declining) in popularity.
3. Why I came to university.
4. Why inflation persists.
5. Why there are fewer (more) jobs in the field of _____.
6. Why more money is spent on _____ than on _____.
7. Why movies are better (worse) than they used to be.
8. Why some restaurants flourish while others flop.
9. Why I sometimes neglect my homework.
10. Why I chose to leave _____.

### Essay 4G

In a process analysis of about 1000 words, explain the events that led up to some crisis or turning point in your life. Note that this also means you will be dealing with cause and effect.

## THE THESIS STATEMENT

Earlier in this chapter we defined the thesis for a given piece of writing as your controlling idea, the point that your essay is all about. It is the main assertion you make about a narrowed topic. An adequate thesis statement guides your thinking as you proceed through the remaining steps of composition: planning your organization, and writing and revising the drafts. But it may turn out that your thesis is not fully formulated until you go through two or three drafts. Sometimes only then can you be certain about what you need to write on this particular occasion for these particular readers. Don't hesitate to refine or change your thesis as you proceed through the rest of the steps.

If you decide to make your thesis explicit early in a paper, it constitutes a kind of contract with your readers. It helps to let them know what you are trying to show them or tell them, to explain or reveal to them, or to convince them of. A carefully worded thesis makes a commitment which the rest of the paper will go on to fulfill.

## Where to Place Your Thesis Statement

It is usually best to put your thesis statement near the beginning of a paper—either at the very beginning (in the first or second sentence) or at the end of the first paragraph. (See the example on p. 160.)

Or you can reserve it for near the end, or at the beginning of the ending; some topics invite this kind of suspenseful technique.

Or you may choose what is probably the most common method: state your thesis both near the beginning and near the end.

Or you may have the kind of thesis that wants breaking up, part of it appearing in one place and other parts in other places.

In any event, here is an important point: The thesis as you put it into your essay need not, and probably should not, appear in the same form as it does in your plan. In your plan or outline you want a carefully and clearly worded sentence to use as a blueprint for constructing your essay: it is likely to be stark and stiff, and all the better for that. In the essay, however, you will usually want to express it more smoothly.

On rare occasions—for example in a piece of pure description—your thesis may not appear at all. Just as sometimes a paragraph is so strong and clear that its topic is clear without a topic sentence, so sometimes an essay's thesis will come through loud and clear even without being explicitly stated.

## The Form of the Thesis Statement

Try to construct your thesis statement in such a way that your narrowed topic appears in the subject part of the sentence and the claim or assertion you are making about that topic appears in the predicate. Take for example the subject of "violence in sport" narrowed further to "violence in minor hockey." This is still only a *topic*, even though it has been narrowed to something that can be handled in a short paper. It becomes a *thesis* when you make a statement about it. For example:

> Violence in minor hockey results from over-enthusiastic parents and coaches.

Or, if you don't believe that violence in minor hockey is a serious problem, you might produce this:

> The claims about excessive violence in minor hockey have been exaggerated by those who don't properly understand the game.

In both of these statements, as you can see, the narrowed topic appears as the subject and a specific assertion about that topic occurs as the predicate.

*Caution:* Try to make your thesis statements either simple sentences or complex sentences. Avoid compound sentences. If you find that you've constructed one in the form of a compound sentence, revise it; if you cannot comfortably revise it into either a complex or a simple sentence, it may turn out to be two separate theses and lead to a badly split essay.

Here are a student's suggested thesis statements—a pair for each of three subjects:

1. *The energy crisis:*
    a. There is a direct relationship between the importance the average North American attaches to the energy crisis and the thickness of the wallet in his pocket.
    b. A sudden surge in interest in human-powered vehicles, both aerial and terrestrial, is one positive result of our obvious fate, as perceived by a society almost totally dependent upon fossil fuels.
2. *The computer revolution:*
    a. Chips, bytes, Algol, Cobol, Fortran, Boolean—a new vocabulary is evolving as computers become a part of life in the '80's.
    b. The silicon chip is playing a larger and larger part in the education of children, with the possible result that future generations will be as helpless without it as we would be without the internal combustion engine.
3. *Violence in sport:*
    a. The famous sting of Ali's left jab fulfills a need in the human spirit to witness, and participate in, some degree of violence and savagery.
    b. I don't know how many gold or silver coins it required 2000 years ago to get a good seat at the "Christians vs. The Lions" spectacles in Rome, but the motivation was the same as people's today when they flock to NHL games: spend a few bucks in the hope of witnessing some good violence.

## Exercise 4K

Comment on these thesis statements. What are their strong points? Do they have any weaknesses? Do some of them sound like lively beginnings, not just dry thesis statements? Is that good, or bad? Is the last one acceptable—can it be revised into a simple or complex sentence? What method or methods of development does each suggest?

## Exercise 4L

Choose two of the following topics, narrow each to something you know about and could handle in three or four pages, and write, for each, two careful thesis statements, each reflecting a different one of the methods of development discussed earlier in this chapter. (In parentheses after each, identify the principal method of development you have in mind for it.)

| | |
|---|---|
| rock bands | student clubs |
| historical novels | cable television |
| the Northwest Territories | a practical education |
| windsurfing | hot tubs |
| skiing | orchestras |

# PLANS AND OUTLINES

Some people find they can write better if they guide their writing from an early stage with a carefully prepared outline. Others find that a roughly sketched plan is enough. And of course elaborate outlines are more useful for some projects than for others.

Using an outline has several advantages:

1. An outline clearly indicates where you have to go.
2. An outline enables you to tell at a glance if you have left out anything necessary or included anything unnecessary.
3. An outline gives you a good sense of the relative proportions of the parts of your project.
4. An outline breaks up the project into smaller elements that you can handle one at a time.

The principal advantage of any outline or plan is that with the project clearly mapped out, you can concentrate on the writing rather than worry about other things while you write. On the other hand, drawing up an elaborate outline during the planning stage might have the effect of closing off your options too early. For many writing projects you need to retain flexibility, for as you revise, you may come up with new ideas that are better than those you could have formalized into an early outline.

An outline shouldn't be a straitjacket, but for most projects you will probably find it useful to provide yourself with at least a rough plan to keep your ideas straight. You can use an emerging outline in conjunction with a tentative thesis statement and develop the two reciprocally. As the thesis becomes more specific, the outline gets more filled in; and adjustments in the outline can help you see how to improve the thesis statement.

Further, the form your outline takes may depend on how you decide to develop your topic. For example, if you are writing a narrative, a list of the events with the more important episodes underlined might be sufficient to keep you on the track and to help you avoid that tendency of many student writers to provide an over-elaborate beginning and then to hurry over the more significant parts. If you are developing your paper by examples and illustrations, you can rough out a plan by simply listing the main points you want to make and, below each one, listing the examples you want to use to support that point. Here is a student's plan for a short paper:

**Thesis Statement:** Although university students are subject to a variety of pressures, the dominant one for many is financial.

**Beginning:** Work 4 months at poorly paid job (temporary) to support 12 months; part-time work detracts from studying.

    I. University expenses:
        A. Tuition
        B. Texts
        C. Other (lab fees, supplies)
    II. Living expenses:
        A. Housing
        B. Transportation
        C. Food & clothing (usually low priority)
    III. Other expenses (necessary for morale):
        A. Trips home
        B. Entertainment

**Ending:** Need for thrift; financial troubles part of university experience; educational value?

Note that, logically, you cannot subdivide a heading into only one subheading: if you have an *A*, you must also have at least a *B*; if you have a *1*, you must also have at least a *2*; and so on.

Or you might find it advantageous to use the more graphic representation afforded by a "branching tree" diagram. Such a diagram can help you see the relations among your ideas as you ask questions about your subject and watch it grow, and it can also help you see the relations between the major parts as you seek the best organization for them. The plan about student expenses, for example, would be represented like this:

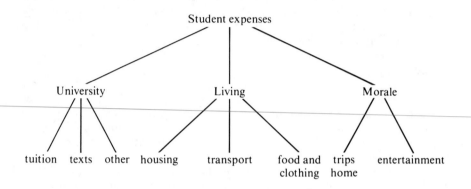

With such a diagram you can see at a glance whether a particular branch needs to be encouraged or possibly, if it stubbornly remains underdeveloped, lopped off. In the latter event, you can try grafting its data onto another branch.

Still another sort of diagram, the "flow chart," is useful for planning a paper analyzing or explaining a process. Flow charts are often used in computer programming to ensure that no step has been left out. In Chapter I we use a relatively informal flow chart to illustrate the writing process: see page 8.

---

### Exercise 4M

Here is a student's plan for a short essay. Examine it critically. The intended method of development is that of examples.

> **T.S.:** Strikes in essential public services are harmful to the public.
> — The postal strike last summer
>   — small businesses ruined
>   — people in remote areas who depend on mail
>   — phones cut off because of unpaid bills
>   — my driver's licence and social insurance card held up
> — Ambulance workers on strike (though only briefly)
>   — danger of emergencies ignored
>   — affects fire-fighters and other groups who have to do the work.

Little more than a glance is needed to reveal that the second section, about ambulance workers, will be inadequately developed compared to the first. Further, the plan has only two main parts, whereas a good essay, as we said earlier (see p. 65) should have from three to seven parts. Revise the plan to get rid of the weaknesses. You will probably want to add more material (the mention of fire-fighters in the last line is suggestive). You may even want to consider a different organization. Is the thesis statement satisfactory, or is it a truism, a tautology? What would be the effect of this harm on the public's attitudes?

## Exercise 4N

From the list below, choose five topics and compose two different thesis statements for each—not just two versions of the same thesis, but two distinctly different ones. These topics have been somewhat narrowed already, but you may need to narrow some even more to arrive at workable theses. (Imagine that you are planning an essay of 1000-2000 words.) Remember that a thesis statement should not be a compound sentence.

bilingualism in Canada
on being a first-year student
the computer revolution
violence in sport
the joys of sport

cable television
how to paint a house
driver education
children's games
living by oneself

After each thesis statement you write, indicate what principal method of development you think would be most appropriate for it.

## Exercise 4O

Combine each of the following groups of sentences into two different possible thesis statements.

1. a. Careful planning is necessary for wilderness exploration.
   b. Accidents happen easily in mountainous country.
   c. Rivers claim lives every year.
   d. Winter can be particularly dangerous.

2. a. Canada should be careful about its exploitation of northern resources.
   b. Mineral resources may be less plentiful than expected.

3. a. Students should not neglect their physical health because of the pressure of mental work.
   b. A program of regular exercise or participation in sport is important for students.
   c. One's physical health influences one's intellectual functions.

4. a. Organic foods are usually more expensive than other foods.
   b. Chemical additives in foods can, according to some people, be bad for one's health.

5. a. Kite-flying is a pleasant pastime.
   b. Outdoor activities are healthful.
   c. Kite-flying is an inexpensive hobby.
   d. People usually fly kites in spring, the loveliest season.

### Exercise 4P

This exercise is designed to let you review the principles of planning.

(a) From the following list of subjects or subject areas, choose five, and by asking questions, narrow each to three different topics. Specify the audience and purpose for each, and the length of the proposed essay.

| | |
|---|---|
| travel | politics |
| summer jobs | mining |
| restaurants | fruit |
| using money wisely | surprise |
| athletics | tact |

(b) Choose two of the resulting sets of topics, and for each of the six construct three different thesis statements; make sure they are substantially distinct from one another.

(c) For each thesis statement, designate the principal method of development for a prospective essay.

(d) For each thesis statement, draw up at least an informal plan showing the major divisions.

### Exploration 4L

Compose six single paragraphs, each using one of the methods of development listed below. Find your own topics. Aim for paragraphs of average length—that is, between 100 and 200 words each; keep your topics fairly simple, therefore, and state them in the first sentence of each paragraph.

1. Example and Illustration
2. Definition
3. Classification
4. Comparison and Contrast
5. Process Analysis
6. Cause and Effect

### Exploration 4M

Construct an outline for this chapter. Use Roman numerals for main headings, capital letters for the first level sub-heading, Arabic numerals for the next, and so on:

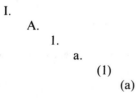

But you should not need to go beyond one or two levels of sub-heading. Does outlining the chapter help you to understand its points and their inter-relationships?

## Exploration 4N

For an essay of about 600-800 words, find a subject (perhaps from the list on pp. 23-24, narrow it to a topic, brainstorm it, run it through the questions for step 3, formulate a thesis question, then a thesis statement and plan, and indicate alongside the entries in your outline both the overall method of development you intend to use for your essay and the methods of development you would use for its major parts. Submit the plan to your instructor and to some of your fellow-students for their comments and criticism.

---

## Essay 4H

After considering the comments and criticisms you receive on the plan in the preceding exploration, proceed to write an essay from it.

## Essay 4I

Think about the different human relations in your life. How many different roles do you play? How many different versions of yourself are there? Have they changed over time? How many "masks" do you wear at different times and on different occasions? Write an essay of 1000-1500 words explaining these different *you*'s. Structure your essay according to a classification of your various identities, and use narrative and descriptive examples and illustrations to help explain each of the categories and sub-categories of your behaviour.

## Essay 4J

Take the narrative you wrote for Chapter I (Essay 1B), condense it, and use it as one of at least three illustrations to support a thesis in an essay of about 1000 words.

## Essay 4K

Think back over the last year and note any significant changes in your life. Formulate these changes (try to come up with at least three) into a thesis statement and write an essay of about 1200 words that develops it by using (a) example and illustration, (b) comparison, (c) cause and effect, and possibly also incorporating some (d) description and narration.

## Essay 4L

Choose one of the following words to define in an essay of 800-1000 words:

| | |
|---|---|
| the good life | virtue |
| myth | love |
| a hero | evil |

Do some brainstorming; use the questions for inventing; take copious notes. Before you begin writing your first draft, lay out a detailed plan. And though definition is your primary method, include in your plan an indication of how you propose to use some of the other methods of development to serve that overall purpose—perhaps example and illustration, classification, comparison and contrast. Hand in the plan with the finished essay; if you find it necessary to revise the plan, hand in both versions.

### Essay 4M

Practise expressive writing. Write a free-wheeling impressionistic description of an object, a person, a building, or a scene. Don't worry about occasion or audience; your purpose is simply to express yourself with relative abandon.

### Idioms 4

In this and the rest of the idiom exercises through Chapter IX, you are to supply an idiomatic preposition to go with each word listed, and compose a sentence using the two words. Many of the words could be followed by more than one preposition, but with little or no difference in meaning. For example one thing can abut *on, upon,* or *against* another. If you think a different preposition does alter the meaning slightly, you can compose an extra sentence to illustrate it. As with the earlier exercises, do as much as you can without help, but to fill any gaps, and to check on the ones you've written, consult a good dictionary or other reference (there are many books on idioms and other matters of usage), or find a friend whose sense of idiom you can trust. Correct any that you've done wrong, and keep a list of them and of the ones you didn't know; keep practising with them until you're familiar with them.

In this and the next idiom exercise all the words are *verbs*. In seeking an idiomatic preposition for each of these, remember that you want one that normally or automatically goes with the verb, one that is almost a part of the verb. For example one could take the verb *collide* and say that two cars collided *at the corner,* or *in the street,* or *on the bridge*. The *at, in,* and *on* here simply introduce "where" phrases, and are not a matter of idiom. The preposition that belongs idiomatically to *collide* is *with,* as in "The car collided with the oncoming bus." The unidiomatic error that sometimes occurs is to use *against* instead of *with*.

Here are the verbs for this exercise:

| | | | | |
|---|---|---|---|---|
| accuse | conform | discourage | grapple | prohibit |
| acquit | convict | dissociate | immigrate | rob |
| arrive | culminate | divorce | infuse | strive |
| border | debar | enlighten | meddle | theorize |
| chide | derive | forbid | object | vie |

### Sentence-Combining 4:  Relative Clauses
### Pattern 4A

Base sentence *a*: A man telephoned me late last night.
Base sentence *b*: He turned out to be a distant cousin.
Result of combining *a* and *b*:
> The man who telephoned me late last night turned out to be a distant cousin.

First, COPY the pattern sentence carefully. Note that you change the word *A* to *The*, that you insert *who* between *man* and *telephoned*, and that you delete *He*.

Note also that you do not add any commas to the sentence.

Second, COMBINE each of the following pairs of sentences into a single sentence modelled on the pattern sentence:

a. A student interrupted the lecturer.
b. She had missed a page reference.

a. One Canadian writer impresses me the most.
b. She is Alice Munro.

Third, COMPOSE two sentences of your own modelled on Pattern 4A.

In this exercise you are making two simple sentences into a complex sentence by changing part of the first into a relative clause—that is, an adjective clause beginning with the relative pronoun *who*. Since the relative clause (*who telephoned me last night*) specifies or limits the noun it modifies (*man*), it is what is called a *restrictive* modifier and is therefore not set off with commas; it is essential to the meaning of the sentence.

## Pattern 4B

a. Some people can count themselves fortunate.
b. They have loyal friends.

RESULT: People who have loyal friends can count themselves fortunate.

Copy the pattern sentence. Note that you drop the vague determiner *some* and that *who* replaces *they*.

Combine each of the following pairs into a sentence modelled on the pattern sentence:

a. Certain people are risking poor health.
b. They don't follow a balanced diet.

a. Some drivers deserve to lose their licences.
b. They drink and drive.

Compose two sentences modelled on Pattern 4B.

In this exercise you are forming a complex sentence by changing sentence *b* into a restrictive relative clause beginning with *who* and then inserting it in sentence *a*.

## Pattern 4C

a. Some people can count themselves fortunate.
b. Their friends are loyal.

RESULT: People whose friends are loyal can count themselves fortunate.

Copy the pattern sentence. Note that you drop the vague modifier *some* and that the possessive (*their*) in sentence *b* becomes *whose*.

Combine each of the following pairs into a sentence modelled on the pattern sentence:

a. Some cars are known as gas-guzzlers.
b. Their engines have to be big.

a. Certain countries are usually the poorest countries
b. Their birth-rates are high.

Compose two sentences modelled on Pattern 4C.

In this exercise you are making a complex sentence by changing sentence *b* to a restrictive clause starting with the relative pronoun *whose* and then inserting it in sentence *a*.

## Pattern 4D

a. The students have all won scholarships.
b. Professor Brown coached them.

RESULT:  The students whom Professor Brown coached have all won scholarships.

Copy the pattern sentence, noting that you replace *them* with *whom* and move it to the beginning of base sentence *b*.

Combine each of the following pairs into a sentence modelled on the pattern sentence:

a. The postman has taken over the route again.
b. Everyone had come to like him.

a. Maybelle has made the man a partner in her law firm.
b. She trusts him the most.

Compose two sentences modelled on Pattern 4D.

In this exercise you are forming a complex sentence by turning sentence *b* into a restrictive relative clause beginning with the pronoun *whom* and then inserting it in sentence *a*. Note that in this pattern the relative pronoun can usually be omitted: The students Professor Brown coached have all won scholarships. Try omitting the pronoun in the two sentences you composed.

## Pattern 4E

a. I intend to buy a personal computer.
b. It will help me manage my everyday finances.

RESULT: I intend to buy a personal computer that will help me manage my everyday finances.

Copy the pattern sentence, using *that* to replace the subject pronoun (*it*) of sentence *b*.

Combine each of the following pairs into a sentence modelled on the pattern sentence:

a. Francis misfiled the student activity reports.
b. They will be needed for Tuesday's meeting.

a. After the talk we went to the reception.
b. It was sponsored by the Gorman Company.

Compose two sentences modelled on Pattern 4E.

In this exercise you are forming a complex sentence by turning sentence *b* into a restrictive relative clause with the relative pronoun *that* as its subject.

## Pattern 4F

a. We are entirely out of copies of the report.
b. Your professor requested it.

RESULT: We are entirely out of copies of the report that your professor requested.

Copy the pattern sentence, using *that* to replace *it* and moving it to the beginning of sentence *b*.

Combine each of the following pairs into a sentence modelled on the pattern sentence:

a. Genevieve has gone to the library for a book on Victorian literature.
b. She needs it for her next English essay.

a. Many people dream about owning expensive things.
b. They will probably never be able to afford them.

Compose two sentences modelled on Pattern 4F.

In this exercise you are making a complex sentence by turning sentence *b* into a restrictive relative clause with the pronoun *that* as its subject. Note that in this pattern it is possible to omit the relative pronoun: We are entirely out of copies of the report your professor requested.

## Pattern 4G

a. The employers' belief turned out to be mistaken.
b. Workers were interested only in higher wages.

RESULT: The employers' belief that workers were interested only in higher wages turned out to be mistaken.

Copy the pattern sentence, putting *that* at the head of sentence *b* and inserting the whole in sentence *a* before the verb.

Combine each of the following pairs into a sentence modelled on the pattern sentence:

a. Ottawa's claim cannot be disputed.
b. It is the nation's capital.

a. My notion could turn out to be expensive.
b. A personal computer will help me manage my everyday finances.

Compose two sentences modelled on Pattern 4G.

In this exercise, as in Patterns 4E and 4F, you are changing base sentence *b* into a restrictive *that*-clause, but this time you are inserting it in sentence *a*, not just putting it at the end.

## Pattern 4H

a. Gloria Diaz volunteered to finish the report.
b. She doesn't mind working late.

RESULT: Gloria Diaz, who doesn't mind working late, volunteered to finish the report.

Copy the pattern sentence. Use *who* to replace *she*, and be sure to put commas around sentence *b* when you insert it in sentence *a*.

Combine each of the following pairs into a sentence modelled on the pattern sentence:

a. The early existentialists were a gloomy lot.
b. They believed life to be meaningless.

a. The minister took full responsibility for the program's failure.
b. He is nothing if not honest.

Compose two sentences modelled on Pattern 4H.

In this exercise, you are making two simple sentences into a complex sentence by changing the second into a relative clause beginning with the pronoun *who* and inserting it in the first sentence. Since the relative clause (*who doesn't mind working late*) does not specify or define the noun it modifies (the name, *Gloria Diaz*, fully identifies the subject), it is what is called a *non-restrictive modifier* and is enclosed in commas; it is incidental information, not essential to the meaning of the sentence.

## *Pattern 4I*

a. The popularity of the Beatles lasted well into the seventies.
b. It was highest in the sixties.

RESULT: The popularity of the Beatles, which was highest in the sixties, lasted well into the seventies.

Copy the pattern sentence. Use *which* to replace *it*, and be sure to put commas around sentence *b* when you insert it in sentence *a*.

Combine each of the following pairs into a sentence modelled on the pattern sentence:

a. The Zipzap 27B computer consistently outperforms its closest competitors.
b. It has only a 32K memory.

a. Large cars are known as gas-guzzlers.
b. They need big engines.

Compose two sentences modelled on Pattern 4I.

In this exercise you are making a complex sentence by converting base sentence *b* into a nonrestrictive relative clause beginning with the relative pronoun *which* and then inserting it in sentence *a*.

## *Playing with Language 4A*

Write a ridiculously mixed extended metaphor. Here is one writer's attempt:

> Getting useful ideas from some textbooks is like pulling teeth, only it's the dentist who suffers the pain. And when the turnip is finally squeezed until it bleeds, the results are like the teeth of the hen in the cliché—scarce. But crying chicken is no use. Omelets, after all, require broken eggs, and if you're trying to become an egghead, your skull must sometimes be put on the block.

### *Playing with Language 4B*

About the middle of the eighteenth century, one minor poet was so overwhelmed by one of the new medical discoveries that he wrote an ode beginning with this line:

Inoculation, heavenly maid! descend!

Look at the world around you. Find some comparable manifestation of technological progress, and write a short paper, or an ode, addressing a similar personification. Find the tap marked *hyperbole* and turn it on full. Let your impassioned writing self get carried away at least a little—but hang onto your controlling intellectual self as you pull the strings. (This topic could be handled as a kind of "modest proposal"; see p. 406.)

*An honest man...appeals to the... understanding. The imposter employs force instead of argument, imposes silence where he cannot convince, and propagates his character by the sword.*

(The Letters of Junius)

# CHAPTER V
# Composing An Argument

The word *argument* probably makes you think of two or more people talking back and forth, perhaps heatedly, with raised voices, about some issue on which they disagree. An argument is a dispute, sometimes even a fight. But for the purposes of *written* arguments, we have to define the word differently: an argument is a piece of writing designed to change the way its readers think or feel about something, and perhaps also cause them to do something they wouldn't have done before.

Straightforward and factual memos and reports and analyses are not likely to be in any sense arguments. But most other pieces of writing, even if they are not what could be called "arguments," will include an element of argument. That is, even if the primary purpose of a piece of writing is not to argue or persuade, there will often be an implicit act of persuasion going on. Further, when your primary purpose in a piece of writing is other than persuasion, you can still choose to sharpen your rhetoric by using some of the techniques of argument. Some instructions on how to do something may not appear argumentative, but implicitly they are trying to persuade readers that the something is worth doing and that this is the right way to do it. Even some kinds of description could be thought of as trying to convince readers that this is the way the object being described actually looks. And though our primary purpose in this chapter is to inform, we also use some argumentative techniques to help persuade you that the information is worth learning and that the procedures we suggest are worth following.

## ARGUMENT AND YOUR AUDIENCE

All the usual principles of good writing apply also to arguments, of course; but many of them take on an extra importance when your purpose is to persuade. Your awareness and understanding and consideration of your audience, for example, are obviously crucial to an effective argument. Unless you are preaching to the already converted, like a politician speaking to the party faithful, your readers will be by definition unsympathetic, even hostile, or at least skeptical and neutral; they will not be on your side at the outset. Your intent is to get them on your side by the end, or at least to persuade them to consider your arguments with an open mind. If you do anything to put them off even the least bit, you will likely lose them, and thus lose any chance of persuading them.

If you know how your readers think and feel about your subject, if you know what they believe and what they disbelieve, if you know their likes and dislikes, you can choose arguments that will appeal to them and avoid ones that won't appeal to them or that might even antagonize them. Trying to write an argument without a clear sense of your audience is like target-shooting in a windowless room with the lights turned out. Therefore when your purpose is to persuade, make thorough use of the questions about audience that we list in Chapter II (see pp. 29, 31-32).

The subject of this chapter is constructing and conducting an argument, on paper. And though it may not be correct to equate an argument, in this sense, with the kind of argument or verbal fight that can lead to a bar-room brawl or a divorce, they are nevertheless similar in important ways, as you will see.

## INDUCTION AND DEDUCTION

The two basic methods of reasoning that you can use in arguing are induction and deduction. These are the main ways people think anyway, but in writing an argument they become highly important. Put most simply, inductive reasoning argues from the particular to the general; deductive reasoning argues from the general to the particular.

Inductive reasoning tries to convince someone of the "truth" of a generalization or assumption by pointing to specific examples that support it. A prosecutor in court argues inductively when he points to evidence in an attempt to convince the jury that the accused is guilty. Or if you were working in a food-testing laboratory and found animal hairs and other impurities in fifteen consecutive bottles of ketchup from one company, you could conclude that the company's quality-control is at fault. If the ketchup was from five different companies, you could conclude that ketchup is simply a tainted food product. But inductive reasoning can never "prove" anything or establish the "truth" of a generalization; it can establish probability—perhaps high probability—but not certainty. Even if the accused is convicted and jailed, someone else could come forward later and confess to the crime. And you conceivably could test a sixth brand of ketchup a week later and find it free of impurities.

Deductive reasoning, on the other hand, does lead to proof, to certainty— but only if the conclusion is based on a generalization or assumption that is true, or accepted as true by the audience. If for example you are trying to persuade a group of reluctant friends to go on to college after high school, you could point out that college graduates, on average, earn higher lifetime incomes than people who stop after high school. If your friends accepted that generalization as a fact, you would have made a dent in their resistance.

When you write an argument, you will probably want to use a combination of inductive and deductive reasoning. If you are consciously aware of just which method you're using at any given point, you can take care to make your arguments as strong as possible. When you are arguing inductively, for example, remember that the more examples you can cite, the stronger your generalization will be. (But don't bring in so many specific pieces of evidence that you overwhelm your readers. They will react negatively if you go past what seems reasonable to establish a point.) When you are arguing deductively, try to start with generalizations or assumptions—premises—that your readers will readily accept; they will then be forced to accept your conclusions. You may find that you need to use *induction* to strengthen a generalization so that you can then proceed with *deduction* from it. For example, if your friends didn't accept your statement about the income of college graduates, you could support it with statistics based on a large number of individual cases.

Deductive reasoning generally follows a series of steps that work from premises to a conclusion. For example a detective's process of deduction might be represented as follows:

a. Only a left-handed person could have inflicted this wound.
b. Only one of the five suspects is left-handed.
c. Therefore that suspect is guilty.

Much of our everyday thinking depends on similar processes, though we seldom think of it as being made up of such steps. For example, if you're fairly careful about what you eat, you could probably represent your reasoning like this:

a. A balanced diet contributes to good health.
b. I wish to be healthy.
c. Therefore I follow a balanced diet.

The detective had an easy case, and no one is likely to argue about the virtues of a balanced diet. But the deductive process is not always so clear-cut. If two of the suspects were left-handed, the detective would have to do some more work to find out who was guilty. And anyone allergic to some foods would have to omit them from the diet, however unbalanced that made it; in other words, you would have to qualify one of the premises if you wanted the conclusion to apply to someone besides yourself. Consider the following argument:

a. Women are not as physically strong as men.
b. Police work calls for physical strength.
c. Therefore women should not be hired to do police work.

Convincing? Unlikely. The fault is a frequent one in argument: overgeneralization. People tend to assume class memberships that aren't always so clear. The greatest culprits are concepts of *amount* and *frequency*. Think about the following two spectra:

NONE ———————————————————————— ALL
NEVER ——————————————————————— ALWAYS

Obviously the terms *half* and *half the time* would occur at the midpoints. Fill in as many other terms as you can on these spectra. Where for example would you place *most, some, a few?* or *frequently, almost always, sometimes, seldom?* When your premises, to be accurate, won't allow the absolute terms *none, all, never,* or *always,* when you have to qualify your nouns and verbs with one or another of the adjectives and adverbs that fall between the two ends of the spectra, then your argument is not self-evident; you have your argumentative work cut out for you. For example:

    a. (Some? Many? Most?) women are not as physically strong as (some? many? most?) men.
    b. Police work (usually? often? sometimes?) calls for physical strength.

Now how would you state the conclusion? And how would you argue toward it?

---

### Exercise 5A

Analyze the following premises and conclusions and revise them as you think necessary. What is being *assumed* in each set?

  1. a. People go to hockey games to see violence.
     b. Owners want to increase gate receipts.
     c. Therefore the owners encourage violence.
  2. a. Safe driving requires good judgment and quick reflexes.
     b. People under 16 have quick reflexes, but do not have good judgment.
     c. Therefore they shouldn't be licensed to drive.
  3. a. Welfare leads to idleness.
     b. Idle people are not productive.
     c. Therefore welfare should not be part of a society that needs to increase its productivity.

---

### Essay 5A

Beginning with one of the following generalizations—facts or widely held opinions—construct a basically deductive argument. If the generalization or assumption you choose seems to you less than convincing or sound, try to strengthen it at the outset—for example by using some inductive reasoning. Do you have to qualify the generalization?

  1. Students who are honest and hardworking should not be penalized for deficiencies in their earlier education that aren't their fault. (You want to argue that you, or someone you know, should not be required to take an extra course, for no credit, to make up a deficiency.)
  2. Since women constitute half the population, they should hold half the positions in government or any other institution. (You want to argue that your school should hire more women than men in order to achieve that balance.)
  3. People who exercise regularly are healthier than people who don't. (You want to argue that all able-bodied students at your institution should be required to take part in the physical fitness program.)

4. Alcohol is a drug, a proven destroyer of mental and physical health and the cause of many fatal or injurious accidents. (You want to argue that alcoholic beverages should not be sold near your school.)
5. Understanding and appreciation of the fine arts enriches people's lives. (You want to argue that all students should take a course in art or music appreciation, or perhaps a studio course.)
6. All citizens have an equal right to a college education. (You want to argue that the government should subsidize students who cannot afford higher education.)
7. Technology and other influences on society are changing it more rapidly than ever before in history. (You want to argue that students should not specialize in something that may not last long in its present form, but that they should take a broad liberal program.)
8. Make up some similar premise and conclusion of your own.

What this assignment asks you to do is fill in the links of reasoning between the generalization and the desired conclusion, something like *If a, then b; if b, then c; if c, then d; Q.E.D.*

---

## METHODS OF DEVELOPMENT IN ARGUMENT

When your purpose is to argue or persuade, to get other people to think and act in new ways, you need to be able to select the most effective strategies from those available to you. You can use any or all of the methods of thinking and development that we discuss and illustrate in the preceding chapter: each of them can be brought to the service of argument. Some may be more frequently used than others, but if you have command of all of them, you can select the best ones for any particular job of arguing or persuading.

### 1. Example and Illustration

This is probably the most common means of using inductive reasoning in argumentative writing. Just as induction draws a general conclusion from a number of attested instances, so examples provide typical, representative instances to support a generalization. They constitute the evidence for the various assertions you make as you proceed with an argument.

Using examples is an informal method of doing what scientists do formally when they use the empirical method of inductive reasoning. They arrive at their generalizations by means of a large number of carefully controlled observations, whether of fruit-fly behaviour or interplanetary radiation. The difference is that the scientific method aims at being exhaustive. That is, a conclusion in science attempts to account for all possible observations and to explain away any apparent exceptions. For instance, if twenty-two samples of an alloy break under a stress of 623 kg/cm², but two samples break under a lower stress, say 497 and 517 kg/cm², then the investigator must try to account for these exceptions. Similarly, and especially in an argument, the examples you use to support a generalization must be representative of the people or objects or events involved if your readers are to understand and, more important, to agree.

## 2. Definition and Classification

Frequently an argument, or the refutation of another's argument, depends on clearly defined terms. Before rational argument can proceed, both parties must agree on what it is they are arguing about. You can use definition and classification to help establish the *common ground* that is necessary for effective argument. It is most often necessary at the beginning of an argument, but it can be useful at other points as well. For example, you may need to define a term or classify a set of concepts in order to get your readers to understand and accept something so that you can use it in a process of deduction.

## 3. Comparison and Contrast

Pointing out how one thing or idea is like another can be a powerful way of getting your readers to see it in a new way. Similarly, by pointing out crucial differences, an argument can, for example, show readers how they have misunderstood an idea or object or event. The resulting clarified concept could then be used as a premise for deduction.

One kind of comparison often used in argument is *analogy* (see p. 80). But analogy as a reasoning process is inherently weak. It can never establish certainty, and usually not even high probability. To argue that because B is like A in certain respects, it will also prove to be like A in another respect, leaves you vulnerable, for an opponent can usually come up with important differences to weaken or destroy your case. If a newspaper columnist, for instance, were to predict that we are headed for a depression as serious as that of the 1930's, pointing to inflation, unemployment, and widespread social instability, the argument would need also to explain away the tighter regulations and controls on currency that prevail today. The argument would be vulnerable at places where the analogy doesn't hold.

## 4. Description and Narration

Although these are methods of presentation rather than analysis, they can help make an argument more compelling and persuasive. A vivid description or brief anecdote can often do more to put a point across than pages of abstract reasoning. They can be used to clarify a point, to serve as an illustration, and to appeal to readers' feelings in such a way as to back up your basic logical argument.

## 5. Process Analysis

Although more often used to convey information, accounts of process can serve argument as well. Sometimes even your primary purpose may be to show that one way of doing something is better than another; your whole argument would then be structured as a process analysis, probably along with some comparison and contrast. Look for example at the deluge of books that purport to tell us the best way to lose weight, or how to influence other people, or how to get rich even though the wheels are coming off the economy. And remember the opening paragraph of "Italian Spaghetti Sauce—Make Your Own" (see p. 33): the student began with an argumentative contrast to set the tone even though the essay that followed consisted entirely of an instructional process.

## 6. Cause and Effect

Clearly, establishing the cause of something can be an important part of an argument. But more often arguments will depend on showing effects. By answering the question "What will it cause?" or "What are the results of this?" you can argue powerfully for or against something. Often simply by sorting out the relations between causes and effects you can get your readers to see something in a new way. Working from effect to cause would be inductive; working from cause to effect would be deductive. Scientific method, for example, commonly uses arguments about causes and effects in order to dispose of competing hypotheses.

# BASIC PRINCIPLES AND TECHNIQUES OF ARGUMENT

If your main purpose in an essay is to persuade, there are special points to keep in mind. Even if an essay is only partly argumentative, handle that part carefully in accordance with these principles.

1. *Go for the brain.* However much they may also appeal to feelings, or emotions, arguments must be primarily directed at readers' intellects. Your aim is to convince your readers through reason and logic. Even if readers are somehow emotionally attracted to an idea, they aren't likely to accept it unless they also believe that it is a logical, reasonable idea. (But the reverse may also be true: see "The Lighter Side" below, pp. 119-120.)

2. *Think of your thesis as a proposition.* In an argument, your thesis is in effect a *proposition*, a statement of a supposed fact or truth or of a proposed course of action, like that enunciated at the beginning of a debate ("Resolved: tuition fees must be increased"), which you then set out to *prove* through logical reasoning. Obviously such a thesis as this sample one cannot be "proved" in an absolute sense; it is not like a law of physics. Rather you try to convince your readers that fees must be raised (a) in order to bring about some desirable result or (b) in order to avoid some undesirable result—or a combination of both. Nevertheless you are likely to be more careful of your argumentative strategies if you think of your thesis as a proposition you are trying to prove or defend.

3. *Argue fact and opinion, not taste. "De gustibus non est disputandum,"* as the Romans put it: There is no disputing taste. Arguments should be about matters of *fact* and should be conducted in terms of facts. But since most arguments are necessitated by different interpretations of the same facts or by people's putting different emphases on different facts, written arguments are usually about different judgments or opinions—but not about tastes.

    *taste:* I like Morley Callaghan's stories because....
    I don't like Morley Callaghan's stories, because....

    *opinion:* Morley Callaghan's stories are worth reading because....
    Morley Callaghan's stories are, I believe, overrated by some critics who choose to focus on....

One could not really *argue* the first pair of propositions; one could only *assert* them. But one could argue either of the second pair by supporting one's opinion with facts and careful reasoning. When people object to a statement by saying "that's only an opinion," they are pointing out that it is not supported by sufficient evidence. By providing such evidence, you turn a statement of opinion into an arguable proposition.

---

### Exercise 5B

Try to identify each of the following as a matter of *fact, opinion,* or *taste.* Which ones could be subjects for formal arguments? Could some of them be in more than one category, depending on how they were handled? If so, explain.

1. Living in the country versus living in the city.
2. Lowering the voting age versus leaving it where it is.
3. Big cars consume more fuel than small cars, or not.
4. Adrienne Rich is a better writer than Virginia Woolf, or vice versa.
5. Higher insurance rates for drivers under 25 are justified, or not.
6. B.C. is a more beautiful province than Ontario, or vice versa.
7. Hitch-hiking should be made illegal, or not.
8. Violence in hockey hurts the game, or not.
9. Violence in hockey should be treated as criminal, like violence on the street, or not.
10. Canada's parliamentary system adequately represents the population, or not.
11. Winnipeg is the crossroads of the continent, or not.
12. Air-ionizers are beneficial, or not.

---

4. *Use convincing evidence. Be precise.* To be convincing, you need to provide facts, statistics, or illustrations that will provide a solid foundation for your assertions. If you don't have, or can't find, good hard evidence, you probably have no business arguing a question. Similarly, support your argument with graphic details. Use narration and description, if necessary, to provide concreteness (see pp. 254-258). For example, offer evidence from your own experience (see pp. 67-68).

5. *Appeal to authority.* Use the statements and opinions of others to back up your own. But be cautious in your use of authorities. Use those who know the subject best, and if possible those who are most widely known and respected. Be up-to-date: what an authority asserted in 1931, or even just a year ago, may have been superseded by later findings. And remember that an expert in one field is not necessarily an expert in another. A prominent athlete or pop-singer may not be the most reliable authority on clothing; an actor who has played a doctor in a television series may not be the most reliable authority on the kind of coffee you should drink.

6. *Appeal to common sense.* You can also appeal to natural or psychological law for support. In our arguments we take as axiomatic many assumptions about external nature and human nature: disease is caused by germs; people can't live long without food; people seldom act against their own best interests; young people are more inclined to rash behaviour than are older

people. Often appeals to such truths are called appeals to "common sense." But keep in mind Alfred North Whitehead's observation that common sense is the sense that assures us that the world is flat.

7. *Begin with sound premises.* Like other chains, a chain of reasoning is only as strong as its weakest link. If that link is a faulty premise, the argument will fall apart. A premise is an assumption about the nature of things that is taken as true because it has been, or is capable of being, verified. The argument, for example, that chimpanzees can be taught to use "language" is based partly on the assumption that what they do with the signs and words they're taught is essentially the same as what we do with our words. Some people accept this as a valid premise; others don't, and for them the argument doesn't stand up. (The difference of opinion also hinges on the lack of a definition of "language" that is acceptable to both sides.)

   Similarly, in *inductive* reasoning, make sure not only that you have enough particulars to support a generalization, but also that those particulars are fair and representative ones. For example, if a college English teacher claimed that "X high school certainly has good English instruction; I've had two or three students from there every year for the past ten years, and they've all been excellent," his argument would quickly collapse because he hadn't established that the few students he'd known were *typical* students from that school; all the others may not have been good enough even to get into college. The particulars you base a generalization on must be a sufficiently high proportion of those possible. Further, you have somehow to explain any negative instances there might be. If another teacher at the college said, "Oh, I had a student from there last year, and he was almost illiterate," the first teacher would have to try to account for this exception. For example he could check to see if that student had gone through all the high school or transferred there in the middle of his last year. Or perhaps the second teacher was wrong in his assessment.

8. *Avoid triviality.* Be careful not to introduce trivial arguments; if you do, treat them as trivial and not as if they were major. That fish make better pets than dogs because fish don't have fleas is a point that might be mentioned along with some other minor points, but it would scarcely be worth leaning on as if it were a major prop of your argument; if you did lean on it you'd almost surely become wordy, but even more important, you'd also lose your readers' confidence in your sense of proportion. So acknowledge the point's triviality, if only implicitly; perhaps even make a joke about it.

9. *Organize carefully.* You must also marshal your arguments in the most effective way. An obvious and desirable order for argument is *climactic* order: begin with your weakest argument and work up to your strongest one. Since the *end* of any piece of writing is its most emphatic part, you would then leave your readers with the strongest possible impression. But since the *beginning* of a piece of writing is its second most emphatic place, you might not want to open with your weakest point, especially if it is much weaker than the others ("Fish don't have fleas, and don't have to be let out at night"). Say you have five main points to develop; number them 1 to 5 in the order of increasing importance. The order for your essay might then be 3-1-2-4-5, or even 4-1-2-3-5, presenting your readers with strength at both

the beginning and the end. But think also about tone: if you want to cajole your readers by amusing them, a remark about fish not having fleas might make an effective beginning.

> *Use soft words and hard arguments.*
> (proverb)

10. *Control your tone.* Nothing antagonizes readers—especially readers who may well be your opponents at the outset—more than being shouted at or made fun of. However great the temptation may be, avoid coming on strong with arm-twisting underlinings and exclamation points and loaded diction and heavy absolutes like *must* and *absolutely necessary* and *at all costs* and *unmitigated disaster* (they often amount to clichés anyway); similarly, avoid sarcasm and ridicule or other aggressive belittling of your opponents or their position or ideas. Generally, be moderate in your tone; present yourself as a reasonable person. Be considerate of your audience, for only then will they in turn be willing to be reasonable and to consider your argument. If you drive your readers into a corner they will likely remain there, embattled, self-martyred, refusing to listen. (But, again, see "The Lighter Side" below, pp. 119-120.)

11. *Be fair; avoid fallacies.* Part of being reasonable is being *fair*. The slightest hint of anything that could be taken as cheating and you will have lost your audience—probably irretrievably. Treating a trivial argument as if it were a major one, for example, is a kind of cheating. This and other such tactics are called "logical fallacies."

  Don't let your enthusiasm for your own argument lure you into adopting shoddy tactics unawares. Here are some other logical fallacies you should guard against:

**Begging the question.** Assuming the conclusion in one of the premises: "This unjust law should be repealed." It is the responsibility of the arguer to prove that the law in question is unjust.

**Circular reasoning.** A kind of question-begging; assuming the truth of the conclusion you're supposedly working toward and using it as evidence.

*Post hoc ergo propter hoc,* "after something, therefore because of it." Assuming that because B followed A, B must have been caused by A: "Soon after we increased Johnny's allowance his grades got worse; obviously having more money is spoiling his performance in school." But Johnny's poor grades could easily have been caused by something else.

**Red herring.** Diverting attention from the real subject by introducing an irrelevant side issue. A false clue, or false scent.

*Argumentum ad hominem,* "argument directed at the man." Diverting attention from the real subject by attacking the character of the opponent; an attempt to demolish the opponent's argument by discrediting the person. In crude form it is what is called "mud-slinging" or "name-calling."

**Hasty generalization.** Arriving at a generalization on the basis of too little evidence; jumping to a conclusion.

*Non-sequitur,* "it does not follow." Any illogical conclusion.

If any of these ploys succeed, then your readers can't be very bright; you're not really arguing but merely swaying your audience, in spite of truth and reason. And in the long run such methods are likely to backfire, for the danger is that, by not recognizing that your arguments are fallacious, you can fool yourself into thinking that you have a good argument when in fact you do not.

12. *Confront the opposition.* Another way in which you must be fair is by considering the opposing view. If there is an argument, there must be two sides. If you present only your side, then you're not arguing but merely asserting, and readers who don't already agree with you will continually be calling to mind all the objections that could be raised. They won't be listening to your argument—or if they are, they certainly won't find it a convincing one.

Unlike a debate, where the opponents are face to face, a written argument provides no immediate opponent, visible and ready to raise objections. Therefore you must recognize and anticipate arguments from the other side. Such a stance not only gives you more credibility, but also gives your writing more energy. The give-and-take of argument produces momentum. Your argument gains in strength when you can anticipate an argument that an opponent might raise and then go on to show that it is unreasonable, or at least vulnerable.

On some occasions, for example when the argument is brief or the issue relatively slight, it may be enough simply to acknowledge the opposition. Indeed writers often use this technique to begin essays that aren't primarily arguments. For example, one could begin with a concession followed by a thesis that leads into an expository essay:

Although many people think that Hemingway is nothing but a *macho* writer, many of his stories reveal elements of quite another temperament and point of view.

This is often an effective way to begin an essay, even one whose primary purpose is not persuasion.

But most arguments of any length or complexity will require more than a nod, a mere opening acknowledgement that there is another side. If you have a number of arguments to bring forward in order to attack a position, then there must be an equal number of opposing arguments that the other side would or could bring forward in order to defend that position. Or, if you are writing what amounts to a defensive argument, then there must be specific arguments attacking your position.

To handle these opposing points fairly and to argue effectively against them, you must not only acknowledge them but deal with them, one by one. Of course you will generally ignore the trivial ones, or treat them lightly, as you will those on your own side; to exaggerate the importance of a trivial opposing point is to commit another kind of fallacy. Rather, you will cite each major opposition argument and then somehow dispose of it. If you fail even to mention an obvious opposition argument, your readers will in effect say "Aha!" and discount your entire argument because it has this large hole in it: it will not hold water.

## Exercise 5C

Compose opening sentences for possible arguments on each side of five of the following topics. Put an opposing point in a concessive phrase or subordinate clause followed by your proposition in the main clause.

EXAMPLE: Vegetable gardening

    a. Although some people think the effort isn't worth it, there are several good reasons why one should grow one's own vegetables.

    b. In spite of the potential savings in money from growing one's own vegetables, the amount of time it takes makes the practice a false economy for most people.

1. Using credit cards: a good idea or a bad idea?
2. Should smoking be banned in public places?
3. Strikes in the public service.
4. The nuclear family: social straitjacket or hope for the future?
5. Import quotas to protect Canadian manufacturers.
6. Nuclear power plants.
7. Vegetarianism.
8. The installation of passive restraints—automatic seat-belts, air-bags—in new cars.
9. Have computers made libraries obsolete?
10. Euthanasia.
11. Weather forecasting: money wasted or money well spent?
12. The Canadian Armed Forces: do we need them?
13. Required courses in the curriculum.
14. Capital punishment.
15. (A similar topic of your own invention.)

## Techniques for Disposing of Opposition Arguments

You can dispose of opposing points in several ways. Some of the more common are as follows (several of these overlap, but we present them separately for the sake of clarity):

1. *Demolish it logically.* If it is in fact illogical, demonstrate that fact carefully and firmly, but politely. Point out errors or weaknesses in an opponent's evidence, or premises, or conclusions. It helps to know at least the more common logical fallacies. ("The claim that opening the new pub last year caused the neighbourhood to decline is a good example of *post hoc* reasoning, for there are at least three other not only possible but more likely reasons for the decline...." "But however sincere the voices raised in objection to what they call the 'unjust bylaw,' they beg the question, for no-one has yet been able to demonstrate convincingly precisely how it is unjust. It harms only those who are guilty of a crime, however minor that crime may be.")
2. *Acknowledge its force,* but provide something even better to replace it.
3. *Acknowledge its immediate virtue,* but demonstrate that its long-term results will be bad.

4. *Acknowledge its validity,* but point out that it only partly covers the ground. ("The massive high-rise apartment development will indeed increase the tax base for the community, but it will also obstruct the view of many and cause serious parking and traffic and policing problems whose solution could well eat up the increased income.")
5. *Point out that it is valid only part of the time.* ("A new open swimming pool would be wonderful in the summer, to be sure, but is the expense justified if the pool will likely be unusable for two-thirds of the year? Wouldn't it be better to spend the extra 40% now for a covered pool that could be used year-round?")
6. *Dismiss it* as essentially trivial or irrelevant—if in fact it is.
7. If there is no way to dispose of it, and if it's too obvious and major an argument to ignore, then you may have no choice but simply to *admit its truth* and hope to counter it with the force of your own points, preferably more than one.

## The Structure of Argument

The more complex and the more formal an argument is, the more it is likely to have the form of a see-saw battle, a ping-pong match, between your points and those of the opposition. It is in this sense that an argument can resemble an oral argument between two participants—with the all-important difference that *you,* the writer, take both sides and thus have complete control over how the argument is conducted. In order to exercise that control to full advantage, you must know exactly what you are doing. Here are some important guidelines to follow and techniques to use when constructing an argument; but remember, you can break most of these "rules" if you do so consciously, for specific reasons dictated by the subject matter you're working with and your particular audience and purpose.

1. In an argument, state your subject and thesis at or near the beginning. And you will probably want to state them, with some variation and re-emphasis, at or near the end.
2. The first major point you make should be a fairly forceful one for your own side of the case. If you want to begin with an opposition point in order to set up the argument, it is usually best to do so in a concessive subordinate clause or phrase (see p. 121); the emphasis will then fall on *your* point in the main clause. This technique is also useful as you begin new paragraphs throughout the essay: an opposition point will occupy a phrase or a subordinate clause, or perhaps a whole sentence or even two or three if necessary, at the beginning of a paragraph, but the rest of the paragraph, usually several sentences, will contain your rebuttal of that point; the paragraph will thus end, forcefully, on your side of the argument.
3. Usually, give no more than one opposing point at a time, or possibly two or three minor or closely related ones. Don't let the opposing side build up momentum.

    An exception to this would be an argument for which you have relatively little to say about the opposition, one whose main purpose is to develop your own side at length. You could then bunch the opposing points together shortly after the beginning and proceed to dismiss them either one by one or all at once and then go on to build your own case.

4. *a.* You may want to start off with a barrage of two or three of your own points before you even give a nod to the opposition; doing so can give an air of strong self-confidence to the beginning of an argument.

   *b.* You will probably want, at one or more places during an argument, to reply to an opposition point with not just one but two or three or more closely related points for your side.

   *c.* You will certainly want to save at least two but more likely three or four or more strong points of your own for the end.

5. It follows that you will need to have more points to make for your side than you have opposition points to counter. This is as it should be: part of the strategy of argument is to emphasize the superiority of your position not only by having better points but also by having more of them.

6. As indicated by 4c, you should reserve the end of your argument, by position the most emphatic part, for one or more of your own points. To end with an opposition point would leave your readers with the other side's view emphatically present in their minds and thus partially if not completely destroy the force of the argument you'd built up for your side. Be sure you end on the right foot: save for your own side the all-important last word.

   *Note*: There is one exception to this principle. You can end an argument with an opposition point if you use a technique called *argumentum ad absurdum*, which takes one of the arguments of the opposition and carries it—or one of its implications—to such a length that your readers can see that it is basically ridiculous.

## Planning an Argument

Because of the importance of structure and proportion in an argument, you should take extra care in planning. For example, you will likely produce a more effective argument—and save a lot of revising time—if you construct a detailed outline rather than depend on a relatively vague sort of plan.

> ABSURDITY, *n. A statement or belief manifestly inconsistent with one's own opinion. (*Ambrose Bierce, *The Devil's Dictionary*)

## The Lighter Side

Lest all this sound as though arguments are relentlessly heavy going, lifeless, and dull, we should point out that few arguments are convincing by virtue of the force of their logic alone. Most of us need to be persuaded by other tactics as well. Even if an argument appeals to logic, readers aren't likely to buy it unless they also *want* to, unless it appeals to them emotionally, as well. You have to make them *like* the idea. In addition to impeccable logical form, then, you will often need to provide the colour and interest and even wit that will keep your readers awake, interested, sometimes amused, and occasionally even indignant. Good arguments—even entirely serious ones—are never dull. Never underestimate the intelligence of your readers. On the contrary, appeal to it. Don't labour obvious points, and inject some irony and humour when appropriate, or make some witty allusion (see pp. 338-339) that you can expect your readers to catch and enjoy. By engaging your readers, wit can help you persuade them.

Notice how Joseph Conrad uses wit and sarcasm in the following paragraph from his article "Some Reflections on the Loss of the *Titanic*" (1912). After criticizing the "modern blind trust in mere material and appliances " and in the sheer size of the supposedly "unsinkable" *Titanic*, he moves on to a crescendo of *argumentum ad absurdum*:

> For my part I could much sooner believe in an unsinkable ship of 3,000 tons than in one of 40,000 tons. It is one of those things that stand to reason. You can't increase the thickness of scantling and plates indefinitely. And the mere weight of this bigness is an added disadvantage. In reading the reports, the first reflection which occurs to one is that, if that luckless ship had been a couple of hundred feet shorter, she would have probably gone clear of the danger. But then, perhaps, she could not have had a swimming bath and a French café. That, of course, is a serious consideration. I am well aware that those responsible for her short and fatal existence ask us in desolate accents to believe that if she had hit end on she would have survived. Which, by a sort of coy implication, seems to mean that it was all the fault of the officer of the watch (he is dead now) for trying to avoid the obstacle. We shall have presently, in deference to commercial and industrial interests, a new kind of seamanship. A very new and "progressive" kind. If you see anything in the way, by no means try to avoid it; smash at it full tilt. And then—and then only you shall see the triumph of material, of clever contrivances, of the whole box of engineering tricks in fact, and cover with glory a commercial concern of the most unmitigated sort, a great Trust, and a great shipbuilding yard, justly famed for the super-excellence of its material and workmanship. Unsinkable! See? I told you she was unsinkable, if only handled in accordance with the new seamanship. Everything's in that. And, doubtless, the Board of Trade, if properly approached, would consent to give the needed instructions to its examiners of Masters and Mates. Behold the examination-room of the future. Enter to the grizzled examiner a young man of modest aspect: "Are you well up in modern seamanship?" "I hope so, sir." "H'm, let's see. You are at night on the bridge in charge of a 150,000 tons ship, with a motor track, organ-loft, etc., etc., with a full cargo of passengers, a full crew of 1,500 café waiters, two sailors and a boy, three collapsible boats as per Board of Trade regulations, and going at your three-quarter speed of, say, about forty knots. You perceive suddenly right ahead, and close to, something that looks like a large ice-floe. What would you do?" "Put the helm amidships." "Very well. Why?" "In order to hit end on." "On what grounds should you endeavour to hit end on?" "Because we are taught by our builders and masters that the heavier the smash, the smaller the damage, and because the requirements of material should be attended to."

## Exploration 5A

In a brief argument (250 words or less) depending primarily on sarcasm and *argumentum ad absurdum*, attack some recent governmental or other official decision, policy statement, or rationale.

## The Vocabulary of Argument

Here is an outline of what the structure of an argument might look like:

1. Beginning: your proposition (your *pro*-position)
2. Your fact
3. a. Opposition point
   b. Your rebuttal
4. a. Opposition point
   b. Your rebuttal
   c. Further rebuttal, with another point
5. a. Opposition point
   b. Your rebuttal
6. a. Your point
   b. Your point
   c. Your point
7. Ending: your final point

Something of this sort is a common pattern for argumentative essays. And there is also a fairly common vocabulary used in such structures, especially for the turning points, the transitions.

### TRANSITIONAL SIGNALS

At 3a, 4a, and 5a, for example, where an opposition point is raised, you would probably use such words and phrases as these as introductory elements:

Some (Many) people claim (think, believe, say, assert)....
One could (might) argue....
It may be true that....
It is true that....
Although (Though)....
I concede that....
Conceding that....
Of course....
I admit that....
No doubt....
Granted....

—or sometimes a combination of them ("Of course it is true that....").

At points 3b, 4b, and 5b, to introduce your rebuttals you would probably use such words and phrases as these:

But....
Nevertheless....
However,....
Even so....

Of course if you use a concessive subordinate clause or phrase to introduce the opposition point ("Although...," "In spite of...," "The fact...notwithstanding,..."), you won't need *But, Nevertheless*, or *However*; you will come straight in with your point. But you may well want to introduce it with, or place within it, phrases like "the fact remains that..." and "it is also true that..."; and such phrases can also occur along with the others: "But the fact remains that...," "It is nevertheless true that...."

At points 4c, and 6a, 6b, and 6c, where you are adding more of your own points to one or more already stated, you will probably use such introductory elements as these:

> Further,....
> Furthermore,....
> Besides,....
> In addition....
> Not only that, but also....
> Indeed,....
> And...also....

And when you get to 7 you may well find that a forceful "Therefore...." is the best word to introduce your logical conclusion.

This list is of course not complete. Nor is it meant to be exclusive or restrictive. For instance, a "But" or "Nevertheless" or "Even so" could easily be used to introduce an opposition point—though they are much more often used to return to your side of the argument. Similarly, at least "It is true that" and "Of course" could be used to introduce one of your rebuttal points—though they are much more often used for opposition points.

---

### Exercise 5D

In the following argumentative essay, written by a student, we have left blanks for you to insert the transitional signals you think would fit best. When you have filled in all the blanks, read the essay through and evaluate its effectiveness.

#### Run for Your Life

For a sound mind and body, go jogging. More and more people are earning the rewards of healthful activity by simply running. Jogging is convenient, economical, and requires little else than two running shoes and some determination.

_____ it takes more than *some* determination to persevere through streaming sweat, gasping breath, and struggling muscles. Perhaps. _____ they have not experienced the more important rewards jogging offers. It not only helps lose embarrassing excess poundage, but also permits one—with a clear conscience—to indulge in life's tasty but fattening little pleasures. _____ jogging helps improve facial complexion, flushing out nasty foreign bodies lodged deep in skin tissue. But more important, jogging builds up muscle tone and strength, which improves your stamina in swimming, cycling, tennis, or even catching the little white man controlling pedestrian crosswalks.

_____ this finely tuned physique comes only at a price—and possibly a painful one at that. _____ joggers are vulnerable to injuries, which come in a wide variety of types and severity—the most common being minor muscle strains of the leg. _____ having experienced a few self-inflicted wounds myself, I can safely say "it doesn't tickle." _____ I can also safely say (and most joggers will agree—the honest ones anyway) that these injuries can be prevented by stretching the appropriate muscles before and after jogging. Other precautions include maintaining an adequate diet, and generally just being careful not to overdo it. _____ major injuries usually need attention—doctors, medicine, bandages, crutches, and so on. _____ what sport does not involve some kind of danger? Or for that matter, what activities in our daily routines? You or I could be harmed by merely walking the dog, taking out the garbage, or whatever.

_____ jogging can be carried to extremes. Some joggers have been known to push their bodies too far, and literally collapse from exhaustion. _____ most joggers are sensitive and respectful of their capabilities, and jog only within their body's limits. _____ many people jog just for relaxation and peace of mind. Jogging is an outlet to vent and relieve frustrations without banging walls, shouting obscenities, or pounding floors. For this reason jogging is often especially beneficial to people with high-pressure jobs. _____ joggers are known to be less prone to heart disease and respiratory ailments.

_____ jogging is fine and dandy but "I haven't got the time." And they may believe it. _____ it's my experience that if people sincerely want to jog, they find the time. _____ the time spent jogging is probably less than one would spend getting to and from gyms or health clubs, especially for those living on the fringes. Jogging is also flexible enough to accommodate any schedule in today's on-the-go society. For those with unpredictable working hours, making participation in structured fitness classes impossible, jogging is the answer.

_____ jogging is partially restricted to appropriate weather conditions. _____ I have seen joggers brave snow, slush, rain, muck, cold—you name it. _____ not only can one jog in almost any conditions, but one can also jog almost anywhere: city sidewalks, hiking trails, sandy beaches, and so on. This gives jogging the added appeal of the freedom of the open air, space, and nature.

_____ jogging is also easy on the bank account. Those of us who can't afford a tennis club or spa membership can be off and running with only a pair of jogging shoes—no white coordinated outfit is necessary. _____ jogging is very much an individual affair: each jogger competes only against personal standards, striving to run a little further or faster than the last time. _____ those thirsting for competition and excitement can find their fun in such events as the Seawall Fun Run or one of the twenty-six mile marathons.

But for any kind of jogger the sense of pride, confidence, and achievement is the same, when goals are attained and exceeded. There is no doubt that jogging is a rewarding activity, for both mind and body—one that can be done anywhere, any time, and most important, by almost any body.

---

## ARGUMENTATIVE TERMS

Here are some other words that are often used in arguments. As you read and write arguments, notice their vocabulary; keep adding to this list.

| | | |
|---|---|---|
| agree | arbitrary | believe |
| ambiguous | argument | claim |
| analogy | because | clear, clearly |

| | | |
|---|---|---|
| consequently | hypothesis | rationalization |
| contradiction | indicate | rebuttal |
| counter, | information | see, observe, perceive, |
| counter-argument | know | understand |
| demonstrate | misinformed | show |
| evidence | obvious, obviously | since |
| fact | opinion | statistics |
| fallacy | oppose, opposition | suggest |
| for | premise | theory |
| generalization | propose | therefore |
| hence | prove | think |

## Exercise 5E

Look for some good arguments in books, magazines, newspapers. Choose two of them and carefully analyze their structures. In the process, list, in the order of their occurrence, all the transitional signals or, in their absence, the whole sentences where the argument turns from pro to con or from con to pro. What terms do you find other than those we list? Add them to your list for future reference. Also, add up the number of separate points made for each side of the argument, and try to decide on the relative strength or importance of the author's points and how they have been ordered.

## Exploration 5B

Select half-a-dozen full-page advertisements from one or two popular or widely distributed magazines. Analyze them to discover what techniques of persuasion they use. What can you infer about the advertisers' attitudes toward their audience? Do you find any logical fallacies? Present the results of your analysis in a report of no more than 300 words.

## Exploration 5C

For a week, read all the editorials in a local newspaper. Then select two or three substantial ones that are clearly argumentative and analyze their rhetoric. Determine where they use induction and where deduction and what methods of development they use. Present the results of your study in a report of one or two pages that concludes by evaluating the editorials' effectiveness as arguments.

OR

Do the same thing with three or four "letters to the editor" on the same subject, drawn from a week's worth of the newspaper. What argumentative stances do the different writers take?

## Exploration 5D

In not more than 250 words, define one of the following terms, using whatever techniques of definition you find appropriate (see Chapter IV). But make your purpose more than just to inform: make your definition partly argumentative, but keep your tone moderate.

| | |
|---|---|
| fast food | euphemism |
| take–home examinations | processed cheese |
| filter cigarettes | humility |
| shoplifting | acupuncture |

## *Exploration 5E*

Find a *small* local issue to argue about—perhaps one you heard a couple of people sounding off about recently in the pub or the cafeteria, or in the dorm, or in the locker room, or in a meeting, or after class. Write a brief argument (no more than 250 words) presenting one side; be forthright, even impassioned. Then stop, back off, and reconsider the issue: write a similarly short argument presenting the other side. Finally, look at both pieces and try to decide how you really feel about the issue; then write a balanced argument supporting your chosen side but acknowledging and fairly representing the opposition.

---

## *Essay 5B*

Compose an argument of between 1000 and 1500 words on one of the following topics. Include a detailed outline.

(a)  Use one of the topics in Exercise 5C (p. 117), taking whichever side of the issue you think is right. You need not stick with the opening sentence you may have written for the exercise.

(b)  "Education is another name for brainwashing." Argue either side of this proposition.

(c)  Argue against something going on in your community which you view as patently absurd but which is nevertheless officially sanctioned.

(d)  If you did Exploration 5C, you might want to follow up by writing an extended argument on the subject of one of the editorials or of the group of letters you analyzed. Write also a short version of your argument as a Letter to the Editor. Send the letter.

(e)  Argue for or against some proposal currently being considered by some authoritative body—for example a national budget, a subsidy program, a spraying program, a new military installation, a new anti-pollution law, a wage or price freeze, an electoral reform.

## *Essay 5C*

Investigate the provisions for the handicapped in your school or your community. Write a short, forceful essay either arguing that these provisions need to be improved or defending them as adequate.

## *Essay 5D*

In a short essay (500-750 words), define one of the following. As in Exploration 5D, make your purpose more than just to inform: make your definition partly argumentative, but keep your tone moderate.

| | |
|---|---|
| horror movies | country music |
| boxing | pornographic magazines |
| pay television | muscle cars |
| Harlequin or similar books | intramural sports |

### Essay 5E

Investigate the attitudes of people on your campus toward one of the following:

| | |
|---|---|
| the athletic program | the grading system |
| food services | student government |
| required courses | tuition policies |
| the size of classes | counselling |

or some similar topic of current local interest and importance. When you have gathered sufficient data, construct an inductive argument that arrives at a generalization or conclusion about the topic and makes a recommendation based on the evidence. (You may want to state your conclusion, or part of it, at the beginning as well.)

OR

Select one section of the published statistics from the last census and use its data as evidence to lead you to a concluding generalization.

### Essay 5F

Find in a current Canadian or American magazine of general circulation an article presenting an argument with which you disagree. Your disagreement should not be with the surface handling of the argument but with one or more unstated, underlying assumptions. In an essay of 1000-1200 words, criticize the argument mainly by pointing out and explaining the underlying assumptions on which it is based. Make it clear why you think one or more assumptions wrong, and explain what you believe the correct ones are. If possible, include in your discussion at least one example of a danger that could result from the position taken by the article. Clip the article (if the magazine is yours) or photocopy it and attach it to your essay.

### Essay 5G

Choose one term from each of the three columns, in 1-2-3 order. The resulting sentence will be your thesis, or proposition, which you should state at or near the beginning of your essay. After some careful planning, develop your material into an argument of about 500 words. Don't be afraid to be funny, if that's how your thesis strikes you.

| 1 | 2 | 3 |
|---|---|---|
| Automobiles | | abolished. |
| Educators | can be | categorized. |
| Food | cannot be | deplored. |
| Government | could be | forgiven. |
| Landladies | must be | ignored. |
| Marriage | must not be | improved. |
| Poetry | should be | investigated. |
| Science | should not be | recycled. |
| Snow | | tolerated. |
| Unions | | welcomed. |

## Essay 5H

Write an argumentative essay of 1000-1500 words on one of the following topics. Choose your side and accumulate the material for the main points you want to make in its favour—but don't forget to bring in at least the major opposing points. Construct an outline before you begin writing; hand it in—revised if necessary—with the finished essay. *Warning*: Some of these are large topics. Be careful to limit your approach and to select your material to keep within a manageable scope.

1. Is reading books a waste of time, with so many other sources of information and entertainment available?
2. Should garbage collectors be considered part of an "essential service" and therefore be forbidden the right to strike?
3. Is humanity the beneficiary, or the victim, of technological progress?
4. Should scientists be able to write well, not just accurately?
5. Does war bring out the best in us, or the worst?
6. Is there any point in studying colonial history?
7. Should Canadian education embrace a "back to basics" philosophy?
8. Should censorship ever be tolerated?
9. Should advertising be permitted on television programs aimed at children?
10. Which are more important, civil rights or property rights?
11. "You've come a long way, baby!" Far enough?
12. Are the rules for issuing drivers' licences strict enough?
13. Should we adopt the American system of having national elections every four years?
14. Should Canada separate into four or five or six self-governing regions, or countries?
15. (A similar topic of your own choice.)

## Idioms 5

See the instructions for Idiom exercise 4, page 100. The words in this exercise are *verbs*.

| | | | | |
|---|---|---|---|---|
| accede | coincide | deviate | frown | obtrude |
| acquiesce | consent | dissent | hint | rid |
| adhere | credit | divest | impose | saturate |
| assent | cure | emigrate | liken | substitute |
| calculate | deprive | exonerate | minister | trust |

## Sentence-Combining 5: Appositives

### Pattern 5A

Base sentence *a*: One of the smallest animals has come to be seen as one of the fiercest.

Base sentence *b*: That animal is the shrew.

Result of combining *a* and *b*:

One of the smallest animals, the shrew, has come to be seen as one of the fiercest.

First, COPY the pattern sentence carefully, keeping only the last word of sentence *b* (along with its article, *the*) and inserting it, enclosed in commas, in sentence *a*, right after the word *animals*, which was also (as *animal*) present in sentence *b*.

Second, COMBINE each of the following pairs of sentences into a single sentence modelled on the pattern sentence:
a. One of my favourite foods is high in both protein and cholesterol.
b. That food is cheese.

a. One of the best-known Greek philosophers left no writings.
b. That philosopher was Socrates.

Third, COMPOSE two sentences of your own modelled on Pattern 5A.

In this exercise you are making two simple sentences into one by reducing the second to either a common or a proper noun and inserting it in the first sentence right after the subject, where it acts as an appositive. That is, it is in apposition to that subject, further defining or characterizing it. Such an appositive is nonrestrictive and must be set off with commas, or sometimes with dashes or parentheses.

### Pattern 5B

a. Ottawa prides itself on being the nation's capital.
b. It is a pleasant place to visit.
RESULT: Ottawa, a pleasant place to visit, prides itself on being the nation's capital.

Copy the pattern sentence, deleting *it is* from sentence *b* and then inserting the rest of *b*, enclosed in commas, in sentence *a*.

Combine each of the following pairs into a sentence modelled on the pattern sentence:
a. Ottawa is a pleasant place to visit.
b. It is the nation's capital.

a. Shakespeare came from the town of Stratford-on-Avon.
b. He was England's greatest poet.

Compose two sentences modelled on Pattern 5B.

In this exercise you are making two simple sentences into one by dropping the subject and verb of the second and inserting the remaining noun phrase in sentence *a*, after the subject, where it functions as an appositive.

### Pattern 5C

a. He came from Stratford-on-Avon.
b. He was England's greatest poet.
RESULT: England's greatest poet, he came from Stratford-on-Avon.

Copy the pattern sentence, noting that you delete *He was* from sentence *b* and put the remainder at the head of sentence *a*. Be sure to insert the comma.

Combine each of the following pairs into a sentence modelled on the pattern sentence:

a. She received the offer on Tuesday.
b. She was the top candidate on the list.

a. He spoke movingly to the rally.
b. He is a refugee from Chile.

Compose two sentences modelled on Pattern 5C.

In this exercise you are again reducing the second sentence to a noun phrase and using it as an appositive in the first sentence. This time, however, you put the appositive phrase at the beginning because the subject of the sentence is a pronoun; the identity of the *he* (that is, Shakespeare) would already be clear from the context.

## *Pattern 5D*

a. "The Hammer" was the name they gave him as a young man.
b. It was a name that came to be feared throughout the West.

RESULT: "The Hammer" was the name they gave him as a young man, a name that came to be feared throughout the West.

Copy the pattern sentence, noting that you delete *It was* from sentence *b* and put the rest, set off by a comma, at the end of *a*.

Combine each of the following pairs into a sentence modelled on the pattern sentence:

a. The board announced the new regulations.
b. They were regulations that ignored all the objections people had raised.

a. Francis misfiled the student activity report.
b. It is a report that will be needed for Tuesday's meeting.

Compose two sentences modelled on Pattern 5D.

In this exercise you are reducing the second sentence to an appositive by deleting the subject and verb (*It was*). The appositive consists of a noun (*a name*) and a relative clause modifying it. The special feature of this pattern is that the appositive begins with a noun that repeats the noun (*name*) the whole thing is in apposition to.

---

## *Playing with Language 5A*

Language can be lovely, but it can also behave illogically. For example, there are many everyday terms that contradict their own meanings, but we use them without thinking of the contradictions. Many such changes in meaning reflect changes in technology, social history, and living habits. Language, then, can also be fun, and instructive. Here are some examples:

We use *black*boards that are nowadays often green.
*Cup*boards are often used to store almost anything but cups.
*Silver*ware is frequently made of stainless steel.
We use *plastic glasses*, both to drink from and to see through.
We use *lead* pencils with no lead in them.
Some golfers now use *metal woods* for their drives.
And we quite normally say that a seaplane *lands* on the water.

Keep a list of other such illogical usages that you come across. Hand it to your teacher. Send it to us.

## Playing with Language 5B

Read through the following paragraph, written by a student:

### The Hike

The peak of our trip was the hike to Lost Lake. We set out when the day was fresh; the sun shone on our backs and we sang tunes to the beat of our steps. Birds flew from the trees as the twigs cracked and crunched from our weight. The path was long and wide—most of the time the three of us walked side by side. When an hour had passed, we stopped in a calm glen and ate the grapes that Lynn had brought. Rays of sun peeked through the leaves and hit the small specks of dust that bobbed in the air. We sat there dazed by the hush...and then moved on. Soon we were back to the tunes we liked so much to sing. One more hour went by. The sun shone hot on us now: yes, we were more than all set for a swim in the lake. Jill was the first to catch sight of it—we ran the rest of the way to the edge of the lake, stopped for a quick test, and ran in: shorts, tops, and all. We dried off in the sun and ate our packed lunch. There we were, just the three of us. We felt as though it was all ours. If time could have stopped for us right there...but the sun had made its way up and down the sky, and it was time to go. We walked down the trail—not one of us spoke—we were all full of deep thoughts.

It is a good description of an outdoor experience, effectively catching the mood and the sense of time and place. But did you notice that it is composed entirely of words of one syllable? Write a paragraph or two of your own—not necessarily narrative or descriptive—entirely in monosyllables. Try to keep it from sounding forced, artificial. It can be done, as the example shows.

# STAGE TWO: Writing

*When a man writes from his own*
*mind, he writes very rapidly.*
(Samuel Johnson)

CHAPTER VI
# Step 6:  The First Draft

With your thesis statement and your plan before you, you are ready to write a first draft. If you've done a good job in the planning stage, writing the draft should be fairly straightforward. With your plan at hand and your readers in mind, you simply flesh out the plan by writing paragraphs.

The first draft is often called a *rough* draft. How rough it is depends partly on how thoroughly you've planned and partly on what kind of a writer you are. Imagine the writers of drafts on a spectrum: at the left end are the hares; at the right end are the tortoises. Although in the fable the tortoise came off best, because "slow and steady wins the race," we recommend that you try to be a hare, for the writing process is not a race against time but a pursuit of quality. "The race," as Lord Tweedsmuir observed, "is not always to the slow." (Paradoxically, for an examination or an in-class essay, where immediate time *is* a factor, you should aim for tortoise-hood.)

The fast drafters, the hares, seldom pause to consider details of either style or content. They don't want anything to interrupt the flow of their thoughts; they want to get those thoughts on paper, fast. If they stop to read over a sentence or two, they do so only to ensure and reinforce the momentum of that flow. They know that when they've finished the draft they can take all the time they need to revise it. But while writing the *first* draft they want to trust their instincts and rely on all the work they've done during the planning stage. They don't want to risk losing an idea or derailing their train of thought by stopping to tamper with a sentence that doesn't seem to be coming out quite right, or to check the accuracy of a particular word, or to worry about whether a paragraph's reasoning process is entirely clear or logical.

The slow drafters, the tortoises, on the other hand, seldom leave a sentence untouched: they rearrange, try different words, different punctuation; they change phrases to clauses, clauses to phrases, phrases to single words; they delete

132

words, insert words, then delete some of those. They even pause to check spelling.

Obviously these meticulous plodders will produce first drafts that are less rough than those of the speedier scribblers. There may indeed remain little to do but prepare a clean copy and do some proofreading. And this is the way it should be if you're writing an in-class essay or an examination. But when you're writing regular essays and are not racing the clock, there are at least two good reasons for preferring the faster method.

The first reason has to do with time and efficiency. The slow drafter does *not* necessarily save time. Halfway or more through a slow drafting process, you may suddenly get a new idea, a new angle on your topic, one that requires you to change your outline or even your thesis. You may then have to scrap a good deal of what you've spent so much time polishing. If you resist the new idea in order to avoid such wasteful and painful cutting, you will be sacrificing quality, settling for a product less good than it could have been.

The second reason also has to do with quality. As we say in earlier chapters, the physical act of writing is itself a generative process. Putting words on paper, making sentences about something, will often lead to new ideas and insights; invention and discovery are still going on. If you stop to fuss and fiddle with individual sentences and words you will likely block these new ideas; the continuing flow of invention will be dammed up.

There's even a third reason: there's often a strong feeling of satisfaction at finishing a draft, a completed unit of writing, however rough it may be. This can be an important psychological boost, especially for relatively inexperienced writers.

So try to be more like a hare than like a tortoise.

## The Importance of Planning

Whatever method of drafting you adopt, fast or slow or somewhere in between, the planning stage is still important. If you're a fast drafter and don't plan thoroughly enough, if you've left too much invention and sense of audience and purpose to emerge *during* the writing of the first draft, you may well have to throw out several drafts before you produce one that isn't too ragged. If you're a slow drafter and don't plan thoroughly enough, your writing of the first draft will be even slower and more tedious and exasperating than otherwise; and you will also have virtually guaranteed that you will have to throw out material in which you've invested a lot of time.

But if your planning has been adequate and your ideas are sorted out, your first draft should go fairly rapidly—especially when you know that you won't have to stop and chew your pencil every few words. You know you can go back and fix it up because you've budgeted plenty of time for revising.

## A Planning Checklist

Since the planning stage is so important, for whatever kind of writer, you should stop and review your entire planning process before you plunge into your first draft. Here is a checklist of questions to help you do that.

STEP 1: *Subject*
Is my subject really as good as I've been telling myself it is?
Is it interesting both to me and to my audience?
Do I know enough about it?

STEP 2: *Topic*
Have I narrowed my topic enough? Have I a limited topic that I can realistically expect to deal with adequately in the time and space that I have?
Is the topic not only interesting but somehow fresh because of the way I'm approaching it?

STEP 3: *Audience and Purpose*
Am I as clear about my audience as I can be?
Have I written a profile of my audience to keep in mind as I write and revise?
Am I clear about my primary purpose, or about my combination of purposes and their proportions?
Have I stated my secondary purpose or purposes as specifically as I can so that I can keep them in mind as I write and revise?
Have I drawn up a list of *do*'s and *don't*'s to keep before me as I write and revise?

STEP 4: *Invention*
Have I asked questions to generate enough pertinent material about my topic?
Have I done whatever research my project calls for?
Have I generated a good deal more material than I need so that I've been able to select the best?

STEP 5: *Organization and Development*
Have I planned the methods of development I'm going to use for the essay as a whole and for its larger parts?
Have I carefully organized my material?
Have I composed as clear and specific a thesis statement as I can at this stage?
Have I constructed a sufficiently detailed plan or outline?

STEP 6: *The First Draft*
Can I now begin writing my first draft and expect to proceed through it with confidence and at a fair rate of speed?

When you can honestly and conscientiously answer "Yes" to all these questions, you're ready to start writing.

## Getting Started

Don't let yourself fall victim to the "blank-paper" syndrome. Most writers have suffered the torture of sitting and staring at that blank sheet; the longer you stare the more frustrating it becomes, and the harder it becomes to get those first words down on the paper. Here are some techniques for avoiding that experience:

1. *Plan carefully.* The more thoroughly you plan, the more confident you will be about your aim and how you're going to achieve it. If you find yourself dithering over a blank sheet of paper, you may have to go back and plan some more.

2. *Think of a title.* If you haven't yet thought of a title, now is a good time to try to come up with at least a tentative one. Even if you decide to change it later, a title at this point can help, for getting even that little bit onto the blank page can help you over the block.

3. *Don't worry about the introduction.* Introductions are notoriously difficult. Rather than attempt this major hurdle at the outset, skip it and start with the first point on your outline. When you've finished your draft you'll have a much clearer sense of your essay than you can possibly have before you start it; you'll then know precisely what it is that needs introducing, and so find it much easier to go back and write your introduction. Even if you do get something down at the outset by way of an introduction, chances are you'll want to change it later; most writers find that introductions written first are best scrapped or drastically rewritten later. So don't let the need for a beginning keep you from beginning.

4. *Try "free-writing"* to get your engine warmed up. Since the act of writing is itself generative, just start scribbling. Write fast, and write anything that comes into your head, even if it isn't something about your topic. This often works like clearing a stopped-up drain: suddenly things begin to flow. Thoughts you didn't even know you had will start pouring out onto the page, and even if they aren't at first directed at your topic, they soon will be. Later you can go back and cross out the stuff you used just to get started. If all else fails, try a tape-recorder: free-associate at it, and then play your ideas back.

## Keeping Going

Momentum is important in writing. Try to complete your first draft at one sitting, avoiding interruptions as much as possible. This will of course be easier to do if your planning has been thorough and if you're writing fast—if you've chosen to be a hare rather than a tortoise. If while you're writing you suddenly come up against an unforeseen problem, such as the need for a transition from one large section to another, it's often best just to skip it—leave a blank space—and come back and work on it later.

If an interruption is unavoidable, or if you're working on an unusually long essay, then when you return to your draft begin by slowly reading over all or most of what you've already written, at the very least the paragraph or two before the break occurred. This should enable you to recapture the lost momentum and get started again. Or you can do what many professional writers do: when a break is unavoidable, stop at a point where you *know* the next thing you're going to say. For example, write a transitional paragraph, or a topic sentence, so that when you sit down again to write, the sentences will flow automatically. You'll have your momentum again, and find it easy to keep going.

One further point. The hare, unlike the tortoise, is free to do one other thing that will improve the quality of his finished essay; indeed he must do it, since his rough draft will almost surely be stylistically loose. A fast drafter will usually, on purpose, write a first draft twenty or thirty or even fifty percent longer than the finished essay is to be. He can then, when revising, weed out weaknesses and generally tighten the prose without fear of ending up with too short an essay.

## Changing Course

If as you're writing you suddenly get a new idea about your topic, a new angle on it or a new way of developing or arranging your material, or a whole new chunk of material to put in—fine. Go ahead and make whatever changes are necessary, as long as you see them as improvements. An outline, including its thesis statement, is not chiselled in stone; you're not irrevocably committed to it.

An outline can be thought of as a road-map, and your writing and revising as a journey during which you use it as a guide. The map will have the intended main route clearly marked, and the side roads will in a sense be closed off. But if as you're driving along you suddenly spot an especially enticing bit of scenery down one of those side roads, you're perfectly free to make a turn and go and have a look at it. If it turns out to be a mirage, a true digression, you can always come back and resume your trip along the original route; but if it turns out to be solid and worthwhile, you can leave it in, altering the route on your map accordingly. It could even lead to other interesting and unexpected things and open up a whole new way of getting to your destination. You may have to follow the new route all the way to the end before you can be sure, but if it turns out better than the originally intended one, take it.

One of the virtues in having an outline in the first place is that although it is flexible, any changes you make in it you will have to make *consciously*. If you were driving without a map you could easily take a side road and follow it to the end without ever knowing that it was a side road. But your reader would know.

## Language and Style

Even if you draft rapidly, you'll inevitably be doing some thinking about language and style. Here are a few questions to begin thinking about as you write your first draft; later, when revising, you should focus on them.

1. *Subject and language:*
   What kinds of language and style are most appropriate for this subject?
   Does it *require* that I use technical terms?
   What sorts of metaphor or allusion does it invite?
   Does the subject clearly *discourage* any particular linguistic and stylistic choices?

2. *Audience and language:*
   How does the nature of my audience constrain my choices of language?
   Do any special terms need defining for this particular audience?
   What kinds of language and style are my readers likely to be unreceptive to or even hostile toward? (For example, depending on the occasion, if your readers are formally educated, you may want to limit your use of slang. If they are relatively uneducated, you'll want to minimize your use of formal or difficult vocabulary and long, involved sentences. What readers might be unreceptive to jargon, or swearing, or macho terms, or liberationist terms, or British usage, or racist vocabulary, or allusions to films and pop music...?)

3. *Writer and language:*
   Can I confidently use the language and style (kinds, forms, levels) required?

What linguistic and stylistic choices are available to me?

What aspects of myself does my language need to reveal—or conceal?

## The Mechanics of the First Draft

Just how you put your first draft on paper can greatly ease or hamper your progress in the revising stage. For example, it is much easier to work with typed copy than with handwritten copy: with typed copy it is easier to read over what you've written, easier to see words and sentences and punctuation marks, easier to judge where paragraph breaks might be needed.

But whether you type or write by hand, always double-space or triple-space. Some writers even quadruple-space. The point is to leave yourself plenty of room for revising—which will probably include rewriting or inserting whole sentences. For the same reason, leave generous margins on all four sides. The more space you leave yourself, the freer you'll feel to make changes. The space *invites* improvements, whereas a single-spaced, margin-less page forbids any but minimal alterations.

Similarly, write only on one side of each sheet, for you will want to spread successive pages out before you, or even, if it's a short essay, to spread out all the pages, so that you can cast your eye over the whole thing at once. Further, one common way of inserting a long sentence or paragraph is to write it on the back of the appropriate page, with an arrow showing where it is to be inserted.

If, like some writers, you know how to type but prefer to compose in longhand, you needn't worry so much about leaving space on your first draft if you do it the rapid way and then type it up into a cleaner and at least double-spaced copy for revising. Some writers even dictate their first drafts into a tape-recorder and have them typed for working copies. Dictating a draft also has the advantage of inducing one to use a tone and vocabulary and syntax that are more natural, a style closer to one's speaking style, than is likely to occur if one composes on paper. Even composing on a typewriter can have something of that effect. And if you have access to and know how to use a word-processor, you might find that it offers a very comfortable way not only to compose your first draft but also to do much if not all of your revising and correcting.

---

### *Exercise 6A*

Start with a simple kernel sentence and, by using imagination and adding modifying words, phrases, and clauses to its basic elements, build an elaborate sentence. Here for example is a simple starter:

> The light streamed in the window.

And here is what a few students did with it. Note that in each one the words of the original simple sentence are retained as the main clause. Note also the way 5 turns the action into a metaphor, and the way 6 picks up the almost unnoticeable metaphor in the word *streamed* and builds on it:

1. When the engine was turned off, the light from the car's headlamps still streamed in the bedroom window.

2. When the drapes were opened, the pale reflected light from the waning moon streamed in the window, casting eerie shadows across the room.
3. a. The light of the streetlamp streamed steadily in through the cracked window.
   b. The harsh light of the crooked streetlamp streamed steadily in through the dusty cracked window of the gloomy old mansion.
4. The morning light streamed in through the window, and from the window it raced to the edge of the bed, and from the edge of the bed it flowed over the rigid corpse.
5. As I sat there alone contemplating the purpose of my existence, passing from one philosophy to another, the faint yet sure light of truth streamed in the window of my mind.
6. The brilliant light streamed in the open window like a torrential spring run-off, flooding the room with brightness and splashing the walls with an autumn sunset's fiery red and gold hues.

Now try your hand at it with these simple sentences:

1. The cat turned and walked away.
2. The building was gray.
3. An idea sometimes wanders into one's mind.
4. A tree stood in the field.
5. Money talks.

## Exploration 6A

Think up some metaphors and similes to express how you would feel in *three* of the following circumstances. Then write a paragraph for each, using some of those metaphors to explain your feelings to someone else. In each paragraph, use at least one simile and one metaphor. (But see p. 104.)

1. getting splashed by a passing car on your way to an important appointment
2. discovering that following your advice has caused a close friend to lose money
3. having to get up and speak in front of hundreds of strangers
4. discovering that a close friend has just betrayed you
5. finding something that you thought was lost forever
6. signing up twenty members for a club you started as a joke
7. getting an *A* on a paper you dashed off after midnight
8. being beaten by a ten-year-old at checkers
9. trying to borrow five dollars from someone you don't much like
10. watering plants for relatives who are on a round-the-world cruise

## Exploration 6B

Take a blank sheet of paper and a pencil. You are going to draw a picture or a diagram. You are allowed only three strokes—that is, your pencil may touch the paper only three times. Think carefully before you begin: *plan* your picture or diagram in your mind. Then draw it. When you've done that, lean back and look at it, and then write a paragraph instructing someone else how to draw the same picture or diagram. Your reader must not see your drawing, but—following your written instructions—must try to reproduce it as exactly as possible. Think carefully about the strategies of an instructional process analysis; try to get your reader to understand and follow your steps precisely.

## *Exploration 6C*

Choose one or more of the following items; for each one you choose, think of some other item with which to compare it in an analogy. Don't come up with something too obvious or clichéd; to be effective, an analogy should strike the reader as at least a little unexpected. For example, would you be struck by the advice that since dogs are in some ways similar to good friends, you should treat your dog like a good friend? Would it be more fruitful to draw an analogy between a dog and a small child? or a mulching machine? or a prison guard? What conclusions might those analogies lead to?

| | |
|---|---|
| your landlady or dorm supervisor | a cat |
| a sports car | taking care of baby brother or sister for |
| a television set | a day |
| a good long novel | the local hockey team |
| poker | a sonnet |
| writing an essay for your English class | dieting |
| being a club president | a currently popular song |

Develop each analogy into a paragraph of at least five or six sentences, with either a stated topic or a clearly implied one. But remember that analogies, however strong, do not establish proof.

## *Essay 6A*

Experiment with writing drafts rapidly and slowly. Try to find out where on the spectrum you feel most comfortable. Here are some topics to use in your experiments. We intend these to require minimal planning, perhaps no more than a couple of minutes of brainstorming:

1. something I ate yesterday
2. how _____ behaved toward me yesterday
3. how I felt when I got up this morning
4. my roommate
5. my favourite extra-curricular activity
6. why I like (or don't like) dogs (or cats)
7. why I watch (or don't watch much) television
8. what I think of this school's athletic program
9. clothing styles on campus
10. why I intend to major in _____

## *Essay 6B*

Find a manageably small controversial topic, and compose a short realistic dialogue (perhaps two pages) depicting a heated argument about it between two people. (They can shout and wave their arms if you want; but no violence, please.) Don't take sides yourself; present the argument as objectively as possible; nobody wins such an argument, though each opponent may feel victorious, if only because of having shouted louder. Then construct two *written* arguments on the same topic, as each of the contenders might write it when cooler heads prevail. How much material from the original dialogue are you able to use in each? And how must you alter it to make it suitable for a reasoned presentation?

### Essay 6C

"The world has never had a good definition of the word liberty," noted Abraham Lincoln in 1864. Has one come along, do you think, in the last 120 years or so? In a short essay, try your hand at defining *liberty*. How much do the different ways people use the word depend on their different points of view or their different stations in life? What other words might be associated with it? Is *liberty* the same as *freedom*? As you plan, write, and revise, have in mind a specific audience and purpose—an occasion for which you are writing.

### Essay 6D

Describe a building. Take your notes while physically observing the building; record everything you can see about it: its size, shape, colour, texture, major and minor features—everything. When you sit down to write, decide first upon some occasion for which you could write such a piece, and upon your audience and purpose. Then decide (1) which points to include and which to omit, (2) which features to emphasize and which to play down, and (3) how to organize the details you decide to use. (Must you use some sort of spatial organization, or is some other order possible?) Try to convey some dominant impression—one you actually felt while observing the building. (See p. 82.)

OR

Do the same thing for a landscape scene viewed from a particular spot.

### Idioms 6

See the instructions for Idiom exercise 4, page 100. In this and the next two idiom exercises, all the words are *adjectives* (including some participles, when that seems the most likely form to be used).

| | | | | |
|---|---|---|---|---|
| addicted | characteristic | exclusive | lacking | receptive |
| alien | conducive | fond | observant | separate |
| analogous | consistent | impenetrable | peculiar | sympathetic |
| approximate | deficient | independent | precluded | vested |
| bent | dissimilar | innate | preparatory | wanting |

### Sentence-Combining 6:  Noun Clauses
### Pattern 6A

Base sentence *a*:  Supply-side economists basically believe one thing.
Base sentence *b*:  Limiting the money supply will slow inflation.

Result of combining *a* and *b*:
>Supply-side economists basically believe that limiting the money supply will slow inflation.

First, COPY the pattern sentence carefully, noting how the word *that* together with sentence *b* replaces the words *one thing* in sentence *a*.

Second, COMBINE each of the following pairs of sentences into a single sentence modelled on the pattern sentence:
a. Most employers at that time naively thought one thing.
b. Workers were interested only in higher wages.
a. The director suggested only one thing.
b. She should learn her lines before the next rehearsal.

Third, COMPOSE two sentences of your own modelled on Pattern 6A.

In this exercise you are turning base sentence *b* into a noun clause beginning with the word *that* and substituting it for a direct object in sentence *a*. (Note: The *that* introducing a noun clause functions as a subordinating conjunction; don't confuse it with the relative pronoun *that* that introduces some adjective clauses.)

## *Pattern 6B*

a. The auditors have told us something.
b. This means that the company is in bad shape.
RESULT:  From what the auditors have told us, the company is in bad shape.

Copy the pattern sentence. Replace the word *something* in sentence *a* with *from what* and move it to the beginning of the sentence; delete *this means that* from sentence *b*; put a comma between the two parts.

Combine each of the following pairs into a sentence modelled on the pattern sentence:
a. I have discovered something about cameras.
b. This shows that one gets the quality one pays for.
a. I know something about gardening.
b. It suggests that it involves more destruction than creation.

Compose two sentences modelled on Pattern 6B

In this exercise you are converting sentence *a* into a preposition (*from*) followed by a noun clause as its object (*what the auditors have told us*); the whole prepositional phrase then acts as an adverb modifying the rest of the sentence.

## *Pattern 6C*

a. Ottawa's principal claim to fame is not the only reason to visit it.
b. It is the nation's capital.
RESULT:  Ottawa's principal claim to fame, that it is the nation's capital, is not the only reason to visit it.

Copy the pattern sentence, adding *that* to sentence *b* and inserting *b*, enclosed in commas, before *is* in sentence *a*.

Combine each of the following pairs into a sentence modelled on the pattern sentence:
a.  The employers' main belief turned out to be naive.
b.  Workers were interested only in higher wages.
a.  Newton's third law of motion is the basis of rocket propulsion.
b.  For every action there is an equal and opposite reaction.

Compose two sentences modelled on Pattern 6C.

In this exercise you are converting sentence *b* into a noun clause beginning with *that* and inserting it after the subject of sentence *a*, where it functions as an appositive (see Pattern 5). Compare these noun clauses with the adjective *that*-clauses in Pattern 4G; how do the two patterns differ? (In some sentences of Pattern 6C you might want to use dashes rather than commas; see p. 305.)

### Pattern 6D

a.  One thing seems likely.
b.  Older people will postpone their retirement.
RESULT:  It seems likely that older people will postpone their retirement.

Copy the pattern sentence. Note that the word *It* replaces *One thing* and that the word *that* together with sentence *b* follows sentence *a*.

Combine each of the following pairs into a sentence modelled on the pattern sentence:
a.  Two things are undeniable.
b.  The brakes were reliable, and the driver had been drinking.
a.  One thing cannot be disputed.
b.  Ottawa is the nation's capital.

Compose two sentences modelled on Pattern 6D.

In this exercise you are turning sentence *b* into a noun clause beginning with *that* and using it as the real subject of the sentence, placed after the verb and the false or anticipatory subject pronoun *it*. (The noun clause can also be viewed as in apposition to the subject pronoun *it*.)

### Pattern 6E

a.  Ottawa is the nation's capital.
b.  This cannot be disputed.
RESULT:  That Ottawa is the nation's capital cannot be disputed.

Copy the pattern sentence, noting that you put the word *That* at the beginning and delete the word *This*.

Combine each of the following pairs into a sentence modelled on the pattern sentence:
a.  Mr. Ricci was late.
b.  This surprised Hilda.
a.  The college raised tuition fees again.
b.  This infuriated many students.

Compose two sentences modelled on Pattern 6E.

In this exercise you are converting one base sentence to a noun clause beginning with *that* and substituting it for the pronoun subject of the other, thus making the clause itself the subject of the new sentence. Sentences beginning with a *that*-clause are unusual and emphatic; don't use them often. And usually they work only if relatively short. For example, note how stiff and awkward this sounds: "That even the best athletes can't be entirely consistent is clear." Such a clause is better put second, as in Pattern 6D.

## *Pattern 6F*

a.  Someone gets to the cabin first.
b.  He usually gets the fire going.

RESULT:  Whoever gets to the cabin first usually gets the fire going.

Copy the pattern sentence, changing *someone* to *whoever* and deleting *he*. Do not insert a comma between the two parts.

Combine each of the following pairs into a sentence modelled on the pattern sentence:
a.  Someone interrupted the lecturer.
b.  She had missed a page reference.

a.  Someone stole my purse.
b.  He has acquired little of value.

Compose two sentences modelled on Pattern 6F.

In this exercise you are making a complex sentence by changing sentence *a* into a noun clause with the subject *whoever* and using the clause as the subject of sentence *b*. (Note that this pattern suggests a way of avoiding the pronoun *he* in a context where gender is unknown.)

## *Pattern 6G*

a.  These exercises teach you something about combining sentences.
b.  This should enable you to exercise greater control over your style.

RESULT:  What these exercises teach you about combining sentences should enable you to exercise greater control over your style.

Copy the pattern sentence. Replace *something* with *what* and move it to the beginning, and delete the word *this*. Do not put a comma between the two parts.

Combine each of the following pairs into a sentence modelled on the pattern sentence:
a.  Isabel learned something about other countries.
b.  This made her more content to stay home.

a.  I have experienced something while studying *To the Lighthouse*.
b.  It makes me want to read more of Virginia Woolf's work.

Compose two sentences modelled on Pattern 6G.

In this exercise you are changing base sentence *a* to a noun clause beginning with *what* and using it as the subject of base sentence *b*. (Note that this pattern suggests one way to avoid beginning sentences with pronouns like *this* and *it* when their reference to an antecedent may be vague.)

## *Playing with Language 6A*

Here is a stylistic point that you should keep in mind: The word *that*, that we used in the preceding sentence, has a way of cluttering up sentences. If you use only one *that* in a sentence, it is unlikely that that *that* will cause any confusion. That is, that that *that* that we used in the first part of the preceding sentence would confuse anyone is unlikely. But now we leave it to you to construct a sentence using the word *that* five times in a row. Have fun.

## *Playing with Language 6B*

"A little learning is a dangerous thing," wrote Alexander Pope. Someone could playfully change this to "A little yearning is a dangerous thing" and use it as a title or as a part of a discussion of puppy-love, or fickleness, or casual romance, or some kind of compulsive but transient greed—perhaps coupling it with "absence makes the heart go yonder." Find five other well-known quotations or proverbs and tamper with them in order both to capitalize on their familiarity and to find a fresh way into a topic. Write at least a few sentences or a short paragraph for each. (If you want, practise on Hamlet's "To be or not to be" soliloquy—but don't count it as one of your five.)

## *Playing with Language 6C*

A newspaper headline: "Road Used to Land Plane." Another: "Government moves slow job growth." And another: "Question of public morality left to judge in 2-year-old nude dancing case." Newspaper headlines can be both amusing and instructive. Often limited in the space and the kind of words they can use, writers of headlines sometimes resort to strange locutions. Make a collection of odd, funny, and ambiguous headlines, and try improving them by rephrasing—but without exceeding the original number of letters and spaces: "Plane Lands on Road," for example. (But it isn't always simply a matter of space, as the third example above demonstrates.) What words seem to come up again and again in headlines? Is their popularity explainable by their brevity—for example *probe* rather than *investigation*? Try your own hand at writing headlines, for either real or fictitious events. Vie with your friends to see who can write the most realistic yet funniest ones.

# STAGE THREE:
# Revising

_____

_____

_____

> *Writing and rewriting are a constant*
> *search for what one is saying.*
> (John Updike)

# CHAPTER VII

# Step 7: Revising

Your first draft finished, you turn to the next step in the writing process: revising Some revising goes on during the writing of the first draft, even if you write rapidly. And probably you even do some revising during the planning stage changing a word or phrase here and there. But during step 7 revising is the principal activity.

Revising is the single most important step in the process of composition Inexperienced or careless writers too often feel that they're virtually done when they finish a draft; all that's then needed, they think, is a few minutes of polishing and proofreading. That's why so much writing—and not just that of students—is hard to read, why it fails to achieve its intended effect. Careful and systematic revision is the key to successful writing.

Follow this rough timetable for any particular writing job:

| | |
|---|---|
| Planning | 30% |
| Writing | 15% |
| Revising | 50% |
| Proofreading | 5% |

Of course these percentages will vary according to circumstances. But however much time you give to any particular piece of writing, we recommend that you devote *at least 50%* to revising. If you are assigned a topic, or have a writing task whose strategies and purpose are already given, it's the planning stage that will be curtailed; then the revising stage may take as much as 80% of the time you spend on the project. Nothing should be allowed to reduce the actual time you spend on revising.

## THE STAGES OF REVISING

You can't revise well if you try to attend to everything at once. Even experienced writers make at least two or three sweeps through their drafts, concentrating on different matters during each sweep; some revise ten or more times. Inexperienced writers should plan to make *at least* three separate sweeps, more likely five or six. (Note: we are speaking of *revising* sweeps; *proofreading* comes later.) As your experience increases so will your efficiency; eventually you will be able to keep your eyes open for more than one thing at a time; then you can reduce the number of revising sweeps you need to make.

Think of revising as occurring in three stages:

1. dealing with the large matters,
2. dealing with the middle matters,
3. dealing with the small matters.

Of course no writer can deal with any one matter in total isolation from the others. If you change sentence structure you'll probably change punctuation as well, and if you change a word or a phrase you may well change punctuation or sentence structure as a result. And changing diction, punctuation, or sentence structure will often affect the structure and strategy of a paragraph, and vice versa. Again it is a matter of emphasis. In the second stage, for example, concentrate on revising paragraphs, letting other changes follow as seems advisable. In a later sweep concentrate on revising diction, making any other changes as necessary.

We recommend that you follow a revising plan at least as detailed as the following:

Sweep 1: unity, emphasis, order, coherence, audience and purpose
Sweep 2: paragraphing, paragraph structures and strategies, coherence
Sweep 3: sentences—clarity, economy, vigour, and grace; ramblers
Sweep 4: diction—clarity, economy, vigour, and grace; jargon
Sweep 5: punctuation

> *Style! I have no style. I merely wait till the mud settles.*
>
> (Goldwin Smith)

### Cooling-off Period

If possible, put your draft aside for a rest before tackling the revision. Usually a couple of days is enough, though even longer periods are increasingly beneficial. Then when you return to the draft you can be more objective than if you begin revising immediately after finishing it. When it's still hot off the press, it's too fresh in your mind; you're too close to it to see it very well.

Nevertheless it is often useful to glance over the larger aspects of a first draft right after finishing it. *Then* put it away for whatever cooling-off period you decide is possible and desirable.

## Early Screening

Immediately after finishing a draft is not only a good time to give it a quick once-over yourself, but also to get one or more other people—perhaps including your instructor—to read it through and give you their impressions—their impressions, that is, of such larger matters as tone, subject, audience, and purpose; leave the smaller stylistic details alone for a while. What your friends tell you about the effects of your draft can help you focus your energies during revision.

---

Please read through my draft and comment briefly on the following:

1. Title:
2. Quality and clarity of ideas:
3. Scope, size of subject:
4. Clarity and placement of thesis:
5. Effectiveness of beginning and ending:
6. Organization: Is the ordering of the material the most suitable?
7. Adequacy of development—overall, and of parts: Is there too much generalization, or not enough specific evidence?
8. Coherence: Does the whole thing hang together? Are the connections between the parts clear?
9. Emphasis, proportion: Is it clear which parts are most important?
10. Is everything relevant?
11. Is anything important missing?
12. Tone, attitude, voice, rhetorical stance: Is it appropriate, clear, and consistent throughout?

I would also appreciate any brief comments you wish to offer on such matters of style and mechanics as diction, sentence structure and variety, paragraphing, punctuation, and spelling.

In your view, what is the major strength of the paper?

_____

_____

_____

_____

What are your principal suggestions for improving it?

_____

_____

_____

_____

---

When you ask others to look over your draft and offer comments and criticisms, you can both make their job easier and make their comments more useful to you if you provide them with a simple form to follow. For example you could give them a sheet listing all the particulars of writing (spelling, punctuation, diction, sentence structure, and so on) and ask them to check off each item on a scale of 1 (poor) to 5 (good). But that sort of chart would be more appropriate later, near the end of the revising process (see p. 315). At this earlier stage you want mainly their reactions to larger matters—though you don't want to exclude comments on style. And you'll also get better information if you ask for written comments rather than just a series of checks in boxes. You might want to use or to adapt the sample form on the facing page in some way:

> *Blot out, correct, insert, refine,*
> *Enlarge, diminish, interline;*
> *Be mindful, when invention fails,*
> *To scratch your head, and bite your nails.*
> (Jonathan Swift)

# Sweep 1: Revising the Large Matters

As soon as you finish a rough draft, look at it as a whole. But prepare for that by self-consciously going back and evaluating your entire planning stage, steps 1 through 5; now that you've finished the draft, you have a new vantage point. You may for example find that your sense of the draft you've just finished doesn't altogether jibe with what you told yourself you were going to do. If there has been any shift in focus, any even slight change in your topic and the way you're dealing with it, or in your audience, or in your primary or secondary purposes, now is the time to weigh the differences and decide whether

(a)  your intentions weren't fully clear or complete, or
(b)  your draft has somehow wandered off course.

If (a), go back to your planning notes and make whatever specific changes are called for; physically making the changes, in writing, will enable you to evaluate them more consciously and hence more clearly. You might want to rephrase your thesis statement, or change something in your plan, or refine your statements of purpose, or revise the profile of your audience. If whatever changes you make seem to hold up, then you can return to the draft and begin revising it according to the new intentions. But don't try to treat any but the larger matters until after a cooling-off period.

If (b), however, if your plans were sound but your draft has somehow not adhered to them, you can set to work revising it right away—again, letting a cooling-off period intervene before you begin working on anything but the larger matters.

But even if you're satisfied that the draft generally fulfills your intentions, you must start the work of revision quite deliberately, for it often happens that one doesn't begin to sense a draft's weaknesses until one gets into it during revision.

Here are some specific ways to examine a draft to find out if it contains any of the large weaknesses drafts are prone to. *Read the draft through—several times*, sometimes slowly, sometimes more rapidly—while asking these specific questions:

1. *Are all the parts of the draft relevant to your purpose?*   You are writing with a specific purpose in mind; you want your essay or letter or report to accomplish something. The parts may be good in themselves, but the piece as a whole will be weakened if some parts don't further your purpose. Suppose that your goal in a piece of writing is to convince people that they should buy and drive smaller cars. You will argue such points as lower initial cost, lower operating cost, easier handling, easier parking; but if you happen to know a good deal about cars and how they work you could easily get carried away, in your eagerness to get all the facts down, and provide more technical information than your readers need. If your audience is the general motoring public, some data about fuel economy and braking distances and repair bills will be in order, but figures about cylinder size, carburetion, gear ratios, and torque will probably only confuse them, distract them from your main point, and thus weaken your argument. If you've used graphs and tables for comparison, for example, you may have included more information than necessary, muddying rather than clarifying your point.

2. *Have you left anything out?*   A main purpose of revising is to let you read your draft *through the eyes of your readers*. (And of course you can take advantage of the responses of others who read it over.) Check to see if you've made any assumptions that were clear enough in your head but that somehow didn't get themselves put on paper. For example, if you're explaining a process that you know quite well, you can all too easily leave out a step that is obvious to you but that would be missed by a reader not familiar with the process. If you're explaining how to play chess and say something like "Usually, one should castle as soon as possible in order to strengthen one's defence," you will only puzzle the poor reader who doesn't know about the move called "castling." Of course if your intended audience is composed of readers who already know the moves and you're writing about various strategies of play, such a sentence would be all right. It's a question, as usual, of audience and purpose.

3. *Are your points accurate and fully explained?*   In the momentum of writing your draft you may have skipped over a figure or date or other fact, intending to look it up later, and then forgotten to do so. Do it now!

Or you may discover that a particular part of the discussion doesn't seem to make much sense. This is a common experience for most writers: something that seemed clear in your mind while you were writing is no longer fully clear even to you; it's therefore unlikely to be clear to your readers. Now is the time to rethink the point, find out what went wrong, and rewrite it, probably adding a phrase or a sentence or two of explanation to make the point clearer.

Or you may realize that a particular generalization doesn't sound as clear or convincing as you thought it would, and decide to add an example or two to support it. You may even decide to clarify a complicated explanatory paragraph by adding—or substituting—a diagram or table or graph or chart so that your readers can see precisely what you mean.

4. *Are your points in the best order?* In your plan you organized your material in what you thought the best order. Now is the time to check how well it works. If for example you're writing an argument, you may have begun with your weakest point and worked up to your strongest; but now you feel that the beginning just isn't forceful enough, so you decide to move your second-strongest point back to the beginning. Or you may be writing some kind of report, and thus have begun with your most important ideas; but now you find the ending too flabby, so you decide at least not to end with your weakest point.

Or you may have discovered a good new idea while you were writing the first draft, and put it in. Now is the time to check its effect on the whole essay. Perhaps the addition disturbs the flow of the original order, requiring you to shift one or more things around to restore coherence. Or the addition may have changed the relative importance of other points, requiring some rearrangement to make the new relations clearer or to restore a climactic order. It may even contradict something you say elsewhere, and so require some major rethinking.

5. *Are the main ideas sufficiently emphasized?* Order, as you know, is only one technique for providing emphasis. Repetition is another; you may for example decide to repeat, toward the end, a point you made earlier, both to emphasize it and to keep your reader oriented. And proportion, or relative length, is another; you might find that an important point needs more detail not just to clarify it but also to keep it from being over-shadowed by its surroundings. Or you might decide to put an important point in a short paragraph by itself in order to emphasize it. Or you might decide to end a paragraph with a short snappy sentence to increase its impact. Or you might even decide to use some graphic device to better emphasize some point or points: a numbered list, for example, or extra white space, or even—in some kinds of writing—lines or boxes to set something off.

*Practical Hint:* When revising a draft, don't make the mistake of blotting things out to the point of illegibility. Rather draw a single line through whatever word or words you're changing, so that you can still read them. You may well want to change it back later on, or lift a passage out for use elsewhere. If you blot it out altogether, you've lost it.

> *Le style c'est l'homme même.*
> (Buffon)

## RHETORICAL STANCE—TONE

For nearly everything you write, you take up a particular rhetorical stance. Usually writers do this automatically, just as when you speak to someone you automatically use a tone of voice appropriate to the occasion. For example, if you're writing a chatty personal letter to a close friend, your style will be colloquial and lively, probably even slangy. But if you're writing a letter of sympathy to a friend who has just lost a close relative, your style will be quite different—more sober and formal. Not only what you say, but also how you say it, will establish your *tone*, and your tone will reflect how you feel toward both your subject and your audience. In the letter of sympathy, your style will indicate that you feel serious, sad, and thoughtful about the subject and friendly and sympathetic toward your reader.

But even though people usually adopt, almost instinctively, a rhetorical stance appropriate to the occasion for a given piece of writing, it nevertheless helps to be able to choose a stance consciously or to be able to control your style so as to reflect a certain stance. For example, in the letter of sympathy you could decide whether you wanted to be a little colloquial so as to be closer, less stiff and formally distant, than you might otherwise sound. And in the chatty letter you probably wouldn't use any formal style unless you did so humorously.

Here then are some simple methods for controlling how you sound. As you proceed through the several sweeps of revision, keep in mind this matter of rhetorical stance. Most of the specific techniques in the following lists are discussed in detail in the following chapters.

In order to make your writing more formal,

> Use bigger and less common words.
> Reduce slang, colloquialisms, and popular phrases.
> Avoid contractions and the pronoun *you*.
> Make sentences and paragraphs longer and more complex.
> Increase the variety of kinds of sentences (simple, compound, complex).

To make your writing less formal, more informal or colloquial,

> Use shorter, simpler, more everyday words.
> Introduce some colloquialisms or even slang.
> Use more contractions and more of the pronoun *you*.
> Use shorter and simpler sentences and paragraphs.

Note that this is not a matter of "level." That is, one style is not higher or lower than another, in the sense of better or worse; it is just different. Formal style is not better than informal style unless the particular rhetorical occasion calls for formality; on many occasions an informal style is far preferable to a formal one.

In addition to the relative formality or informality of your style on a given occasion, you can also control its complexity or intricacy. In a formal letter of condolence, for example, you would probably want to avoid anything stylistically fancy. But in a light or popular piece, such as a sports column, you'd probably want your style to be both colloquial and lively. If you're writing a speech, even for a serious occasion, you'll probably want to include some stylish, oratorical flourishes. Or in a narrative you might choose to be informal or even colloquial, but still to avoid anything fancy in order to keep the style from calling attention to itself.

On occasions when you want to make your writing livelier, then—to raise the temperature and the noise-level, so to speak—

> Increase the vividness and vigour of your verbs; cut down on the verb *be* in all its forms.
> Use more concrete and specific nouns.

Increase the number and variety of modifiers.

Use more metaphors and similes, and even patterns of sound, like alliteration, as long as you stay in control of the effect.

Use more parallelism and balanced structures in your sentences and paragraphs, and increase the variety of sentence length.

And on those occasions when you want your prose to be subdued, temperate, more restrained—when you want it quieter and cooler—

Use quieter, less lively verbs, and more *be* and *have*.

Use fewer specific and concrete nouns; make your diction more general.

Cut back on the number and variety of modifiers.

Cut down on figurative language, sound patterns, and rhythm in sentences.

Most serviceable prose takes up a moderate stance. It avoids the extremes both of formality and slanginess and of extravagant liveliness and dull sobriety. You can assure yourself of having adopted such a stance by checking your style during revision. Generally, you will want to

Use both big words and small words, but more medium ones.

Use some unusual words, but keep mostly to familiar, everyday ones.

Use some contractions and *you*'s, but not many.

Make your sentences mostly short or average length, and see that at least half of them are simple or compound.

Keep most of your paragraphs near the average length.

Use a mixed diction—some lively words, some quiet; some concrete and specific, some abstract and general.

Use a moderate number and variety of modifiers.

Use some figurative language, sound patterns, parallelism, and balance—but not a lot.

But sometimes you will want to get away from a moderate stance. For example, here is a paragraph describing the experience of watching the 1975 World Series on television. The assignment was to find a subject that could be treated in a lively and colloquial style and to work up a paragraph on it. Note the techniques the writer uses:

### The Annual Bash

Did you watch the World Series? Baffling bunts and howling homers, slippery singles and doughty doubles, cud-chewing pitchers and testy batters; the outfield awaiting, the infield jumping, the umpires guessing; the catcher crouched like a mushroom behind the plate; the pitcher unwinding like a forkful of spaghetti; frenetic fans and enthusiastic announcers—what's it all in aid of? Suspense. Competition. Excitement. Sometimes boredom. Everybody's happy? Sports fans eat it up, and even non-fans are chained to the tube, hoping it won't go to seven and spoil another night's TV-dinner schedule. You can't stand to watch it, and you can't stand not to watch it. Errors and assists, RBI's and steals: the statistics flood the screen, and you wonder if it'll go on forever. So you watch; so you wonder; so you retch (the announcer again) and you cheer. At last it's over. The Red Sox blew it, the Reds socked it. It's been a joy, and a torture, and a nuisance—and I wouldn't have missed it for the world. Wait'll next year?

Note that the writer did not rely on slang to achieve the colloquial tone he wanted.

Here is another single-paragraph composition—longer, serious, more formal, as the writer felt to be appropriate to the subject matter:

### The Brotherhood

Ever since Cain slew Abel, consanguinity has seemed to offer minimal assurance of peaceful relations. Indeed it might well be thought to foster animosity, for some of the most brutal conflicts down through history have been intestine ones. The soil of much of the Iberian peninsula, for example, was in the 1930's incarnadined by Spaniards of opposing political opinions. Closer to home, Americans in the mid-nineteenth century, disagreeing about slavery—among other things—were incapable of settling their differences by means other than bloody conflict, sometimes with members of a single family fighting on opposing sides. And if one considers recent circumstances in Northern Ireland, Lebanon, and Central America, one must acknowledge that reasoning together amongst citizens of one nation seems to be no more popular in the contemporary world. The bitter strife between peoples within various African nations adds appreciably to the list. Nor is such uncivil bellicosity unique to the western world: the Vietnamese experience, and the Laotian and Cambodian struggles that accompanied it, argue the universality of the tendency. The recent altercations in Iran and the protracted wars earlier in the century among Chinese of various persuasions augment, at both ends of the scale of magnitude, the list of evidence of the apparent proclivity of homo sapiens to fraternal and internecine violence. Innumerable minor conflicts could no doubt be adduced to further increase the negative statistics. Even the nuclear family is no stranger to violent arguments; but it is in the family of man at large, now its own kind of terrifyingly nuclear family, that man's truest nature is perhaps demonstrated. One does not wish to embrace pessimism unadvisedly, but it would seem that the keeper, as often as not, has not only abandoned, but also turned against, his brother.

Examine the techniques the writer used to achieve a tone of sober formality. Do you think he pushed it too far? Or does the style effectively convey his attitude? Are such phrases as "the brotherhood" and "the family of man" inherently sexist? Should they be changed, and if so, how? If they are sexist, does it matter?

---

### *Exploration 7A*

Rewrite the above paragraph. Keep it relatively formal, but reduce the number of Latinate words, and introduce as much stylistic complexity as you think it will bear—a complexity almost completely lacking in its present form. What different occasions might the two versions be appropriate to?

---

A particular tone or rhetorical stance is often appropriate to a particular subject, of course. But sometimes a subject may be treated quite differently under different circumstances. In the following three paragraphs, for example, the student was demonstrating how a single topic can be handled for three different kinds of occasion:

## Automotive Dependency: A Change in Attitude

Automobiles form an integral component of North American life. Such a pervasive automotive society has developed around the expanding use of these individual transportation units that it would be difficult to imagine modern North America without the presence of the motor-car. Many new economic and cultural developments have been forged in the automotive foundry of North American society. The list includes motels, drive-in theatres, drive-in restaurants, drive-through banks, and even drive-in churches. The zenith of the automotive age occurred in the mid-twentieth century. In the 1950's and 1960's parking lots and freeways, both engendered by the automotive revolution, become synonymous with general economic progress. Even today some younger members of society revere particular models and devote a great deal of time to their maintenance and restoration. But in 1973 an event occurred that began to alter the automotive mentality of North America: the increase in the price of world crude oil. Presently a new attitude towards automobiles appeared. Gone are the days of luxurious but inefficient automobiles. Today North American society is demanding efficient, more compact, and higher quality automotive products.

## Thinking Small

Cars are an important part of North American society. We all rely on them to a large extent as our primary means of transportation. Try to imagine what life would be like without our horseless carriages. Difficult, isn't it? For our social and economic structure has developed around the use of the automobile. Motels and drive-in banks, restaurants, and movie theatres are all examples of the automotive culture. During the 1950's and 1960's the parking lot became a symbol of progress. In the U.S.A. billions of dollars were spent on massive interstate freeways that web throughout the country. Some young men even go so far as to worship some particular models as if they were gods. But unfortunately (or fortunately?) all this may be coming to an end. The price hikes in world oil that occurred in 1973 have dramatically changed attitudes toward cars in North America. Where bigger, faster, flashier was once the norm for automotive design, people are now demanding smaller, better built, and more efficient cars.

## No More Big Wheels

In North America cars rule. What would we do without them? We'd be up the creek, that's what! We depend upon our wheels for almost everything we do. We travel from motel to motel, eat at drive-in restaurants, bank at drive-in banks, go to drive-in movie theatres, and even worship at drive-in churches—in sunny, funny California anyway—all because of the boom in car-ownership. In fact the whole continent's daily life revolves around four wheels. This motor madness has gone so far that some guys make a particular model like a 'Vette or Mustang their golden calf. Consequently the great expanses of blacktop called parking lots and the thousands of miles of U.S. interstate freeways became symbols of progress in the '50's and '60's. But the bubble burst in 1973 when gas prices shot up. Unfortunately (or luckily?) this changed everybody's feelings about our four-wheeled friends. Where once we all wanted snarling, gleaming gas-pigs, now we're crying for econo-boxes.

Think of the different kinds of publications these could appear in. The first might be at home in a business or economic journal; the second would fit a somewhat less staid magazine or perhaps a newspaper's editorial page; the third might fit some popular and lively magazine.

---

### Exercise 7A

Here are four paragraphs written by students in response to various assignments. Analyze their techniques and decide what rhetorical stance each adopts. How appropriate is the stance to the subject matter and the apparent occasion of each? Present your conclusions in a brief report. Since the paragraphs lack titles, suggest one for each.

**1.**

Money, money, money. It makes the world go round. Whether you have too much of it or not enough of it, you seem to have too many problems because of it. And whether you like it or not, you need money to survive in a society where overconsumption is the name of the game. Food, shelter, clothing, entertainment—everything has a price, except perhaps love. Money may not be able to buy love, but then love can't pay the bills either. Associations of wealth, prosperity, and happiness surround that precious, glimmering dollar sign, and so do feelings of envy, greed, and deceit; money always brings out the worst in us. It is a shame that instead of being satisfied with who and where we are in society, we use money to help us scramble to the top—only to discover that, rich or poor, everyone is equal in the end.

**2.**

The natural beauty of untouched wilderness is what makes the Gulf Islands, off B.C.'s southwestern coast, a favourite among vacation spots. These islands are visited most frequently by boaters and campers any time from April to September. Kendrick Island is my favourite of them all. It is the smallest, and perhaps the least well-known. One side of Kendrick provides a sheltered, peaceful spot for anchoring a boat. A soft breeze often ripples the water, providing good conditions for wind-surfing. The other side of the island faces the Gulf of Georgia; on a clear day one can see the coastal mountain ranges beyond Howe Sound. Fierce winds often blow from the Gulf, sending crashing waves up onto the smooth rock formations, but this seems not to bother the family of seals that play among the seaweed reefs. Once on the island, a person can spend a whole day discovering its secrets: crabs hiding in the crannies of the rocks, oysters clinging to the barnacles, wild-flowers and thickets harbouring lazy garden snakes and field mice, and the tall evergreens swaying in the breeze while small birds fly to and from their nests.

**3.**

Have you ever had a flat tire? It can be quite the experience, especially if you're travelling along at a snappy speed—say 60 km/h or more. First there's a loud

BANG, which in itself is enough to send you flying, but then you lose control of the car, and if you're not careful you're liable to go into a spin. Most people would immediately slam on the brakes, but they say this is the worst thing to do—you're supposed to come to a gradual stop. O.K., so now you've stopped the car. Do you have a spare tire—inflated—in the trunk? Maybe. Do you have a jack? Probably not. Even if you had both, you can't do anything without a wrench to loosen the lug-bolts. This is when you decide to give in and hitch-hike to the nearest phone and call a tow truck. You're dialing the number and you start thinking how much it's going to cost. Right then and there you vow to join the BCAA first thing in the morning.

**4.**

The old woman who lives three doors down from us is a witch. They say she casts evil spells on anyone who dares to disrupt her privacy. Rumour has it that five years ago one poor fellow was caught nosing around her porch, was yanked into her house, and hasn't been seen or heard from since. But even if that isn't true, I wouldn't go near her house if you paid me. She's got two weird black cats that sit posted on either side of her gate like sentinels. Their amber eyes penetrate into your very soul; it makes you feel as if they could suck it right out of your body. They're also armed with pretty sharp claws. I can easily do without spiritual and physical piercing, thank you very much. Maybe I'm foolish, but I feel a lot safer on this side of the fence.

# BEGINNINGS AND ENDINGS

During the first sweep of revision, take a close look at the beginning and the ending of a piece of writing. You will make further refinements during later sweeps, but at this point you should check the effectiveness of the way you've chosen to begin and end. If you're like most writers, you'll find that in the first draft your beginning and ending are feeble, perhaps even perfunctory. In writing the draft you were primarily interested in getting your ideas down on paper; you didn't worry much about either the beginning or the ending, knowing that the problems they present can best be tackled when the body of the draft is complete. Now is the time to focus on them.

There are several principles you should be aware of for both beginnings and endings, and both beginnings and endings can be classified into a few common kinds. But first an important general principle and some rules of thumb.

## Proportion

There is no rigid rule about how long the beginning or ending should be in relation to the rest of a piece of writing. But some students seem to think that there is, probably because some teachers and even some texts have given them a simple formula to follow. For example there is one standard kind of school essay which could be called "The Five-Paragraph Theme." Its formula looks like this:

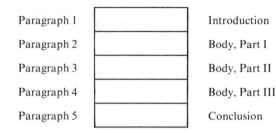

| Paragraph 1 | | Introduction |
| Paragraph 2 | | Body, Part I |
| Paragraph 3 | | Body, Part II |
| Paragraph 4 | | Body, Part III |
| Paragraph 5 | | Conclusion |

The implication is that the "Introduction" and the "Conclusion" each take up about 20% of the essay, leaving 60% for the "Body" with its three parts. There is nothing wrong with this formula—if it fits the requirements of a given essay: if for example the topic has three main points, and if each can be developed adequately in just one paragraph, and if the material or the occasion, or both, require a fairly long and detailed introduction, and if the whole thing is sufficiently complex to require a similarly long and elaborate concluding paragraph. But most of the time such a formula would be highly artificial; adhering slavishly to it or to any other formula means imposing a structure on the material rather than letting the material and the occasion determine the structure. Bad tactics.

And chances are a writer following such a formula would begin the final paragraph with the phrase "In conclusion," a practice which should be reserved for only the most stiffly formal and patterned business or technical reports, whose readers may expect it. In other kinds of writing avoid it.

Partly to get away from such unwanted stiffness, we avoid the terms *introduction* and *conclusion* and speak of *beginning* and *ending*. Indeed, an essay may just "begin" and "end"; it may not need anything that could be called an "introduction" or a "conclusion." If you can get into the habit of thinking of beginnings and endings rather than of introductions and conclusions, you will more easily avoid the all too common compulsion to provide a formal introduction and conclusion for every essay, whether it needs them or not. Such discrete, unitary "introductions" and "conclusions" also run the serious risk of seeming tacked on, not integrated with the essay as a whole.

Here is a better way to think of the proportions of a piece of writing:

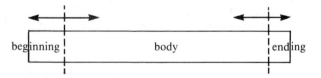

The two vertical lines setting off beginning and ending are movable; they can slide back and forth as required for any particular piece of writing.

Another common assumption is that the beginning and the ending should be approximately the same length. Not so. E. M. Forster's essay "My Wood," for example, has a fairly long beginning (about 15% of the whole essay), then four distinct and enumerated parts for the body of the essay, and an ending that is merely the last sentence of the fourth part. It's quite effective.

Notice that in our diagram we've drawn the vertical lines so that the beginning is about twice as long as the ending. Follow this rule of thumb:

> Beginning . . . . . . . . . . 10%
> Body . . . . . . . . . . . . . 85%
> Ending . . . . . . . . . . . . 5%

Those proportions, or something fairly close to them, are quite common and quite effective—especially for what most of us think of as "essays." But remember that it is only a rough guideline; depart from it when and how you need to, but do so consciously and because you perceive a need to do so for a particular piece of writing.

## Beginnings

The beginning of a piece of writing is (after the title) the first part your readers see. It deserves your special attention because it automatically, by its position of strong emphasis, gets your readers' special attention. A poor beginning can cause you to have no readers at all. A good beginning will encourage your readers to read on with interest.

### BASIC PRINCIPLES OF BEGINNINGS

A good beginning to any piece of writing must do two things: it must identify the subject and it must interest readers. But you can usefully think of a beginning as doing five things:

1. It identifies the subject, and often states the topic; it may also indicate something about how the writer is going to handle the topic.
2. It gets a reader's attention and interest.
3. It establishes the writer's rhetorical stance.
4. It suggests or identifies the occasion and establishes the reader's role.
5. It provides whatever is needed by way of background.

Not every beginning needs to do all these. If you're writing a report or a memorandum, for example, or a paper for a course, you can usually assume your reader's interest, and the occasion and the reader's role will be obvious. But when your audience is broader and your subject one of more general interest, you should consciously consider all five of these functions to make sure they are being carried out adequately. They enable you to establish your *credibility* as a writer on a given occasion.

1. *Identify your subject and, usually, state your thesis—or part of it.* Even if your title identifies the subject, the beginning of the essay must do so. Your first sentence may well announce your subject. Or, if you're using a delayed beginning (see below), you may lead up to it gradually. But you can seldom delay the clear identification of the subject beyond the first paragraph. Your readers want to know what's going on; they will become impatient if you keep

them in the dark too long. Think of the times you've begun reading something and then quit because you got tired of waiting for some clear indication of what it was all about.

The thesis, too, usually comes no later than the end of the first paragraph, or perhaps the beginning of the second. Sometimes you can hold back a thesis until at or near the end of an essay; some subjects can effectively be developed that way—for example, moving from the general to the specific—but only rarely, and only if you are firmly in control. And sometimes you can state a complex thesis one part at a time—for example a first part at the beginning, a second part a third way of the way through, a third part two thirds of the way through, and then the three parts tied together at the end.

Here, for example, is the beginning paragraph from a draft of a student's essay:

> DRAFT: Fitness centres are growing rapidly. Although they seem expensive, joining one is a good investment. If you want to get involved in a fitness program, there are two options available. You can join a fitness centre, or you can go to fitness classes at a community centre. The difference between the two is that by joining a fitness centre you can go to any one of the many scheduled classes throughout the week, but community centres offer only a very limited number of classes. In the long run joining a fitness centre is more beneficial.

Note how the opening sentence just hangs there; it seems to have almost no connection with the rest of the paragraph. And note that the second sentence, which is part of the thesis statement, does not flow into the next sentence; there's no logical coherence between them. Note further that the final sentence is also a part of the thesis. What's to be done? You've probably decided already. Begin by either deleting the first sentence entirely, or make it into a subordinate clause or phrase for use elsewhere in the paper. Then begin with the third sentence; the paragraph is not only a beginning paragraph but a paragraph that is developing a contrast—and the third sentence is the natural beginning of that; it also helps to get the word *you* right there at the start, to involve the reader. Finally, move the second sentence to the end of the paragraph where it belongs. The writer first thought that the thesis should be stated right at the beginning, but this is a good example of a thesis that comes naturally at the end of the first paragraph.

2. *Get the readers' interest.*   Even if you have a guaranteed or captive audience, you want your readers to be interested in what you are writing. You want them to *want* to read your words, and to want to go on reading until the end. A letter which begins "Well, Christmas has rolled around again and I thought I'd better let you in on what I've been up to for the past year" isn't likely to arouse the recipient; the clichés and the general tone of tiredness and duty will invite at best only a dull or cursory kind of attention. Often the title of an essay can spark interest, but the beginning of the essay itself must also do the job. Here are some points to keep in mind:

a. Arouse curiosity, but don't puzzle your readers unnecessarily or for too long.
b. Point out the importance of the topic.
c. Open with something vivid and concrete; or, if you open with a generalization, get specific as soon as possible.
d. Avoid tired or vague language.

  e. Make clear to your readers what they can expect from the rest of the essay.
  f. Generally, begin as concisely as possible; don't waste your readers' time.
  g. Avoid a string of overlong sentences. If you begin with a long sentence, follow it with one or more shorter ones. Consider beginning with a two- or three-word sentence, or even one or more minor sentences, each of which could consist of only one word.

3. *Establish the rhetorical stance you want to use throughout; assume a role.* At the beginning of any piece of writing you are making an implicit promise to your readers; you are not only announcing a subject and an approach; you are also committing yourself to a certain style. The voice readers hear at the outset is the voice they will expect to hear throughout the essay. Sometimes you will want to begin lightly or humorously and then become relatively serious (though not likely the other way around), but other major shifts are not advisable. For example, if you open with a formal level of diction, don't suddenly switch to colloquialisms or slang. If you begin with predominantly short sentences (perhaps because of the nature of your intended audience), don't change to predominantly long and involved sentences later.

Of course this doesn't mean that you should use a monotonous sameness of style throughout an essay. You want a pleasant variety, and you may want to shift briefly in order to startle your readers or to emphasize a point. But generally you should stick close to the stylistic base-line you establish at the outset.

4. *Identify the occasion and assign your readers a role.* Avoid the feeling of a void. If the occasion for a piece of writing is not implicitly clear, make it as explicit as necessary. If you begin indirectly, don't keep your readers in suspense too long. Be sure that it is soon clear—implicitly, if not explicitly—just why you are writing the piece and just why they should be reading it. If you mentally cast your readers in a certain role, if you think of them in a particular relation to you and to the subject, chances are that what you write will convey the sense of this role to them.

Here is the title and beginning paragraph of a student's draft for an essay:

### Physical Fitness

Physical fitness means 1) being able to meet the demands of one's daily life tasks, 2) being able to handle emergency situations, 3) preventing degenerative health disorders, and 4) having a positive physical self-image. There are five major components to physical fitness, which are 1) cardiovascular fitness, 2) strength, 3) muscular endurance, 4) flexibility, and 5) body composition.

Do you feel like reading on? The writer asked herself just who *would* feel like reading on. Probably no-one. There is no voice—except a kind of computerized, mechanical one. Since she wanted to inform and interest and perhaps influence an audience wider than those who would read a textbook, she knew she had to revamp this beginning, or rather supply a new one. Here is the new first paragraph—along with a new title, as well:

### Looking Good, Feeling Good

Do you find yourself yawning at your desk, feeling drowsy all day, being prone to tantrums, getting fatigued from minimal exertion, being too tired to pursue leisure activities, feeling nervous and jittery, having difficulty relaxing, being subject to worries and moods, having an irritable disposition towards others? According to Dr. Kenneth Cooper, in his book *The New Aerobics*, any one of these symptoms may be associated with less than adequate standards of physical fitness. Are you as fit as you think? Think back to what your appetite was like when you were 20 years old. Have you retained the same eating habits? If so, chances are you are a candidate for creeping obesity, because most people's activity level drops after age 24. After the age of 20, if you continually gain one pound a year, by the time you are 50 you will be 30 pounds heavier, and most of us cannot afford this excess.

Now there's someone talking. And now too there's someone listening, for the new beginning clearly defines its audience. In her original audience profile, the student had said, weakly, "anyone who is interested in physical fitness," and produced the weak beginning. But the new opening would also *create* an interest in many readers who didn't have one before, especially those who find themselves being described in the long opening sentence—precisely the people the writer is aiming at. Not until she had begun revising did she get a clear sense of her audience. And from then on it was easy. See also the two examples of beginnings on p. 33.

5. *Provide any needed background information.* If you are describing a process, your beginning may have to include some discussion of the purpose or the setting of the process. Or if your subject requires you to use one or more unfamiliar or specialized terms, you may have to devote part of your beginning to defining them. As always, keep your readers in mind. Don't assume they know something that they may not. It is better to risk insulting their intelligence by telling them something they already know than to risk puzzling them or causing them to wonder what your purpose is. Even knowledgeable readers won't be insulted if you establish a tone of good will and if you provide the information efficiently and diplomatically, for example by putting it in subordinate parts of your sentences.

## KINDS OF BEGINNINGS

Think of beginnings according to their directness. The more direct the beginning, the shorter it will be; the less direct, the longer. Short essays usually have short, relatively direct beginnings. Longer essays can not only accommodate longer, less direct beginnings; they also often require them. But unless you have good reason to do otherwise, choose the more direct beginning.

**Direct Beginnings**    Here are the principal kinds of direct beginnings:

1. A straightforward statement of your opinion or your proposition. Explain your thesis; state your purpose.
2. A reference to or statement of an opposing idea which you intend to argue against, to refute or otherwise dispose of.
3. An analysis of your subject or topic. This can be handled in two main ways:
   a. it can be a way of narrowing down to the specific part or parts you intend to focus on or emphasize;
   b. it can lay out the major divisions of your topic, providing your readers with what amounts to a brief plan of the essay to follow.

**Less Direct Beginnings**   Some beginnings are still fairly direct even though the statement of the thesis is delayed for a bit after the subject is identified. Here are three common kinds:

4. A broad, general statement followed by a progressive narrowing through increasingly specific points until you arrive at a specific statement of your thesis. When this occupies the whole of a single paragraph, as it often does, it is what is called a "funnel" or a "wedge" paragraph; it wedges its way into the essay.
5. A definition of one or more key terms relating to your subject or thesis.
6. Some interesting historical or factual background, or a setting for what you're going to discuss. Similarly, a report or research paper might begin with a summary of previous work on your subject.

**Beginning with Hooks**   Some beginnings use what are called "hooks" to snag readers' attention. The degree of directness depends on the nature of the hook and on how long specific mention of the subject and thesis is delayed. The dangers with these opening devices are (a) that you may be tempted to use them too often, to depend on them when a more straightforward beginning would serve better, and (b) that some of them can too obviously appear to be gimmicks, to call attention to themselves and thus distract your readers from your real point. Be careful with them. Here are some commonly used and effective kinds:

7. A quotation directly or indirectly related to your subject or topic. Such a quotation can be from your focussed reading about a topic or from your general reading, for example in a magazine or newspaper. Or it can be one you've purposely dug up from such a reference book as *Bartlett's Familiar Quotations* or *The Oxford Dictionary of Quotations*.

   Similar to this is a beginning that uses a well-known proverb or aphorism, which you may not need to quote directly. But watch out for "the cliché effect": a paper that begins with "A stitch in time saves nine" or "Too many cooks spoil the broth" would not have much of a ring of originality about it. Sometimes you can overcome this by treating an all-too-familiar proverb in a fresh way. For example how might you develop an essay that began "Not enough cooks even tried to spoil the broth in my house" or "A stitch in time saved only 8½ last April..."? Try playing with some others. (About seventy-five years ago, Ambrose Bierce in *The Devil's Dictionary* provided some examples of what he called "old saws fitted with new teeth," such as "A bird in the hand is worth what it will bring," "Half a loaf is better than a whole one if there is much else," "Strike while your employer has a big contract," and "Where there's a will there's a won't.")
8. An interesting or even provocative question that will arouse your readers' curiosity; often you can use one or more questions to lead to a narrowing of focus on your topic. (But don't lean too heavily on "rhetorical questions"— questions whose answers are obvious and thus not stated; they can put a reader off, especially if they come in bunches.) Sometimes even your thesis itself can usefully be put in the form of a question; the rest of the essay then constitutes an answer to that question.

9. A brief narrative or description, something lively and stimulating to serve as an interesting illustration or example. This could be a vivid descriptive sketch, an anecdote, or a dramatic incident—perhaps from personal experience. Sometimes you can begin a narration *in medias res*, "in the middle of things," in order to create suspense and arouse your readers' curiosity about what led up to the event. Such an opening could also take the form of a few lines of dialogue—something that you read somewhere, or overheard and wrote down, or even made up for the occasion.

   Here for example is an effective dramatic beginning for a student's essay called "Save Our Wrecks," arguing for the better preservation and treatment of underwater archaeological sites:

   > On a stormy night in February, 1872, the American barque *Zephyr* was out-bound from Nanaimo to San Francisco with a cargo of sandstone blocks and columns. The sandstone, quarried from Newcastle Island, was destined for use in constructing the new United States Mint. The ship never left British Columbia. Lost in the storm, the *Zephyr* foundered on the rocks of Mayne Island.

10. An interesting or even unusual and striking fact or statistic, or some important figures bearing on your topic. Or you could open with a startling or sensational statement or detail or illustration, or a striking analogy or contrast, or some dire or outrageous prediction, or something otherwise bizarre or mysterious. (But be careful that you don't force such a beginning, or prolong it; let it speak for itself as much as possible, and keep it brief.)

11. A contrast, for example pointing out a change. A good beginning might be one that says, in effect, "I used to think so-and-so, but now I think such-and-such."

12. A reference to some widely shared attitude or emotion or experience, some common problem or pleasure. (But don't make it sound too obvious or commonplace; make it interesting.)

13. A reference to some well-known recent historical or other event that is (or can be made) somehow pertinent to your topic; or a reference to some famous person recently in the news. The more nearly *current* such a reference is, the more potent a hook it will be.

14. A figure of speech, or a play on words, or something else humorous. (But be careful: don't be arch or coy; don't get carried away with your own cleverness. Such a hook must be a small one; keep it brief.)

15. And of course you can use a carefully thought out *combination* of two or more of these kinds of beginnings.

## THINGS TO AVOID IN BEGINNINGS

1. Don't start too far back. If you're going to discuss a modern novel, don't begin with the narrative techniques of the ancient Greeks. If you're writing about the latest Ferrari racing car, don't begin by speculating on the invention of the wheel. Sometimes a *brief* reference to something remote in the past—by way of contrast or analogy, for example—can spark the beginning of a paper; but if such a hook is to be effective it must be brief: don't dwell on it.

2. Don't use the trite "dictionary" opening, such as these:

   *The Concise Oxford Dictionary* defines *altruism* as...
   According to the *Gage Senior Dictionary*, a *boondoggle* is....

   Put definitions in your own words and direct them at your topic in an efficient way. For example:

   Altruism, the habit of being unselfish, of thinking first of others, is becoming more and more rare, especially among people packed into large cities.

   Probably the only time you would need to quote a dictionary is when you were specifically comparing the way different dictionaries define a particular term.
3. Avoid beginning with the weak "It has been said that" ploy; it is evasive, passive, vague, limp—about as engaging as a wet handshake.
4. Don't begin with—especially don't devote a complete sentence to—so obvious a commonplace that it doesn't need saying:

   Many people these days find themselves in dire economic straits.
   Pierre Trudeau first became Prime Minister in 1968.
   Peanuts are rich in protein.

   These are in effect "empty" beginnings. Readers confronting such an opening sentence will immediately feel that their time is being wasted; they will be disinclined to read on. If you need to include such information, put it in subordinate parts of your sentences.
5. Another sort of empty beginning is that which wanders around, seemingly aimlessly, often in broad generalities, circling a topic instead of facing it. The best remedy for such a beginning is to scrap it and start again—with exaggerated directness, if necessary. Sometimes just throwing out your first paragraph will do the trick.
6. Except for certain kinds of business or technical reports whose standardized format may call for it, avoid the "editorial" opening which tells the reader what you're going to do rather than just going ahead and doing it. Such statements make your intentions and your chosen structure too obvious. So don't write such things as "In this essay I will discuss three aspects of so-and-so" or "In this paper I will try to prove that so-and-so...." Save words, and the reader's patience, by being direct: show, don't tell. "So-and-so has three important functions:...." "So-and-so, as the following evidence will show, is...."
7. Don't apologize ("Although I am no expert at analyzing poetry, and so will probably do a poor job of it....") or complain ("Since it is necessary for me to try to make sense of the Riel Rebellion in order to satisfy this assignment....") or otherwise dwell autobiographically on your problems as a writer at the moment of writing. Such things leave a bad taste in a reader's mouth.
8. Don't write too long a beginning. If the question even arises in your mind whether a beginning is too long, it probably is. Student writers often produce excessively long "beginnings" or "introductions"; sometimes they take up half the essay, or even more. If you find yourself doing that, or if when you

critically examine your draft you find that you have done it, go back to your plan and rethink it. Almost always the cause of such grotesque disproportion is the writer's having thought of as introductory what should have been seen as a major part of the main body of the essay.

---

### Exercise 7B

Here is an example of a weak beginning:

> An assessment of the present global economic system is a rather complex task. No longer does an examination of the political relationships between nation states suffice to reveal all of its aspects.

The implicit apology or complaint in the first sentence puts readers off, and the weak reference of *its* and the weak word *aspects* in the second don't restore confidence. Try revising the two sentences into a single sentence that would be a more effective beginning.

---

## Endings

The ending of a piece of writing occupies the most emphatic position of all. As the last part that readers see, it contains much of what they carry away. A good beginning is important because first impressions are important; a good ending is important because it is your last chance to make an impression—and this final impression, whatever it is, is the one that will stick. A good ending can do little to save a weak essay, but a weak ending can ruin an otherwise strong essay.

### BASIC PRINCIPLES OF ENDINGS

The one thing any good ending must do is somehow convey a *sense* of an ending, a tone of finality; it must give readers a satisfying feeling of completeness or completion. One way you can achieve this sense of an ending is through some shift in tone or level, some heightening of style.

An ending should leave no questions to be asked.

An ending will usually be better if it is forceful. But don't come on too strong; don't overreach. Be emphatic, but be consistent, and be as modest as the circumstances will allow. And sometimes a sudden shift to a quiet tone will be appropriate and effective.

Like beginnings, endings should be interesting. Nothing can be worse than a dull, flat, stale, tacked on, perfunctory statement or summary.

Rather than perpetrate a dull ending, it is sometimes best just to *stop*: your own instinctive "sense of an ending" will have done the job; there will be no need for an explicit, self-consciously added ending that would probably sound perfunctory anyway. Here for example is what a student's draft provided as a concluding paragraph:

> DRAFT: The ideas in this poem are made very clear by repetition and used in different contexts.

Utterly flat and perfunctory. Here's a first attempt at revision:

REVISED: The ideas in this poem are made very clear by repetition, parallel, and contrast.

Some improvement, because slightly more specific. Eventually the writer arrived at this version, which may not be great, but it's far superior to the early version:

REVISED: The poet, then, uses repetition, parallel structure, and striking contrasts to emphasize the meaning. The poem's impact is unmistakable.

Still a summing up, but it's put more forcefully and specifically. It's also improved by being put in the active voice rather than the passive (see pp. 223-225). And the final short sentence at least takes a generalizing step beyond mere summary.

Here is another weak ending. Note how whatever force the ending has is frittered away by the empty jargon of the last five words:

DRAFT: Each is unique, but both man and snowflake become repetitive when viewed in the context of large numbers. Their distinctive and identifying features are lost in this frame of reference.

Attempting to revise, the student writer changed "frame of reference" to "situation." The jargon was even worse (see pp. 268-275). Finally the writer saw that he didn't need such a final phrase, that *lost* is a good forceful closing word.


## MAIN KINDS OF ENDINGS

Like beginnings, endings are of different lengths. Usually the longer the essay the longer the ending it will support or need. Most endings will be relatively direct (the more formal the essay the more direct), and most will fit into one of three categories:

1. *A direct restatement of the thesis* (or sometimes a first statement of it). This usually occurs at the *beginning* of the ending. If the ending is a brief one, it may consist of little more than such a restatement.

If the thesis is only alluded to or otherwise obliquely referred to, the ending will seem less direct.

A longer ending will also seem less direct. An extended ending will usually consist of a reference to or restatement of the thesis, followed by some new material—a further generalization, for example, or a shift to a different pespective.

A particularly effective ending is the kind some call the "So what?" ending. Designed to keep readers from asking that embarrassing question, it details at least the important implications of what the body of the essay has demonstrated.

2. *A summary*, perhaps reminding the reader of the main points of an explanation or argument or the main steps in a process. This also of course reemphasizes those main points. But be sure the essay is long or complex enough to need a summary: a summary at the end of a short essay will insult the intelligence of readers who still remember quite clearly what they have just been reading.

3. *A "conclusion"*—that is, some sort of logical conclusion coming at the end of a process of reasoning, or some other kind of final piece in a pattern of

development. And though you should not label your whole ending a "conclusion," it would be perfectly all right to follow a long discussion or analysis or argument with a paragraph that opens something like this: "Several conclusions emerge from these quite different experiments. The first, and easiest to act on...."

## PARTICULAR STRATEGIES FOR ENDINGS

1. **Called-for Endings**   The primary purpose of an essay and its overall method of development often dictate or suggest an appropriate ending. For example:

a. A process of inductive reasoning naturally leads to a final generalization based on the particulars discussed.

b. A process of deductive reasoning naturally leads to a final logical conclusion based on the factual evidence analyzed.

c. A narrative might naturally culminate in a climax of some sort.

d. A description of a process might well be followed by an evaluation of the process, a reemphasis of its purpose and usefulness.

e. A cause-and-effect essay could build to an emphatic climax pinpointing the main effect or the main cause.

f. A comparison-contrast essay could end with a final pulling together of the main points of comparison or contrast, or perhaps an evaluation based on the comparison.

g. A thesis-illustration essay could end with one final, important illustration or example.

h. A technical report might end with a formal summary of major points or a set of recommendations.

i. An argument can often be effectively ended with a call to action of some sort. (But it is seldom good tactics to demand or insist upon something; rather, modestly propose or suggest or recommend some change or some course of action.) Sometimes a good way to end an argument is simply to dispose of one final opposition point.

> *Beginning and ending shake hands.*
> (German proverb)

2. **Frames and Echoes: Beginnings and Endings Working Together**   It is often useful to think of a beginning and an ending as constituting a frame for a piece of writing. The beginning and the ending are often best when their close relationship is made explicit. For example:

a. If the beginning included an explicit (or even implicit) question or series of questions, or if the thesis itself was put in the form of a question, the ending could well (with or without repeating the question) present the answer, perhaps drawing together the parts of the answer expressed along the way into a final overall answer to round off the essay.

b. The *echo* effect: Question and answer can be handled as in part an echo. But other kinds of endings can also be given added punch by artfully picking up something from the beginning or even from the title—a word or phrase or sentence or image or metaphor or analogy or quotation—in order to make the essay come full circle.

3. **Endings with Clinchers**   Just as beginnings often use "hooks," so endings often use what are called "clinchers"—devices to bring about a sharply effective ending. Some of these are similar to the hooks used in beginnings; in fact they often combine with their beginning counterparts to bring about a frame or echo effect. For example:

a. An ending that reemphasizes the importance of an idea mentioned at the beginning.
b. An anecdote—perhaps one that refers back to the beginning.
c. An allusion—again perhaps one that picks up an idea from the beginning.
d. A quotation, or a proverb or aphorism—perhaps one that picks up an idea from the beginning. In any event, it is usually best not just to tack one on, hoping it will be effective. Rather, make the quotation or proverb a part of your own syntax—or at least follow it with your own final comment; your readers will feel better at the end if you demonstrate that you remain in full control by having the last word.
e. A question or speculation or prediction that provokes further thought on the subject (but not an entirely new idea, for that would be like beginning a new essay rather than ending a present one).
f. An ironic or otherwise surprising twist, perhaps some kind of sharp contrast or unexpected analogy.
g. Something humorous. If the subject and tone permit, a light touch, a joke or witticism or play on words at the end can be very effective. But resist the temptation to end with a jest when it might spoil the overall effect; remember that the last few words constitute the flavour you leave in your readers' minds. Make the final taste exactly the one you want.

### THINGS TO AVOID IN ENDINGS

1. Don't label or announce your ending as such. Unless you're writing a business or technical report that necessitates it, do not begin your ending with "In conclusion," "In summary, then," or even "Thus we see that"—or anything of the sort. In any non-technical piece of writing, such an ending usually sounds tacked-on, perfunctory. Such labelling makes an "ending" into a "conclusion": it makes it too obvious, destroying any sense of smoothness and control you've built up in the essay itself. If it seems appropriate, announce your ending instead with a quiet "so" or "then," usually carefully tucked into a sentence beginning your ending: "It would seem, then, that...," "So it turns out that...," "The result, then, is clear."

   Be especially wary of the word *thus*; it may sound good in your mind, but to others it often sounds unnecessarily stiff and awkward, especially at the beginning of a sentence. Thus you see that one can't be too careful about the way one begins an ending.
2. Don't apologize. As in the beginning, don't in the ending offer apologies, disclaimers, or complaints. Don't let slip—or appear to let slip—your command of the subject or the occasion. Similarly, don't end with a weak

statement, a qualifying remark, an irrelevant comment, or anything that contradicts your main point. Don't end with afterthoughts or mere minor details. End strongly by referring back to your main purpose and your overall subject.

3.  Be wary of introducing any wholly new ideas in an ending; make sure that anything fresh you bring in is linked to or builds on what has gone before. Certainly don't introduce anything that could be taken as a new *topic*.

4.  A snappy ending can be effective, but too abrupt an ending may jar readers. Unless you have specific reasons for doing otherwise, let your readers down easily at the end.

5.  When you restate your thesis in an ending, don't *merely* restate it, but do so in a new way, one that incorporates the new light you've shed on it in the body of the essay. Similarly, if you summarize your main points, don't provide a dull, flat, *mere* summary. Except in some technical reports, an ending should not be a mere recapitulation.

6.  Don't overreach or exaggerate. If you've made a small matter clear or proved a small point, don't come on grandly and pretentiously at the end as if you'd done much more. Don't make assertions in the ending that aren't backed up by what you've said in the essay. Be wary of absolutes.

---

## Exercise 7C

Examine the beginnings and endings of at least ten pieces from an anthology of non-fictional prose—perhaps one you're using in the writing course you're taking. Copy out the beginnings and endings and try to identify what kind each is; for each, list whatever devices or strategies you find.

How many of them consist of whole single paragraphs? Do any take up more than one paragraph? For how many is it difficult to put your finger on exactly where the beginning ends or the ending begins? Do any of them simply start or stop, with nothing you can call a separate beginning or ending?

## Exercise 7D

Select ten of the following familiar sayings and quotations. For each, either explain how it could be used as—or in—a title, or incorporate it in a possible beginning or ending. "Seeing is believing," for example, could become "Seeing Is *Not* Believing" or, for an ironic title, "Seeing Is Believing?" Could the old saw about pouring oil on troubled waters be given an ironic application in these days of disastrous oil spills? Often you can give a tired proverb or maxim a clever twist to make it function freshly. For example an essay describing a funny family could be titled "Hilarity Begins at Home," or the sentence could be worked into a beginning or ending. But beware of being *too* cute and clever. Are any of these sayings such clichés as not to be usable? Do any of them actually suggest possible topics?

| | |
|---|---|
| Actions speak louder than words. | Bad news travels fast. |
| All cats are gray in the dark. | Barking dogs seldom bite. |
| All's well that ends well. | Better late than never. |
| All roads lead to Rome. | Boys will be boys. |
| All that glitters is not gold. | Brevity is the soul of wit. |

| | |
|---|---|
| *Carpe diem.* | Let sleeping dogs lie. |
| *Caveat emptor.* | Might is right. |
| The child is father of the man. | Money is the root of all evil. |
| Comparisons are odious. | Nature abhors a vacuum. |
| Crime doesn't pay. | A new broom sweeps clean. |
| Don't change horses in mid-stream. | No news is good news. |
| Easy come, easy go. | Nothing ventured, nothing gained. |
| Every cloud has a silver lining. | Once bitten, twice shy. |
| Every rose has its thorn. | Rome wasn't built in a day. |
| Forbidden fruit is sweetest. | Sweet are the uses of adversity. |
| Good fences make good neighbours. | A thing of beauty is a joy forever. |
| Haste makes waste. | Variety is the spice of life. |
| It never rains but it pours. | Where there's smoke there's fire. |

Or find some others to work with; there are several dictionaries of proverbs you can consult. And consider using two proverbs together; for example, what do you make of the relation between "He who hesitates is lost" and "Look before you leap," or between "Too many cooks spoil the broth" and "Two heads are better than one"?

### Exercise 7E

Select one of the propositions you constructed for Exercise 5C (p. 117) and write two different beginnings for an essay arguing that proposition. Assume that at least half of your readers are people who don't agree with your position.

When you have finished, look closely at the two results. Which one do you think would be the most effective: Write a paragraph explaining why.

### Exercise 7F

Select two of the narrowed topics you came up with for Exercise 2D or 2E (pp. 26-27), and for each topic write five (or more) different possible beginnings; use a different kind of strategy for each one. Then write a possible ending to go with each beginning; try as many different kinds of endings as you can, but be sure that each ending you write is somehow appropriate to the beginning with which you pair it. For the purposes of this exercise, don't worry about whether your beginnings and endings consist of whole paragraphs or not.

### Exercise 7G

Here is a student's short essay from which we have removed the ending. Write three different possible endings for it (remember, they need not be whole paragraphs) and then briefly evaluate the three. (We have also removed the title, since it in part prepared for the ending. For each ending you write, then, supply a title that fits it.)

My old high school is in the middle of a field once owned by the Canadian Forces. It is a simple looking school, but it conveys a creepy feeling to most people who pass by. It looks like a jail.

The icy grey concrete walls and the slit-like windows give the school the look of a penitentiary. The long unkempt grass growing in the gopher-ridden field adds to the sense of isolation. The only break in the monotony is the old runway which nearly cuts the field in two. A tall, cold, heavy-gauge wire fence surrounds the field and the school. It seems to tell people to keep away: "Don't come near this place."

Now and then there is a sign of life. It's usually a glimpse of the football team slaving away like inmates, or a student or two lingering at one of the exit doors, having a quick smoke before the next class.

---

### Exploration 7B

Return to an essay or article you read recently and found effective; choose one of some length, say of about ten or twelve closely reasoned paragraphs. Analyze it carefully and draw up an outline of it. Does outlining it help you understand it and how it works? Did you have any difficulty locating its thesis? What techniques of beginning and ending does it use?

### Exploration 7C

Select one of the following topics, or make up a similar one of your own. Frame a topic sentence calling for supporting details, and compose a paragraph developing that topic. Arrange the details in the order of increasing importance—that is, *climactic* order.

> things I learned in school last year
> my impressions of a foreign country
> the right attitudes for either a participant in
>     or a spectator of a particular sport or game
> getting along with roommates
> what it was like at the party
> table manners
> being a collector

### Exploration 7D

In a single paragraph, relate as vividly as you can a recent experience you had, one that made you think—however briefly—about yourself, your ideas or ideals, your life, your future. Then add a few sentences indicating how you might use this paragraph, or a version of it, to begin an essay.

### Exploration 7E

Using fictitious names, write one paragraph about someone you know and like and another paragraph about someone you know and dislike. Choose as subjects two people who are at least superficially similar—that is, of the same sex, of similar age, perhaps with similar relationships to you (fellow students, fellow-club-members, fellow employees, teammates, former teachers). Then combine the two descriptions into one unified paragraph organized by comparison and contrast. Decide whether you want to make your topic or thesis explicit or to leave it implicit.

---

### Essay 7A

Take one of your earlier *narrative* pieces and revise it. Cover the same incident or incidents from a different point of view; or completely change the time sequence;

or change the *purpose* or point you mean the narration to support or illustrate. Hand in the original essay along with the new version, and include a brief note explaining your different intentions.

## Essay 7B

Write a short essay (about 500 words) that could be entitled "Tweedledum and Tweedledee" (you can surely come up with a better title). Your purpose is to compare two things or ideas commonly accepted as alike, or so nearly alike as would make no difference, and to show that they aren't so alike after all. If a good metaphor depends partly on showing unexpected likeness in two things usually considered different, reverse the process and show unexpected differences between two things considered similar. This is a good way to destroy, or at least combat, some cliché analogy—for example that a successful business executive will make a good premier, or that the school of hard knocks is as good as a formal education, or that rock is essentially the same as Bach. But try to find your own subject.

---

## Idioms 7

See the instructions for Idiom exercise 4, page 100. In this exercise, the words are all *adjectives*.

| | | | | |
|---|---|---|---|---|
| adept | clear | faced | obedient | redolent |
| aloof | confident | grateful | paranoid | solicitous |
| angry | consonant | incongruous | pertinent | tired |
| averse | destitute | indigenous | prejudiced | void |
| bereaved | enamoured | inseparable | propitious | wary |

---

## Sentence-Combining 7: Participial Phrases

### Pattern 7A

a. Mahmoud heard the telephone ring.
b. He was locking the door of his office.

Result of combining *a* and *b*:

    Locking the door of his office, Mahmoud heard the telephone ring.

First, COPY the pattern sentence carefully, deleting *He was* and putting the rest of sentence *b* at the head of sentence *a*. Be sure to insert the comma.

Second, COMBINE each of the following pairs of sentences into a sentence modelled on the pattern sentence:
a. Ingrid thought of a new argument.
b. She was waiting for the meeting to begin.
a. Phillip and Doris discovered they both knew Mr. Lasky.
b. They were chatting during the break.

Third, COMPOSE two sentences modelled on Pattern 7A.

    In this exercise, you are reducing the second sentence to a participial phrase and attaching it at the beginning of sentence *a*. To do so, you merely drop the pronoun (*he*) that repeats the subject of *a*, and the auxiliary part of the verb (*was*) leaving only the present participle or -*ing* part of the verb. When attached to sentence *a*, the participial phrase functions as an adjective modifying the subject, *Mahmoud*. In this pattern the two base sentences, or the two parts of the combined sentence, refer to actions occurring at the same time; each combined sentence could in fact lead off with the word *While*.

### Pattern 7B

a. The prisoner stood on his chair.
b. He was shouting angrily.

RESULT:   The prisoner stood on his chair, shouting angrily.

Copy the pattern sentence, deleting *He was* and inserting a comma before you add the rest to sentence *a*.

Combine each of the following pairs into a single sentence modelled on the pattern sentence:
a. The children went on with their game.
b. They were pretending not to notice us.

a. The economy continued to fluctuate wildly.
b. It was showing no signs of settling down.

Compose two sentences of your own modelled on Pattern 7B.

In this exercise, as in Pattern 7A, you are converting sentence *b* to a participial phrase and attaching it, with a comma, to sentence *a*—this time at the end. (Could it just as well be put at the beginning?)

### Pattern 7C

a. The building's wiring was defective.
b. This posed a fire hazard.

RESULT:   The building's wiring was defective, posing a fire hazard.

Copy the pattern sentence. After deleting *This,* change *posed* to an -*ing* form and put sentence *b* after sentence *a*; be sure to precede it with a comma.

Combine each of the following pairs into a sentence modelled on the pattern sentence:
a. The vacuum cleaner's bag burst.
b. It spewed dust all over the room.

a. Some crossword puzzles tease the mind with witty cryptic definitions.
b. They challenge solvers and give them a great deal of pleasure.

Compose two sentences modelled on Pattern 7C.

In this exercise you are again converting sentence *b* into a participial phrase and putting it after sentence *a*. Note that this time the relation between *a* and *b* is one of cause and effect. Note also that using this pattern is one way to avoid subject pronouns (*This, It, They*) whose reference to an antecedent is vague or ambiguous.

## Pattern 7D

a. The committee lacked a clear precedent.
b. They could make only tentative recommendations.

RESULT: Lacking a clear precedent, the committee could only make tentative recommendations.

Copy the pattern sentence. Note that you replace *They* in sentence *b* with *the committee* from sentence *a*, change *lacked* in sentence *a* to an *-ing* form, and insert a comma between the two parts.

Combine each of the following pairs into a sentence modelled on the pattern sentence:

a. André moved quickly and easily up the ladder.
b. He made it to vice-president in two years.

a. Most employers thought workers were interested in nothing else.
b. They focussed on wages.

Compose two sentences modelled on Pattern 7D.

In this exercise you are converting the first of two sentences to a participial phrase by changing the verb to the present participle (*-ing*) form. The phrase, put at the head of the second sentence, then modifies the subject, *the committee*, which you've moved over from the first sentence to replace the pronoun in the second. Note that again the relation between *a* and *b* is one of cause and effect.

## Pattern 7E

a. After the talk we went to the reception.
b. It was sponsored by the Gorman company.

RESULT: After the talk we went to the reception sponsored by the Gorman company.

Copy the pattern sentence, deleting *It was* and putting the rest of *b* after sentence *a*. Note that you do not put a comma between them.

Combine each of the following pairs into a sentence modelled on the pattern sentence:

a. Francis misfiled the student activity reports.
b. They will be needed for Tuesday's meeting.

a. Ms. Nordstrom demonstrated the new intercom system.
b. It was designed by a student architect.

Compose two sentences modelled on Pattern 7E.

In this exercise you are turning two simple sentences into one by reducing the second to a participial phrase and adding it to the first. Dropping the subject pronoun (*It*) and the auxiliary part of the verb leaves only the past participle (*sponsored*), which in the finished sentence functions as an adjective modifying the noun it follows (*reception*). Note that reducing the second sentence to a participial phrase enables you to avoid using the passive voice.

### Pattern 7F

a. Sarah was experienced at gardening.
b. She knew it involved more destruction than creation.

RESULT: Experienced at gardening, Sarah knew that it involved more destruction than creation.

Copy the pattern sentence, replacing *She* with *Sarah*, deleting *was*, and putting a comma between the two parts.

Combine each of the following pairs into a sentence modelled on the pattern sentence:
a. The biologist was frustrated by repeated failures.
b. He considered abandoning the experiment.
a. The car was washed and polished.
b. It looked almost new again.

Compose two sentences modelled on Pattern 7F.

In this exercise, as in Pattern 7E, you are converting one base sentence to a past participial phrase by dropping its subject and the auxiliary part of its verb. This time, however, the adjective phrase goes at the beginning of the finished sentence, and the deleted subject of *a* replaces the pronoun (*She*) to become the subject of the sentence. Note that, as in Patterns 7C and 7D, the relation between the two parts is one of cause and effect.

### Pattern 7G

a. The repair crew finished sooner than we expected.
b. They had frequently dealt with such problems.

RESULT: Having frequently dealt with such problems, the repair crew finished sooner than we expected.

Copy the pattern sentence. Note that you delete *They*, change *had* to *having*, and put sentence *b* in front *a*; be sure to insert the comma.

Combine each of the following pairs into a sentence modelled on the pattern sentence:
a. You'll be able to write leaner and cleaner prose.
b. You have learned how to combine sentences.
a. Carlos was fluent in English, French, and Spanish.
b. He had been born in Venezuela and had grown up in Montreal.

Compose two sentences modelled on Pattern 7G.

In this exercise you are again converting one base sentence to a participial phrase and putting it in front of the other sentence, whose subject it then modifies. You delete the subject pronoun of *b* (*They*) and change the auxiliary part of the verb (*had*) to the *-ing* or present participle form (*having*) to go with the past participle (*dealt*), yielding a participial phrase in the present perfect tense. Note that once again the relation between the two parts is one of cause and effect.

## *Pattern 7H*

a. Combining sentences can save words.
b. It can also sharpen meaning.

RESULT: Combining sentences can both save words and sharpen meaning.

Copy the pattern sentence, noting that you delete the words *it can also* from sentence *b* and that you insert the words *both* and *and*.

Combine each of the following pairs into a sentence modelled on the pattern sentence:
a. Buying back Canadian oil and gas assets has cheapened the dollar.
b. It has caused a decrease in production, as well.
a. The computer revolution is changing the lives of many ordinary people.
b. It is also making a lot of money for some manufacturers.

Compose two sentences modelled on Pattern 7H.

    In this exercise, as in Pattern 1H, you are changing a second simple sentence into part of a compound predicate; but this time you are also emphasizing the parallel structure by using a pair of correlative conjunctions, *both...and*, instead of just the coordinating conjunction *and*. Note that the word *both* includes the sense of *also* or *as well*.

---

### *Playing with Language 7A*

Take the object you described for Exploration 4H and make it the subject of a one-paragraph narrative. It doesn't have to be funny, but you'll probably find it easier to treat such a simple object involved in some sort of action if you use at least some humour. Even consider making the object itself the narrator of the paragraph—the "I."

### *Playing with Language 7B*

TV series these days continue to be mostly dreadful—but popular. Invent a new and "sure to be popular" series that incorporates, satirically, prominent features of several programs that are now or were recently popular. Try to do it in no more than about 400 words; that is, you'll have to select carefully from the vast body of available material. Perhaps pretend you are writing a studio's publicity release for the media.

---

*An old tutor of a college said to one of his pupils: Read over your compositions, and wherever you meet with a passage you think is particularly fine, strike it out.*

(Samuel Johnson)

CHAPTER VIII
# Sweep 2:  Revising Paragraphs

A first sweep of revision will probably include some tinkering with paragraphs. In any event, the second sweep is the time to focus your attention on paragraphs. Check each paragraph in your draft to see if it is about one topic and if the topic is clear. Ask yourself if each paragraph develops its topic adequately. And check it for coherence: do its sentences stick together? Finally, check it for emphasis: does the paragraph just trail off, or does it make its point effectively? If the end seems weak, try adding a sentence or a clause or phrase that specifically looks back to the topic sentence; this should clarify the point and round off the paragraph. Check mainly the following matters:

1. Paragraphing—the division into paragraphs
2. Paragraph length
3. Paragraph parts and structure—beginning, middle, and end
   a. Topic sentences—the three functions of the beginning
   b. Paragraph development—the body
   c. Paragraph endings
4. Paragraph unity
5. Coherence within paragraphs
6. Beginning and ending paragraphs; transitional paragraphs
7. Rhythm in paragaraphs
8. Emphasis in paragraphs

And while you're at it—and not just in argumentative papers—check your reasoning processes in each paragraph to make sure you haven't let any logical fallacies or other weaknesses slip in.

178

## Kinds of Paragraphs

There are generally three kinds of paragraphs:

1. Substantive
2. Beginning and ending
3. Transitional.

A substantive paragraph is one that states and develops an idea. A beginning or ending paragraph, or even a transitional paragraph, may also develop an idea, but its principal purpose is to begin or end a piece of writing or to provide a bridge from one part to another.

Except for item 6, the following discussion focusses on substantive paragraphs.

## What Is a Paragraph?

Paragraphs are the building-blocks of prose. Each paragraph is a unit in itself, but when paragraphs are put together they build an essay or other piece of writing. A regular substantive paragraph is a miniature essay. It is unified because it has a single topic which it develops. It has parts within it (sentences) just as an essay has parts within it (paragraphs). Most principles that apply to essays also apply to paragraphs—and vice versa. (It is possible for an essay—a short one—to consist of only one paragraph, though some people resist calling such pieces "essays." You have probably already written some single-paragraph compositions, and you will probably be asked to write others. Whether you think of them as "essays" or not isn't really important, though they do follow the same principles.)

## 1. PARAGRAPHING—DIVISION INTO PARAGRAPHS

Try to imagine reading an extended piece of prose without any paragraph divisions. Or better still find and read some prose published long ago, when paragraphs often went on for pages and pages. You'll come away convinced—if you need to be—that paragraphs are good things. A principal function of paragraphs is to give readers' eyes and minds a brief rest, a chance as it were to take a breath before plunging into the next stretch. Paragraphs are a form of typographical manipulation; call it eye-spacing. And that function is very important.

But as prose techniques developed over the centuries, paragraphs increasingly became units of thought as well. And though one can sometimes re-paragraph a piece of prose and still find it quite readable, its readability will still depend on its being divided into units of thought.

Check the paragraph divisions you made during the writing of your first draft. You may decide to make some preliminary changes (even though you may decide to change them back again later).

Here are three paragraphs from the middle of a short essay on some public misconceptions about "the soft life" students lead:

It is commonly held that the average student is a "pencil-pusher"; the only thing he exercises is his mind. In fact, however, a student who suffers from intellectual exhaustion usually engages in some form of physical exercise to give his mind a rest. When a typical labourer comes home from work, on the other hand, he usually relaxes his tired muscles by putting his feet up and reading the paper.

Another commonly held misconception about students is that their work week, which consists of the hours they spend in class, is relatively much smaller than the forty-hour week of the average labourer. Indeed, fifteen to twenty hours a week of classes is a fairly short week. What is not understood by most people, however, is that going to school is a full-time job. Once the worker goes home, he can tune his job out for the night; but once a student comes home, he has exams to study for, term papers to write, and classes to prepare for.

There is also the problem of finances. A student has only four months to make enough money to support himself and his studies for the next year. A working person, on the other hand, has a cheque coming in every month. But it is the student who supposedly has it "soft"!

This is from the second draft. The method of comparing and contrasting is working well. Yet when the student set about tightening her prose, she discovered that she could cut these three paragraphs a great deal—in fact, cut them down to one paragraph, with the last sentence functioning as an effective topic sentence:

Many people think students are mere pencil-pushers, exercising only their minds, whereas most students make it a point to rest their minds by exercising their bodies as well, just as labourers might relax their tired muscles by putting their feet up and reading the paper. Another misconception holds that students work only a few hours a week rather than the average labourer's forty; but labourers can go home and forget their jobs, whereas students go home and study for exams, write papers, and prepare for the next day's classes. And remember the problem of money: a student must earn enough in only four months to last through the next academic year, whereas a jobholder gets a cheque every month. Yet it is the student who supposedly has it "soft"!

The illusion that there were three paragraphs' worth of material was replaced by the perception that the basic contrast between student and labourer could be more forcefully presented in one paragraph. The sentences may be longish, but they are straightforward and easy to follow. And because the whole uses about one-third fewer words, it comes across much more effectively. Compare the two versions closely to see how the cutting and tightening were accomplished.

## 2. PARAGRAPH LENGTH

There is no ideal or "correct" length for a paragraph. A paragraph can consist of one word or hundreds of words. A paragraph can contain one sentence or dozens of sentences. The longer and more formal a piece of writing is, the longer its paragraphs are likely to be, partly because its content is more complicated, its units of developed ideas larger. The paragraphs in informal writing will generally be shorter, as will the pieces themselves. But since one of the reasons for paragraph divisions in the first place is to promote ease of reading, even formal prose can often be made easier to read by being divided into shorter paragraphs.

Writing done for newspapers or for magazines printed in columns will have relatively short paragraphs: in the narrow columns the paragraphs look longer than they would if printed in a book. They look "normal." It's largely a visual matter, less a matter of units of developed thought.

When you write essays for a class you are operating partly under something like those conditions. Since a paper submitted in a class must be double-spaced, its paragraphs will look twice as long as they would if printed in a book. And if you submit handwritten work instead of typed work, your paragraphs will—depending on the size of your handwriting and the spacing of the ruled lines on the page—probably look three or four times as long as they would if printed in a book. Therefore you must be careful not to let this merely visual factor overwhelm considerations of adequate paragraph development.

## HOW LONG SHOULD A PARAGRAPH BE?

The only reasonable answer to this question is "long enough to get from the beginning to the end."

But that's not much practical help. Let's instead do something presumptuous: let's establish what constitutes a "normal" paragraph, and then consider departures from that norm.

In most modern nonfictional prose (excluding journalistic prose), normal paragraphs vary from 3 sentences up to 10 or 12 sentences; the average is about 6 sentences, or a little more. But of course sentences themselves vary a great deal in length and complexity, so here's another way of figuring it: normal paragraphs vary in length from about 50 words to about 300 words; the average length is about 150 words. Here's yet another rule of thumb: most paragraphs contain between 4 and 9 sentences, and between 75 and 225 words.

---

## *Exercise 8A*

Check our presumptuous figures. Examine several contemporary essays by different authors, for example in a convenient anthology, to determine the number of words and sentences in the paragraphs, and compute the average. (Don't count words; count the words in a few lines to establish the average number of words per line, and then count lines.) You might want to broaden your survey by doing the same thing with sample chapters in two or three textbooks.

Write up your findings in a brief report. How closely do your results agree with ours? If any particular work you examined departs widely from our supposed norm, try to account for the variance.

---

## CHECKING AND REVISING PARAGRAPH LENGTH

We've defined our norm fairly loosely in order to accommodate the wide variety of paragraph lengths found in everyday writing. If you agree that our figures are about right, here's how to use them during revision.

**Short Paragraphs:**

Whenever you find that you've written a paragraph less than three sentences long, check to see if it is justified. A paragraph of only one or two sentences can serve as a perfectly good transitional paragraph or a beginning or ending paragraph, but a *substantive* paragraph of only one or two sentences or of fewer than fifty words probably calls for revision in one of four ways:

a. Develop the paragraph further, for example by providing more illustrations to support the topic sentence.

b. Combine the paragraph with either the preceding or the following paragraph. A frequent weakness of student writing is a string of several short paragraphs that should be combined into a single paragraph under one topic sentence.

c. If the paragraph is merely an assertion of a single point, or a mention of a single example, try to find a home for it somewhere else. Sometimes such a "paragraph" gets out of sequence; it really belongs with one or more things that occur elsewhere in the paper, where it can be properly integrated. Consult your plan.

d. If you decide that the paragraph can't be developed and that it doesn't belong anywhere else in the essay, you should probably delete it. And check your plan to make sure that such a revision is acceptable.

If you decide to retain a substantive paragraph of only one or two sentences, make sure that you can justify your decision in one of the following ways:

a. You want to set off a point in a paragraph of only one or two sentences in order to give it special emphasis. It does fit smoothly just where it is in the development of the essay.

b. The sentence (or especially the second sentence of two) is itself a relatively long and complicated sentence: for example it could be one with a statement followed by a colon or a dash introducing a series of phrases, or it could consist of a series of three or more independent clauses which could, if you chose, be punctuated as separate sentences—in other words, it could be a sentence something like this one, which *could* have been written as four or more separate sentences and which, in any event, is substantial enough for a paragraph by itself (and note that the word-count is over a hundred).

c. You have other special reasons for one or more short paragraphs. For example you might want to set off several short consecutive steps in a process essay.

**Long Paragraphs:**

Whenever you find yourself with a paragraph of more than 12 sentences or more than 300 words, consider whether it would be easier to read if it were broken into two paragraphs. If you decide you want to divide it, try to find a place where some natural division falls, such as a step from one stage of a process of reasoning to the next, or the beginning of an extended example. You may have to rephrase the beginning of the new paragraph to make it a better topic sentence. If you decide to leave a long paragraph intact, be able to justify it:

a. It has to be long to develop its single idea adequately. It offers no place where you could divide it without doing harm to the unity of its topic. Long as it is, it is more effective than it would be if it were broken up.

b. It is long because you want to emphasize the weightiness of its particular topic.

c. It has more than 12 sentences because you have deliberately chosen to use predominantly short sentences that could have been combined.

**Variety:**

A string of paragraphs of similar length can be monotonous. Try to mix short, medium, and longer paragraphs so that your essay as a whole has a pleasing rhythm to it.

But check to see if your *average* paragraph length is about 6½ sentences and about 150 words. And check to see if at least half of your paragraphs fall between 4 and 9 sentences, and 75 and 225 words. If you're far off these figures, decide whether you want to do something about it or leave it as it is in confidence that it is appropriate to your subject, your audience, and your purpose.

## 3. THE PARTS OF A PARAGRAPH

A regular substantive paragraph has three main parts—beginning, middle, and end. The beginning, in most paragraphs the so-called "topic sentence," announces what the paragraph is to be about; the middle, or "body," develops the topic; and the end ends the paragraph. In many paragraphs—especially those of greater length and complexity—there is also a fourth part: the second sentence is often a second topic sentence, or partly an extension of the topic sentence and partly the beginning of the paragraph's development.

### The Topic Sentence

Most paragraphs begin with a topic sentence because that is usually the best way for a paragraph to begin. And a good topic sentence has three important jobs to do:

(1) It somehow refers to the overall subject or topic or thesis of the essay.
(2) It provides a smooth transition from the preceding paragraph.
(3) It introduces the topic of the paragraph.

And a good topic sentence is usually also efficient, doing a fourth job:

(4) It begins developing the topic, or at least narrows it or otherwise says something *about* it; it doesn't merely name the topic. In this way it is similar to a good thesis statement.

The main exceptions to these principles occur in narratives, or in narrative parts of other kinds of writing, where a paragraph might begin simply "Then" or "And then" or "Next" or even just with the next occurrence in chronological order, without even a transitional word. And sometimes a strong topic sentence can effectively cover two or even three successive paragraphs, especially if it has two or three distinct parts.

Sometimes a topic sentence occurs elsewhere than at the beginning of a paragraph. It may be the second or third sentence, or come about the middle of the paragraph, or even at its end. And some paragraphs have an *implied* topic;

that is, there is no topic sentence as such, but the paragraph's topic is so clear that it is automatically inferred by the reader.

Many of the principles and devices discussed under "Beginnings" in the preceding chapter (pp. 159-166) apply also to the beginning of paragraphs. One of the most important of these is that a good beginning will somehow set up expectations in your readers' minds about what is to come. For example, after a generalization your readers will expect some specific illustrations; after a question they will expect an answer; after a statement implying subdivisions they will expect detailed treatment of those subdivisions. A paragraph that fulfills the implied promise made by its opening will be unified and coherent; it will not frustrate readers, but satisfy them.

## THE SECOND SENTENCE

A paragraph's second sentence is frequently also a kind of topic sentence. That is, it may partly restate the topic but in narrower or more specific terms. Such a sentence often begins the actual work of development. (Sometimes even a third or fourth sentence can partly carry on the work of stating a topic, though it is often difficult to determine the borderline between topic sentence and development of topic.) Here for example are the first two sentences of a student's descriptive paragraph. Note how the statement of the topic is not complete until the end of the second sentence, and how that sentence has more to do with setting up the coming development than has the first.

> A pencil is a charming instrument. In its unpretentious and humble position it lords it over the self-righteous pen in several rather discreet and clever ways.

Note also how the writer is using personification to enliven the description.

## The Body

The body of a paragraph consists of the development of its topic. That development usually follows one or another of the methods discussed in Chapter IV, or some combination of two or more of them. Here for example is a student's topic sentence that effectively sets up the structure of the paragraph to follow: a series of details demonstrating the several ways in which the theory is suspect:

> Dr. Luscher's colour theory is problematic in a number of ways.

## The Ending

Like endings of whole essays, a good paragraph ending gives a satisfying sense of completion. But seldom does a paragraph need a formal or explicit tying off. Often an effective way to end a paragraph is in some way to refer back to or partly restate the topic sentence, but it should be no more obvious than that. Usually you'll want to make the reference or the repetition oblique or indirect. And again, some of the specific techniques for ending essays can also be used for paragraphs (see pp. 166-170).

Frequently you will find that a paragraph just comes to an end naturally, without your having to round it off. Indeed, it is usually better simply to let a paragraph stop than to try to tack on a self-conscious ending, for a paragraph ending that calls attention to itself by in effect saying to the reader "Hey, lookit me! I'm a paragraph conclusion!" is almost always damaging.

Here are two other kinds of paragraph ending to be on guard against:

(1) Don't let a paragraph end weakly. End strongly, not with anything wishy-washy or trivial or qualifying or contradictory. Here for example is a paragraph ending that dribbles away its energy in a weak concluding phrase:

> DRAFT: They cause the movement of money, which in turn stimulates economic growth, among other things.

All that is needed to turn this into an ending that sounds like an ending is a change in word order:

> REVISED: They cause the movement of money, which in turn, among other things, stimulates economic growth.

But it might be just as well to delete the phrase "among other things."

(2) Don't make the mistake of trying to include in a paragraph ending a transition to the next paragraph, for that almost unavoidably not only calls attention to itself but also deflects the paragraph's course or dissipates its energy. It is the job of the beginning of the new paragraph to provide whatever transition is needed.

## 4. PARAGRAPH UNITY

Keep your readers in mind. They expect a paragraph to be limited to one topic and to develop that topic by explaining it, analyzing it, describing it, or in some other way supporting it. And they expect that topic to be clearly evident, usually by its being announced early in the paragraph by a topic sentence.

If a paragraph has a good topic sentence, and if every other sentence in the paragraph is directed at that topic, the paragraph will be unified. Check your paragraphs carefully to make sure they don't disconcertingly shift from one topic to another. If one does, you may have to divide it into two paragraphs, each with its own separate topic sentence.

## 5. PARAGRAPH COHERENCE

Just as the paragraphs in a piece of writing must clearly stick together, so must the sentences within a paragraph cohere. Usually this coherence will occur as a matter of course. But if it does *not* occur naturally, you must take pains to establish it. Any break in continuity will jolt your readers, throw them off their stride.

The first requirement is that your paragraph be unified. If it is not, no amount of tinkering can make it cohere successfully. Given that necessary unity, then, coherence can come about in several ways:

a. *Patterns* If a paragraph has a discernible pattern, it will likely be coherent. For example, a paragraph comparing or contrasting X and Y should be coherent if it follows an alternating pattern, bouncing back and forth from X to Y. Or it could dwell on X for one or more sentences and then turn to Y. Or a paragraph can maintain coherence if its sentences alternate between questions and answers, or if it moves from a series of related questions to their answers. Or a paragraph can alternate between positive and negative, or the pros and cons of an argument, or some other pair of opposites.

b. *Movements* Sometimes the movement of a particular method of development through a paragraph can establish coherence. For example, a paragraph could consist of a generalization followed by a series of specific examples—or it could move the other way, from specific illustrations to a general statement, and thus end with its topic sentence. Or it might establish a kind of pattern by starting with a generalization, then getting a little more specific, then a little more specific, and so on until it ends with a fully narrowed, specific point— a process sometimes called "down-shifting." Or a paragraph might move through a series of details from least important to most important (the order of climax), or from small to large, or simple to complex. Or it could simply follow a clear chronological or spatial order.

c. *Parallelism* If two or more successive sentences in a paragraph are parallel—that is, if they have the same syntactic structure—they will naturally hang together. It is seldom advisable to carry such parallelism beyond two or three sentences, but if the sentences themselves are fairly long, or the paragraph relatively short, or both, such parallelism can be the principle or even the sole method of achieving coherence in a paragraph. (See the discussion of parallelism in Chapter IX, pp. 233-235.)

Here is a paragraph from a student's paper on how he would direct a scene of *Hamlet*. Note how he has shaped the paragraph around a series of comparisons and contrasts, and how he has used parallel and balanced sentence structures to enforce the contrasts. Such paragraphs seldom just happen, nor are they casually thrown together; rather they are carefully made:

> We are dealing with only two actors in this scene. Polonius is an old man. He is dignified and regal—though not compared to the King. He likes to talk and is poetic and witty—though not compared to Hamlet. His clothes are not as bright as those of the younger lords and ladies but they are in sharp contrast with the grim blackness of Hamlet's attire. Ophelia is a very pretty young lady. She is somewhat humbler yet more graceful than Gertrude and the other ladies of the court. She is dressed simply, in light colours (probably white), to contrast with both the loud colours of the court and the black of Hamlet.

d. *Transitional Signals* If coherence is not provided by pattern or movement or parallelism, or is not otherwise implicitly clear, then you will probably have to use some explicit transitional signals. There are many words and phrases that function in this way, words and phrases we naturally use all the time to build bridges between sentences. Here are the most common ones, grouped according to the kinds of connections they establish. Many of them will naturally occur at the beginning of a sentence ("Moreover," "On the other hand") or near the beginning ("There are, on the other hand"); but you would not begin a sentence with *Too*, or even *As well* (though *As well as* would be all right). (See also the discussion of some of these connectors in Chapter V, pp. 121-122.)

*Adding a point or introducing a comparison:*

| | | |
|---|---|---|
| and | another | likewise |
| also | a second point | similarly |
| besides | in addition | equally |
| next | further | too |
| or | furthermore | in the same way |
| nor | as well | by comparison |
| moreover | as well as | again |

*Moving from general to specific; introducing examples or details:*

| | | |
|---|---|---|
| for example | namely | for one thing |
| as an example | such as | for another |
| for instance | that is | specifically |
| to illustrate | the following | in particular |
| as an illustration | in fact | in essence |

*Emphasizing a point:*

| | | |
|---|---|---|
| especially | in fact | chiefly |
| above all | indeed | certainly |
| in particular | (even) more important | primarily |
| to repeat | most important | unquestionably |

*Restating a point:*

| | | |
|---|---|---|
| in other words | to put it another way | that is to say |
| in simpler terms | again | in brief |
| in effect | that is | in short |

*Introducing a contrast or qualification or concession:*

| | | |
|---|---|---|
| but | despite | unless |
| however | surely | even though |
| frequently | nevertheless | even if |
| occasionally | nonetheless | all the same |
| usually | notwithstanding | to be sure |
| provided | otherwise | certainly |
| whereas | still | no doubt |
| after all | though | doubtless |
| on the other hand | although | admittedly |
| on the contrary | unfortunately | of course |
| in contrast | yet | in a sense |
| by contrast | conversely | I admit |
| generally | unlike | granted |
| in general | rather | naturally |
| in spite of | if | it is true |

*Showing cause and effect:*

| | | |
|---|---|---|
| as a result | consequently | then |
| because | accordingly | thus |
| since | for | therefore |
| for that reason | since | so |
| it follows that | hence | and so |

*Showing connections in time:*

| | | |
|---|---|---|
| at the same time | before | afterward |
| at this time | earlier | ago |
| simultaneously | previously | in the past |
| while | hitherto | then |
| now | once | when |
| nowadays | tomorrow | thereafter |
| meanwhile | next | lately |
| in the meantime | shortly | subsequently |
| at present | soon | last |
| at times | immediately | at last |
| since | in time | eventually |
| until | in the future | ultimately |
| formerly | later | final |

*Showing connections in space:*

| | | |
|---|---|---|
| above | across | distant |
| below | adjacent | in the distance |
| under | near | in the background |
| behind | nearby | here |
| in front of | beyond | there |
| in the foreground | far | elsewhere |
| on (at, to) the left | far away | opposite |
| on (at, to) the right | farther | beside |

*Showing sequence with numbers and other terms:*

first, second, third, etc.
first, secondly, thirdly, etc. (do not use *firstly*)
in the first place, in the second place, etc.
at first, to begin with; next, also, then; at last, finally, at the end

*Ending:*

| | | |
|---|---|---|
| on the whole | final | therefore |
| all in all | lastly | accordingly |
| altogether | as a result | hence |
| so | in short | thus |
| finally | then | consequently |

Avoid *in conclusion* and the like except where they are clearly appropriate (see pp. 167-169).

e. *Using personal pronouns*   If you refer to someone by name at the beginning of a paragraph, the rest of the paragraph will naturally cohere simply as a result of using the appropriate personal pronouns. For example if the opening sentence (or even the preceding paragraph) identified Emily Carr as the topic, succeeding sentences could begin something like this, and carry the thought through to the end with clear and strong coherence:

...Emily Carr.... She.... She.... She also.... She.... To her.... Hers was.... And she.... Her....

There's a little connective help from an *also* and an *and*, but the main strength of such a paragraph's coherence would lie in the repeated pronouns. If you felt that it would be effective, you could repeat the name itself at or near the end.

f. *Using demonstrative adjectives and pronouns*   The words *this, that, these,* and *those* can establish strong coherence by referring back to some early point in a paragraph.

*demonstrative adjectives:*

Building the railroad.... *That* project.... *That* massive achievement....

The fathers of confederation.... *That* body of men.... *Those* men....

*demonstrative pronouns:*

Modern economic theories.... *These* are.... *These* can be....

The right to an education.... *This* is not.... Nor is *this* any....

Note that such references could also be followed by or interspersed with personal pronouns:

*That* project.... *It*.... *That* achievement....

*These* are.... They.... *These*.... *They* also....

*Note:* You will usually be safer if you use demonstrative *adjectives* rather than demonstrative pronouns. A lone *that* or *those* or—especially—*this* can often be confusing because of the remoteness or vagueness of its antecedent: This *what?* the reader will ask; so write This *idea*, This *fact*, This *process*, This *group*, This *theory*, and so on.

g. *Using other words*—indefinite pronouns, enumerators—that, like demonstratives, carry on a topic by referring back to a specific point:

| | | |
|---|---|---|
| some | several | either |
| many | each | neither |
| all | such | one, first, *etc.* |

h. *Repeating*   Another way to help tie a paragraph together is to repeat key words, phrases, or ideas. Inexperienced writers often avoid repetition because they mistakenly think it is wrong; in fact it is one of the best, because most natural, ways to achieve coherence. Of course, dull and unnecessary repetition is weak. But if you avoid repeating a word just for the sake of variation, you are more likely to puzzle your readers than to help them. Therefore let nature take its course: don't be afraid to repeat key terms, or to repeat key ideas in slightly different terms, throughout a paragraph. That is probably the surest way of keeping your readers oriented. And you can always revise out, later, any repetition that you decide is excessive—too flat or wholly unnecessary.

### Exercise 8B

List the words and phrases in the preceding paragraph that contribute to its coherence. We have used several kinds, so label them by groups. You should be able to find at least thirty.

*A Final Warning about Paragraph Coherence:* Don't overload a paragraph with devices of coherence. Surprisingly often the paragraphs you write will, if they are unified, also be sufficiently coherent. They will stick together of their own accord. But if, after rereading a paragraph, you feel that its coherence is weak, or better yet if someone else reads it over and tells you that it is, then strengthen it. Sharpen or clarify the pattern or movement; increase parallelism; or draw upon the many transitional signals that can, like road signs, point the way for your readers.

When you do use these signals, choose the ones that most accurately point out the connections between the parts of your paragraphs: don't send your readers off on an unnecessary detour, for they might not find their way back. And use only as many of these signal words as you think are necessary. To tack a *besides* or a *moreover* or a *conversely* or a *therefore* or a *later* or a *that is* onto the beginning of every sentence would result in an annoyingly stiff, mechanical, awkward paragraph. Use those you need, but sometimes tuck them a word or few into the sentence.

### Exploration 8A

Here is a paragraph from a student's personal experience narrative about a juvenile escapade. As you can see, the writer was overzealous about providing coherence: at the beginning of almost every sentence he repeats material from the last part of the preceding sentence. The result is a monotonous and wordy paragraph whose sentences are far too similar in kind and length. Revise the paragraph by tightening it; combine some sentences, break up others—whatever you think will help.

We entered the construction site with the sole intent of toying with the morbidly appealing forklift. Before reaching the forklift we went into the hollow shells of some unfinished buildings. The buildings gave a somewhat ghost-like warning to stay away from the place. Ignoring the ominous warning of the buildings, we left in the direction of the portable john. We pushed over the john, which caused us to break out in unrestrained laughter. It was the laughter that motivated us to continue on our destructive path. After pushing down a partially completed wall, we proceeded to the forklift itself. Upon reaching the forklift we proceeded to remove its spotlights. Using a pair of bolt-cutters we found, we removed the lock on the engine cover. At that moment I looked up, and saw a police car driving in towards us. We split up and ran, but the attempt was futile, for they had already surrounded the construction site.

### *Exploration 8B*

Compose a paragraph which, like that in the preceding Exploration, achieves coherence primarily by linking the sentences. Each sentence should pick up something—a word, phrase, or idea—from the preceding sentence and then use it to get itself going. It may for example repeat something, use a synonym for it, refer to it with a pronoun, or cite what is obviously a specific example of a preceding generalization. Vary the kinds of links you forge between the sentences, and try to avoid making it all look or sound too mechanical. For this exploration, do *not* use narration, description, or process analysis.

### *Exploration 8C*

Choose a paragraph from something you wrote earlier in the year, one that you now realize has decidedly poor coherence. Revise it.

### *Exploration 8D*

Compose several separate paragraphs, each depending *primarily*, though not necessarily exclusively, on a different one of the following techniques of achieving coherence:

| | |
|---|---|
| pattern | personal pronouns |
| movement | demonstrative adjectives |
| parallelism | indefinite pronouns, enumerators |
| transitional signals | repetition |

---

## Unity and Coherence of the Whole Essay

During your first revising sweep you checked your essay's unity and coherence by looking at the relations between its larger parts to make sure that they were all relevant and that they hung together. Now is a good time to double-check those matters and to do whatever fine tuning is necessary. Simply look at the opening sentence of each paragraph (after the first one) to make sure it does these two things:

    a. refers in some way to your overall subject or narrowed topic or thesis statement. If it does, and if the paragraph follows that opening sentence in a unified way, then it is almost guaranteed that your essay as a whole is unified, that all its paragraphs pertain to the central point.

    b. provides some kind of transition from the preceding paragraph. If each new paragraph establishes such a connection, then all your paragraphs will necessarily stick together and the essay as a whole will be coherent.

To illustrate how successive topic sentences can help to bind an essay together, here are the topic sentences of three successive paragraphs from George Woodcock's essay "The Novels of Callaghan." Note how each both looks back at what has just preceded and sets up the topic for the paragraph to come; and note that each refers clearly to the essay's overall subject:

> Similarly, in Callaghan, we see a progression in his earlier novels toward the simplification of structure.

> Callaghan, even at this point, rarely resorts to obvious metaphor.

> It is to this quasi-metaphorical use of imagery that Callaghan turns abundantly in his second novel, *It's Never Over*.

## 6. TRANSITIONAL PARAGRAPHS, AND BEGINNING AND ENDING PARAGRAPHS

### Transitional Paragraphs

Transitional paragraphs usually consist of one or maybe two or three sentences. They form bridges between large parts of an essay. Unless you're writing a relatively long and complicated essay, you probably won't need any transitional paragraphs; all the transitions you need can be provided in the opening sentences of your substantive paragraphs. But if you have two or three or more large blocks of material, you may decide that a separate transitional paragraph is the best way to get from one to the other and to keep your readers clearly informed of just where they are. A transitional paragraph customarily does two things:

(1)  it glances back at what has gone before, perhaps by briefly recapping it;
(2)  it briefly introduces what is to come, perhaps by stating part of a complex thesis.

For example, here is a good one-sentence transitional paragraph from a student's process essay on how to get, set up, and stock an aquarium:

> Once you have all the necessary equipment, the work of setting up the tank begins.

It marks the border between the first and second large sections of the essay. And note how the following transitional paragraph, from an essay by Mordecai Richler, looks both backward and forward, effectively bridging the gap between two large parts:

> If once the arts in Canada were neglected, today, such is our longing, they are being rushed into shouldering a significance not yet justified by fulfilment, which brings me to the importance of Northrop Frye.
>
> ("Introduction" to Canadian Writing Today)

### Beginning and Ending Paragraphs

As discussed earlier (see pp. 157-159), beginnings and endings of essays need not consist of whole paragraphs. But sometimes a paragraph— especially if it is relatively short—can make an excellent beginning or ending. Such paragraphs, like transitional paragraphs, have a simple job to do. They are beginning or ending a piece of writing; they are not developing topics; they are not substantive paragraphs.

But often, especially in relatively short essays, the beginning or ending will not occupy an entire paragraph. Rather it will be a part of a paragraph that is also developing a topic. A beginning paragraph might for example spend a few sentences getting things going and then settle down and start developing the thesis. Similarly, an ending paragraph will often start off as a normal substantive paragraph, developing the final point of the essay, and then in maybe no more than the last sentence or two bring the essay—and the paragraph—to a satisfactory end.

## 7. RHYTHM IN PARAGRAPHS

A paragraph whose sentences are all approximately the same length almost inevitably puts readers' minds to sleep. During this second revising sweep, while you're still looking at your paragraphs as units, give at least some thought to their rhythm as determined by the lengths of their sentences. You can carry on with this part of revising as you proceed with the next sweep, focussing on sentences—for example, there should also usually be a variety of *kinds* of sentences in paragraphs. Or you might decide that working on sentence lengths, with an eye to paragraph rhythm, is a good way actually to start that next sweep.

In any event, here are four paragraphs, all written by students. First read each of them through, and then try to decide which ones you found easier or more pleasant to read, and which more difficult or less pleasant:

a. Gerry Sorenson's form was hair-raising but she managed to capture the Gold Medal at the World Alpine Ski Championships in Schladming, Austria. Excitement (as well as anxiety) began to build as she leaped over a metre in the air bursting from the starting gate. By the time she had screamed past the ninth gate and gone into her crouch, the crowd knew she meant business. With her skis scraping and chattering against the icy slope, she crouched even lower to get up more speed. Exploding over the final jump, she touched down a split second before rounding the last gate, already tasting the victory just ahead. As she shot across the finish line, her hands flew in the air, triumphantly, for another Crazy Canuck had done it.

b. The life of a student is hard. It is hard because there is too much work and not enough time. Many people, however, think just the opposite is true. They think students spend most of their time protesting, carousing, and getting into all sorts of trouble. I must admit that these people are not entirely mistaken, for there are students who come to university solely to have a good time. But I hardly think this characterizes most students. It certainly doesn't characterize those who take their studies seriously. It doesn't characterize me.

c. The most corrupt piece of literature existing today is not the violent comic book or the pornographic novel. Rather, this debauching classic is the woman's fashion magazine. As she leafs through page after glossy page of anorexic models with immobile hair and faultless complexions, even the most confident female is susceptible to feelings of inadequacy. The modern woman is not infallible, yet according to *Vogue* and *Cosmopolitan* , she should appear to be. It is distressing that in a society of emerging opportunities for women, an intrinsic element of their success is still physical beauty. Until this myth is eradicated, the full potential of women will not be realized.

d. It seems that everywhere we shop today, the pressure is on us to buy, buy, buy. With the high-pressure and subliminal sales tactics that stores use, it is very hard for the average shopper to resist the temptation to spend. Slogans such as "Sale—50% off!" and "Limited Time Offer!" often cause us to come home from the shopping centre with several unnecessary—and often unwanted—items. The policy of "buy now, pay later," which most stores are constantly advertising, further encourages this impulse buying. Although you probably do not need or cannot afford that cute striped dress, it is so easy to pull a credit card out of your wallet to pay for it. It is easy because you do not have to worry about the bill coming until the end of the month.

Of course sentence length isn't the only factor affecting the readability of these or any other paragraphs, but it definitely plays a part—sometimes quite a large part. Chances are you found paragraph *a* the *least* readable, with *d* not far behind, and paragraph *b* the *most* readable, with *c* close behind. Here are profiles of the four paragraphs, by sentence length (in number of words):

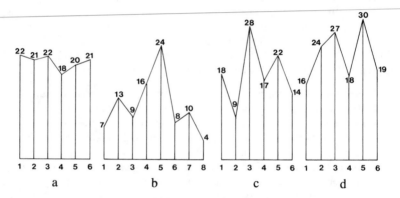

With its lively subject matter and diction, paragraph *a* may be highly interesting, but it still comes across as unnecessarily flat, just as its graph shows it to be. Paragraph *b*, in contrast, has distinct shape, or rhythm, and therefore reads more easily in spite of its quiet, relatively general subject matter. Note the particular effectiveness of its very short final sentence. The up and down rhythm of paragraph *c* helps its readability, whereas *d*, though it has one dip and shorter beginning and ending sentences, is somewhat harder to read because, relatively speaking, it has a general sameness or flatness.

## 8. EMPHASIS IN PARAGRAPHS

When you decide that a particular point in a paragraph is especially important, emphasize it. There are five main ways of achieving such emphasis:

a. by varying sentence length
b. by repeating a word or a phrase
c. by putting the important material in prominent positions
d. by shifting the style
e. by using typographical devices.

## *Exercise 8F*

If you take apart a tightly coherent paragraph and mix up the sentences, it should be possible for someone to put them back in their original order. Here are three student paragraphs whose sentences we have scrambled. Try to put them back in their original order. You probably won't find it easy to do with the first two, but fairly easy with the third; see if you can figure out why.

1. a. She is so smart that at times she seems almost human.
   b. She is one of my best companions because she listens to everything I say and doesn't give a smart comment in reply.
   c. She is also a good watchdog.
   d. Who can a person turn to when he has to talk to someone but feels that all his friends are against him?
   e. My dog is very well behaved, so she doesn't cause any trouble in the house.
   f. As soon as someone comes into the yard she gives me a warning.
   g. Therefore when I talk to her it's not like talking to an inanimate object like the wall.
   h. The house never seems empty, even if no one else is there, because my dog is around.
   i. My dog is the answer for me.
   j. I would feel lost without my loyal companion, my dog.
   k. When I am feeling lonely, or just feel like being by myself, I always know my dog is there, and she comforts me.

2. a. I live in an apartment and that's why I don't own a dog.
   b. The apartment-bound are a sad, comfortless lot trapped by their environment, their landlords, and themselves.
   c. I wonder if the average suburban house-dweller really knows just how much of a luxury it is to be able to recline before a crackling fire with a steaming mug in one hand and a clump of eager, puppy-warm fur in the other?
   d. Many people are just not able to own a dog.

3. a. He swears that all dogs have an odour and leave a mess all over the furniture and floors when they shed their hair.
   b. Having a dog would also limit the kind of housing facilities I could rent when I am through school.
   c. My mother's allergy to dog hair presents yet another obstacle to having a dog in the house.
   d. Since I am still living with my parents the biggest obstacle to having a dog is my father.
   e. Although I am fond of dogs, I do not own one.
   f. He is strongly against having a dog in the house.
   g. For another thing, I am aware that a dog would severely limit my mobility, for I would be unable to take a holiday without first finding someone to look after it.
   h. All things considered, I shall remain dog-less.
   i. I can be sure my parents wouldn't be willing to.

## Exploration 8E

Try revising one or both of the first two paragraphs in the preceding exercise in order to improve their coherence.

## Exercise 8G

Take apart two or three paragraphs from writing you've done recently. Scramble the sentences, and then let someone else try to put them back in their original order.

## Exploration 8F

Here is a list of the main facts about a particular historical event:

> Date: 21 October 1805.
> Combatants, commanders, and forces:
>   British, Viscount Horatio Nelson, 27 ships.
>   Allies, Admiral Pierre de Villeneuve, 34 French and Spanish ships.
> Statue of Nelson, completed 1843, in London's Trafalgar Square.
> Napoleon threatened to invade England.
> Event known as battle of Trafalgar; occurred near Cape Trafalgar on Spanish coast (Atlantic) near Gibraltar.
> Nelson's signal at outset: "England expects that every man will do his duty."
> Villeneuve's fleet sailed in lone long and uneven line.
> Nelson split his fleet into two columns: he leading one in the flagship *Victory*, Cuthbert Collingwood the other in the *Royal Sovereign.*
> British fleet penetrated allied line at two points; could then attack from both sides.
> Allied fleet cut off from base at Cadiz.
> Nelson had lost an arm and an eye in previous battles.
> Words of Nelson's opening signal now famous.
> Bullet from French ship *Redoutable* mortally wounded Nelson.
> Twenty-two allied ships captured, and one destroyed.
> Villeneuve taken prisoner; later released, and committed suicide (1806).
> British lost no ships.
> The battle ended Napoleon's power at sea.

Compose a single paragraph from these facts. Decide on a clear purpose, select whatever facts you need, and arrange them in whatever way will best achieve that purpose. Don't decide too quickly: test different selections and arrangements in order to discover the material's potential.

## Exploration 8G

(a) Write a paragraph of 150-200 words using one of the following, or a similar one you make up, as an opening topic sentence. Develop the paragraph in any way you want.

> Singing stars aren't what they used to be.
> Getting to campus is sometimes more interesting than being there.
> People change as the seasons change.

Fast-food outlets deserve a better press.
Changing a tire isn't as hard as you may think.

(b) Rewrite the paragraph so that the topic sentence, revised if necessary, comes somewhere about the middle.

(c) Rewrite it again so that the topic sentence comes last.

## Essay 8A

In an essay of about 1000 words, compare and contrast the items in one of the following pairs:

1. two modern paintings or sculptures by different artists who use similar techniques
2. two current films of the same genre (for example science fiction, western, domestic comedy, crime story)
3. two reviews of a recent best-selling novel—one you've read
4. two short stories or two poems on a similar theme
5. two pieces of professional landscaping near your school

In this essay your purpose is to judge relative quality; you will essentially be writing argumentatively. For this essay, draw up a *topic sentence* outline—that is, one consisting of the actual topic sentences you intend to use (review the characteristics of good topic sentences, pp. 183-184). If you need to change your plan during writing and revising, submit the new version as well.

## Essay 8B

Take the classification scheme you drew up for Exercise 4D and use it as the basis for an essay of 800-1200 words.

## Idioms 8

See the instructions for Idiom exercise 4, page 100. In this exercise, the words are all *adjectives*.

| | | | | |
|---|---|---|---|---|
| adjacent | compatible | fascinated | obliged | scared |
| amenable | consequent | ignorant | partial | superior |
| appended | contemptuous | inconsistent | piqued | unmindful |
| based | disengaged | inimical | prejudicial | vulnerable |
| blasé | estranged | jealous | punishable | worthy |

## Sentence-Combining 8: Infinitive Phrases
## Pattern 8A

Base sentence *a*: Mrs. Narayan will conduct the seminar.
Base sentence *b*: She promised it.
Result of combining *a* and *b*:
    Mrs Narayan promised to conduct the seminar.

First, COPY the pattern sentence carefully, noting that *Mrs. Narayan* replaces *She*, that the rest of sentence *a* replaces *it* in sentence *b*, and that *will conduct* becomes *to conduct*.

Second, COMBINE each of the following pairs of sentences into a single sentence modelled on the pattern sentence:
a. Rose operates both machines.
b. She learned it in less than three hours.
a. Stanley met with the volunteers.
b. He had arranged it.

Third, COMPOSE two sentences of your own modelled on Pattern 8A.

In this exercise you are reducing base sentence *a* to an infinitive phrase (*to conduct* is the infinitive form of the verb *conduct*) and using it as a direct object of the verb in base sentence *b* (*promised*).

### Pattern 8B

a. The storm should arrive just in time to ruin the weekend.
b. Mr. Reimer expects it.
RESULT: Mr. Reimer expects the storm to arrive just in time to ruin the weekend.

Copy the pattern sentence, noting that sentence *a* replaces *it* in sentence *b*, and that *should arrive* becomes *to arrive*.

Combine each of the following pairs into a sentence modelled on the pattern sentence:
a. You may attend the banquet as well.
b. Your registration receipt will permit it.
a. Mrs. Mueller reported her travelling expenses.
b. Her counsellor advised it.

Compose two sentences modelled on Pattern 8B.

In this exercise you are converting sentence *a* to a noun or pronoun followed by an infinitive phrase, the whole then becoming the direct object of the verb in sentence *b*. Note that in both Pattern 8A and Pattern 8B different tenses of verbs get changed to the same form of infinitive, namely the present tense.

### Pattern 8C

a. Mr. O'Malley had been quickly promoted.
b. This delighted him.
RESULT: It delighted Mr. O'Malley to have been quickly promoted.

Copy the pattern sentence, noting that *had been* becomes *to have been*, that *This* becomes *It*, and that *Mr. O'Malley* moves over and replaces *him*.

Combine each of the following pairs into a sentence modelled on the pattern sentence:
a. Sally had broken her promise
b. This distressed her.

a. The professor had been seen by the two students.
b. This embarrassed him.

Compose two sentences modelled on Pattern 8C.

In this exercise you are changing the first sentence to an infinitive phrase which is then used as the subject of the new sentence (the word *It* being a false or anticipatory subject). (Compare the similar Pattern 6D). In this pattern, the verbs are changed into the only other possible tense of the infinitive beside the present (see Pattern 8B), namely the perfect tense, where *to* is followed by *have* and the past participle of the main verb.

## *Pattern 8D*

a. The professor was seen by the two students.
b. This embarrassed him.

RESULT: To be seen by the two students embarrassed the professor.

Copy the pattern sentence, noting that *the professor* moves over and replaces *him*, that *was* becomes *to be*, and that you delete the word *This*.

Combine each of the following pairs into a sentence modelled on the pattern sentence:
a. Annette won the scholarship.
b. This was a great satisfaction to her.

a. Sharon visited the Pyramids and the Parthenon.
b. That made her vacation complete.

Compose two sentences modelled on Pattern 8D.

In this exercise, as in Pattern 8C, you are reducing a sentence to an infinitive phrase which then becomes the subject, only this time at the beginning rather than the end.

## *Pattern 8E*

a. Bill Andreski had only one goal that year.
b. He wanted to win the men's downhill.

RESULT: Bill Andreski had only one goal that year, to win the men's downhill.

Copy the pattern sentence, noting that in sentence *b* you drop everything up to the word *to* and insert a comma.

Combine each of the following pairs into a sentence modelled on the pattern sentence:
a. The government expects us all to help.
b. It expects us to carry our share of the burden.

a. These exercises have one purpose.
b. They are intended to help you learn to write better sentences.

Compose two sentences modelled on pattern 8E.

In this exercise you are reducing a sentence by dropping its subject and verb and keeping only an infinitive phrase, which you then use as an appositive at the end of the other sentence. *Note*: In this pattern you could use a colon or a dash, instead of a comma, to set off the appositive.

### *Pattern 8F*

a. Ottawa's claim cannot be disputed.
b. It is the nation's capital.
RESULT: Ottawa's claim to be the nation's capital cannot be disputed.

Copy the pattern sentence, deleting *It*, changing *is* to *to be*, and inserting sentence *b* after *claim* in sentence *a*.

Combine each of the following pairs into a sentence modelled on the pattern sentence:

a. Your ability is improved by practice.
b. You write good sentences.

a. His hope was realized last year.
b. He travelled all the way up the Amazon.

Compose two sentences modelled on Pattern 8F.

In this exercise you are reducing one sentence to an infinitive phrase and inserting it in another sentence as a modifier of the subject (*claim*).

### *Pattern 8G*

a. I bought a smaller car.
b. I save money on fuel.
RESULT: I bought a smaller car to save money on fuel.

Copy the pattern sentence, noting that you delete the repeated *I* from sentence *b* and that *save* becomes *to save*.

Combine each of the following pairs into a sentence modelled on the pattern sentence:

a. I skipped the season but watched the World Series.
b. I saw how it all came out.

a. Many people are eating less and exercising more.
b. They keep their weight down and stay in better shape.

Compose two sentences modelled on Pattern 8G.

In this exercise you are reducing one sentence to an infinitive phrase and adding it to another sentence to express purpose—a common use of the infinitive. Sometimes you will want to emphasize the sense of purpose by putting the words *in order* in front of the infinitive: "I bought a smaller car in order to save money on fuel." Try adding *in order* to the other sentences you wrote. Does it help? Don't use it unless it distinctly aids the emphasis, for otherwise it will simply be wordy.

### *Pattern 8H*

a. Will Mr. Ricci be late?
b. That would surprise Hilda.
RESULT: It would surprise Hilda for Mr. Ricci to be late.

Copy the pattern sentence. Note that sentence *a* ceases to be a question, that *for* replaces *Will*, that *be* becomes *to be*, and that *It* replaces *That*.

Combine each of the following pairs into a sentence modelled on the pattern sentence:
a. Will the college raise tuition fees again?
b. That would infuriate many students.
a. Will the turnout be larger than expected?
b. That would delight the planning committee.

Compose two sentences modelled on Pattern 8H.

In this exercise you are converting the first sentence to an infinitive noun phrase and using it as the delayed subject of the sentence. You end up with what is called a *conditional* sentence that could also be expressed as follows: "If Mr. Ricci is late, Hilda will be suprised." Compare Pattern 6E, where the sense is that of a fact rather than of a possibility.

---

## Playing with Language 8A

A *lipogram* is a piece of writing that avoids using one or another letter. For example, here is a student's paragraph that avoids one common letter. Do you see which one?

### Sunsets

Watching a sunset can be a stirring experience. A spectacular sunset is relatively rare—especially in a rainy climate—and at dusk when the sky is clear and I have a few free minutes I frequently drive my car anywhere I can get a perfect view. There I stand, camera in hand, awaiting that certain instant when the sky blazes deep blue, scarlet, pink, and amethyst. But I can never quite capture this instant with my camera; it invariably eludes the lens. With a sigh, I get back in the car, start up the engine, and drive away. But I'll be back, persisting in believing that my luck will change next time.

Write some lipograms of your own. First write a paragraph omitting the vowel *a*, then one with no *e*, then one with no *i*, then one with no *o*, and then one with no *u*. The letter *e* is the most frequently used in English: was that the letter you found most difficult to leave out?

Try also a paragraph with no *t*, or no *n*, or no *s*, or no *h*, or no *r*. The challenge is to write such a passage without its sounding forced and artificial.

## Playing with Language 8B

The opposite of a lipogram is a piece of writing in which every word contains a particular letter. Try writing a paragraph in which every word contains an *a*, or an *s*, or a *t*, or an *n*. For a rougher challenge, try one with the letter *u*. As with the lipograms, try to make the prose sound natural, not forced or artificial.

## Playing with Language 8C

Compose a conversation between two people in which each speech consists of only one word. That is, speaker A says one word, then speaker B says one word, then speaker A says another word, and so on. Do not use any other words—no labels such as "he said" or "she shouted" to describe either the speakers or their manner of speaking; the single words they say must convey all the necessary information all by themselves. Try to make your dialogue go on for at least a dozen words from each speaker, but don't try to go beyond about twenty-five— that is, about fifty words altogether.

*By being so long in the lowest form
I gained an immense advantage
over the cleverer boys....I got into
my bones the essential structure of
the ordinary British sentence—
which is a noble thing.*

(Winston Churchill)

CHAPTER IX

# Sweep 3: Revising Sentences

Sentences are the most important elements in writing, the basic units of expression. Even if everything else is perfect, bad sentences will ruin any piece of writing; and good sentences can often go a long way toward compensating for weaknesses in other matters. Although you will naturally be working on your sentences at every stage of the writing process, they deserve your special and concentrated attention during one sweep of revision.

This chapter gives you practical advice on how to check your sentences for weaknesses and on how to improve them. The goal is to make your sentences effective. To be effective, a sentence must have the following four qualities:

1. Clarity
2. Economy
3. Vigour
4. Grace

These qualities often overlap: a sentence that is not economical will not be vigorous; a sentence that is not vigorous will not be as clear as it could be; a sentence that is not graceful will probably be neither as vigorous nor as clear as it could be. Nevertheless, each quality is worth focussing on separately.

But first a brief review.

## SENTENCES: PARTS AND KINDS

What is a sentence? A sentence is a satisfyingly complete utterance. A sentence can consist of any number of words, from (on occasion) one to (on occasion) hundreds. However long it is, it conventionally begins with a capital letter and ends with a period (or question mark or exclamation point).

Sentences contain subjects, verbs, objects, complements, modifiers, and function words. Sentences are made up of clauses and phrases. (If you need to, brush up on these and other terms by consulting the Glossary or a good handbook).

The four grammatical kinds of sentences are as follows:

*simple* (a single independent clause):

Calculators are handy devices.

*compound* (two or more independent clauses):

Calculators are handy; many people rely on them.

*complex* (one independent clause and one or more subordinate clauses):

Although calculators are handy, some people become overdependent on them.

Calculators are handy devices, which causes some people to forget what they knew about arithmetic.

*compound-complex* (two or more independent clauses and one or more subordinate clauses):

Some people use calculators as if there were no other way; other people, however, manage to use them without letting their brains atrophy.

*Practical Hint:*   The best way to inspect single sentences for possible errors or other points needing revision is to read your draft backward, sentence by sentence. Because you won't then be caught up in the flow of meaning from sentence to sentence, you'll be more likely to catch fragments or other errors or awkwardness in the individual sentences.

## Minor Sentences and Fragments

A *fragment* is by definition a non-sentence; it usually lacks either a subject or a verb, and needs to be combined with one of the sentences next to it. A *minor sentence*, on the other hand, is a word or group of words that doesn't constitute a normal or "major" sentence, but is acceptable because it is a satisfyingly complete utterance. Answers to questions, for example, are frequently such minor sentences:

Where did you go?
Out.
What did you do?
Nothing.
When did you leave?
Early in the evening.

Or even questions themselves:

I feel terrible this morning.
Why?
Because I ate too much last night.

The last example, beginning with "Because," is also a minor sentence, and therefore acceptable, but only because it is the answer to a question ("Why?");

otherwise "because," since it is a *subordinating* word, would make that utterance unsatisfying, a fragment. Look at the following, from a student's essay on gardening:

> DRAFT: Nature often supplies enough of the basic nutrients so that even if we don't add them the garden will still get by. At least for the first few years. Although up to a certain point, the more nutrients there are in your soil, the more productive your garden will be.

The first part is a normal sentence. But the second and third parts are not. "At least for the first few years" is merely an adverbial phrase. And the *Although* that introduces the third part is a subordinating word: readers expect such a subordinate clause to be followed by an independent clause; when it is not, they are jolted, and disappointed. In the hands of a skilled writer, something like this might work. But usually it is safer to treat such obviously subordinate elements as parts of other sentences. Here combining solves the problem and produces a good clear solid sentence:

> REVISED: Nature often supplies enough of the basic nutrients so that even if we don't add them the garden will still get by—at least for the first few years—although up to a certain point, the more nutrients there are in your soil the more productive your garden will be.

Clearly the writer originally set off the adverbial phrase in order to get a certain tone and some emphasis; in the revised version, setting the phrase off with dashes provides exactly that tone and emphasis.

Often the desire to end an essay (or a paragraph) with something different leads students to write a fragment as the final "sentence" of an essay—an embarrassingly bad way to end, since the final position in the essay then emphasizes something the writer would prefer readers not even to notice. Since this urge for some kind of stylistic fillip is almost always subconscious, it is worth taking an especially careful look at how you end an essay. Don't mistake a fragment for a minor sentence.

Used carefully, however, and with the writer in full control, minor sentences can be extremely effective. Here's part of a student's personal essay:

> So what's so hard about a job interview? That's the attitude I took, and look where it got me. Broke.

The word *broke* could have been introduced by a colon, but it works perfectly well, and gets even more emphasis, set off as a minor sentence. Here's the beginning of a short essay by another student using minor sentences effectively:

> A man's club, until recently, was considered to be the last male bastion. Exclusive. Dignified. Inviolate. Men only. But no more.

And another:

> Money, money, money. It makes the world go round.

By all means, then, use the occasional minor sentence for emphasis or other effects. But be sure of what you're doing: don't commit a fragment; don't set off as a sentence a word or group of words that could just as well —and should—be attached to an independent clause. Read it aloud and you will usually be able to hear if it sounds like something that can —or cannot—stand alone. Fragments are undesirable in serious writing for two reasons:

1. They distract or mislead readers.
2. Most educated readers expect to read complete sentences; a fragment reflects unfavourably on the writer.

# 1. CLARITY

If your readers are to understand a sentence, it must be clear; it must say what you want it to say, and only what you want it to say. Here are a number of specific things to check your sentences for, things on which clarity often depends.

## a. Unity

A good sentence is a unified sentence. It is about one thing. Here is an example of a sentence that is not unified:

> The weather was almost ideal that day, and our car broke down almost exactly halfway between Calgary and Edmonton.

It is virtually impossible to think of a logical reason for putting those two statements in the same sentence. Here is another sentence:

> It was almost time for the first act to begin, and my headache was getting worse.

Here the sentence may seem disunified, but in the context of a personal narrative about someone's first experience performing in a play, it could be quite justified.

What sometimes happens is that in the rush of writing a first draft one's mind jumps ahead of one's pencil, resulting in two or more unassociated ideas getting themselves jammed into one sentence. Check your sentences to make sure they are unified. Be on the lookout for compound sentences: keep their proportion small. If a sentence appears disunified, be sure the relation between its parts is made sufficiently clear by the context; otherwise, break the sentence up as necessary.

## b. Logic

A disunified sentence is of course an illogical sentence. But there are some other and more common kinds of logical breakdowns in sentences. An ad claimed that a particular kind of new car was now selling "for the lowest price it may ever sell for again!" Think about it. A news report about a particular dispute said that both sides had met with a mediator, and then added that "neither side met face to face, however"—as if one side could have met "face to face" without the other. Such lapses in logic can be amusing, of course. But in an essay, whether they are amusing or not, such illogicalities will at least briefly upset or distract readers and at worst confuse them or destroy their confidence in the writer. Here are a couple of examples from students' writing:

> DRAFT: The trip takes just over a week, depending on how fast one wants to travel.

It is impossible to know just what the writer intends to say, but some such revision as the following is clearly necessary:

REVISED: The trip can take anywhere from five to ten days, depending on how fast one travels.

(Note that, to be precise, it is not how fast one *wants* to travel but how fast one actually travels that determines how long the trip will take.)

DRAFT: We have indulged in the luxury of clothes since the beginning of time, and, therefore, have not allowed our bodies to develop any natural protection against extreme temperatures.

Here the word *therefore*, emphasizing a logical step, backfires, for readers will shake their heads, thinking it much more likely that early man first donned clothing at least in part as a protection against extreme temperatures. The reference to "the beginning of time," so obviously an exaggeration, will further put readers off. Carefully check your statements for instances of illogical thinking or illogical uses of language.

## c. **Alignment**

A particular kind of logical slip we call an *alignment* error—that is, an illogical alignment of two elements of a sentence. Most often the two elements that somehow don't get along are the subject and verb (and the error then is sometimes referred to as one of *predication*). In any event, illogical alignments are easy to commit and often hard to catch. After all, *you* know what you mean, so what you've written will seem perfectly all right. But if you can put yourself in your readers' minds and realize how *they* will read the sentence, you'll see the need for revision. For example one could easily write something like this, and feel satisfied with it:

The purchase price of even a modest house these days is simply too costly for most families who are just starting out.

But if you read it slowly and carefully, and *think* about it as you read, you soon realize that it isn't the *price* that is costly, but the *house*; the price could be said to be high but not—at least not logically—*costly*. You probably wouldn't even think of saying something like "My, that price is costly!" But when several other words intervene, it is easy to overlook the slip. Reread carefully. Even two words side by side can easily be misaligned, as in the often-heard phrase "at a young age," which should of course be "at an early age." Here are some other examples, written by students:

DRAFT: The premiers' concern about the situation is urgent, as the Prime Minister's should be.
REVISED: The premiers see the situation as urgent, as should the Prime Minister.

Another example, where *consisted of* is obviously an illogical verb:

DRAFT: The new defense policy consisted of several changes.
REVISED: The new defense policy included several changes.

Check your sentences for instances of illogical alignment. If necessary, read each sentence through extra slowly, perhaps even aloud, and think about the meanings of its words.

---

### Exercise 9A

Revise the following sentences to get rid of poor logic and alignment.

1. The efficiency and speed with which a computer processes data usually pays for itself very quickly.
2. Her attitude toward art is mentioned several times throughout the novel.
3. The pace of this scene moves very quickly.
4. Expressionist paintings concentrate on a psychological rather than a natural focus.
5. There are five sports in the curriculum from which you can choose which one you want to do.

---

### d. Coherence: Misplaced Modifiers, Dangling Modifiers, Weak or Ambiguous References, Agreement, Shifts, Faulty Comparisons

Any sentence that isn't clear or that doesn't hang together logically could be said to be incoherent, but there are several particular ways in which sentences can go wrong syntactically and throw your readers off balance. You should familiarize yourself with each of these so that you can guard against them and catch them during revision.

#### (1) Misplaced Modifiers

If a modifier—usually an adverb—is in the wrong place, not next to or near the word it is supposed to modify, the meaning of the sentence will often be ambiguous or otherwise unclear. A magazine report included the following sentence:

> There were strong calls for an immediate ceasefire in the UN Security Council.

Readers will quickly understand the intended meaning, of course— but probably not before seeing a vision of a shootout in the Security Council's meeting room. The prepositional phrase "in the UN Security Council" obviously belongs either at the beginning of the sentence or immediately after the word *calls*, and therefore nearer the verb *were*, which the phrase modifies.

Be particularly careful with words having to do with relative degrees of time or amount, innocent-looking little words like *only*, *merely*, *nearly*, *scarcely*, *hardly*, *always*, *just*, and *even*. Make sure you put them where they will make your intended meaning clear to your readers. In conversation, for example, where tone and stress would help, no one would be likely to misunderstand this sentence:

> DRAFT: He only suggested that his students follow three rules.

But in writing, unless you actually mean that "He only *suggested* it; he didn't *insist* on it," you'd be better off to write either

> REVISED: He suggested only that his students follow three rules.

or

> REVISED: He suggested that his students follow only three rules.

—whichever conveys the meaning that you want your readers to understand.

## (2) Dangling Modifiers

A modifier is said to dangle when it does not clearly or logically modify any specific word or phrase in the sentence to which it is attached. Usually the writer has in *mind* the word to be modified, but has not made sure that the specific word appears in the sentence. Watch especially for sentences beginning with an *-ing* verb form and ending with a clause in which the actor-subject has not been specified:

> DRAFT: While leaving the house, the phone rang.

What an agile telephone! Not all dangling modifiers are so unintentionally funny, but many of them are. The problem here is that the participial phrase "While leaving the house" has no logical noun to modify: it dangles. But of course what happens in the reader's mind is that the phrase attaches itself to the only available noun, *phone*, producing the unwanted humorous result. The fault can be revised in two ways. Either provide the logical noun or pronoun for the phrase to modify:

> REVISED: While leaving the house, *I* heard the phone ring.

or change the phrase to a subordinate clause that therefore won't dangle:

> REVISED: As I was leaving the house, the phone rang.

Here is another student sentence:

> DRAFT: Once viewed from every angle, readers get to know the protagonist of the novel.

Here the phrase "Once viewed from every angle" does have its logical noun to modify (*protagonist*), but it still dangles; it wants to attach itself to the noun *readers* because that noun comes first and is also the subject of the sentence. Again, there are two ways to revise the sentence. Either make the logical noun the subject and put it first:

> REVISED: Once viewed from every angle, the protagonist becomes clear to the reader.

or change the phrase to a clause that won't dangle:

> REVISED: Once they have viewed him from every angle, readers get to know the protagonist of the novel.

### (3) Weak or Ambiguous Reference

Check your draft carefully to make sure that wherever you've used such pronouns as *which* and *this*, you've used them clearly. Look at the following sentence, for example, from a student's essay on exercising:

> DRAFT: Millions of people are currently involved in jogging, but many of them neglect such things as warm-ups and cool-downs, which could be dangerous.

Intelligent readers can probably soon figure out that the *which* refers to the whole preceding clause and not just to "warm-ups and cool-downs"; it is the *neglect* of those exercises that is dangerous. But readers should not have to pause to figure out such things. If you make them do so, they will not like you for it. Often the best way to revise is to get rid of the pronoun and use an appropriate noun instead:

> REVISED: Millions of people are currently involved in jogging, but many of them neglect such things as warm-ups and cool-downs; such neglect could be dangerous.

Here's another student's sentence, discussing Joseph Conrad's *Heart of Darkness*:

> DRAFT: Because a snake is evil the river metaphorically associated with it must be seen as evil, and this is supported by subsequent events in the story.

The *this* here is at best vague. Does it refer to all of the preceding part of the sentence? Probably not. A revision helps clarify the meaning—and also gets rid of the loose coordination that is almost inevitable with the *and this* pattern:

> REVISED: Because a snake is evil the river metaphorically associated with it must be seen as evil, a conclusion supported by subsequent events in the story.

(See also p. 189, on demonstratives.)

Even a simple little pronoun like *it* can get you into trouble with your reader:

> DRAFT: People's opinions seldom change. If they do it is usually caused by some disaster or other.

Not all readers would be annoyed by such a sentence, but many would. They would wonder what *it* refers to; the word *change* is clearly the one the writer had in mind, but it's a verb, not a noun. Don't take a chance on having extra-tolerant readers; revise, even at the cost of having to add another word or two:

> REVISED: People's opinions seldom change. If they do, the change is usually caused by some disaster or other.

---

### Exercise 9B

Here, from student drafts, are a few sentences to practise on. Try to rephrase them so as to get rid of a vague *this* entirely, or at least change it from a pronoun to an adjective—that is, give it a noun to modify. (See also Sentence-Combining patterns 6G, 7C, 9A, 9B, 9C.) Also revise anything else that needs it.

1. Both passages are very graphic. This is achieved by the author relating his story as a first-hand experience.
2. Shakespeare skillfully moulds the concepts of astrology into his plays to provide emphasis and to heighten the mood of the play. This is exemplified by his use of astrological imagery in Horatio's speech.
3. The roads were improved by trying to straighten them out; new surfaces were tried to accomplish this.
4. Grace Poole is not surprised by his visit. This is odd because Rochester does not see his wife very often.
5. The novel confirms that using phrenology to evaluate one's acquaintances was quite common. Mrs. Dent does this when she looks at Jane.

---

## (4) Agreement

Lack of grammatical agreement in a sentence is a serious writing error. Educated readers will frown upon it even if it doesn't make the meaning unclear—which it often does. If you find yourself making this error, you should make an extra effort to conquer it, probably by studying a comprehensive handbook. Agreement can break down in two ways: between subject and verb, and between pronoun and antecedent. Briefly, here are the principles:

**Subject-Verb Agreement**   Verbs must agree with their subjects in person and number. The matter of *person* (first, second, or third) seldom causes any trouble; but the matter of *number* (singular or plural) can trip up even good writers on occasion. Errors in subject-verb agreement most often come about in these circumstances:

1. When other words—such as a prepositional phrase—come between subject and verb:

   The theme of the entire collection of essays *is* (not *are* ) that language is important.

   The singular *is* agrees with its subject, *theme*, not with the word *essays*.

2. With compound subjects:

   Jean and his dog *are* (not *is*) out in the yard.

   But don't be confused by phrases like *as well as* and *in addition*; they are not conjunctions, and therefore do not form a compound subject:

   Jean, as well as his dog, *is* out in the yard.

3. With singular subjects joined by *or*; the verb should be singular:

   Either Sally or her brother *is* going to cover for me.

   If only one of the two is singular, the verb agrees with the one closest to it:

   Either Sally or her brothers *are* organizing the party.
   Either the reindeer or Santa *needs* a bath.

4.   When for one reason or another a subject follows its verb:

> There *are* (not *is*) simply more of them around.

The plural *them* signals that the pronoun *more* in this sentence is plural; had the phrase been "of it," the correct verb would have been *is*.

**Pronoun Agreement**   Pronouns must agree in person, number, and gender with their antecedents, the words they refer to or stand for. The most common trouble occurs with such indefinite pronouns as *everyone, no one,* and *anyone*; these are singular, as the element *one* in each clearly indicates:

> Everyone who wasn't satisfied got *his* (not *their*) money back.

Note that even people who would use *their* in such a sentence wouldn't dream of saying "Everyone who weren't satisfied," as they should if they wanted to be consistent. But it is now widely considered unacceptable to use the generic pronouns *he, his, him,* or *himself* to refer to a singular antecedent of unspecified gender. You can substitute *he or she, his or her,* and so on, but such pairs, if they occur more than once or twice in a short piece of writing, quickly become wordy and tedious. And to substitute the unsightly *he/she, his/her,* and so on, is even worse. Often the simplest solution is to change from singular to plural:

> All those who weren't satisfied got their money back.

The problem of pronoun agreement then disappears. (See also pp. 267-268.) Watch out also for another kind of agreement error; here's a sentence from an advertisement:

> How does our company keep their prices so low?

Since the verb *does* indicates that the noun *company* is being considered singular, the shift to the plural pronoun *their* is incorrect.

**Reference of Pronouns**   Pronouns must not only agree with their antecedents, but also refer to them in a clear way. Here is an example of ambiguous reference:

> The business has been in my family since its inception.

What does the pronoun *its* refer to? Here the probable antecedent, *business,* is farther away than the other possible one, *family.* Keep pronouns and antecedents as close together as you can. The more remote an antecedent is from a pronoun, the harder it is for readers to make the connection and understand what you're saying.

### (5) Shifts

Pronouns, then, also have to be watched for consistency of number and person. Note for example how in the following sentence the student shifts from plural *their* to singular *its* and then back to plural with *they*:

> Any major company that has their own training facilities for its employees knows that good quality education will eventually pay back costs in better quality workmanship and also much sooner than if they had a poorer program.

All that's needed is to change *their* to *its* and *they* to *it*. In the next example the shift is from third person to second:

> Writers must keep on their toes as they revise; you have to watch for all sorts of things that can go wrong.

Changing *you* to *they* corrects the fault. And occasionally something written rapidly will contain an awkward shift in the tense of verbs:

> The next day, when I met him in the library, he was very upset. He begins by accusing me of stealing his calculator.

To keep the tense consistent, change *begins* to *began*.

Another kind of shift that can easily occur when one is writing fast is called a "mixed construction"—a shift from one syntactical pattern to another in mid-sentence. The result is an incoherent sentence; once spotted, such errors are easily revised:

> DRAFT: I based my entire judgment of people by deciding whether or not I liked the shoes they wore.
>
> REVISED: I based my entire judgment of people on whether or not I liked the shoes they wore.

> DRAFT: This untutored writer, working without benefit of a ghost writer nor editorial guidance, places her world on view.
>
> REVISED: This untutored writer, working without benefit of a ghost writer or editorial guidance, places her world on view.

### (6) Faulty Comparisons

Check your draft for places where you've made comparisons; make sure that each is logical and complete. A sentence such as this, for example, could easily slip past even a careful writer:

> DRAFT: The new tanker is longer than any ship afloat.

But it is itself now a ship afloat, and since it can't be longer than itself, revision is needed:

> REVISED: The new tanker is longer than any other ship afloat.
>
> REVISED: The new tanker is the longest ship afloat.

Another way in which an omitted word can make a comparison incomplete is illustrated by the following sentence:

> DRAFT: As for homeowners, the new policy treats them as fairly, if not more fairly, than the one it replaces.

Another *as* is needed to make the statement of comparison complete:

> REVISED: As for homeowners, the new policy treats them as fairly as, if not more fairly than, the one it replaces.

But the unwieldy construction can easily be avoided:

> REVISED: The new policy is at least as fair to homeowners as the one it replaces.

Here is another example, one that begins with a dangling modifier and then gets tangled up with first an incomplete comparison and then an illogical one:

> DRAFT: Coming from high school just three months ago, the new environment is very different. It hardly compares with the first day of high school.

Here is how the student revised this mess; combining the two sentences not only gets rid of the looseness of the original but also helps get rid of the problems with comparison:

> REVISED: Compared with that of the high school I came from just three months ago, the environment here at university is totally different.

---

## Exercise 9C

Here are some sentences to practise on. Revise them to get rid of the various kinds of incoherence they contain.

1. By reading some books, it will help you in your writing and your speaking.
2. No matter how you feel about a particular assignment, one should always do the best one can with it.
3. Hydro is run like a business, and like all businesses a product is supplied to a demanding market.
4. After putting all my energy into fighting the fire for so many hours, the climb back up the hill was a test of muscle and willpower.
5. The moderator ordered both the speaker as well as the heckler to remain quiet.
6. People from all parts of the world immigrate to Canada because of its consideration and freedom which it shows to its society.
7. He only seems to regard the rules as informal guidelines.
8. Vegetation fights and overwhelms Europeans and their attempts to spread their civilization throughout the story.
9. She promised to attend the Saturday rehearsal, and then she leaves town for the weekend.
10. Not a day passes without noticing someone on television or radio stressing how important it is to be physically fit.
11. Although the committee was at first unanimous in its decision to promote her, they later decided to let the dean make the decision.
12. The team won five special awards last year, and that's more than any team has ever won.
13. Almost all of her characters that she puts in the novel are capable of surprising the reader.
14. Nonsmokers are injured as much and, according to some sources, more by cigarette smoke in offices than the actual smokers are.
15. In each paragraph I examined revealed more clumsy organization.

---

## e. Emphasis

Part of making a sentence say what you want it to say is making sure that what you <u>want</u> emphasized is what <u>gets</u> emphasized. In the sentence you just read we used repetition, underlining, and parallelism to achieve emphasis; we also put the parallel structure at the end of the sentence, where it gets the most emphasis. Elsewhere in this book we discuss and illustrate these and other methods of achieving emphasis. Here, then, is just a brief review or list as a reminder of ways to emphasize something in a sentence—or to avoid emphasizing the wrong thing:

(1) Usually, put main ideas in independent clauses rather than in subordinate parts of a sentence.
(2) Put the most important points at the beginning of a sentence or, better, at the end.
(3) Repeat a word or phrase.
(4) Shift the style: use a different level of diction, or stylistically heightened syntax—such as parallelism, absolute phrases, or minor sentences.
(5) Depart from normal word order (another kind of shift in style). Since in English sentences the normal order is subject-predicate, anything not in that order tends to stand out. And since adjectives normally precede the nouns they modify, putting them after, instead, makes them stand out. Here is a student's descriptive sentence that uses both of these inverted orders:

> Through billows of steam and smoke, black and gritty, erupts a terrifying din.

Note that putting the adverbial phrase at the beginning of the sentence also contributes to the emphasis by delaying the main point of the sentence until the end.

(6) Use punctuation for emphasis. (See Chapter XI, especially pp. 285-286.) But don't underline or italicize if you can get desired emphasis in better, less mechanical ways. Similarly, don't depend on exclamation points or quotation marks; it is juvenile to use quotation marks or exclamation points to signal irony.

---

## Exercise 9D

Compose a group of sentences emphasizing the same word or idea in at least three different ways; or perhaps you'll want to work with a short sentence from one of your earlier papers.

*Example (written by a student):*

> It was an ancient story, but it was new to her. *(diction level)*
> It was an old, old story, but it was new to her. *(repetition)*
> Even though it was new to her, the story was an old one. *(position)*

---

## f. Other Matters of Clarity

Sometimes sentences miss being clear for still other reasons. You simply have to keep your eyes open for sentences that are ambiguous or that in other ways somehow don't quite make sense. For example a magazine described the plot of a television episode as follows: "Janet inadvertently fixes up Terri with a guy she's interested in." Devotees of the series might know which of the two characters the *she* refers to—but could even they be sure? It will be easier to catch such slips if you put your draft away for a few days, for if you re-read a sentence shortly after you write it, you can all too easily believe that it says what you *think* you wrote rather than what it actually says. Here are some examples from student papers:

> When the top of the omelette glistens with just a thin film of the egg mixture, slide the omelette onto a waiting, warmed plate by tilting the pan, and fold the remaining half of the omelette on top of the first with a flick of the wrist as it glides from the well-greased pan.

Obviously there needed to be some mention of the *first* half of the omelette sliding onto the plate before the instruction about "the remaining half." (The sentence needs other kinds of revising as well; try your hand at it.)

> The structure of the sentence in this section of the novel indicates Mrs. Ramsay's mind is leaping about.

Here simply inserting a clarifying *that* in front of "Mrs. Ramsay's mind" prevents the momentary misreading of it as the direct object of the verb *indicates*.

> DRAFT: One area of argument is in the structure of the computer itself.

Here the problem is partly diction (*area*; see p. 270), but the main fault is simply the fuzziness of the statement. It is easily revised:

> REVISED: One argument has to do with the structure of the computer itself.

### Faulty or Loose Coordination; Subordination
(see Sentence-Combining 1 and 2)

Clarity is also affected by the way you coordinate and subordinate. When you decide to coordinate two independent clauses by joining them with a coordinating conjunction, be sure to use the conjunction that most accurately expresses the relation between them. Trouble most often occurs with *and, but,* and *for*:

> FAULTY: The assignment was unusually heavy, *and* I managed to finish it two days early.
> REVISED: The assignment was unusually heavy, *but* I managed to finish it two days early.
> FAULTY: I had forgotten to stop for gas, *and* the engine soon sputtered and died.
> REVISED: The engine soon sputtered and died, *for* I had forgotten to stop for gas.

Sometimes it is better to use no conjunction at all, but a semicolon (or period):

> FAULTY: Usually history papers are difficult for me, and chemistry reports are much easier.
> REVISED: Usually, history papers are difficult for me; chemistry reports are much easier.

The second clause is not in an *and* relation to the first; it is not an addition to it, but simply a statement naturally following it. Sometimes the coordination is less faulty than just loose:

LOOSE: It was threatening to rain, *and* I decided to leave the gardening until the next day.

REVISED: I decided to leave the gardening until the next day, *for* it was threatening to rain.

Sometimes, especially when the conjunction *for* is present, it is preferable to revise by *subordinating* one clause:

REVISED: Since it was threatening to rain, I decided to leave the gardening until the next day.

An earlier example can be treated similarly:

REVISED: Since I had forgotten to stop for gas, the engine soon sputtered and died.

When you subordinate, do it logically:

WEAK: Frumbley mounted the horse very carelessly, immediately falling off and breaking his collarbone.

REVISED: Mounting the horse very carelessly, Frumbley immediately fell off and broke his collarbone.

In this example the subordinate element is a participial phrase rather than a clause, but the principle is the same: in the revised version, the lesser of the two facts is subordinated to the more important one.

> *Words are like leaves; and where they most abound,*
> *Much fruit of sense beneath is rarely found.*
> (Alexander Pope)

## 2. ECONOMY: AVOIDING WORDINESS

We discuss sentence length elsewhere (see pp. 193-195 and 228-229), and you may think that economy is only a matter of sentence length. No. Don't confuse *economy* with *conciseness*. There is of course a virtue in brevity. Short sentences are often effective sentences. And a sentence that goes on and on, that tries to pack too much in between the capital letter that begins it and the period that ends it, will often, however unified and coherent it may be, be unnecessarily confusing to a reader: it will need breaking up. But there's nothing in principle wrong with a long sentence if it takes a long sentence to say what you want to say. What *is* wrong, or weak, is a sentence that takes more words than it needs in order to say what it says. The most economical form for any particular sentence is not the shortest possible form but the most effective. Economy means avoiding waste. Perhaps if you let the word *economy* suggest money, and if you imagine that words cost money—say a dollar each—you will be less inclined to spend them carelessly.

(You will find more advice on avoiding certain kinds of wordiness in the next chapter, on diction: see pp. 252-254.)

*The strain of constructing prose sentences
is clearly marked even in the speech of the
most articulate people. That is to say, the
point I want to make is, all of us use, sort
of, filler phrases to conceal our nervousness,
or something, in working out our, you know,
sentence structure.* (Northrop Frye)

## a. Removing Deadwood

Unnecessary words in sentences are called "deadwood." They should be cut out
to keep the sentence healthy. A sports reporter informed his readers that "Both
teams were tied at seven-all." This is *redundant*; it says the same thing twice, or
even three times: "The teams were tied at seven." "Both teams had seven runs."
"The score was seven-all." Economy. A government official's remark to a reporter
is redundant to the point of absurdity: "Matters are so uncontrollable that we
can't control them." Consider the following sentence written by a student:

> DRAFT: Imagining themselves to be superior beings, proud and vain people act
> condescendingly toward those they consider to be inferior.

Now a pruned version:

> REVISED: Imagining themselves to be superior, proud and vain people condescend
> toward others.

No meaning has been lost, though a third of the words are gone. One could cut
even more, but there's no need to; the object is not to make every sentence sound
like a cable or a telegram but to get rid of waste.

> DRAFT: The design is rectangular in shape and is predominantly blue in colour.

The deadwood is obvious:

> REVISED: The design is rectangular and predominantly blue.

## b. Reducing Clauses

Some sentences that we write in our drafts are longer and more complex than
they need to be because we have put into clauses what could have been expressed
in a phrase or even in a single word. We could shorten—and improve—the
preceding sentence, for example, by changing "that we write in our drafts" to the
phrase "in our drafts" and "they need to be" to the word "necessary." Take a
particularly close look at relative clauses (those that begin—those beginning?—
with such words as *who, that,* and *which*); they are often easily reduced.

> DRAFT: By the end of the novel, it has become a struggle between two great
> powers, which are America and Russia.
> REVISED: By the end of the novel, it has become a struggle between two great
> powers, America and Russia.

Especially watch out for the "He is a man who" pattern:

> DRAFT: He is a man who likes to travel.

Such sentences can almost always be improved by cutting:

> REVISED: He likes to travel.
> DRAFT: This is a matter that should be brought to the manager's attention.
> REVISED: This matter should be brought to the manager's attention.

## c. **Reducing Clutter: Prepositional Phrases**

Hastily written sentences sometimes suffer from unnecessary clutter, particularly that of prepositional phrases. There's nothing wrong with prepositional phrases; we used two in the preceding sentence, and there are three in this one. But if they can be cut—for example reduced to a word—the sentence will usually be improved.

> DRAFT: Irony can be found throughout both novels in several forms.

Rephrasing gets rid of one prepositional phrase, considerably improving the sentence:

> REVISED: Both novels contain several kinds of irony.

The idea of "throughout" did not add anything useful. (Part of the weakness was also the *passive voice*: see pp. 223-225 below.)

Especially harmful are prepositional phrases that come in bunches:

> DRAFT: The more frequent the author's change in style, the less interesting the novel becomes because of the development of confusion in the mind of the reader.
> REVISED: The more often the author's style changes, the less interesting the novel becomes because of the growing confusion in the reader's mind.

Still two prepositional phrases—but a vast improvement.

---

### *Exercise 9E*

Revise the following sentences to make them more economical.

1. If we invest heavily enough, we shouldn't experience any setbacks in the immediate early short term.
2. The hero of the day was a sixteen-year-old teenager.
3. Not only does the great Congo River show temptation to Marlow, but it also provides for him the only means of ingress into the interior of the continent of Africa.
4. The leaf has an elliptical shape and is light yellow in colour.
5. She is a woman who prefers gardening and cooking to other activities that she doesn't enjoy as much.
6. It is a fact that many ex-convicts sooner or later get back into trouble with the law again.

7. In the back of my mind I was thinking of some of the things about which I'd forgotten in the process of making preparations for going on this trip into the mountains.
8. There is potential danger involved in experiments like this, and I would like to give a short summary of the possible dangers.
9. The settings for the show are far too fantastic and unreal as well as being grossly extravagant.
10. In the report the committee recommends that the strength of Canada's armed forces should be considerably increased.

### d. Combining Sentences to Reduce Wordiness

Sometimes wordiness overlaps from one sentence to another. For example, a good intention to provide an explicit transition might lead you to start a sentence by repeating something from the preceding sentence. But the repetition, especially if too mechanical, might hide the fact that the two sentences would be better combined. Here for example is the beginning of a student's essay; it's a weak beginning, and its weakness is made all the worse by the slavish repetition:

> DRAFT: I have had a few first impressions of this university. Some of my impressions have been favourable, such as of the setting and the number of services that are available to the student; however, others have not been as favourable. My unfavourable impressions include those of the line-ups and a general confusion about what to do and how to do things for classes.

The revision gets rid of at least the worst of the problems:

> REVISED: I have both favourable and unfavourable first impressions of the university. I like the setting, and I'm pleased by the many services available to the student; but I'm not so pleased by all the line-ups, and I'm still confused about just what I'm supposed to be doing, especially in getting ready for classes.

Since some words had to be added simply for clarity, the saving is only about 15%, but the tedious repetition is gone, the parts of the sentences are now combined more logically, and the implicit parallelism has been used to advantage. Economy—that is, effectiveness, efficiency—is much improved.

### Exercise 9F

Here are two sets of sentences from students' original drafts. Revise and shorten each by combining sentences.

1. Hockey is a fast-moving, exciting sport. It is enjoyed by both the players and the spectators. Although it is one of the most exciting games, it seems to be deteriorating among the professional ranks in the National Hockey League.

2. Dickens's characters do not change so much. An example of this is Joe Gargery, in *Great Expectations*. Joe's character does not change throughout the entire novel even though many things happen to change his life. Examples of these events are Mrs. Joe's being attacked and Pip's going away to the city.

---

> *In composing, as a general rule, run your pen through every other word you have written; you have no idea what vigour it will give your style.*
>
> (Sydney Smith)

## 3. VIGOUR

We don't mean the heading of this section to imply that every sentence you write should come on with lights flashing and siren blaring. But quiet sentences, even delicate sentences, nevertheless can and should be strong sentences. Any sentence that is *weak*, for whatever reason, will simply not perform its job as well as it should.

Wordiness of course weakens any sentence. The less economical a sentence is, the more likely it is to be flat, tedious, dull, even mushy; it will be less easy to understand; it will be relatively ineffective. But there are a few other causes of weakness to guard against; and there are a few techniques for making your sentences as vigorous as you want.

### a. Passive Voice

One of the prime sappers of strength is the passive voice. Whenever possible and appropriate, change verbs in the passive voice to verbs in the active voice.

Transitive verbs in English have two "voices," the active and the passive. The active voice is the more direct; the subject of the sentence *does* something to an object:

ACTIVE: Fido chewed my slipper.
Janet will play the guitar.
The demonstrators shout their approval.
Mr. Bellamy has found the missing file.

The passive voice inverts the subject and the object; what was previously the object (*slipper, guitar, approval, file*) becomes the subject of the sentence. Note that the passive versions are all longer:

PASSIVE: My slipper was chewed by Fido.
The guitar will be played by Janet.
Approval is shouted by the demonstrators.
The missing file has been found by Mr. Bellamy

You can easily recognize a verb in the passive voice: it contains a form of the verb *be* (in the examples, *was, will be, is,* and *has been*) or occasionally *become* or *get*, followed by the past participle of the verb (*chewed, played, shouted, found*). (*Note:* Passive voice has nothing to do with tense; any tense can be passive, as the examples show.)

Clearly the passive voice is less direct than the active, which is why the active voice is usually clearer and stronger. But the passive voice does have some advantages. For example you can use it to control word order so that you can get a desired word at the beginning or end of a clause, for emphasis. Or you can use it when you are not sure who performs an action, or when the identity of the performer is not relevant to your point. You might choose to write "The missing file has been found," leaving Mr. Bellamy entirely out of it, when what is important to your readers is not who did the finding but the reassuring fact that the file has been found. The point is that you should consciously *choose* to use the passive voice, or to let it stand in your draft where you find that you have used it.

But too often writers use the passive voice to evade responsibility or to withhold information unnecessarily. Think how you would feel if you read this in your school newspaper:

> It has been decided that all students will pay an extra $10.00 fee to the Student Council this semester.

You'd probably think "Hey! What's going on here?" You'd probably right away want to know just who made this decision: some student bureaucrat? a committee? somebody in the school administration? "It has been decided"—*by whom*, you'd like to know. But the sentence doesn't tell you. That's precisely how readers often react to an unnecessary use of the passive voice that doesn't identify the performer of an action. But even when the performer *is* identified, an unnecessary passive voice will usually at least be muddy, or lead to wordiness, or misunderstanding, or even grammatical error:

> PASSIVE: By cutting down on the passive voice in your writing, habits of responsibility are also learned.

The sentence stubbornly refuses to identify the learner; even though it is fairly obviously the implied *you*, the omission is annoying to the reader. Worse, the passive voice in the second part of the sentence leads to the creation of a dangling modifier in the first part. Changing the verb to the active voice eliminates the dangling modifier:

> REVISED: By cutting down on the passive voice in your writing, you also learn habits of responsibility.

In the following example, the passive voice ruins the otherwise good ending of a student's piece on a car accident; the final paragraph describes the after-effects:

> I finally reached home and headed straight for my bed. It felt strange to me, like a coffin. My body felt cold, my mind empty. Sleep could not be achieved; my eyes kept staring at the blank ceiling, projecting on it a continuous rerun of the crash.

Changing "Sleep could not be achieved" to something in the active voice—"Sleep eluded me," or "I couldn't sleep," or "I tried in vain to get to sleep, but"—makes all the difference. In the next example, passive voice again goes hand in hand with a dangling modifier:

> DRAFT: In addition to feeding the fish up to four times a day, the water should be partially changed every few weeks.

The sentence is slack and vague, as well. Revision makes it crisp and vigorous:

> REVISED: Feed the fish three or four times a day and change half the water at least once a month.

## Exercise 9G

Try to convert each of the following sentences from the passive voice to the active voice. The nature of the passive voice will make some harder to revise than others; when necessary, use your imagination. If you prefer to leave any of these sentences in the passive voice, explain why.

1. These mats were woven by my grandmother, but she didn't dye her own yarn.
2. You will find the company's policy explained on the enclosed form. If your payment is not received within 30 days, steps will be taken to see that it is collected.
3. The meeting was called to order, and the treasurer's report was read.
4. Schecter was knocked out in the third round, but it was decided, since he got to his feet shortly after the bell had been rung, to let the fight continue.
5. Rules are made to be broken.
6. The minister's motion was ruled out of order, and after a few minutes' commotion the business of the house was allowed to proceed.
7. Justice should not only be done, but should manifestly and undoubtedly be seen to be done.
8. Tab A should first be inserted in slot B, after which it should be easy to deal with tabs C and D; and though leads X and Y must eventually be connected to their respective terminals, it should not be difficult to negotiate the intervening steps, remembering always that Z is to be left open.
9. The investigation has been authorized by the chief constable, who in the end will be held responsible for any infractions that may be committed by the members of the special team.
10. It has been decided that no one will be allowed to report for duty tomorrow without shoes having been shined and scarves freshly pressed.
    [signed] Commander Ross.

## Exercise 9H

The following is not an especially strong paragraph, but we have made it even weaker by changing some verbs from active voice to passive voice. Try to restore it to the student's original version by changing passive voice to active voice. Are there any verbs that should stay in the passive voice? If you think so, explain why.

> Vincent van Gogh is today considered a great painter. Yet during his lifetime almost no recognition was given him. It is hard to believe that van Gogh's painting was not appreciated by the people of his era. Intensely expressive effects were created by his brilliant colours and slashing brush strokes, working together. Van Gogh was a remarkable painter. It is a shame, therefore, that the praise he justly deserved was not received by him until after he was dead.

> *Le mot, c'est le Verbe, et le Verbe,*
> *c'est Dieu.*            (Victor Hugo)

## b.  Verbs: The Hearts of Sentences

Sentences live in their verbs. The only action in sentences comes from their verbs and verbals. Everything else just lies there, inert, waiting for a verb to come along and give it a shove, set it in motion. If you use too high a proportion of verbs that don't do much, that don't move, that themselves just lie there, then your sentences will just lie there, your paragraphs will just lie there—your prose will just lie there. If your prose doesn't move, it will probably not move your readers except perhaps to put it down or go to sleep.

Now look at another version of the preceding paragraph, with some of the verbs changed. Though not an aggressively lively paragraph in the first place (but lively enough, we hope), it has become relatively flat and dull in the following version:

The life of sentences is in their verbs. The only action in sentences is that of their verbs and verbals. Everything else is motionless, inert, until a verb is present to make it move. If your sentences have too high a proportion of verbs that aren't active but static, that are themselves motionless, then your sentences will also be motionless, your paragraphs will be motionless—your prose will be motionless. If your prose has no movement, your readers will probably not be moved by it—except perhaps to put it down or go to sleep.

We changed some of the verbs to forms of *be* and *have* (*is, are, has*), and the prose has gone limp. There's nothing wrong with *be* and *have*; we all use them a great deal, for they are extremely useful, even essential, for many things we want to say. But if you let them constitute more than about half of your verbs, they may seriously weaken your style.

When revising, then, look for sentences that depend on a form of the verb *be* or *have* to see if you can improve it. Look for example at a student's sentence about a descriptive passage in a novel:

DRAFT: A point that is emphasized in the description is the character's clothing.

Two *is*'s. The result: wordiness, an unnecessary prepositional phrase, and an unnecessary instance of the passive voice. (Alignment is also weak: "clothing" is not logically a "point.") A dull sentence. To fix it, look for some sort of action. Ask "What is going on here?" or "Who or what is doing something?" In this example *what* is going on is an act of *emphasizing*, and the *who or what* doing the emphasizing is the *description*. Revising the sentence so that those two items become respectively *verb* and *subject* gets rid of the wordiness, the prepositional phrase, and the passive voice; even the alignment problem disappears. The result: a crisp and vigorous sentence that makes its point without any muddiness:

REVISED: The description emphasizes the character's clothing.

Here's another example from the same context:

DRAFT: The visual image and the character hinted at are in contradiction to each other.

This time "what's going on" is an act of contradicting; instead of using the noun *contradiction* as the object of the preposition *in* following the verb *are*, try putting the action itself into a verb, and you come up with a stronger sentence:

REVISED: The visual image and the character hinted at contradict each other.

Now the action is where it belongs, in the verb, not hidden away in a noun that depends on a form of *be*.

A similar weakness stems from unnecessarily depending on such forms as *it is, there is,* and *there are.* Such expressions often enable us to say something the way we want to, but used when they aren't necessary they can cause wordiness and general weakness. When you find yourself using one of them, check to see if you can improve the sentence by framing it another way. For example:

DRAFT: In my home town there are many people who are out of work.

Note the increased tightness and strength of the revised version:

REVISED: In my home town many people are out of work.

The main verb is still *are*, but cutting "there are" as well as "who" makes a great difference. But don't get carried away. "There was no one I could turn to for help" sounds natural and emphatic; to change it just to get rid of "There was" would probably produce awkwardness or wordiness or obscure the meaning: "I could find no one to turn to for help", "No one was there for me to turn to for help"; "I could turn to no one for help." No, leave it alone.

## c. Negatives

When possible, avoid negative constructions. A positive statement is usually more forceful than a negative one, and often more economical as well:

NEGATIVE: There was no one present at the meeting who had not read the report.
POSITIVE: Everyone at the meeting had read the report.

The second version also avoids the doubling up of negatives (*no, not*), which can become confusing.

It is probably preferable to say

I disapprove of their proposal.

than

I am not in favour of their proposal.

But sometimes a negative carries a tonal punch. To write that

She was aware of his feelings.

is clear. But if the context supports it, you could write

She was not unaware of his feelings.

which carries a subtle something extra.

Negatives can also sometimes cause ambiguity, especially when followed by a *because* clause or phrase, or even just a modifier with the sense of *because*:

AMBIGUOUS: The President's route was not made public for security reasons.

The sentence seems to imply, however illogically, that the route was made public for some other reason. Simply inserting a comma before the modifying phrase or clause will usually reduce the potential ambiguity (see p. 299); but putting the first part positively instead of negatively removes the ambiguity entirely:

REVISED: The President's route was kept secret for security reasons.

In the next chapter you will find further techniques for increasing the vigour of your sentences; see especially Abstract and Concrete, pp. 254-258, and Modifiers, pp. 258-259.

## 4. GRACE

Not every sentence should be "graceful" in the strictest sense. Some sentences need to sound harsh or strident or otherwise unpleasant in order to create a particular desired effect. But even such sentences should be graceful in the sense that their sounds and rhythms are just what the writer wanted them to be. The point is that no sentence should be unintentionally or unnecessarily ungraceful.

In other words, don't confuse *grace* with *elegance* or *refinement*. Think of it rather as similar to *appropriateness, suitability, decorum*. Straining for false elegance is just as bad in one direction as committing grammatical blunders is in the other.

Instructors often use the symbol *awk* or *k*, meaning "awkward," to mark sentences that somehow seem wrong but that don't fit any other particular category. Many sentences marked *awk* simply lack grace. The advice that follows should help you clean up such trouble-spots before they get marked, and it should also help you improve other sentences. You will find other advice on these and related matters in the next chapter (see pp. 264-275) and in the discussions of level and tone (see pp. 151-157). Here we focus on variety, word order, rhythm, sound, and figurative language.

### a. Variety

Successive sentences should vary in length both to achieve emphasis and to avoid monotony (see pp. 193-195). But you also want your sentences to be of different kinds and structures, for a string of several sentences of one kind also risks monotony or some other undesired effect. For example, a long string of similar simple sentences may make you sound like a kindergartner. A string of similar compound sentences could do the same—or, depending on their structure, they could be ponderous, making your prose sound like a hippopotamus in slow motion. And a long string of complex sentences (or compound-complex) is apt to be difficult to follow, to put too heavy a burden on your readers. Try to ensure that you have a judicious mixture of sentences. (But see *simple sentence* in the Glossary: obviously you must use judgment in this matter.) Examine the sentences in the following paragraph:

DRAFT: The Institute will enroll students from all over the province who will attend various programs that will range in length from three days to three weeks. The students will attend seminars covering many subjects that will depend upon their interests, which will include those of volunteer firemen, security guards, and ambulance drivers. The seminars will be taught by professionals who will be seconded to the Institute from the relevant fields of law enforcement, fire protection, and health care.

These three sentences contain no grammatical errors, and each by itself is reasonably clear. But when they're put together something happens. Even such a brief paragraph is downright dreary, if not actually difficult to read, because the sentences are so alike in both length and structure. Each is twenty-six words long, and each begins with the main subject and verb of the sentence and ends with one or two subordinate clauses. Now read a revised version:

REVISED: The Institute will offer programs varying in length from three days to three weeks. Coming as they do from all over the province, and with their different backgrounds as volunteer firemen, ambulance drivers, and security guards, the students will attend seminars on different subjects related to their interests. The seminars will be taught by professionals seconded from the fields of fire protection, health care, and law enforcement.

This is certainly not great prose, but it is serviceable. The revised version is much easier to read, and also clearer, because the sentences are more varied (and the eight *will*'s have been cut to three). Instead of 26:26:26 the lengths are now 14:33:19. And to break the relentless similarity in structure, the longer second sentence now begins, not with the main subject and verb, but with a long modifying -*ing* phrase.

As a final note, here's what one student wrote on the subject of sentence variety:

Short, medium, long. Sentences can be any length. Many people, however, write one length of sentence exclusively. No variation. This can create a piece of writing that falls flat, both on paper and in the reader's mind. Luckily, the solution to this stylistic problem is simple. Write sentences of different lengths. Short, medium, and long sentences, in various combinations, will help create a piece of writing that looks interesting on paper and sounds interesting in the reader's mind. Try it; you'll like it.

> *Proper words in proper places,*
> *make the true definition of a style.*
> (Jonathan Swift)

## b. **Word Order**

One kind of faulty word order, the misplaced modifier (see pp. 210-211), offends primarily because it clouds meaning. Other kinds of faulty word order can affect grace, smoothness, the flow of a sentence. A couple of examples:

DRAFT: That Jim stays behind, while the others flee, to face the inquest sets him apart from the captain and the engineer.

Such sentences can happen in the rush of writing a draft: ideas don't always occur to us in the best order.

> REVISED: That Jim stays behind to face the inquest, while the others flee, sets him apart from the captain and the engineer.
> DRAFT: The winter camper is usually active so wool is good to wear which can be worn in layers.

The *which* clause is of course a misplaced modifier of a sort, but here it doesn't confuse the meaning so much as make the sentence read awkwardly:

> REVISED: Since the winter camper is usually active, wool, which can be worn in layers, is a good material to wear.

Subordinating the first clause gets rid of the informal coordinating conjunction *so*. But the *which* clause could also be left in place if it is changed to an independent clause:

> REVISED: Since the winter camper is usually active, wool is good to wear, for it can be worn in layers.

You can easily overlook even such obviously awkward sentences as these unless you read your draft *aloud*; the awkward order will likely strike your ear more forcefully than it will your eye.

Another kind of awkward word order is the split infinitive:

> DRAFT: Once his followers have left, Laertes starts to laboriously strut toward Claudius.

Here the infinitive *to strut* is interrupted, split, by the adverb *laboriously*. Occasionally you may have to intentionally split an infinitive to avoid awkwardness or stiffness, but here the interruption is unnecessary:

> REVISED: Once his followers have left, Laertes starts to strut laboriously toward Claudius.

The adverb comes quite naturally after the infinitive.

## c. Rhythm

Awkward word order often produces awkward rhythm. But rhythm can come out badly for other reasons as well. For example, after a good topic sentence the following passage begins to get bumpy:

> DRAFT: Changing a diaper can be a frustrating experience. However, if a carefully planned routine is maintained things will go smoothly. Yet, it must be said at the outset, routine isn't everything.

Punctuation is partly at fault (this is treated more fully in Chapter XI), but that isn't the real problem. The trite "it must be said at the outset" is worth cutting entirely. The "However, ..." and the "Yet, ... " are both rythmically awkward; they even call attention to each other by their similar sense. Unless you want table-pounding emphasis, equivalent to underlining it, *However* at the beginning of a sentence is almost always stiff and unnatural. The unnecessary passive voice of *is maintained* lumpishly adds to the heaviness.

> REVISED: Changing a diaper can be a frustrating experience. But if you follow a carefully planned routine, things will go smoothly. Routine, however, isn't everything.

The "But" (*without* a comma, note) smoothly replaces the "However," and a "however"—put *after* the subject—replaces the "Yet."

You don't usually want your prose sentences to sound like lines of verse, with regular metrical feet. But prose does often have rhythm, at times even approaching that of poetry: "Changing a diaper can be a frustrating experience." (Four beats or five? What difference would it make?) Short sentences often have such beats. And such rhythm automatically goes with parallel structure:

> Expressionist paintings describe intangible worlds with new techniques and new symbols, discordant colours and distorted shapes.

Two-part sentences (here a compound predicate) often have a balanced rhythm:

> He remembered travelling down the highway but forgot the details of the accident.

> *Take care of the sense, and the*
> *sounds will take care of themselves.*
> (Lewis Carroll)

## d. Sound

Patterns of sound sometimes accompany patterns of rhythm. The phrase "discordant colours and distorted shapes," in an example just above, is not only parallel but contains in its two parts two words with similar sound, *discordant* and *distorted*. They almost rhyme. When nearby words begin with the same sound, the pattern is called *alliteration*. Note the alliteration of the *r* sound in the following, along with the perfect balance:

> To write is to risk.

The student who wrote that sentence used sound and rhythm—and a short sentence—to emphasize something he felt about writing, and it works superbly.

In prose two alliterating words in a sentence are usually enough. Sometimes one can get away with three, especially if they aren't right next to each other. More than that is decidedly risky, for you might end up with something ludicrous like "A mellow moon shone like a melon in the mist while my mandolin murmured its melancholy music." If you're not after laughter (is that rhyme acceptable?), avoid too-obvious sound patterns.

Another kind of sound pattern to be on guard against is that of the accidental echo or partial rhyme. It's not likely, for example, that the words "statistics" and "mystics" would go very happily together in the same sentence—at least not in serious prose. Here's a student's sentence:

> DRAFT: Marlow on his adventure eventually discovers the dark part of the human mind.

The alliteration of *discovers* and *dark* is good. But unfortunately the stressed *vent* sound in both *adventure* and *eventually* spoils the sentence.

> REVISED: Near the end of his adventure Marlow discovers the dark part of the human mind.

Now it sounds all right. The slight similarity of sound in *end* and *adventure* isn't harsh, as was the other.

As you read through your draft—out loud—listen for the unwanted patterns of sound and rhythm that can creep in. But also be on the lookout for places where you can use rhythm and sound to add grace and emphasis to your thoughts.

You can also introduce vigour and rhythm into your sentences by using contrasting diction. Into a pool of biggish words, toss a pebble of a word: it can make quite a splash. Or vice versa. Or juxtapose a big formal word and a small (perhaps colloquial or slangy) one for effect: *continental chic, sentimental guff, incomprehensible junk, dull platitudinousness, monumental stink*; sometimes alliteration and other sound patterns help: *implacable imp, doddering dodo, philandering fop, silly sententiousness, puff portentously*. But always be sure that your context can accommodate the tone that results from this technique.

> *A man's reach must exceed his*
> *grasp or what's a metaphor?*
> (Marshall McLuhan)

## e. Figurative Language

In an instructional essay on hiking equipment and technique, an essay that could have been very dull and dry, a student began one paragraph with this sentence:

> A backpack is a hiker's house.

The rhythm (a regular metrical four beats which succeeds because the sentence is short), the alliteration (*hiker's house*), and most of all the metaphor (*backpack is house*) combine to make this a striking and most effective topic sentence for a paragraph about the importance of a properly constituted backpack. Another student made a sentence vivid with both a striking figure ("eating...your imagination") and good alliteration at the end:

> When you're alone in a strange country and eating nothing but your imagination the only thing real is the muttering growl in your gut.

Here is a richly metaphorical passage from Henry David Thoreau's *Walden*—the final paragraph of the second chapter, "Where I Lived, and What I Lived For":

> Time is but the stream I go a-fishing in. I drink at it; but while I drink I see the sandy bottom and detect how shallow it is. Its thin current slides away, but eternity remains. I would drink deeper; fish in the sky, whose bottom is pebbly with stars. I cannot count one. I know not the first letter of the alphabet. I have always been regretting that I was not as wise as the day I was born. The intellect is a cleaver; it

discerns and rifts its way into the secret of things. I do not wish to be any more busy with my hands than is necessary. My head is hands and feet. I feel all my best faculties concentrated in it. My instinct tells me that my head is an organ for burrowing, as some creatures use their snout and fore-paws, and with it I would mine and burrow my way through these hills. I think that the richest vein is somewhere hereabouts; so by the divining rod and thin rising vapors I judge; and here I will begin to mine.

No paraphrase can do justice to such a passage, but stripped of its metaphors the paragraph would be something like this—and note that much if not most of its effectiveness has disappeared along with the metaphors:

I search for the secret of things not just in the relatively short period of known history but in the wider area of eternity and the universe. My ignorance is proportional to my age, and I wish to use my appropriate faculty, my intellect, and not be distracted by everyday material concerns. My immediate environment seems to me as good a place as any to commence my search.

Dull—and not even very clear. Thoreau's meaning is in the metaphors.

By all means try to inject life and clarity into your sentences with metaphors and similes. They are best when they come naturally; they seldom come on command. But don't overreach, or force them, as did one student trying to emphasize her state of mind during a crisis:

My mind was drenched in confusion.

The verbal metaphor of *drenched* just doesn't work; it doesn't call up a logical picture to fit the circumstances. And don't make the kind of mistake one MP did in an attempt to add colour to his remarks during parliamentary debate:

It's time to stop milking a dead horse.

When he reached for a metaphor, what he grabbed was a cliché—and he then proceeded to use it in a hilariously wrong way.

# PARALLELISM

One of the most effective techniques you can use to make your writing both clear and vigorous is parallelism. To use parallelism you follow one simple but powerful rule: elements that are similar in meaning or function should be similar in form.

First, you should use parallel structures when you are in any way listing anything at all, whether the list consists of single words, verbs, verbal phrases, prepositional phrases, clauses, or even whole sentences. Here are some examples of parallelism in each of these levels of structure:

PARALLEL NOUNS: When writing you must be careful with *grammar, spelling,* and *punctuation.*
PARALLEL ADJECTIVES: She is *fair, fat,* and *forty.*
PARALLEL VERB PHRASES: The instructor will *administer the test, mark the papers,* and *analyze the results.*

PARALLEL INFINITIVE PHRASES: On weekends it is his responsibility *to cut the grass, to weed the garden, to vacuum the floors,* and *to wash the dishes.*

PARALLEL SUBORDINATE CLAUSES: The chairman recommends *that you arrive on time* and *that you be properly dressed.*

PARALLEL SENTENCES: *His novels are mainly romantic adventure stories. His poems are mainly lyrical meditations.* (If you wanted to emphasize a close relation between the two, you could of course join them with a semicolon rather than separate them with a period.)

Even larger units, such as short paragraphs, can be structured so as to be parallel.

A good rule of thumb is that elements that *can* be made parallel *should* be made parallel. If you follow that principle your sentences and paragraphs will flow smoothly and rhythmically and your ideas will come through clearly and emphatically. Your prose will be easier to follow, for your readers will know not only where they have been but also where they are going. And if you can work out ways of expressing your ideas in parallel structures, you will find that many problems of organization and coherence will be solved in advance.

Notice for example how Hugh MacLennan uses parallelism both to develop and to tie together this paragraph from his essay "By Their Foods...":

> If a wise maturity accounts for the food of England, masochism must be held responsible for what the Scotch eat. Believe no Scotchman who tells you that his countrymen can afford no better. When Lord Strathcona was a millionaire many times over, oatmeal porridge, so I am told, remained his favourite dish. Believe no Scotchman who attributes the national diet to the barrenness of Scottish soil. Scotland is surrounded by billions of the finest food fish in the world, and the Scotch are skilled fishermen. If they boil their salmon and halibut till no taste remains, if they bake out of their haddock the last drop of moisture, if they serve these ruined fish with a dry, grey potato and (for variation) boiled turnips and sprouts, if they offer for dessert soggy rice pudding with bloated raisins bulging out of it, if they equate a distaste for haggis with disloyalty to Scotland herself—let nobody pity them or wonder why they eat as they do. They prefer this diet because it gives them the pleasure of being miserable.

After a topic sentence that is also transitional from the preceding paragraph, the second and third sentences form a pattern which is repeated by the fourth and fifth sentences, and the long sixth sentence consists mainly of five parallel clauses all beginning with "if they."

If you use elements that can be made parallel, but are not, the result will often seem awkward or even confusing to your readers. The following sentence, for example, is awkward because the writer has not taken advantage of an opportunity to use parallelism:

DRAFT: Harold irritates easily, is not organized, and arrives late.

The sentence can be quickly improved by making the three elements in the series parallel:

REVISED: Harold is irritable, disorganized, and often late.

In the following sentence, you can see that the third element needs to be made parallel with the first two:

DRAFT: The aims of the new system are to save time, conserve energy, and that fewer employees will be required.

Change the *that* clause to an infinitive like the others:

REVISED: The aims of the new system are to save time, to conserve energy, and to use fewer employees.

Notice here how you can emphasize the parallel structure merely by repeating the little word *to* at the beginning of each part of the series.

An important use of parallelism is that which occurs with such paired terms (known as correlative conjunctions) as *either... or, neither... nor, not only... but also,* and *both...and.* The parallelism in such constructions is a powerful way to gain emphasis and to express similarities and contrasts. Note the following sentence:

Mr. Domenico gave them not only his sworn promise but also a signed statement.

—much stronger and clearer than, for example, "Mr. Domenico gave them his sworn promise and a signed statement," or even "Mr. Domenico gave them his sworn promise and a signed statement as well." Of course you must be sure to make the elements that follow each term of these pairs parallel; otherwise the sentence will be awkward, like this: "Mr. Domenico gave them not only his sworn promise but also signed a statement." That won't do. It may help you avoid such errors if you think of the sentence written this way:

<pre>
                            not only his sworn promise
Mr. Domenico gave them  <
                            but also a signed statement.
</pre>

## Faulty Parallelism

But though parallelism can be a powerful stylistic technique, it is also liable to a couple of easily made slips that you need to guard against.

Whenever you use one of the sets of correlative conjunctions, be sure that the words or groups of words following each half of the pair are syntactically parallel. Look at this example:

DRAFT: The extras in this scene can wear Elizabethan costumes, but they should be neither striking in design nor colour.

The terms "striking in design" and "colour" are not properly parallel; readers feel as if they've driven over a large bump in the road. Revision is simple:

REVISED: The extras in this scene can wear Elizabethan costumes, but they should be striking neither in design nor in colour.

The rhythmic balance now helps both clarity and emphasis. The road is smooth.

The force of parallel structure is such that it controls what's in it. In this sentence a student let the parallel structure contradict the sense:

DRAFT: Both of these kinds of hiking boots provide protection from water, dirt, and other abrasive materials.

This makes *water* an abrasive material, which of course it isn't. Revising the sentence to clear it up, one can use a different kind of parallelism:

REVISED: Both of these kinds of hiking boots provide protection from water and from dirt and other abrasive materials.

## Exercise 9I

Compose sentences similar to those at the beginning of this section, using two, three, or four parallel elements of the following kinds:

1. nouns
2. adjectives
3. adverbs
4. verb phrases
5. infinitive phrases
6. participial phrases
7. prepositional phrases
8. subordinate noun clauses
9. subordinate adjective clauses
10. independent clauses, or sentences.

## Exploration 9A

Compose a paragraph that uses the same or nearly the same patterns of parallelism as MacLennan's paragraph quoted above (p. 234).

## RAMBLERS

One final point. Many of these problems and principles overlap, as we noted earlier. Many of the examples could have appeared under other headings. But one particular kind of sentence deserves singling out as offending in all four ways: the rambling sentence. A sentence that rambles is out of control. It will probably be incoherent and disunified or otherwise unclear; it will likely be wordy; it is bound to be weak; and it will almost surely lack grace. Such sentences don't often occur—or rather they don't often get left in draft form; they're easy enough to write during the relatively free-wheeling composition of a rough draft. Here's how part of a draft of an instructional essay on vegetable gardening looked:

DRAFT: Once you have prepared the soil and planned your garden, the next step of gardening, which consists of the planting and cultivating, is generally specific for each particular vegetable, and by following the instructions that are printed on each packet of seeds, and your own intuition, it will be quite simple, and you can look forward to spending your summer gardening time taking care of such things as thinning, staking, weeding, cultivating, and supplying an adequate amount of water to your garden, if nature doesn't do it for you, and maybe some fertilizing (which can be overdone, so be careful), and of course trying to control various kinds of pests, which are all necessary if you are to get a satisfactory harvest.

Too much to pack into one sentence: it badly needs breaking up into more manageable units. The ideas are all related, but loose coordination, the multitude of subordinate elements, the sometimes awkward structures and dislocations, and the repetition and general wordiness make it almost impossible to follow. Readers' minds can keep only so much up in the air at one time; if you ask them to juggle too many items of information they will start dropping them and lose the sense of what you're saying. Effective sentences usually don't require readers to keep in their minds more than three or four elements before they come to some kind of a stop (for example a comma, semi-colon, or period), some kind of "closure" which enables them mentally to take a breath before going on to the next group of items.

---

## Exercise 9 J

For practice, revise the rambling sentence on gardening. You will probably want to break it up into a least three or four sentences, to do some cutting and rearranging, and to reduce the subordination.

---

Even a relatively short sentence can in effect ramble, and therefore be difficult to follow, if long phrases or clauses separate a subject from its verb:

> DRAFT: This method of soil preparation, although it requires you to spend many long hours spading and clearing and composting, work that sometimes requires rather heavy physical labour, will save you time and effort in the long run.

Not impossible to follow, perhaps, but at the end you probably had to look back to the beginning in order to remind yourself what the subject of the verb "will save" was. Changing the syntax makes such a sentence much easier to read:

> REVISED: Although preparing the soil this way requires long hours of sometimes heavy work spading and clearing and composting, it will save you both time and effort in the long run.

But let a student have the last word; here's how he summed up the matter of ramblers for us:

### A Stylistic Sin

All students, or other people who, by necessity, have to put their thoughts onto paper, have, at some time, committed the unforgivable stylistic sin of writing unnecessarily long and verbose sentences, the meaning of which is all too often hidden in a maze of phrases and clauses, and it is to these people that the following piece of advice is directed: don't write sentences like this one.

## *Review Exercise: Sentences*

Each of the following sentences or groups of sentences needs revising according to one or more of the principles discussed in this chapter.

1. That evening, upon returning home and finding my friend waiting for me, caused so much excitement that it made my heart palpitate.
2. At the beginning of the reading lesson the interest of the children should be motivated. This can be achieved by discussing different things that relate to the story.
3. World transportation is dependent upon fossil fuels.
4. There has never been more than 850 people living on Anticosti Island.
5. Upon arrival at our destination, my self-assurance was quickly shattered.
6. By sentencing convicted murderers, specifically mass murderers and child-killers, to death we would be permanently removing those people detrimental to society.
7. Some dental plans require that their members visit the dentist at least once a year and failure to do so results in cancellation of membership.
8. The tendency for such firms is to hire increasingly college-trained people.
9. The entire plan fell through when Stevie stumbles and explodes the bomb.
10. No only can jogging be done in any conditions, but also anywhere: city side-walks, hiking trails, sandy beaches. This gives jogging the added freedom of open air, space and nature.
11. I have sensed a real unawareness of the value of music education among the masses.
12. We cannot afford to go on having the unique qualities of our minds suffer any more abuse.
13. This is an important qualification, since it allows exceptions for some characters from this rule.
14. The Irish love of life and land is surpassed only by their love of horses. A passion that spans over two thousand years.
15. We invite you to compare its flavour to any other brand.
16. If negotiations are delayed, unnecessary lives will be lost.
17. While struggling to free my boot, a large dog appeared on the other side of the fence.
18. When hiking a general objective, goal, or destination is to be reached.
19. Many people are killed or die in the story.
20. The statistics are obviously affected by the policies that are in effect.
21. The contract was not renewed on the recommendation of the manager.
22. When you get up into the mountains you breathe air which you have never breathed before, maybe because it is clean.
23. The casual friendliness of all these strangers is very rewarding and the park seems to breed this characteristic, which is as memorable as the physical beauty of the park itself.
24. The reason why I haven't any very strong feelings about these historical events is due to the fact that the events themselves can be classified as mild.
25. And I feel that I can understand what an adopted person must feel like and I will never forget that feeling.
26. Children are our most important resource, and therefore we must provide an opportunity to educate them to their full potential.

27. There is about a dozen characters in each story.
28. There was also an interest in chivalry and romance presented through allegory.
29. Why would Britain and France willingly place themselves under American protection? There are three reasons for this.

And finally, here is a short paragraph (describing the setting of a short story) that is badly in need of revision. It is choppy, monotonous, poorly organized (note the unnecessary repetition), and contains poor reference and faulty coordination, and perhaps other weaknesses as well. Revise it. You may want to try some sentence-combining. Given the materials, make it as good a paragraph as you can.

30. The town itself is a small town with a dirt road. There is only one restaurant, and their dance hall had closed down because the summer was over. The town is near a lake; it is very popular with city people. They have summer cabins around the lake. During the summer the town is alive with tourists, and when summer is over the town dies down.

---

## *Exploration 9B*

Write a paragraph beginning with a deliberate minor sentence (or more than one). Perhaps you can contrive to end it with one as well.

## *Exploration 9C*

Write a paragraph of at least 150 words, on any topic, using no verbs other than forms of *be* and *have*. Then rewrite the paragraph without using any forms of *be* and *have*. The second paragraph will likely be not only more vigorous, but also shorter. But both paragraphs will be extreme in their verbs, and therefore probably awkward in one or more ways. Write the paragraph again, using a judicious mixture of verbs; it should prove not only easier to write, but more effective as well.

## *Exploration 9D*

Do a statistical survey of the paragraphs six or more sentences long that you wrote for earlier assignments. Find the one whose sentences are (a) nearest to uniform in length and (b) least varied in structure and kind. If necessary, settle on two different paragraphs to work with, one with each qualification. Revise the one or two paragraphs, introducing as much variety of both kinds as you think they will bear. Then ask someone to read the two versions and tell you which one is the more effective.

---

## *Essay 9A*

Write down the names of twenty or so people who figure in your life. Then draw up at least three or four different schemes of *classification* for them. For example you could classify them according to their degree of importance to you, or the degree to which you like or trust them, or the closeness of their relation to you, or perhaps their professions or their stations in life. Choose the scheme that seems to reveal the most useful ideas or the most interesting slant—perhaps a way of looking at these people that you hadn't thought of before—and use it as the basis of an essay of 500-700 words. (Try to classify them into at least three categories in each scheme; schemes with only two categories—for example male and female, or relatives and non-relatives—are less likely to produce enough useful or varied material. Classifying them as either young or old would get you less far than if you set up four or five age categories.) Include a thesis statement and a plan, complete with a statement of audience and purpose.

### Essay 9B

Write a review of a film you have recently seen. Evaluate it, and make clear to the reader the criteria on which you base your evaluations: technical matters, direction, acting, expressed or underlying values, originality, and so on. Don't go off on rambling tangents of philosophizing about life, art, and film-making; keep your and your reader's attention focussed on the film in question. But do make your own values and assumptions clear enough so that a reader will know whether or not to agree with you. Your purpose is either to encourage others to see the film, or to discourage them from wasting their time and money on it. Your editor has allotted you space for 750 words: you must come quite close to that.

---

### Idioms 9

See the instructions for Idiom exercise 4, p. 100. In this exercise, the words are all *nouns*.

| | | | | |
|---|---|---|---|---|
| analogy | fondness | insight | prerequisite | resemblance |
| confidence | friend | martyr | pride | respect |
| distaste | hindrance | motive | pursuit | solution |
| equivalent | incentive | opposition | regret | tendency |
| fascination | influence | precedence | repugnance | want |

---

### Sentence-Combining 9: Gerund Phrases

### Pattern 9A

Base sentence *a*: The treasurer forgot to deposit the cheques.
Base sentence *b*: She admitted this.

Result of combining *a* and *b*:
   The treasurer admitted forgetting to deposit the cheques.

First, COPY the pattern sentence carefully, noting that *The treasurer* from sentence *a* replaces *She* in sentence *b*, that *forgot* becomes *forget* and takes on an *-ing* ending, and that sentence *a* then replaces *this* in sentence *b*.

Second, COMBINE each of the following pairs of sentences into a single sentence modelled on the pattern sentence:
a. Alan works the late shift.
b. He enjoys it.

a. The supervisor met strong opposition.
b. He didn't anticipate this.

Third, COMPOSE two sentences of your own modelled on Pattern 9A.

In this exercise you are changing the verb in sentence *a*, whatever its tense, to the gerund form of that verb. The gerund phrase then functions as a noun, replacing the direct object *it* or *this* in sentence *b*. The gerund, you notice, with its *-ing* ending, is identical in form to the present participle. They differ only in function: a gerund functions as a noun, whereas a participle functions as an adjective.

## Pattern 9B

a. I will buy a home computer.
b. This will help me manage my everyday affairs.
RESULT: Buying a home computer will help me manage my everyday affairs.

Copy the pattern sentence, noting that *I will buy* becomes simply *Buying*, and that *This* is deleted.

Combine each of the following pairs into a sentence modelled on the pattern sentence:
a. She won the scholarship.
b. This was a great satisfaction to Annette.

a. They eat less and exercise more.
b. This helps people keep their weight down and stay in shape.

Compose two sentences modelled on Pattern 9B.

In this exercise you are reducing the first base sentence to a noun phrase beginning with a gerund (*Buying*) and using it as the subject of the new sentence—replacing the weak *This*.

## Pattern 9C

a. Mark smoked continually.
b. This annoyed the others at the meeting.
RESULT: Mark's continual smoking annoyed the others at the meeting.

Copy the pattern sentence. Note that you omit *This*, and that you change *Mark* to *Mark's* and *smoked* to *smoking*. And note that *continually* loses its *-ly* ending and changes places with *smoking*.

Combine each of the following pairs into a sentence modelled on the pattern sentence:
a. He flirts occasionally.
b. This amuses the whole class.

a. Shelly drove carefully and confidently.
b. This reassured Mary Jane.

Compose two sentences modelled on Pattern 9C.

In this exercise, as in Pattern 9B, you are again converting base sentence *a* to a gerund phrase and using it as the subject of the new sentence. Note that since the gerund functions as a noun, the noun or pronoun in front of it must be a possessive.

### Pattern 9D

a.  Ottawa's main attraction is only one of the reasons for visiting it.
b.  It is the nation's capital.

RESULT:  Ottawa's main attraction—its being the nation's capital—is only one of the reasons for visiting it.

Copy the pattern sentence, noting that you change *It is* to *its being* and then insert sentence *b* into sentence *a*, setting it off with dashes.

Combine each of the following pairs into a sentence modelled on the pattern sentence:

a.  Annette's achievement was a great satisfaction to her.
b.  She won the scholarship.
a.  One of Bill's habits amuses the class.
b.  He flirts.

Compose two sentences modelled on Pattern 9D.

In this exercise you are reducing a sentence to a gerund phrase which you then insert as an appositive after the subject of the other sentence. Since such an appositive causes an abrupt break in the flow of a sentence's syntax, dashes are usually appropriate to set them off, although commas or parentheses would serve (see p. 305). Note that the possessive pronoun (*its* in the pattern sentence) can be omitted.

*Note*: Sometimes a gerund followed directly by another noun (its object) will sound awkward or ambiguous unless you put the word *of* between them; for example: *your writing of essays, his painting of pictures, our driving of cars.* Without the *of*, the *-ing* forms can sound like participles rather than gerunds.

For another use of gerunds, see the pattern sentence for 3A, where in the phrase *of weeding and fertilizing*, the gerunds *weeding* and *fertilizing* are objects of the preposition *of*.

---

### Playing with Language 9A

Compose some deliberately ambiguous sentences, sentences that can be understood in two ways. For example:

Flying airplanes can be dangerous.
The dog looked longer than the cat.
She hit the man with the big stick.
Too many chefs spoil the sauce.
He is not a man to trust.

Then revise them (start with those above) so that they are no longer ambiguous—but do so by making the least possible change to each.

## *Playing with Language 9B*

The sounds of words, even when they are read silently, can contribute to the effect they have. Consider *moon, orb, globe, round.* (Does their shape also contribute—all the *o's* emphasizing roundness?) Onomatopoeia—the sound matching the sense—can be a strong element in prose as well as in poetry. Consider such words as the following, whose sound (and perhaps also appearance) reinforces their meaning:

| | | |
|---|---|---|
| willow | chop | slim |
| smooth | peregrination | superfluousness |
| click | bark | ripple |
| flip-flop | huff | brick-bat |
| gulp | prolong | plump |
| clip | *Weltschmerz* | sinuosity |
| snip | orotund | wisp |

Do *tunnel, funnel, runnel* and *gunwale* have anything in common besides their sound? Is there anything special about a lot of words that start with *p*? (poison, pain, pang, peevish, panic, peril, pallid, pimple, poor, prison) or *h*? (happy, hello, health, high, holy, home, hedonism, holiday), or are we being unfairly selective? How about words beginning with *d*?

Keep your own list of words notable because of their sound. Do you have a few pet words, words you're especially fond of simply because of their sound? Almost everyone does.

Compose some sentences using some words in a way that takes advantage of their sound. Can you also make use of the shape of some words?

## *Playing with Language 9C*

Write a paragraph in which as many words as possible begin with the same sound. Here is how one student incorporated an alliterative paragraph into a short piece with a clear purpose:

### America—Acquit Alliteration!

In recent years there has been an unsettling trend toward using more alliteration in writing. It all began in New York when an obscure ad-man named Jonathan Jingle discovered that a short, rhythmic phrase with repeated sounds was easy to remember. A new dimension was thus added to American Life —the dimension of Alliteration. Alliteration in its original "pure" form has all but died out under the tremendous output of words and sounds during the "Alliteration Explosion."

Sensing the imminent extinction of alliteration as an effective mode of writing, 237 literary men and women met last summer in Boston. They reasoned that since the "Alliteration Explosion," the reading public had become insensitive to the "repetition for emphasis" effect. One or two repeats per line were no longer enough to catch the eye of a complacent public. The answer was clear. In the spirit of a similar decision by Marie Antoinette, who, it may be remembered, said "If they're bored with bread, court them with cake," the Alliteration Association of America (or the AAA, as it prefers to be known) recently issued the following statement in New York, outlining its proposal:

Succinct Sirs,

    All around America, alliteration always arouses an apathetic attitude. Accordingly, Americans abhor almost all additional alliterative axioms appearing at all aggrandized. Alternatives allow an amiable amalgamation among alliterative alliances. Adroit advice advocates alertness and alacrity, although advancement alters as altercations amass against anticipated achievements.

    "Act Against Academic Apathy!"

                                  Sincerely,
                                  Sara S. Sikes
                                  Secretary

    To my present knowledge no further action has been taken on the proposal by the AAA. Word has it that the AAA has split into two opposing factions, with one side adhering to assonance, the other comfortable with consonance.

### Playing with Language 9D

Think of some topic with lots of action in it, something *dynamic* (a sports car race, blasting out an excavation for a new building, demolishing an old building, the collision of two trains, part of a football game....) and write a paragraph describing it—but write the paragraph entirely in *passive voice*. When you have finished it, read it through aloud to find out what has happened to the vigour.

### Playing with Language 9E

Compose a short paragraph about some weakness or error in writing. Add to the point by committing the weakness or error yourself and making your sentences or your paragraph comment on it. Then do the same for some stylistic strength. (For example, see the student paragraphs on pp. 229 and 237.)

*We should be as careful of our*
*words as of our actions.*
(Cicero)

# CHAPTER X
# Sweep 4:  Revising Words

The effectiveness of any piece of writing obviously depends a great deal on the quality of the words in it. Because inexperienced writers often wrongly assume that any words that convey the intended meaning will be satisfactory, they tend to accept pretty much the first ones that come to mind. Experienced writers, on the other hand, recognize the importance of diction; they know that their words deserve close scrutiny. Like the proverbial missing nail that caused the loss of a battle, just one or two poorly chosen words can ruin a sentence, and thus a paragraph, and thus a whole essay.

This chapter gives you advice about certain weaknesses to look for while revising and also about some techniques for improving your diction in any given piece of writing. As with sentences, here again we focus on the four essential qualities: clarity, economy, vigour, and grace. And also as with sentences, these four categories overlap a good deal.

*A powerful agent is the right word. Whenever*
*we come upon one of those intensely right*
*words in a book or a newspaper the resulting*
*effect is physical as well as spiritual,*
*and electrically prompt.* (Mark Twain)

## 1. CLARITY: CHOOSING THE RIGHT WORD

### a.  Wrong Word

Any word that doesn't do the job in the best way is of course a "wrong" word. But there are some particular kinds of "wrong word" that you should be aware of so that you can be on the lookout for them as you revise.

Even professionals slip. A news story about the sudden collapse of a bridge included the following sentence: "Seconds later a pickup truck *hurdled* through the air and landed near the car." At first *hurdled* may sound right, and it may come close to describing the action, but a second's conscious thought—and if necessary a trip to the dictionary—would have led to the substitution of the correct *hurtled*. A government ad referred to a certain man as "one of Canada's leading sculptures." Of course these may have been spelling errors, but if so they are due to confusing two similar words. In the spelling section you will find a list of words often confused in that way (see pp. 332-333); study it, familiarize yourself with the words, so that you won't make such embarrassing careless errors. And reread your drafts carefully, for no such list can include all the potential troublemakers; the *hurdle-hurtle* and *sculpture-sculptor* pairs wouldn't appear on conventional lists of this kind—yet each tripped up an experienced writer. Some other often confused pairs are included in Exercise 10B below (pp. 251-252).

"Wrong word" choices that can't be blamed on spelling can be troublesome too. Even if readers can figure out what a writer intended, they won't enjoy having to do so—and their estimate of the writer's intelligence will plummet. A news account included this sentence: "Officials think the incidence of computer crime is not nearly as great as tends to be purported." The writer evidently didn't know that *purported* is not a synonym for *reported*; perhaps he was also reaching for some meaning like "proposed" or "estimated." In any event, the wrong word makes him look ignorant. A student wrote this:

> I call the committee's decision regretful.

But the last word should of course be *regrettable*. Another news account referred to "the number of deaths that emerged from that incident." But the word *emerged* is simply not logical in that context; *resulted* would be right.

## b. **Idiom**

The exercises in idiom elsewhere in this book deal mainly with what prepositions are idiomatic with certain other words for certain meanings. But there are other kinds of idioms as well. No one familiar with English should have any difficulty understanding expressions like "put in an appearance" or "behind the times" or "not cut out for," though they would sound odd if translated literally into another language. Idioms are often metaphorical, proverbial, or colloquial or slangy, and often they are clichés as well: mind your *p*'s and *q*'s, know your onions, spill the beans, lay an egg, in the soup, on the carpet, behind the eight-ball, bolt from the blue, fly-by-night, put your foot in it, and so on. But the main trouble writers have with idioms—aside from those with prepositions—is in failing to use everyday words in the way that they idiomatically work in English. The result is often similar to a "wrong word" choice. For example, the student who wrote

> DRAFT: She obviously enjoys lavishing herself in colourful clothes and jewellery.

didn't understand how the verb *lavish* works. Two kinds of revision are possible. Change the word:

> REVISED: She obviously enjoys dolling up in colourful clothes and jewellery.

(the slangy term is at least more acceptable than the error), or rephrase to use the verb idiomatically:

REVISED: She obviously enjoys lavishing colourful clothes and jewellery on herself.

Here's another student sentence:

DRAFT: I have long come to realize how precious time is.

The first part needed revising to make it idiomatic; again, there's more than one possibility:

REVISED: I have long since come to realize how precious time is.
REVISED: I long ago came to realize how precious time is.

Another example:

DRAFT: The circumstances demand you to pay close attention.

To someone whose native language isn't English, the words *demand* and *require* may seem almost synonymous in such a context; but English idiom won't allow *demand* followed by an infinitive like *to pay*:

REVISED: The circumstances require you to pay close attention.

Or, if the word *demand* is preferable, then changing the infinitive to a *that*-clause makes it idiomatic:

REVISED: The circumstances demand that you pay close attention.

An example from a newsmagazine:

The Pope officiated the beatification ceremony.

The trouble here is that the verb *officiate* is not transitive; it shouldn't be used with a direct object. Here it should have been "officiated at." Another student's sentence:

Such quality is characteristic of his work on a whole.

The writer confused two idiomatic phrases; "on a whole" has to be changed to either "on the whole" or "as a whole." Similarly, the following pairs are often misused: *for his part* and *on his behalf, take part in,* and *partake of;* make sure you use the phrase that means what you want to say.

> *"When I use a word," Humpty Dumpty said, in a rather scornful tone, "it means just what I choose it to mean—neither more nor less."*      (Lewis Carroll)

## c. Denotation and Connotation

Words that *denote* much the same thing can *connote* quite different things or attitudes. For example, if you disapproved of someone's being slow to part with his money, you would call him *stingy, cheap, mean, niggardly,* or—somewhat less negatively—*parsimonious, tightfisted, close*; if you approved of his saving ways, however, you would call him *thrifty, economical, frugal.* And for the opposite sort there is a similar range of adjectives: *profligate, spendthrift, extravagant, liberal, generous, lavish, munificent.*

---

## Exercise 10A

Label each of the following words or phrases as having *positive, negative,* or *neutral* connotations; underline any which you think could have different connotations depending on context, tone, or some other variable.

| | | |
|---|---|---|
| frivolous | stewed | rustic |
| fatty | decrepit | ignorant |
| smooth | rich | stupid |
| oak tree | sapling | textbook |
| Cadillac | dictionary | overstuffed chair |
| grapefruit | pale | electrifying |
| limpid | green | snowy |
| neat | white | yellow |
| black | raunchy | satisfactory |
| painted | sham | tiny |
| simulated | slender | competent |
| maverick | nice | punctual |
| rebel (noun) | miserly | prodigal |

For at least five of those you underlined, compose sentences using them in order to illustrate their different connotations. For example:

It was a perfect afternoon for something as frivolous as a frisbee match.
She's so frivolous about her studies that she deserves to fail.

---

## Exploration 10A

A thesaurus can be an excellent aid. It can not only help you find better words to express an idea, but it can also help you to think, to discover ideas. During *inventing*, for example, you can use a thesaurus to turn up synonyms and near-synonyms that spark new trains of thought, different ways of looking at a subject, slight shades of difference in meaning that can open up new approaches and perspectives.

By all means avail yourself of the help a thesaurus can provide. But at the same time beware of the main danger of a thesaurus: what are often listed as synonyms are not words that mean exactly the same thing. Far from it. For example, under *patience* in one thesaurus you can find such widely different words as *persistence, submission, constancy,* and *inexcitability*, words not at all alike in denotation, let alone in connotation. When you use a thesaurus, the best safeguard against going astray with your use of words (especially words you aren't fully familiar with) is to consult your dictionary at the same time. You should never use a thesaurus without having your dictionary open in front of you as well.

By way of exploration, look up in a thesaurus the words *elegance* and *transparent*. List and define (using your dictionary) all the synonyms you can find for each. (You should be able to find at least twenty for each). When you have done that, choose one of the groups of synonyms, select five words from that list, and write two or three paragraphs explaining the differences among them. To do so, you will probably need to use the methods of classification, definition, and comparison and contrast. Further, use concrete and specific examples and illustrations to make the meanings clear.

Or do the same for some other word that you find interesting and that has a plethora of supposed synonyms.

---

> *English usage is sometimes more*
> *than mere taste, judgment, and*
> *education—sometimes it's sheer*
> *luck, like getting across the street.*
> (E. B. White)

## d. Usage

Certain words and phrases are especially prone to misuse—and not just by inexperienced writers. For example a book review contained the following sentence:

> The prairie landscape dominates with its enormity.

The writer should have known that *enormity* does not mean "enormousness"; *enormity* has nothing to do with physical size; rather it means "extreme wickedness" or "outrageousness."

Another published review included this:

> The subject of her new novel, equally intriguing as that of her first, is the behind-the-scenes action in the advertising world.

But *equally...as* is weak usage. It should have been "as intriguing as" or, after mention of the first novel's subject. "The subject of her new novel is equally intriguing."

Another professional wrote this:

> It is not too fulsome to say that some of the best television plays have been seen on *Masterpiece Theatre*.

The attempt at suavity backfires for readers who care about the language, for *fulsome* means cloying, offensively excessive, loathsome, disgusting. Just remember that the *ful-* part of this word is related to *foul*.

We frequently read and hear sentences like

> There are presently nine people on the committee.

and

> A report is expected momentarily.

The second sentence would be correct if it said "A report is expected presently," since *presently* means "soon" or "in a little while"; *momentarily* is the adverbial form of *momentary*, which means "lasting a little while." The confusion surrounding these words in the minds of many people is such that you probably should avoid them both—unless you use them correctly in something written for an audience whose sophistication you are sure of. Otherwise, say "now" or "at present" or "soon" or "shortly" or "in a moment" or "for a moment" or "temporarily"—whichever best suits the meaning you want.

Here is a sentence from a student's essay:

> The most essential factor in cold-weather camping is choosing the right equipment.

The weakness of words like *factor* will be taken up later in this chapter (see Jargon, pp. 268-275); here it is the word *essential* that demands our attention. It is what is called an "absolute": something is either essential or it's not; one thing can't be more or less essential than another. The student should have used the word *important* instead. Here are some other such absolutes, words that do not admit of degree; if you find one in your draft, make sure you haven't modified it with a word like *more, most, less, least, rather, somewhat,* or *very,* or that you haven't otherwise compared it:

| | | |
|---|---|---|
| essential | final | perfect |
| necessary | right | unique |
| full | wrong | absolute |
| empty | unanimous | equal |

Note that you can still express degree without violating such absolutes by using such phrases as "almost empty," "more nearly perfect," and "closer to unanimous."

A magazine article included this:

> Last week the new MP stood in the local school gymnasium addressing a small crowd comprised of the faithful and the curious.

Since *comprise* means "consist of" or "include," this sentence should have used the word *composed.* Keep the two words distinct in your mind. Here is how they should be used:

> Canada comprises ten provinces and two territories.
> Canada is composed of ten provinces and two territories.
> Ten provinces and two territories compose Canada.

You can avoid many slips if you remember never to use *of* after *comprised*; use it only after *composed.*

Try to avoid the word *as* in the sense of *for, since, because.* It can be ambiguous:

> There is to be no ceremony or hearse for Lycidas as he is being carried off by the tides.
> During that period things were not looking gloomy in the arts either, as they were becoming more creative.
> I have stopped biting my nails, Father, as you have asked me to.

The word *person* is a perfectly good one, of course. But its recent over-use, probably to avoid the sexually specific sense of *man*, has left it almost unavoidably tainted. Therefore try to avoid the word *person* unless you modify it with an adjective, for then it has less of the flavour of jargon: *a talented person; an informed person; a peculiar person.* If you want a plural sense, use the word *people*, not *persons*.

Similarly, the word *individual* has been so over-used to mean simply *person* that you should try to use it only as an adjective: *an individual design; individual requests.* If you're careful, you can use it to mean *a single person seen as distinct from all other people.*

The word *use* is also a perfectly good one, though it too is over-used, especially as a noun in wordy phrases like *the use of.* But don't try to aggrandize it by substituting *utilize* or *utilization*; nor can you expect to get away with substituting the pretentious *employ* and *employment.* Because of what we are writing about in this book, we often use the word *use*—usually, we hope, as a verb and with some justification. But we're sure you can find places where we could have used some other locution. (Try your hand at this paragraph, for example).

One final word, *hopefully*, is undeniably common, and there is some justice in the claim that it is a legitimate sentence modifier, like *truthfully* or *finally.* But many people frown on its being used as a synonym for *It is to be hoped that* or *I hope.* It can still be used acceptably, as in this sentence from Roderick Haig-Brown's *Fisherman's Fall*:

> The first type [of small-stream estuaries] is the most difficult and I suspect the least productive; the fish are usually scattered and one can only wade out hopefully with the last of the ebb and retreat gradually before the flood.

If you don't use it like this, as an adverb clearly modifying a particular verb, don't use it. In fact you might prefer to avoid it altogether, for it has become hopelessly muddied by loose use.

These and other examples of weak usage will not offend everyone, of course. But why take chances on your audience's being composed entirely of people who don't care enough about the language to be annoyed (not *aggravated*) by such careless usage? As a student, you know that your instructors will probably care. Familiarize yourself with the common pitfalls so that you can avoid them in your writing, and in your speaking as well. If you consistently avoid them, you'll never have to worry about their alienating anyone in your audience. Even more important, if you develop habits of precision and good usage you will be building your own confidence in writing for *any* kind of audience.

---

## Exercise 10B

Here is a list of some commonly confused pairs and other often misused terms. In a good dictionary—preferably one that includes notes on usage—look up each word. Copy out the definitions and advice on usage for all those whose meanings and correct usage you were not already sure of. Then compose a sentence using each of the words correctly. Keep these notes handy as a checklist to use when you are revising diction.

| | |
|---|---|
| affect, effect | individual, person |
| aggravate, annoy | individuality, individualism |
| alternate, alternative | infer, imply |
| amount, number | less, fewer |
| belabour, labour | lie, lay |
| between, among | material, materialistic |
| can, may | persons, people |
| continual, continuous | real, realistic |
| disinterested, uninterested | simplistic, simple |
| fortuitous, fortunate | varying, various |

PLEONASM, *n. An army of words
escorting a corporal of thought.*
(Ambrose Bierce, *The Devil's Dictionary*)

## 2. ECONOMY (AVOIDING WORDINESS)

The preceding chapter includes advice on cutting deadwood out of sentences (see pp. 220-223). Here is more advice on avoiding wordiness, this time focussing on certain kinds of words and phrases that cause it.

Some all-too-common phrases are redundant because the idea expressed by one part is present in the other. For example:

| | |
|---|---|
| absolutely perfect | general consensus |
| advance planning | mental attitude |
| advance warning | necessary prerequisite |
| basic fundamentals | new innovation |
| character trait | new record |
| circle around | other alternatives |
| close scrutiny | past history |
| completely destroyed | personal friend |
| consensus of opinion | precautionary measure |
| continue on | reflect back |
| end result | regress back |
| enter into | return back |
| erode away | revert back |
| exact same | serious crisis |
| fellow colleagues | share in common |
| final outcome | stereotyped image |
| final result | surround on all sides |
| flee away | true facts |

Each of these needs only one word to say the same thing; for example *trait* (or *characteristic*), *scrutiny, continue, erode, consensus, record, precaution, regress, stereotype.*

Other phrases that produce wordiness are similar to clichés in that they spring ready-made to people's lips and pens. These should almost always be reduced to their shorter equivalents:

at a later date (later)
at the present time (now)
at the same time that (while)
by means of (by)
despite the fact that (though, although)
due to the fact that, because of the fact that, on account of the fact that (because)
during the course of (during)
for the purpose of (for, to)
for the reason that (because)
in all likelihood (likely, probably)
in all probability (probably)
in connection with (about)
in height (high)
in length (long)
in the event that (if)
in the near future (soon)
in the not too distant future (soon)
in the neighbourhood of (about, near)
is of the opinion (thinks)
period of time (period, time)
previous to (before)
prior to (before)
up until, up till (until, till)
with the exception of (excepting, except for)

Note that almost all these reductions get rid of unnecessary prepositional phrases.
Still other such phrases are usually mere fillers, like "um" and "uh" and "y'know" in colloquial speech. Surprisingly often they can be cut entirely:

in fact
in character
in colour
in nature
in number
in shape
in size
manner, in manner
is a person who
is one of those who
personal, personally
the fact that
use of, the use of, by the use of, through the use of, usage of

Cutting one of these will occasionally force you to change another word or two, but not often.
Some other such phrases, even if they can't be entirely cut, can usually be reduced. Like *there is* and *there are* constructions, they are often signals that the

sentences in which they appear are wordily constructed:

> in the form of
> on the part of
> with the result that

Note that they inevitably include at least one preposition. If you examine your drafts carefully for unnecessary prepositional phrases, as suggested earlier (see p. 221), you'll spot these.

All these wordy phrases blur meaning and blunt effectiveness. The more you can eliminate such excess baggage, the easier your readers' task will be and the more effective your writing will be.

*How forcible are right words!* (Job 6:25)

# 3. VIGOUR: CHOOSING EFFECTIVE WORDS, AVOIDING WEAK DICTION

> *Particularity will keep you from*
> *sentimentality.*       (Theodore Roethke)

## a.  Abstract and Concrete; General and Specific

Concrete words refer to objects or qualities we can know about through one or more of our physical senses, things we can see, hear, touch, taste, smell, or feel as movement. Abstract words refer to ideas or qualities we can know only with our minds. For example:

| *concrete* | *abstract* |
|---|---|
| roommate | companionship |
| Lake Louise | beauty |
| Toronto | urban |
| pain | illness |
| University of Manitoba | education |
| airplane | transportation |
| Charlie Chaplin | comedy |
| shiver | temperature |
| quiche | gastronomy |
| battery | power |

A related distinction is that between the general and the specific. General terms refer to classes of things like cats, trucks, and cities; specific terms refer to members of those classes, like Blue-point Siamese, pickups, and provincial capitals. Blue-point Siamese are specific members of the class *cats*; pickups are specific members of the class *trucks*; provincial capitals are specific members of the class *cities*. But such more specific terms sometimes themselves designate classes. For example Dodge pickups are specific members of the class *pickups*;

Fredericton is a specific member of the class *provincial capitals*. When you reach a single specific member, such as *Fredericton*, you are at the end of the line. *Dodge pickups* is quite specific, but there's still further to go if one wants to.

Usually, abstract words are more general, concrete words more specific. But the correspondence is not exact. Consider the following range of terms (think of a spectrum), which moves from the most specific to the most general:

IBM Selectric (#98-57061)—IBM Selectric—typewriter—office equipment—liquid asset—wealth

As you see, the first item in this sequence refers to a specific, individual object, one of a kind. Each succeeding term is more general, denoting a larger class: there are many Selectrics, but only one numbered 98-57061; there are more typewriters than there are Selectrics; there are many more pieces of office equipment than there are typewriters. And so far all these terms are concrete. But with the phrase "liquid asset" we are on the thin line between concrete and abstract. And with the final term, *wealth*, the language has become entirely abstract.

---

## Exercise 10C

Starting with each general and abstract term on the left, compose a list of at least five items that are increasingly specific and concrete.

*Examples:*

art—literature—fiction—novels—Canadian novels—*The Stone Angel*
history—European history—European wars—the Napoleonic Wars—the Waterloo campaign—the Battle of Waterloo

entertainment—
industry—
science—
protection—
athletics—

---

If you have a choice between an abstract term and a concrete term, you should usually choose the concrete; it will make your writing more precise and more readable. And rather than try to make do with a vague generalization, supply a concrete example or illustration. Rather than "He is very wealthy," write "He has lots of money; he holidays in the Caribbean every year." Rather than write a memo to your boss saying something like "It is my belief that we need to improve our security arrangements," try "I'm convinced that this store needs better locks on its doors and an alarm system for the rear ground-floor windows." In a letter home, don't write, "I've found interesting ways to occupy my limited leisure time"—or if you do, follow it with something like "During the few hours a week I can spare from my Economics, English, and History texts, I've found that chess is a good relaxation, and for physical exercise I've joined the hiking club."

Of course we all need to use abstract and general terms; much formal and intellectual writing depends on them. And writing that was entirely concrete could be tiring and hard to follow. The point is that most of us can improve our writing by making it more concrete and specific.

Here is a one-paragraph piece written by a student. Note the generous sprinkling of vivid concrete details, and note how much the effectiveness of the paragraph depends on them. As you read, your mind latches onto those concrete details; their cumulative effect is such that by the end you have a solid feeling of the tangible realities of the north. The concrete details pull you closer to the prose and what it's saying. (The rather wooden phrase "The procurement of supplies" is the only part of the paragraph that pushes the reader away). And note the effectiveness of the concluding analogy.

### The True North

Many of us who live comfortably in the lower mainland of British Columbia entertain false impressions of life in northern Canada. We fancy cozy log cabins with crackling fireplaces, handsome mountains, and virgin forests enveloped by shimmering white snow. The picture is appealing and romantic. But we fail to realize that although the north is breath-taking, it is also uncomfortable, inconvenient, and potentially dangerous. We forget that the snow is present for three quarters of the year, and when the warmer months do arrive, they bring with them wet, muddy ground and the constant plague of mosquitoes. In any season, road travel is difficult because of snow, mud, or below-freezing temperatures. The procurement of supplies is a lengthy and costly procedure in remote areas, usually requiring helicopters to traverse rough terrain. Also, most areas up north are located far from any kind of medical attention—a circumstance worth considering in a region of frostbite, avalanches, rockslides, and wild animals. The north can be compared to an exquisite, yet hard and uncompromising woman. We worship its natural beauty, but we must be prepared to meet all its moods.

Here are two students' one-paragraph definitions of *erosion* . The concreteness in the first helps some, but even that is mostly quite general; the slightly more specific list of eroding agents at the very end marks the first place where the paragraph begins to come alive—but it's too late to save it:

Erosion is a natural process in which the earth's surface is worn away by actions of air, water, and changes in temperature. It is the wearing away of earth or rock. This natural process works very slowly but over the period of hundreds of thousands of years a mountain can be worn down to a plain. The earth's surface is always being eroded by rainfall, running water, ice, and wind.

Now read the second one:

### Erosion

We observe its presence in all corners of the earth—no form of matter is safe from its attack. The process may be violent, like the barrage of the wind against the craggy peak, or the scraping of rock beneath the raging glacier. Also, it can be gentle: the delicate caress of the mist upon the seashore. Whatever its mood, it gnaws persistently, consuming our lands, our society, perhaps even our nerves and our bones. Its hunger can never be appeased. It is the passage of time.

This paragraph is full of concrete and specific images, and though the final metaphor turns to the abstraction of *time*, even that remains strong because it is supported by the concreteness leading up to it. Strong concrete verbs and nouns like *barrage* and *caress* and *gnaws* bolster the effect. Even "corners" adds some concreteness. (Perhaps "raging glacier" is forced, though the writer could argue that she intended the paradoxical personification of the imperceptibly moving glacier as yet "raging," doing violent things to the earth beneath it.) Even assuming that the two writers may have had different purposes in mind, which could affect the amount of specific and concrete diction they used, the second paragraph works better.

---

## *Exploration 10B*

Here are two comparisons of the words *ignorance* and *stupidity* . The first is especially well written, for example making excellent use of parallel sentence structure; but its only concreteness is in the words "books, newspapers, and television"—not much help. The second has some vague concreteness in the first half, but is especially effective because of the example with which it ends.

### 1.

*Ignorance* is defined as the state of being unaware, uninformed, backward, or destitute of knowledge. *Stupidity* is defined as the state of being slow of mind, lacking in intelligence or reasoning power, or being given to unintelligent decisions or acts. The only similarity between the two states is that they are both used to describe a general lack of knowledge. The two terms, however, are definitely not interchangeable. Ignorance is a state in which knowledge is lacking, not because of a lack of intelligence, but because of a lack of exposure to things, such as books, newspapers, and television, which would give knowledge. Stupidity is a state in which knowledge is lacking, not because of a lack of exposure to things which would give knowledge, but because of a lack of intelligence, or an inability to transform information into knowledge. Ignorance and stupidity, which are often considered to be the same, are actually two terms with completely different meanings.

### 2.

#### Stupid Idiot, Ignorant Fool

How many times have you heard someone being called "stupid idiot" or "ignorant fool"? The two words, "stupid" and "ignorant," are often used interchangeably by people who don't realize that the two words have different meanings. Ignorance is a lack of knowledge regarding a fact. Stupidity is the failure to employ the knowledge one possesses regarding a fact. Even though they have different meanings, these two states of mind, stupidity and ignorance, can bring about the same result. For example, a person who is ignorant of the fact that walking in front of a car is dangerous will achieve the same result as the person who, knowing that it is dangerous to walk in front of a car, is stupid enough to do so anyway. Both these people will get hit by the car. Two different states of mind leading to the same result.

The first is more formal, yet it could benefit from some of the concreteness of the second; and the second could benefit from some of the parallelism and tighter coherence of the first. Try combining the two paragraphs into one that includes the best features of both, perhaps increasing the concreteness. While you're at it, get rid of the unnecessary repetition of "the two words" in the second sentence of number 2; you can do it by changing the passive voice to the active voice. You might want also to reduce that sentence's "who" clause to a participial phrase. And is the ending of number 2 a fragment, or is it a justifiable minor sentence?

---

*In order to write good stuff, you have to hate adverbs.*

(Theodore Roethke)

## b.  Modifiers

(1)  Which of the following two sentences is the more effective?

   (a)  The little dog barked loudly and sharply at my left ankle.
   (b)  The puppy yapped at my left ankle.

If you chose (b), you have the right instincts. Its relative shortness makes it snappier, of course; but both the shortness and its general superiority are due mainly to its greater particularity. It depends less on weak modifiers; instead it expresses its meaning through the more specific noun and verb. The general noun *dog* with its adjective *little* has been replaced by the single more specific noun *puppy*; the general verb *barked* with its two adverbs *loudly* and *sharply* has been replaced by the single more specific verb *yapped*.

As you work your way carefully through your draft, look for opportunities to increase the vigour of your style by substituting more precise nouns for adjective-noun combinations and more precise verbs for verb-adverb combinations. Look especially for places where you've used two or more adjectives or adverbs to prop up a weak noun or verb. Particularly in narrative and descriptive writing, your prose will usually be more effective the less it depends on modifiers and the more it expresses its meaning through specific nouns and verbs.

---

### *Exploration 10C*

a.  Compose a brief paragraph describing some simple object, perhaps one within your view at the moment (a plate of food, a vase of flowers, a favourite stuffed animal, an unmade bed, a potted plant, an ornate paper-weight, a piece of furniture...). Use no adjectives, not even verbal ones (present and past participles); depend primarily on vivid nouns.

b.  Compose a brief paragraph describing a simple action, some event or movement which you can see occurring or which you can remember having seen recently (a point during a tennis match, a car pulling away from a curb, a dog rooting in a garbage can, a kid on a bicycle, a sailboat going past, a friend doing a high dive, wind blowing papers off your desk...). Use no adverbs; depend instead on specific verbs.

---

(2) Also check your modifiers for redundancy. For example, the phrase "cruel tyrant" is weaker than simply "tyrant," which contains the sense of *cruel*. To write that someone is "constantly plagued" is redundant, since the sense of *constantly* is sufficiently present in *plagued*. Whenever you can get rid of a modifier without changing meaning, you will increase the effectiveness, for such modifiers do not, as you might think, emphasize the meaning; rather they blur it.

ACTUALLY, *adv. Perhaps; possibly.*
(Ambrose Bierce, *The Devil's Dictionary*)

(3) Look especially for places where you've used such weak qualifiers and intensifiers as these:

| | | | | | | |
|---|---|---|---|---|---|---|
| rather | somewhat | quite | significant | some | very | certainly |
| extremely | actual | actually | real | really | literally | virtually |
| completely | definitely | true | truly | considerable | total | totally |

You can almost always sharpen your meaning either by simply omitting these words or by revising sentences to get rid of them. Look for example at the following sentence:

DRAFT: As long as they keep setting up study panels, there is no real sense of really tackling the problem.

REVISED: As long as they keep setting up study panels, they are not tackling the problem.

The apparent attempt to get emphasis with *real* and *really* produced a muddy "there is" clause with clumsy repetition. The revised version is actually more emphatic. (Should that *actually* be removed?) Here are two more examples; simply cutting the unnecessary word sharpens the sense:

DRAFT: The company has been rather successful in attracting well-qualified applicants.

REVISED: The company has been successful in attracting well-qualified applicants.

(The "rather" may have been intended to create a slightly ironic tone; if its qualifying sense was not ironic, it could be changed to "moderately" or "highly" to convey the precise meaning intended.)

DRAFT: Unfortunately, his explanation did very little to clarify what he meant.

REVISED: Unfortunately, his explanation did little to clarify what he meant.

Such intensifiers as *very* and *really* often have an effect just the opposite of what a writer intends; rather than strengthen the meanings of the words they modify, they make readers think those words weak because they needed propping up. Particularly try to avoid the almost automatically weak phrases "very important" and "very significant."

## c. **Vague Words**

Some of the words discussed above, such as *very* and *rather*, are often empty words. Empty or unnecessarily vague words don't pay their way. They contribute little or nothing to a sentence, and since they nevertheless take up space, both on the page and in readers' minds, they slow the sentence, dissipate its energy. As you revise, be on the lookout for empty or vague terms like these:

| | | | | | | |
|---|---|---|---|---|---|---|
| thing | something | manner | character | nature | a number of | |
| some time ago | position | occurrence | concern | quality | person | |
| beautiful | nice | pleasant | good | bad | certain | deal |

There's no law against them, and they can be used effectively. But they and words like them are potentially dangerous because they invite vagueness. They're worth checking on when you find you've used them. Usually you can strengthen your meaning by substituting more precise, concrete, and specific words. Why call someone a "bad man" when you can more effectively label him a scoundrel, a hypocrite, or a thief? What would readers get from a sentence like "My uncle was a very nice man"? Not much—unless it was followed by a catalogue of his "nice" qualities; and if that were handled well the sentence with "very nice" would be unnecessary anyway. Don't let yourself get trapped into almost empty sentences like this: "Three important things resulted from this occurrence which should concern us all." Words are like expensive gasoline: you want to get the most mileage you can out of them. Don't say "It was a valuable experience" (or "very valuable"); describe what made it valuable. Don't say "That book was very worthwhile"; drop the *very worthwhile* and say what made you feel that reading the book was worth your while. Be specific.

Similarly, check your nouns and—especially—your verbs. Rather than say you "like" or "dislike" something, be as specific as the context will permit: say you adore it or hate it, admire it or despise it, enjoy it or loathe it, relish it or abhor it, revere it or disapprove of it, and so on. A thesaurus, used along with a dictionary, can sometimes help you find words to express your desired meaning most precisely. Sometimes you will want the quiet neutrality of "She entered the room," but don't settle for saying that someone "came" or "walked" into a room if you can sharpen your point by using a more specific verb. Here for example are some possible alternatives:

| | | | | | | | |
|---|---|---|---|---|---|---|---|
| ambled | banged | barged | blew | bounced | bounded | bowed | bowled |
| breezed | brushed | bumbled | burst | cantered | charged | chugged | |
| clomped | clumped | crawled | crept | danced | dawdled | dived | |
| dragged | drifted | eased | edged | flounced | flowed | galloped | |
| gallumphed | inched | jostled | jumped | kow-towed | leaped | limped | |
| loped | lunged | made her way | marched | meandered | minced | | |
| oiled her way | oozed | popped | pounced | pounded | pranced | | |
| progressed | quested | railed | ran | rolled | romped | rushed | sailed |
| sauntered | scampered | scraped | scrounged | shrugged | sidled | skipped | |
| slid | slipped | sloped | sneaked | sped | spun | squeezed | staggered |
| stamped | stole | stomped | straggled | streaked | strode | strolled | |
| struggled | strutted | stumbled | swam | swept | swung | teetered | |
| toddled | tooted | toppled | traipsed | tramped | trampled | tripped | |
| trod | tromped | trundled | twisted | waded | waddled | wafted | |
| wandered | wangled her way | whizzed | wobbled | worked her way | | | |

If the subject is plural, still other verbs are possible:

crowded    erupted    filed    paraded    streamed    surged    swarmed

Some of the verbs listed above are metaphorical, but one could use even stronger metaphors:

browsed    bruised    charmed her way    clawed her way    fiddled    galoshed
groaned    ground    pomped    queened her way    snailed    snow-shoed
shaked    sneered his way    swanked    sailed with all flags flying

Don't settle for vague or neutral terms unless their vagueness or neutrality is precisely what you want. When possible use livelier words; otherwise your prose may be lifeless.

See also Abstract and Concrete above (pp. 254-258); other vague and empty words are discussed under Jargon, later in the chapter (pp. 268-275).

---

### Exercise 10D

For each of the neutral verbs below, supply as many livelier, more specific alternatives as you can think of. When you can't think of any more, turn to your dictionary and a thesaurus for help. As you list them, think about the different connotations of each.

| | | | |
|---|---|---|---|
| get | talked | took | wanted |
| saw | put | threw | hit |
| said | found | ate | cut |

---

## d. Clichés, Trite Expressions

Clichés are phrases that have been used so much that they are too familiar. They are so familiar that they pop into our heads without our needing to think about them. And that makes them dangerous. For if we use a cliché without thinking about it, it will probably be weak and wordy. "He never touched liquor in any shape or form" is much less vigorous and effective than "He never touched liquor." A cliché-ridden style is a boring style; there's scarcely enough to keep the mind awake:

> She knew deep down inside that he was no great shakes, just a common or garden variety fellow, but she knew also that her friends looked upon him with favour. So in order to make them green with envy she left no stone unturned in her efforts to make him fall for her hook, line, and sinker. And to him she came out of nowhere, like a bolt from the blue, and soon he was well and truly caught in her net. But lo and behold, once she had him in her power she fell head over heels in love, and she knew in her heart that she would stick with him through thick and thin.

Boring. Occasionally a cliché can be used on purpose to convey an idea quickly and easily; for example in a sentence that is already heavy with information, a cliché can come as a welcome relief for a reader. (Is "welcome relief" a cliché?) But if you let clichés creep into your writing without your knowing it, they are almost sure to bore from within. (Occasionally too a cliché can be used successfully if it is given a humorous twist or otherwise made unusual; did we succeed with "bore from within" in the preceding sentence? Or is that twist itself a cliché by now?)

Many clichés were once lively expressions, vivid metaphors and the like, often with alliteration or a folksy charm, all of which makes them tempting, especially to less experienced writers. It was their attractiveness that led to their overuse in the first place. If you're not sure about some expression you feel tempted to use, ask the opinion of someone else, preferably someone with more experience.

Thoughtless use of clichés can also cause other weaknesses and errors, such as the misspelled "on tenderhooks." A television commentator covering an election informed us that "all three parties are running neck and neck," ("And neck," one wants to add.) A student, trapped by the apparently innocent little phrase "in my eyes," produced an unintended chuckle by seeming to attribute to them an olfactory sense:

> It is the rose's beautiful, velvet petals, and its entrancing, sweet fragrance that in my eyes make it so beautiful.

(How effective is the repeated *beautiful* in that sentence?) Another, thinking—or rather not thinking—of the clichés "turn the tables on someone" and "turn things around," confused them, and the reader, with

> They could turn the tables around.

And another combined clichés to produce this delightful mixed metaphor:

> That is really the problem with politicians: they're too busy circling their wagons and shooting inwards to see the forest for the trees.

Clichés that are also metaphors are especially dangerous because a writer who uses one without thinking sometimes won't even realize that a metaphor is present. And so one finds such embarrassing errors as "tow the line," "the dye is cast," "a long (or tough) road to hoe," and (in a recent newspaper article) "It's time Albertans reigned in their expectations." If you use clichés, use them carefully and consciously; otherwise your readers will think you're writing in your sleep.

Clichés are far too numerous for any collection to be complete. And more are always on the way, for today's clever phrase will likely become tomorrow's cliché. But here is at least a brief list to suggest the sorts of phrases we all need to be on guard against:

| | |
|---|---|
| any way, shape or form | bigger and better |
| abreast of the times | a slave to custom |
| drastic action | blushing bride |
| takes the cake | once in a blue moon |
| quantum leap | born and bred |
| acid test | dissolved in tears |

| | |
|---|---|
| green as grass | crying one's heart out |
| plain as the nose on your face | wreathed in smiles |
| happily ever after | as good as gold |
| cute as a button | fighting like cats and dogs |
| bored to tears | down in the dumps |
| blue Monday | bright-eyed and bushy-tailed |
| smoke-filled room | bright as a new penny |
| beat a hasty retreat | budding genius |
| hard as nails | far and above |
| serves no useful purpose | as a matter of course |
| in the long run | seeing is believing |
| various and sundry | ran the gamut of |
| take someone to task | last but not least |

Almost any trite, hackneyed language—including such clichés, some slang, mere fillers, and much jargon—is weak and wordy simply because it is worn out from overuse. Tired words and phrases lack the strength to express an idea forcefully, let alone deliver a punch. Even worse, like weeds that deprive other plants of nourishment, such words and phrases sap the strength of their surroundings, weakening whole sentences and paragraphs. Cultivate your garden carefully.

But by all means begin an essay with "Once upon a time" if you can make it work, perhaps ironically, humorously—in other words, if you know what you're doing.

---

### Exercise 10E

Here are some flat, vague, general, abstract, and just plain dull, uninteresting sentences for you to practise on. Liven them up in any way you think will work. Use your imagination on the possible contexts. Even be outrageous (once or twice).

1. I think there is possibly one thing which might make me think differently about it someday.
2. No one who was present in the room at the time evinced any reaction whatsoever by way of movement.
3. He said something funny.
4. The construction had a beautiful look about it, somehow.
5. Arnold isn't very interesting to be with.
6. It was a nice sort of remark to hear.
7. Having arrived, we took our seats among those who were already assembled.
8. I went into the corral with some trepidation, and finally put a saddle on the old horse.
9. Like a bolt from the blue, I though of what to do.
10. This unpleasant experience caused me to reconsider the motivations I might be harbouring with a view to making a different kind of impression the next time I found myself in anything like such a situation.

---

## 4. GRACE

Grace is more a quality of sentences and paragraphs than of diction—though a major destroyer of grace, jargon, is the subject of the next section. There remain only a few smaller matters to point to here.

### a. Tone

A good deal of what we mean by "tone" has to do with rhetorical stance, the major discussion of which is in Chapter VII (see pp. 151-157). Here we need only remind you that during revision you should check to see if you stuck to the stance you chose early on. You might, as you revise, even find that your choice didn't work out quite as you expected, and decide to make some changes. For whatever reason, now is the time to adjust the tone. Do you want to refer, for example to *the movies*, to *film*, or to *the cinema*? If your draft seems a little too formal, you can substitute some less formal words for some formal ones, perhaps even throwing in a few contractions. If it seems too impersonal, inserting only a few *you*'s can make a great difference. If it seems too flat or staid, you can increase the amount of concreteness and specificity, add a little alliteration, introduce a few metaphors and similes. Or vice versa.

### b. Slang

Whatever your rhetorical stance, you will not likely want to use much slang. A little goes a long way. At this point, you will want to make sure that you haven't introduced any slang unconsciously. Especially be sure that you haven't unthinkingly mixed one kind of diction with another. Slang can be particularly damaging. Look for example at the badly mixed diction in this paragraph. The student seemed to want to be slangy and formal at the same time, but the two kinds of diction clash:

#### One Far-out Movie!

What a great flick! It was a tale about this cool ex-jock who had the book thrown at him for working-over a cop and ripping off a car. While doing time in the joint he is coerced into moulding a prisoner's football team to take on the guards. It was immediately apparent that many of the cons desired an opportunity to get square with the guards who they felt had been shafting them. The context evolved into a battle which pitted the symbolic factions of good and evil against each other in a confrontation of unbelievable intensity.

---

### *Exercise 10F*

Revise the preceding unfortunate paragraph. Get rid of the slang; aim for a medium, informal rhetorical stance, with some colloquialism (for example *doing time* might stay, but *joint* should go). Is any of the language too formal? Try not to lose any of the liveliness along with the slang; in fact, you might want to increase the complexity of the style.

---

### Exploration 10D

(a) Write a one- or two-paragraph definition of the word *slang*. Consult as many dictionaries or other sources as you think necessary, but make your definition depend in part on your own experience: use some examples current in your own vocabulary.

(b) By consulting your own experience and interviewing a few friends, compile a short list (say twenty terms) of slang words and phrases currently in fashion. Then, for each term on your list, write a sentence using it and a second sentence that says essentially the same thing without using it.

(c) In another paragraph, using at least two examples, explain why it is risky to use slang in most writing. To what degree does the risk hinge upon questions of audience or purpose?

## c. Coined Words

Occasionally—but probably no more than once in any one piece of writing, unless perhaps a highly descriptive or humorous piece—occasionally you can add a touch of sparkle by making up a new word or using a word in an unconventional way, for example as a different part of speech. In the sample essay in Chapter I, for instance, the writer made the noun *torrent* into a verb, *torrenting*. Another student turned a noun into a verb in this sentence:

> It rained and snowed and hailed and stormed: then it blue-skyed.

Perhaps one could get away with combining *mud* and *puddle* , if the context was clear, and write of stepping in a *muddle*. Someone coined the word *verbicide* to describe the way some people murder the language. Another writer came up with *blandeur* to characterize the kind of music heard at Hollywood galas. But be careful not to make up new words accidentally; they will get marked *nsw* (no such word), for they are obviously unintentional, careless substitutes for perfectly good words that already exist. Words like these should never have got past the reviser's eyes: *sarcastism, incentivated, resoluted, reflectance, solitudity, obstination*. A professional writer even wrote of "such illuminous guests," evidently not content with *illustrious*, or confusing it with *luminous*, which wouldn't comfortably carry the sense of *luminary* anyway. And remember that, properly speaking, there is no such word as *irregardless*.

## d. Variety

Variety is usually a virtue. Different kinds and lengths of paragraphs and of sentences give a desirable variety to a piece of writing as well as enabling you to emphasize what you want (see pp. 151-157, 193-195 and 228-229). Similarly, even within a chosen rhetorical stance you will want to vary your level of diction. For example, if you are writing a formal letter of application, try inserting just one or two less formal words or phrases, perhaps even something slightly colloquial, to add a personal touch, to let your readers know that you're a human being rather than a machine. And now and then shift your level of diction to emphasize a word. For example, note how in the following sentences the student writers have shifted their diction one way or the other to make a single word stand out amid its surroundings.

> While the wind blows caressingly and the birds sing harmoniously and the sky is filled with vivid blue, I sit in my room and do homework.

(The word *homework* is also emphasized by being placed last.)

> When the snow had melted and spring came, the flowers mysteriously opened.
>
> Taking an industrial first-aid course will greatly augment your chances of getting a job.
>
> He attempted to persuade me in the most eloquent terms to get lost.

See also the example paragraph on p. 195.

Nevertheless it can be dangerous to introduce variety simply for variety's sake. If you consciously use a different word just to avoid repeating a word, you may fall into the trap called "elegant variation." Read the following sentence:

> Fear is a subjective human experience characterized by anxious anticipation of pain or distress; paranoia is an extreme kind of fear identified by suspicion or mistrust of people.

The student wrote *identified* in the second clause merely to avoid repeating *characterized*. But such variety only confuses readers: they instinctively want to know why the different word was used when the circumstances seem so similar. Here the parallel structure of the two clauses is itself enough to demand that *characterized* appear in both.

In a recent book about the attack on Pearl Harbor, the author describes the approaching Japanese planes in the following over-written paragraph (we have omitted the details about various altitudes so that the verbal structure of the sentences stands out more clearly):

> High over the Pacific, Nagumo's airmen winged their way toward the target. Lining the center of the formation...streaked ten triangles of high-level bombers under Fuchida's personal command. Flanking to port...sped Takahashi's...dive bombers. To starboard Murata's...torpedo planes roared....Covering the entire force... snarled Itaya's fighters.

For the sake of variation, and perhaps in an attempt to make it all seem more dramatic, he used a different verb in each sentence: *winged ...streaked...sped ...roared...snarled.* The result is almost silly; *flew* and *were* would be better (an instance where the more specific words are not in the best); or perhaps some restructuring of the sentences would remove the necessity for five separate verbs. (And note the four parallel sentences in a row—"Lining....Flanking....To starboard....Covering...." Only "To starboard" slightly breaks the pattern. Would some variety of sentence structure improve the paragraph? Here is a sentence from *Funeral Games*, Mary Renault's novel about the heirs of Alexander the Great:

> At all the gates, with a hubbub of shouting men, wailing children, burbling camels, bleating goats and cackling poultry, the country people who feared war were pouring into the city, and the city people who feared famine were pouring out.

Here the appropriate variety of vivid participles modifying their various nouns works superbly. And in the last part of the sentence she repeats the verb *pouring* in the two parallel clauses; it would be much less effective if, just for variety, she had changed the second one to something like *streaming*.

### e.  Avoiding Sexist Language

Historically, the noun *man* and the pronoun *he* were understood to refer either to all humanity or to a male, depending on the context. Today, however, more and more people understand them to refer specifically to the male sex. Times change. What was formerly considered standard expression is now perceived as sexism in language. Therefore it is increasingly important for a writer to avoid sexism in his use of language. A sentence like the preceding, for example, with its masculine pronoun *his* referring to *writer*, should be revised; there are probably more women writers than men, and the pronoun *his* unfairly and unrealistically implies that any given writer must be a man. Some people choose to substitute *he or she* or *his or her* in such instances:

A writer should avoid sexism in his or her use of language.

But many readers find this annoying, especially if it occurs often. And the form *his/her* strikes many readers as awkward and visually cluttering. (The *s/he* dodge is close to absurd: not only is it impossible to pronounce, but it also offers no equivalents for *his* and *her, him* and *her,* or *himself* and *herself*.) One can of course alternate between masculine and feminine pronouns, using *she* in half of such instances and *he* in the other half. But this too, over a succession of pages, sounds gimmicky or like tokenism, and becomes tiresome. Usually the easiest way to accommodate reality is to switch from singular to plural:

Writers should avoid sexism in their use of language.

If it is clear from the context that the topic is *writers*, one can sometimes use the pronoun *one*, which often sounds too stiff and formal, or you can shift to the more informal second-person pronoun *you*:

You should avoid sexism in your use of language.

But often the best way to avoid the problem is to revise out the pronouns entirely—and achieve a tighter prose while you're about it:

A writer [or *Writers*] should avoid using sexist language.

Sexism also appears in language that enforces stereotypes. Not all cooks are women—far from it. Not all athletes are men—far from it. Many men are frail and frivolous; many women are robust and raunchy. Women, as well as men, drive trucks; men, as well as women, take care of babies. The generalization

A lawyer should have a good rapport with his client.

could as well be written as

A lawyer should have a good rapport with her client.

But it could also be put in the plural:

> Lawyers should have a good rapport with their clients.

or even—avoiding the pronoun altogether—

> Lawyers and clients should have a good rapport.

or

> A lawyer and a client should have a good rapport.

Try to avoid even implicit sexism in your writing—and your thinking. If you refer to Earle Birney, don't follow by referring to *Ms. Atwood*; say *Margaret Atwood*. If you later refer to *Birney*—using the surname only—refer also to *Atwood*. If Birney is a *poet*, so also is Atwood a *poet*: don't call her a *poetess*.

Your language reveals the way you perceive the world. Make sure your readers perceive you the way you want them to. You can improve both your prose and your image by cutting out sexism, whether it's explicit or only implicit. Since we are all conditioned by usages customary in the past, we should attend particularly to these matters in the present, during revision.

---

> *Utterances in jargon are like bird calls:*
> *they identify the species and little more.*
> (Ben Ross Schneider, Jr.,
> *Travels in Computerland*)

> *But if thought corrupts language,*
> *language can also corrupt thought.*
> (George Orwell, "Politics
> and the English Language")

## Jargon

Jargon is a kind of language that virtually precludes clarity, economy, vigour, and grace. Jargon is gobbledygook, bafflegab, doublespeak, and often simply gibberish. It is the kind of language favoured by many bureaucrats and other people in government, including the military; by many scientists and social scientists and other professionals, including teachers; and unfortunately by many ordinary people and students because they hear and see it so often and, unthinkingly, associate it with prestige and power. In various degrees, it is characterized by

> a. fuzziness rather than clarity,
> b. wordiness rather than economy,
> c. weakness rather than vigour,
> d. awkwardness and ugliness rather than grace.

In his 1946 essay "Politics and the English Language," George Orwell quoted the following verse from Ecclesiastes:

I returned and saw under the sun, that the race is not to the swift, nor the battle to the strong, neither yet bread to the wise, nor yet riches to men of understanding, nor yet favour to men of skill; but time and chance happeneth to them all.

He then translated this "good English" into a jargon-filled paragraph which he calls "modern English of the worst sort":

Objective consideration of contemporary phenomena compels the conclusion that success or failure in competitive activities exhibits no tendency to be commensurate with innate capacity, but that a considerable element of the unpredictable must invariably be taken into account.

This he admits "is a parody, but not a very gross one." It seems mild compared to the kind of unintelligible language so common today. Here is an announcement from a school board:[1]

Programmatic assumptions will be specified, competencies identified, a rationale developed and instructional objectives stated. Pre-assessment, post-assessment, learning alternatives and remediation will be an integral part of instructional modules within the framework of program development.

What does it mean? And how about this one, from a U.S. government office having to do with education:

This matter will be critiqued and augmented through individual and iterative reviews by individuals representing the scholarly, school and localized community of sufficient range to obtain replicability consensus of breadth of views to form substantial documentation which will record the needs assessment.

Even in just these examples you can recognize several of the stylistic weaknesses discussed elsewhere in this book, such as

— passive voice
— overdependence on the verb *be*
— clutter of prepositional phrases
— unpleasant sound patterns and lack of rhythm.

Obviously, whatever jargon creeps into your drafts can be attacked at any time during the revising process. But we've included jargon in this chapter because it is often recognizable by its diction: big words where small words would do, unnecessary words, vague and abstract and general diction, and "vogue" words,

---

[1] For these and some of the other examples quoted in this chapter, and for many more similar examples, not only of jargon but of other abuses of English, as well as other interesting discussions of language, see the following: Joseph Gold, ed., *In the Name of Language!* (Toronto: Macmillan of Canada, 1975); William Lambdin, *Doublespeak Dictionary* (Los Angeles: Pinnacle Books, 1979); Leonard Michaels and Christopher Ricks, eds., *The State of the Language* (Berkeley, Los Angeles, London: University of California Press, 1980); Edwin Newman, *Strictly Speaking* and *A Civil Tongue* (Indianapolis and New York: Bobbs-Merrill, 1974, 1976); William Safire, *On Language* and *What's the Good Word* (New York: Times Books, 1980, 1982); John Simon, *Paradigms Lost* (Markham, Ontario: Penguin, 1981); Hugh Rawson, *A Dictionary of Euphemisms & Other Doubletalk* (New York: Crown, 1981).

terms that suddenly become popular and that therefore quickly get themselves overused. (Vogue words, we might add, are also often vague words.) Further, certain words and phrases turn up over and over again. Whenever you come across any of these while you are revising, treat them as danger signals; you can almost always improve the quality of your writing if you revise such terms out of it.

*Potentially empty or vague words:*

| | | |
|---|---|---|
| activity | factor | position |
| angle | field | posture |
| area | framework | profile |
| aspect | function | realm |
| case | level | situation |
| facet | mode | status |

Although nouns can be perfectly good modifiers (*school* book, *bath* towel, *railroad* station), these empty words are particularly likely to have nouns stuck in front of them to create wordy jargon; for example: retrenchment mode, thunderstorm activity, power-play situation, loss position, playground area.

*Words from science, technology, commerce, and other disciplines:*

| | | |
|---|---|---|
| access (verb) | impact (verb) | parameter |
| bottom line | input, output | replicate |
| feedback | interface | target (verb) |

*Vogue words and other terms and suffixes that often produce or accompany jargon:*

| | |
|---|---|
| concept | ongoing |
| cope | relevant |
| experience | relate to |
| identify with | self-image |
| in depth | supportive |
| interpersonal relationship | type, -type |
| -ize, -ized, -ization | viable |
| lifestyle | -wise |

*Wordy terms, jargony phrases:*

along the lines of
as far as…is concerned
at this (any, that, some) point in time
basis, on a…basis, on the basis of, based on
connection, in connection with, in that connection
considering, in consideration of
evidenced by
frame of reference
from the perspective of
in relation to
in the final analysis

in (with) reference to
pertaining to
regarding, in (with) regard to
respecting, in (with) respect to
standpoint, from the standpoint of
terms, in terms of
time frame
vantage point

This is not a complete list. No such list can be complete, for new terms are added almost every day, especially slangy vogue terms like *uptight, jawbone, fallout, hang-up, hassle, scene.* And you can also add to it many of the terms listed under "Clarity," "Economy," and "Clichés" earlier in this chapter.

But many of these terms can be used in reasonable, smooth discourse; we have used several of them here and there in this book. And some of the technical and scientific terms are fine when they're kept in their own back yards. The verb *access* is part of the growing vocabulary having to do with computers. In a technical context *parameter* is precise and clear. And this is an accurate use of *interface*: "There's little computer interface between government departments." Those are examples of "jargon" narrowly defined: the special vocabulary of a particular discipline. In their home territory such terms are not only legitimate but often even necessary for efficient and precise communication among specialists. But when such terms escape into the outside world they join the much larger throng of "jargon" in the broader sense. Here are some more examples of the way some of these terms often get used; these are all from printed sources, such as textbooks, announcements by universities and businesses, articles by engineers and social scientists.

> We expect our profit-and-loss picture to constitute an ongoing situation.
>
> We have exceptional game plan capabilities together with strict concerns for programming successful situations.
>
> I too am concerned with the evolution of viable constructs by which complex problems at the medical-legal interface can be effectively resolved for social usefulness.
>
> The purpose of this letter is to historize the philosophical infrastructure Craig Computer Centre abides, regarding applicant referrals.
>
> This falling off of extra returns is a consequence of the fact that the new "doses" of the varying factor inputs have less and less of the fixed resources of factors to work with.
>
> It has come to be rather widely recognized in the sociological field that social stratification is a generalized aspect of the structure of all social systems, and that the system of stratification is intimately linked to the level and type of integration of the system as a system.

In these examples you can see some of the vocabulary in action. Try to familiarize yourself with the kinds of habits that produce such writing so that you can guard against it—and also recognize it in others' writing and speaking. For example, verbs like *familiarize, criticize, alphabetize,* and *characterize* are standard and acceptable. But jargonauts get carried away, adding *-ize* to other words—usually nouns—to make new verbs; and so we get ugly and often confusing words like *personalize, finalize, concretize, randomize, prioritize,* and *annualize.* Worse yet, such verbs then get turned back into nouns by the addition of still another suffix, so that we now encounter monsters like *fascistization* and *televisionization.* Given the potential for jargon in the word *parameter,* what does *parameterization* mean? And it's difficult to believe another one: *funeralized.*

Jargonauts also like to use nouns as verbs even without adding anything; for example *impact.* (We have not yet seen *impactize* or *impactization,* but perhaps we just haven't looked hard enough. But since jargonauts like prefixes, too, we do find the new verb *deimpact.*) Verbs such as *critiqued* and *authored* are no longer uncommon. Even *defencing* turns up. There may be some justification for the verbal noun *parenting,* but its jargonistic flavour was given away by the almost simultaneous appearance of the grotesque *parenthooding.* Adjectives are also vulnerable; thus we read of something being *obsoleted.*

A particularly virulent form of jargon we call "the noun disease." As if any noun was equally an adjective, we find phrases like "pupil station" for desk, and "learning resource centre" for library, and "artist creation of the proposed development" (instead of "artist's rendering"; jargonauts are naturally careless about diction in general), and "viewer mail" (mail from viewers of television programs) and "the area of administrative systems programming development" and "staff quality assurance mechanisms" and "social activity deprivation" (being sent to one's room?) and "residence hall living unit grouping."

Jargonauts are fond of the word *type* and—worse—of tacking it onto other words as a hyphenated suffix. So we hear a wordy weather forecaster say, "We're looking for a showery type of precipitation" (we expect showers). Another weather report referred to "emergency-type conditions."

The similar fondness for -*wise* produces a ballet director telling us that dancers "have to be good technique-wise" and a government official saying that "Energywise, economywise and environmentalwise, we have become obsessed with the problems." And one of our students once admitted that he was "weak, grammaticalwise."

The word *condition* seems innocent enough, but the phrase "emergency-type conditions" turns it into jargon. The heavy offender of this type (whenever you feel that you want to use the word *type,* if possible substitute the word *kind*)—the heavy offender of this kind is the word *situation.* It is almost always weak unless it refers to a physical *site,* or at least does so metaphorically. Otherwise, its emptiness is glaringly apparent: we hear not of a crisis, but of a "crisis situation"; not of an emergency, but of an "emergency situation." A class, or even a classroom, in these days is known as a "learning situation." A factory lunchroom is an "in-plant feeding situation." One teacher even wrote of "the patently artificial situation of any examination situation." Indeed, the magnetic vacuity of the word *situation* is so strong that it attracts jargonautical companions aboard, so that we hear a publicity stunt being referred to as a "gimmick-type situation" and a crisis as, not merely a "crisis situation," but the much more ominous "crisis-type situation."

Other jargonistic items often clump together as well. We find a professor remarking that "The colleges, trying to remediate increasing numbers of…illiterates up to college levels, are being highschoolized." Another thicket of jargon occurs in the following notice: "Computer services are available to members on a partial cost recovery basis." The double-headed noun modifier "cost recovery" squats in the midst of the wordy phrase "on a...basis."

The perniciously prevalent "on a...basis" allows one to use four words instead of one. An in-flight magazine: "Headsets will be provided by your flight attendants on a complimentary basis." Here the passive voice enabled the writer to use even more words. Why not "Your flight attendants will provide complimentary headsets"? And of course the five-syllable *complimentary* translates as *free*. Again: "The authorities claim they can deal with offenders on a successful basis" (that is, they can deal with them successfully). Another: "There was one thing that happened on a positive basis" (One good thing happened). And another: "Their reports are received on a round-the-clock basis." One almost constantly hears of something occurring or being done "on a daily basis" or "on a monthly basis" or "on a yearly basis" (yearly) or "on an annual basis" (yearly) and even (again the jargon virus feeds on itself) "on an annualized basis" (yearly). Try to keep "on a...basis" out of your writing. (One official found a way to avoid *basis*: "We'll have to look at any further applications on a case-by-case situation.") The similarly wordy phrase "in terms of" beclouds many sentences. Said a civic official, "The slowdown hasn't cost the city much in terms of jobs"—that is, it hasn't cost the city many jobs. A social worker said, "I've dealt with this patient in terms of long-term care"—the repetition makes it sound even worse.

Even the little word *case* is usually empty—and who wants an empty case? "In many cases, people were forced to dip into their savings"—not only wordy jargon, but also an odd image of people rummaging around in various kinds of "cases" to get at the money they'd stashed; "Many people were forced to dip into their savings" says it all. And you can't duck this one merely by substituting the impressive-sounding *instances*: "A regular appointment requires a college degree in most instances." Translate that one yourself.

The lists of jargonistic terms will help you spot potential trouble. In the following sentence, for example, the offending words are dead give-a-ways: "Another factor frequently mentioned is the difficulty encountered by the colleges in finding business executives with some teaching experience, thus enabling them to relate to undergraduate students." The sentence is a syntactical mess anyway, with its passives and its awkwardly dangling "thus enabling," but *factor* and *relate to* add jargon to its sins. (The word *experience* here is not jargon; it appears jargonistically in phrases like "An unforgettable dining experience!" Advertising copy-writers are fond at least of the vogue-word component of jargon.) Another: "In his new book he projects how this new industrial revolution will impact all aspects of human activities." (Can't you just see those poor impacted aspects lying all over the place? What is an "aspect" of an "activity"?) An advertising company's promise: "We will also strategize with the clients on ways to optimize usage of the spots by broadcast management." (As you see, the *-ize* have it.) Sometimes you can smell the jargon even without any of the tell-tale terms: "A downturn in income would have a negative effect on our ability to maintain a positive cashflow." Jargon: *downturn, negative effect, positive cash-flow.* But this company spokesman made it even easier for us by going on to say that "the results are negative, in terms of effects."

Wordiness alone is sometimes enough to reveal the jargonaut. In jargon one doesn't just "like" something; one "manifests an interest in" it or "evinces a preference for" it. One doesn't "apply for" something; one "makes application for" it. "It's too soon to decide" becomes "It's too soon to make any determination on that." Police seldom "catch" criminals any more; they "apprehend" them—and some even go so far as to "make apprehension." You also have to guard against a string of heavy *-tion* nouns; even just two can be deadly, as in this statement: "Finalization of the implementation of the program which, it had been decided by the faculty, would facilitate forward movement toward goal achievement was made operational in the penultimate semester." Even *operation* adds its *-tion* weight; and one can't help wondering what the *which* refers to: there are three choices of antecedent. And there are other things wrong. For practice, try revising it; and shun *-tion*.

Appalling stuff, to be sure, and clearly harmful to its perpetrators, who come off sounding foolish to anyone who appreciates clarity and grace in language. But such language—or un-language—can be harmful in other ways too. Just a few years ago, for example, a dam in the western United States was officially listed by government inspectors as being "in a failure mode." Three years later it collapsed, drowning people and wreaking immense damage. Perhaps if they had instead listed it as "Dangerous!" or "Weak!" or said that "It could burst at any moment," someone would have been alarmed enough to do something to prevent the disaster. The softness of "in a failure mode" instead probably put people to sleep.

In at least one part of Canada, what used to be known as "hazardous wastes" are now officially referred to as "special wastes"; *special* almost makes them sound like something you'd just love to have in your home town, if not in your own back yard. When "special" wastes turn up in the news, there's bound to be a great deal less public attention given them than if they were still called "hazardous."

These are examples of *euphemism* ("good-speak"), glossing over the true nature of something by substituting a pleasant, or less unpleasant, term for a harsh or supposedly offensive one. We all employ euphemisms; they're necessary in civilized society. We don't ask a bereaved widow at the funeral if she wants to "look at the corpse"; we say instead "view the body". And perhaps some "senior citizens" acquire a little more dignity from being so labelled, though many continue to think and speak of themselves more forthrightly and accurately as "old people." In any event, when euphemistic jargon is used to deceive, when it tries to hide or palliate a truth that would be better kept frankly in the open, then of course it is dishonest. A city dump is called a "sanitary landfill"—sounds like something healthful to have near where you live. Used-car dealers call their wares "pre-owned cars" or even "pre-owned units"—just well broken-in, of course. The poor are called "needy"; the needy are called "deprived" or "under-privileged," and then became the "socio-economically disadvantaged"—and so the abstractness removes us even farther from the concrete reality of their poverty. We might think to make up some Christmas baskets for the poor, or even the needy, but for the socio-economically disadvantaged? Hardly. Someone else, the "system" maybe, is obviously looking after them, if they've been given so scientific-sounding a label as that.

And so on. Don't get sucked in by such euphemisms, whether they are intentionally dishonest or not. And don't get in the habit of using them yourself. Be honest in your language. Unnecessarily cruel or harsh words can hurt people unnecessarily, and it's right to soften them, out of consideration for others' feelings. But the unnecessary jargon of euphemism can hurt people, too. And as

Orwell notes, "The inflated style is itself a kind of euphemism."

Why is jargon so common? Because people are unthinking and insensitive to language. Because they think big words and technical words and more words and voguish words and convoluted syntax will make them sound more important.

And with so much of it around, and with so much of it issuing from positions of prestige and power, it is little wonder that defenceless students write sentences like these:

I believe it fair to say that most of us have experienced the negative personal characteristics aired by certain individuals at some point in time.

An individual's feelings concerning the future are often motivated by the kinds of life events he has experienced.

The most important factor in cold-weather camping is choosing the right equipment.

Physical Education may provide a basis from which a student may find that he is very good in a certain sport.

Expressionism delves into the innermost realms of emotional and psychological states.

Accounting facilitates the informational aspect of the business process.

The existing job vacancies were quickly filled and we now have a condition of market overload.

Although the decline in teacher hiring coincides with the drop in the economy, another major factor that has contributed to this problem is the socio-educational change.

Since the massive oil price hikes of 1973 were implemented, energy has become the most important factor influencing world geopolitics.

---

## Exercise 10G

Try translating the above sentences into better English.

---

Jargon, then, is bad news—especially in its pervasiveness. But there's good news as well: you probably noticed that the students' sentences, just above, were in general less offensive than those we quoted earlier; some of those are untranslatable. As a student, you are probably only beginning to be exposed to jargon in any great quantity. And the rest of the good news is that you are no longer defenceless. We hope you now have some idea of what to look for and guard against.

Remember, your readers will get the image of you that you present to them. Unless you want to come across as a jargonaut, keep such stuff out of your prose.

---

## Review Exercise: Diction

Revise the following sentences to get rid of whatever weaknesses and errors in diction you find in them. (All of these sentences are real; that is, they were all written by students or professionals.)

1. Ultimate decisions concerning project approval lie within the jurisdiction of the provincial government through its utilities commission.
2. He looked questionably at her.
3. Properly used, this two-day test will prove to be of use in the classroom.
4. Typically, these insignificant men are disillusioned with visions of self-importance.
5. The crowd who comprise the islanders in the film are unintentionally funny.
6. They are accused of perpetuating evils, but are really scapegoated by the very people who try to suppress them.
7. We must look with suspect at someone who claims to be an authority yet can show us no credentials.
8. The youngsters were hooping it up on the public beach.
9. Meteorology is not an exacting science.
10. The building was not installed with a smoke-detection system.
11. He did his upmost to win the match.
12. The commission was suddenly dumped with the problem of holding hearings.
13. They all found it a very worthwhile learning experience.
14. What exactly are our services to the public comprised of?
15. The truth is that the U.S. does not impose regimes with tanks.
16. So far four applicants have applied for the new channel.

---

### Exercise 10H

English offers a number of idiomatic equivalents for more formal, sometimes even ponderous, Latinate diction. You can choose to say *slow down* rather than *impede*, or *make up* rather than *constitute* or *compensate*. If you want to lighten the tone of your writing, you can often use these more colloquial idioms instead of the heavier equivalents—or you can do the opposite. Here are just a few examples to experiment with. Choose a verb from the list on the left and match it with as many as possible of the words on the right, then see if you can come up with a more formal equivalent for it. (Look up the more formal word in a dictionary to see if it comes from Latin or Greek.) The word *bring*, for example, can go with at least eight of the other words to form common two-part verbs: *bring about , bring back, bring down,* etc.

| | | |
|---|---|---|
| bring | about | off |
| come | after | on |
| go | aside | out |
| keep | away | over |
| pull | back | through |
| put | down | to |
| run | forth | under |
| set | forward | up |
| take | from | upon |
| throw | into | with |

Sometimes one of the verbs will combine with two of the other words to form an idiom: *come up with* = *propose, produce, discover; put up with* = *tolerate.* And note that some of the resulting phrases can appear only with one or two nouns, as in "*put forth* all her *effort*." Why do you suppose some of the idioms from this exercise sound more colloquial than others?

---

### Exploration 10E

Write a one- or two-paragraph analysis of the following passage—part of a narrative and descriptive piece by a student. Comment on as many as you can of the elements that contribute to its effectiveness:

> In contrast to the chaotic daytime, it was a quiet evening on the pier. Hours had passed since the last lift-truck had rattled down the dock. All the engine-blocks of the fishing boats were probably quite cold. The cannery machines, with their shoulder-hunching teeth-gritting whine, were also quiet. The wind and water were the only noise-makers left to fill the void.

Do you find anything at all to criticize adversely?

---

### Essay 10A

Here are five quotations. Each is a metaphor or analogy expressing a general point about life. Choose one of them, and quote it verbatim. Then rephrase it in abstract terms, two or three times, gradually focussing on a thesis. Then support that thesis in an essay of about 500 words by using specific and concrete examples.

1. Expect poison from the standing water. (Blake)
2. Lilies that fester smell far worse than weeds. (Shakespeare)
3. The road of excess leads to the palace of wisdom. (Blake)
4. The bird a nest, the spider a web, man friendship. (Blake)
5. Be not so lengthy in preparing the banquet, lest you die of hunger. (Pater)

### Essay 10B

From a single episode in your own experience, write a short essay that illustrates one of the following:

| | |
|---|---|
| frustration | apprehension |
| annoyance | regret |
| chagrin | elation |

### Essay 10C

The contrast between illusion and reality is a common literary theme. Try your hand at it, but at least for now stick to truth. Write a personal essay on disillusionment, on the irony of expectations unfulfilled. Focus on the contrast between what you once thought would happen and what actually happened, between what you once thought you'd get and what you actually got, between what you once thought someone or some group stood for and what you later discovered that person or group actually stands for.

---

## *Idioms 10*

In this last idiom exercise, you are to revise sentences that contain unidiomatic usage. Some of the errors are with prepositions like those you've been dealing with in earlier exercises, but a few involve different kinds of idioms, as discussed in this chapter. Improve the sentences in other ways if they need it.

1. He credited his wife, Christine, for the idea.
2. She weighed in the order of one hundred kilograms.
3. If we are paranoid of flying, we may not remember of being scared by something when we were small.
4. The winner of the downhill credited his good time with improved equipment.
5. The reporter had a lot of questions of the minister.
6. He came here to lend his support for the association in its fight.
7. The narrator makes this point very clear in the beginning of the novel.
8. He is woefully ignorant to the fundamental reasons for the decision.
9. He wrote an essay along a similar theme.
10. Khan pirates a ship and sets out after the *Enterprise,* hell-bent not only for revenge, but also for the secrets to the Genesis Effect, a new invention with the capacity both to destroy and create life.
11. We are so confident in our quality that we can offer this amazing guarantee.
12. Novels are able to enlighten readers to some part of human character.
13. The pride and prejudice of the main characters are the obstacles in the union of those characters.
14. It was during his pursuit for a better education that he discovered the value of what he had left behind.
15. He becomes prejudiced at the rural and less wealthy people
16. She has pride of her social class and prejudice of his.
17. She has a very strong prejudice to him.
18. Later on he confides with her.
19. There was an attempt, but only at the last moment, of avoiding hostilities.
20. He made no attempt at explaining why he had behaved as he had.

## *Sentence-Combining 10:  Absolute Phrases*

### *Pattern 10A*

Base sentence *a*: The minister was nothing if not efficient.
Base sentence *b*: His report was ready in two days.

Result of combining *a* and *b*:

   The minister being nothing if not efficient, his report was ready in two days.

First, COPY the pattern sentence carefully, noting that *was* becomes *being* and that a comma follows the first part of the new sentence.

Second, COMBINE each of the following pairs of sentences into a single sentence modelled on the pattern sentence:

a. The program for the festival had been decided upon.
b. The committee could return to routine business.

a. No precedent was established.
b. The committee could make only tentative recommendations.

Third, COMPOSE two sentences of your own modelled on Pattern 10A.

In this exercise you are reducing base sentence *a* to what is called an *absolute* phrase—meaning a phrase that has no syntactical connection with the rest of the sentence but is simply juxtaposed to it and set off with a comma. Think of an absolute phrase as modifying all the rest of the sentence, not any specific part of it. Most absolute phrases consist of a noun (for example *minister*) along with some other word or phrase—adjective, adverb, or even noun—but most often either a past or a present participle (for example *being*). Absolute phrases most often occur in narrative and descriptive contexts.

## Pattern 10B

a. The committee could return to routine business.
b. The program for the festival was decided upon.
RESULT: The program for the festival decided upon, the committee could return to routine business.

Copy the pattern sentence, noting that you delete the word *was* and put base sentence *b*, followed by a comma, in front of base sentence *a*.

Combine each of the following pairs into a sentence modelled on the pattern sentence:
a. Henry Lebrun sat at his desk.
b. His arms were folded stiffly across his chest.
a. The president of the student body stood up to speak.
b. An expression of controlled rage was on her face.

Compose two sentences modelled on Pattern 10B.

In this exercise, as in Pattern 10A, you are reducing a sentence to an absolute phrase—but this time you accomplish the change by merely deleting the verb. Note that sometimes this pattern is reversible—that is, the absolute phrases in the sentences above can either precede or follow the independent clauses they modify.

## Pattern 10C

a. Annabelle submitted her report to the committee.
b. The bad news was neatly underlined in red.
RESULT: Annabelle submitted her report to the committee, the bad news neatly underlined in red.

Copy the pattern sentence, deleting the word *was* and putting a comma between the two parts.

Combine each of the following pairs into a sentence modelled on the pattern sentence:
a. The petition will be circulated next week.
b. The letter from the political prisoner will be printed in full.
a. The results of the election were finally coming through.
b. My choices, as usual, were not winning.

Compose two sentences modelled on Pattern 10C.

In this exercise you are again deleting verbs to turn sentences into absolute phrases which you use to modify other sentences. Note that the sentences above—unlike those in Pattern 10B—are not reversible: the absolute phrases here are comfortable only at the ends of their sentences.

Be sure that you set off absolute phrases with a comma or a dash; if you should slip and put in a period, you would be making it into an awkward fragment (see pp. 206-208).

## Pattern 10D

a. The Ferrari took the turn at over 150 km/h.
b. Its engine was roaring and its tires were screaming.
RESULT: Its engine roaring and its tires screaming, the Ferrari took the turn at over 150 km/h.

Copy the pattern sentence, noting that you drop both *was* and *were* from sentence *b* and that a comma follows it.

Combine each of the following pairs into a sentence modelled on the pattern sentence:

a. Julie skated and whirled gracefully around the pond.
b. Her eyes were aglow, her long hair was streaming in the wind, and her cheeks were red from the cold.

a. The sentry spoke into the darkness.
b. His face was drawn and white, his hands were trembling, and his voice was a mere whisper.

Compose two sentences modelled on Pattern 10D.

In this exercise you are again reducing one sentence to an absolute phrase. Note that you can effectively compound two or more elements in an absolute phrase.

## Pattern 10E

a. The Ferrari took the turn at over 150 km/h.
b. Its engine was roaring and its tires were screaming.
RESULT: Engine roaring and tires screaming, the Ferrari took the turn at over 150 km/h.

Copy the pattern sentence, noting that you drop *its* and *was* and *its* and *were* from sentence *b* and that a comma follows it.

Combine each of the following pairs into a sentence modelled on the pattern sentence:

a. Julie skated and whirled gracefully around the pond.
b. Her eyes were aglow, her long hair was streaming in the wind, and her cheeks were red from the cold.

a. The family settled down to watch a favourite golden oldie on television.
b. Our supper was over and the dishes were washed and put away.

Compose two sentences modelled on Pattern 10D.

In this exercise you are again reducing one sentence to an absolute phrase—but note that this time you truncate it even further than in Pattern 10D: not *Its engine roaring* but just *Engine roaring*. The effect of absolute phrases can be quite dazzling: don't use them too often.

___

### Playing with Language 10A

Compile your own list of clichés to add to the one provided on pp. 262-263. Copy down every one you hear or read during a week, and add any others you can think of. Then, using as many of these clichés as you can, write a brief narrative. Make it as tiresome as possible.

Keep adding to your list. Perhaps someday you can provide the world with the definitive list of clichés—definitive, anyway, until a few days later.

### Playing with Language 10B

Select one or more of the proverbs or familiar quotations from the list on pp. 170-171 or elsewhere and rewrite them as they might have been written had they just occurred to some government or other official today. You'll probably want to be wordy, abstract, pompous, and jargony—but try to stay within reason, or "real-life situations"; that is, try to write them the way they would actually be written today by someone who had never heard the old familiar versions.

*Example:* Too many cooks spoil the broth.

> If more than the requisite number of workers are utilized in the culinary section, the result will likely be the production of either a vegetable- or a meat-based stock that will be found to be inferior to the normal or expected quality. Please leave the chef alone.

OR

Go all out. Take some well-known proverb, or some short, well-known piece (such things as Hamlet's "To be or not to be" soliloquy and "Little Miss Muffet," for example, have been humorously treated this way), and jargonize it as much as you can, somewhat in the way Orwell treated the verse from Ecclesiastes, but even more outrageously. Use all the jargonaut's techniques you can.

### Playing with Language 10C

Choose ten clichés from your own experience or from the list on pp. 262-263. Compose a sentence using each, and then rewrite each sentence so as to get rid of the cliché. Then select five of those you used, and write a sentence or two using each cliché in a fresh way.

*Example:*
> He came back from his holiday looking brown as a berry.
> He came back from his holiday with an enviably attractive deep tan.
> I may be brown as a berry now, but when my tan starts to fade I'll look sallow as a squash.
> I don't tan; I freckle: I look about as brown as a half-ripe salmonberry.

### Playing with Language 10D

Sports-writers seem to have a rule that they can never use the the same verb twice, in one report, to describe the same thing—like one team beating another. Pretend you are a sports reporter. Write a feature sports-page story, or the script for a TV sports announcer. Write about a single game in whatever sport you prefer, or about a particular team, or about a particular series; or do a retrospective on a whole season, or a profile of one player; perhaps make it a weekend wrap-up—whatever you decide you'd most enjoy. Use the sports-writers' particular kind of elegant variation and whatever other stylistic gimmicks you want. Make your prose sound at least as silly as some of that done by professionals. If you need to refresh your memory, read the sports pages and watch the sports commentators on TV for a few days, perhaps making notes. Aim for around 750 words for your piece.

### Playing with Language 10E

This exercise is intended to strengthen your vocabulary as well as to test your ingenuity in invention and in constructing sentences. Use each pair of words in the list below in a single simple or complex sentence—not compound. In at least some sentences, make use of parallelism.

| | |
|---|---|
| ebullient—depression | despotic—hierarchy |
| inception—stamina | ameliorate—onerous |
| injurious—salutary | querulous—denizen |
| proclivity—noxious | alacrity—disparage |
| perspicuous—cogent | bellicose—calamity |
| perspicacity—hindsight | pandemonium—docile |
| naive—conciliatory | cajole—obviate |
| enthrall—deter | chagrin—affable |
| haphazard—hilarious | elicit—manifest |
| exhaustive—scanty | adulation—rudimentary |

Prologue (Peter Quince):

*If we offend, it is with our good will.*
*That you should think, we come not to offend,*
*But with good will. To show our simple skill,*
*That is the true beginning of our end.*
*Consider then we come but in despite.*
*We do not come, as minding to content you,*
*Our true intent is. All for your delight,*
*We are not here. That you should here repent you,*
*The actors are at hand; and, by their show,*
*You shall know all, that you are like to know.*

Theseus:

*This fellow doth not stand upon points.*

Lysander:

*He hath rid his prologue like a rough colt; he*
*knows not the stop. A good moral, my lord:*
*it is not enough to speak, but to speak true.*

(A Midsummer Night's Dream)

# CHAPTER XI
# Sweep 5:  Revising Punctuation

When you speak to someone you can vary the loudness of your voice; you can vary your pitch from high to low; you can speed up and slow down, even stop for a pause; you can wave your arms and hands around; you can raise or lower one or both eyebrows, widen or narrow your eyes, shake or nod your head, wrinkle your nose, perhaps even wiggle your ears. You automatically use the sound of your voice and such physical gestures to help convey meaning when you speak. But when you are writing you are not communicating by sounds and your audience isn't present to see you gesture or make faces; you are deprived of all those useful means of communication.

But when you are writing you have something to take their place: punctuation. Punctuation is not an arbitrary contrivance invented by schoolteachers just to make life difficult for students. Rather it is, basically, the tool writers use to tell readers how their writing should be read—in large part how to *hear* it. And what you may think of as rules of punctuation you can instead think of as *conventions*, mechanical devices people have agreed upon so that they can communicate more easily with one another in writing. We all accept the convention, for example, that a sentence begins with a capital letter and ends with a period (or question mark or exclamation point). If someone wrote you a letter and ignored that convention, you'd be annoyed because of the extra work you'd have to do to try to understand it.

Here's a short paragraph written by a student. We've removed all its punctuation and capitalization. Try to read it:

> the human voice is music itself it rises and falls it pauses it gets louder and softer if this music were not present in our voices we would all speak in monotones and conversation would soon become very tedious our speech pattern is song and it reflects our emotions happiness anger sorrow fatigue and nonchalance all show up in our voices thus we can see that music is man's chief way of expressing his inner emotions whether he realizes it or not

You were probably able to understand the paragraph, but in order to do so you must have mentally supplied some punctuation marks. And even then you proably found it flat, monotonous, tedious—all because of the lack of punctuation. Try punctuating it yourself, the best way you can think of (you can compare yours with the student's original version, later in the chapter), and then read it again. This time you should be able to hear it. Before, it didn't speak; your mind was listening, but without punctuation there was little or no voice to hear. With punctuation, it has acquired a voice.

The purpose of almost all the rules or conventions of punctuation is to enable us to make sure that readers will read our sentences the way we want them to, to make sure that they will understand the syntax and meaning the way we have constructed them, and hear the intonations, emphases, and pauses that we put into them with our commas, semicolons, colons, dashes, periods, question marks, and exclamation points. The word *punctuation* comes from the Latin *punctum*, meaning a pricked mark, or point (compare *puncture*); we don't have to poke holes in our pages, but it's worth remembering that punctuation marks *point* to your meaning so that readers can understand it clearly.

During this final sweep of revision, look closely at how you have punctuated each sentence in your draft. Check your punctuation in two ways:

1. Make sure you haven't punctuated incorrectly—that is, that you haven't used a punctuation mark, or omitted one, in a way that would break the conventions and send your readers the wrong signal.
2. Consider revising punctuation to improve the clarity, emphasis, or rhythm of your sentences.

Punctuation is not difficult. The principles of good punctuation are mostly simple mechanical ones; the rules you need to know are few. People who have trouble with punctuation simply haven't taken the time to learn the principles and the rules; their sloppy punctuation reveals them to their readers as lazy and uncaring.

Study the following discussions to familiarize yourself with the principles and rules of good punctuation, and use them as a guide during revision. You might even want to memorize some of the rules so that you can avoid error and so that you can develop the habit of punctuating well.

*Practical Hint:* Since punctuation is so often a matter of sound and rhythm, you will find punctuation much easier if you get into the habit of reading your sentences aloud. Learn what each punctuation mark can do, and then punctuate your sentences the way you want them to be *heard* by your readers. Even though sound is not an infallible guide, your ear for good punctuation will develop along with your knowledge of the conventions.

(For *apostrophes*, see Chapter XII; for *quotation marks*, see Chapters XII and XIV.)

## END-PUNCTUATION MARKS

Only three marks appear at the ends of sentences: the period (.), the question mark (?), and the exclamation point (!). These serve to mark off the three basic kinds of sentences: the statement, the question, and the exclamation.

### 1. Periods

You don't need to be told that periods end most sentences, for most sentences you write are statements. But you do need to make sure that the groups of words you put periods after are true sentences, not *fragments* (see pp. 206-208). Periods are also called "full stops"; they bring readers to a complete halt and force them to pause briefly before beginning the next sentence. They also are intended to coincide with that feeling of satisfactory completeness that comes at the end of a sentence. If you put a period after a fragment, it will jolt readers, for what it is saying to them ("This is the end of a sentence; you are to experience a sense of satisfactory completeness") will jar because they will not be experiencing that sense. Their experience will contradict what the period is telling them. The slight drop in pitch that a period signals will conflict with such a drop's being prevented by the fragmentary structure. (Omitting a necessary period is even worse: see "Run-on Sentences," pp. 292-293.)

### 2. Question Marks

Again, you don't need to be told to put a question mark at the end of a question. If you read your draft aloud, you'll often hear a rising intonation and not forget to put in the question mark. But be sure that you put question marks only after direct questions, not indirect ones. Indirect questions are questions embedded in statements:

> DIRECT: What did she want?
> INDIRECT: I wondered what she wanted.

> *Exclamation points are the most irritating*
> *of all. Look! they say, look at what I just*
> *said! How amazing is my thought!*
> (Lewis Thomas, *The Medusa and the Snail*)

### 3. Exclamation Points

Except perhaps in personal letters or sometimes when you are representing dialogue, your writing will be more effective if you minimize or even avoid the exclamation point. It is merely a way of making a sentence sound more emphatic; you'll usually do better if you make the sentence emphatic on its own rather than depend on the sometimes cheap effect of an exclamation point. For example:

> They claimed they couldn't let me move into the dorm until September!

To emphasize your unhappiness about the inconveniencing delay, try rearranging:

> They couldn't let me move into the dorm, they claimed, until September.

The interrupting phrase "they claimed" has the effect of putting more emphasis on the last two words; an exclamation point isn't necessary. Again:

> The other driver denied that he had been speeding! I was astonished!

This is better rendered as follows:

> Astonishingly, the other driver denied that he had been speeding.

The long introductory word, followed by the comma and the pause it forces, gives the sentence all the emphasis it needs.

You may have noticed that in many comic strips the characters almost always speak in exclamations, even to say the most mundane things—a cheap effect. Unless you want your writing to sound like comic-strip dialogue, severely restrict your use of the exclamation point.


# INTERNAL PUNCTUATION MARKS

> *I have grown fond of semicolons*
> *in recent years.*  (Lewis Thomas)

## 4. Semicolons

Semicolons are also "stops," almost as "full" as periods. There are basically only two uses for semicolons:

a. In place of a comma when a heavier stop is needed. This is a minor and infrequent use, and is illustrated later. (See p. 300.)
b. To join independent clauses. This is its major use; all you need to remember in order to keep from going wrong with it is this: use a semicolon only in a place where you *could* use a period instead. For example:

> Riding a motorcycle can be dangerous; one should take every possible safety precaution.

Since the semicolon could be replaced with a period, all is well. Otherwise a semicolon will confuse a reader, as in this sentence from a student's rough draft:

> DRAFT: In a big city there are always people nearby; hundreds and thousands of them.

A period in place of that semicolon would make the last group of words into a fragment; in effect, the semicolon does the same thing because it is virtually a full stop. A semicolon signals to readers that an independent clause is coming; here we get only a phrase. The semicolon must be changed:

> REVISED: In a big city there are always people nearby, hundreds and thousands of them.

The comma is best, though a dash or a colon could be used. Here's another example:

> DRAFT: She is a strong character in the novel; mainly because she is harsh and often cruel and unfair.

Again the semicolon sends the wrong signal to readers: it says that an independent clause is coming, but only a subordinate clause arrives. Again the final group of words is in effect a jarring fragment; readers expect the subordinate *because* clause to lead them to a later independent clause—but instead they bump into the period at the end of the sentence.

> REVISED: She is a strong character in the novel, mainly because she is harsh and often cruel and unfair.

---

### Exercise 11A

Compose three sentences which use only a semicolon to join two independent clauses. (See also Sentence-Combining pattern 1B.)

---

## 5. Commas

The most commonly used—and abused—mark of punctuation is the comma. It is commonly used because the places where it is needed to send certain signals occur more often than those that call for other marks; it is commonly abused because writers carelessly ignore a few simple rules governing its use. Although you might at first think that commas are used in a bewildering variety of ways, in fact their principal uses as punctuators of sentences can be boiled down to only three:

a. To join independent clauses that are already connected with one of the coordinating conjunctions (*and, but, for, or, nor, yet, so*):

> Her argument sounds convincing, but it is based on a false premise.

b. To separate items (words, phrases, or clauses) in a series of three or more:

> We returned from the hike hot, tired, and dirty.

or to separate a series of two or more adjectives in front of a noun:

> Her graceful, intelligent prose has won her many readers.

*Note:* Put commas between such adjectives only when you could put the word *and* there:

> They live in a big red barn of a house.

Since you would not say "a big and red barn," you do not put a comma after *big*. But you could say "Her graceful and intelligent prose." If you're not sure, try reading such phrases aloud to see if you feel the need for the slight pause that a comma would cause.

c.   To set off parenthetical beginnings or endings of sentences, whether words, phrases, or clauses:

> Indeed, it was her best performance of the season.
>
> With a good deal of help from his friends, he managed to make it through the winter.
>
> Because she is harsh and domineering, she stands out among the novel's characters.
>
> It was not a good day for their opponents, however.
>
> He walked out of the meeting at four, taking his clique with him.
>
> The suggestion came as a complete surprise, which made it seem all the more attractive.

or to set off parenthetical interrupters—at both ends:

> It was not, however, a well-written article.
>
> Eileen, my silly sister, is off to the beach again.
>
> His latest film, like its predecessors, depends heavily on melodrama.
>
> The experiment, which she performed successfully, satisfied her instructor.

Other conventional uses of the comma are probably familiar to you:
After a noun of direct address:

> Jennifer, please write me before you leave for Europe.

After the informal salutation of a letter:

> Dear Jennifer,

After the complimentary close of a letter:

> Yours truly,

To separate the elements of place-names:

> He is from Shelburn, Nova Scotia, Canada.
>
> Orillia, Ontario, was the model for Stephen Leacock's Mariposa.
>
> (Note the conventional comma *after* the name of the province as well as before it.)

To separate the elements of dates:

> July 30, 1983, was an unusually warm day.
>
> (Again, note the comma *after* the year.)

With a verb of speaking before or after a quotation:

> And then André said, "Of course I'll lend you the money."

And occasionally to indicate the omission of a word, as after *forgive* in Alexander Pope's well-known line:

> To err is human; to forgive, divine.

Like periods and semicolons, commas are also sometimes technically referred to as "stops." But this can be misleading, for commas don't *stop* you; they just slow you down a little. Commas induce a slight pause.

## 6. Colons

A colon is also a stop—and it does stop readers cold. But paradoxically, just a split second after it stops them, it pushes them into the next part of the sentence. Periods and semicolons do not do this; readers must move on by their own effort. Colons, however, give them a shove: colons have an anticipatory force that draws readers on to what follows (usually an explanation or elaboration of what came before the colon, as in this sentence). If you noticed the colon as you read the preceding sentence, you should subconsciously have had a slight feeling of being impelled onward, a slight sense of expectation, perhaps even curiosity, about what the next part of the sentence was going to say. Examine the way we have used colons in sentences elsewhere in this book; try to get a feel for the kinds of relations between the two parts. And look at this one from Morley Callaghan's *That Summer in Paris*:

> A whisper had gone the rounds that Greenwich Village was washed up: Paris was the new frontier.

and this, from Northrop Frye's "The Motive for Metaphor":

> Many animals and insects have this social form too, but man knows that he has it: he can compare what he does with what he can imagine being done.

It is of course this "looking forward" quality that makes colons so useful to introduce lists, examples, and quotations, as we do throughout this book. Colons indicate that something follows. You no doubt use them that way without even thinking about it. But don't overlook their use in other kinds of sentences; where the relation between the two parts is right, the colon can be the best mark to use. At the same time, however, don't get so carried away that you overuse them. One per paragraph would probably make a safe upper limit, though even that might strike some readers as overdoing it, as a bit too fancy.

### Exercise 11B

Compose three sentences using a colon as a sentence punctuator—not to introduce a list, but to indicate that the second part of the sentence will contain an explanation or something similarly sequential following the first part.

*Warning:* There is one misuse of the colon that you should be careful to avoid. Like the semicolon between clauses, a colon should be used only after a syntactically complete construction—that is, after an independent clause. For example, avoid using a colon to introduce a series after any form of the verb *be*, as in the following:

> DRAFT: The obstacles between us and our goal were: poor equipment, too few volunteers, and out-moded procedures.

Since the series is merely the complement that completes the verb phrase, there should be no punctuation after the verb. Or it could be revised in another way:

> REVISED: Three obstacles stood between us and our goals: poor equipment, too few volunteers, and out-moded procedures.

Similarly, don't put a colon between a preposition and its object:

> DRAFT: The firm has branches in: Alberta, Manitoba, and Quebec.

Either omit the colon in such a sentence or make what precedes the colon a complete sentence:

> REVISED: The firm has branches in three provinces: Alberta, Manitoba, and Quebec.

(*Note:* In a formal letter, a colon conventionally follows the salutation.)

## 7. Dashes

Although the dash is a highly effective punctuation mark, its very strength means that you should not use it often. If used too often, dashes quickly lose their effectiveness and make prose choppy. Certainly you should never use a dash as a casual or lazy substitute for any other mark, such as a comma or a semi-colon. Reserve it for those places where it is the most appropriate mark. Like the colon, the dash often in effect says something. Wherever it appears, a dash calls attention to itself—or rather to whatever is set off by it. It can suggest emphasis; it can mark a sharp or unexpected or ironic turn of thought in a sentence; or it can indicate an abrupt syntactical break. Look at the following sentence (from the introduction to Henry Rossier's *The New City, a Prejudiced View of Toronto*):

> This is Toronto the Good—smug, solid, respectable.

In this sentence Pierre Berton could have used a colon effectively, but he chose a dash instead because it sets off the series with a sharper emphasis than a colon would have offered. Vincent Massey gets a similar effect in the following sentence (from "Uncertain Sounds"), where again a colon could have appeared:

> I want to talk about the mainspring of all human affairs, that special mark of humanity by which mankind stands or falls—language.

He could have ended the sentence with "falls, namely language," using the word *namely* to provide the emphasis; but the dash does it better, more sharply, more economically. In the following sentence, Pierre Berton uses a dash rather than a comma to set off—and thus emphasize—the long concluding appositive:

> When they were not laying track across the soft porridge of the muskeg they were blasting it through some of the hardest rock in the world—rock that rolled endlessly on, ridge after spiky ridge, like waves in a sullen ocean.
>
> *(The National Dream: The Great Railway 1871-1881)*

In the following example, Hugh MacLennan uses a pair of dashes to set off an interrupting independent clause both because he wants to emphasize it and because the clause breaks sharply from the syntax of the rest of the sentence, so sharply that a pair of commas would be confusing:

> The chief competitor of modern fiction—of this there can be no doubt—is the great fiction already written.
>
> ("The Novel as an Art Form")

In the next example the writer uses a dash to mark a shift in tone:

> The employees are prepared to go back to work, all right—but only, it seems, on their own terms.

A matter-of-fact comma would simply not be appropriate to the ironic edge (a tonal quality clearly indicated also by the phrases "all right" and "it seems"). In the following sentence, the student writer similarly uses a dash to mark the ironic humour of the final clause:

> Those of us unable to afford a tennis club or a spa membership can be off and running with only a pair of jogging shoes—no white coordinated outfit is necessary.

A flat semicolon would not support the tone.

---

### Exercise 11C

Compose six sentences,

(a) two using a dash to emphasize something;
(b) two using a dash to mark an ironic turn of thought;
(c) two using a dash to indicate an abrupt syntactical break.

---

## STRATEGIES OF EFFECTIVE PUNCTUATION: MAKING CHOICES

From some of the preceding examples illustrating the uses of the different punctuation marks, it is clear that you are often not restricted to one "correct" mark in a given spot; you often have choices. In any given instance you should choose the mark that best creates the effect you are trying to produce. The following discussion and examples will help you understand how to make choices for several different kinds of sentences.

## 1. Joining Independent Clauses

Imagine that in your draft you wrote the following two short sentences (a student did):

a.  Summer is over. The school year begins.

You decide not to combine them by subordinating one to the other; you want to keep the rhythmic effect of the two short independent clauses. And you decide not to combine them with a weak *and*. But now you have to decide whether to leave them as separate sentences, separated by the period, or to join them with some other punctuation mark. Try the different possibilities; read them over, slowly, first to yourself and then aloud:

b.  Summer is over; the school year begins.
c.  Summer is over, the school year begins.
d.  Summer is over—the school year begins.
e.  Summer is over: the school year begins.

Each of the five possibilities creates a slightly different effect. Leaving them as two sentences (a) dramatically emphasizes each clause by itself and lets the reader make the obvious connection between them. In (b) the rhythm is about the same, but the emphasis on the separate clauses is much less, for the semicolon pulls them together, establishing their connectedness. In (c) the slighter pause of the comma pulls them even closer together and speeds up the reading. In (d) the dash not only emphasizes the connection between the two but also throws heavier emphasis on the second clause, perhaps with a suggestion of shoulder-shrugging and "Well, here we go again" (the context would help establish the tone). In (e) the colon not only connects the two clauses and, like the dash, puts emphasis on the second, but even defines the connection as one almost of cause and effect. With the colon in it, the sentence reads something like this: "Summer is over, and that means the school year begins."

You have five versions to choose from, then, and you can choose the one that best carries out your intentions. The semicolon is the most neutral choice, the quietest choice. Leaving the clauses as separate sentences is a little noisier, and is fine if there aren't many other short sentences in the vicinity. The comma is dramatic, even a touch defiant and risky (see Comma Splice, below), not the sort of thing you'd want to do often. And both the colon and the dash make quite a bit of stylistic noise; they too should be used sparingly.

---

### *Exercise 11D*

Compose a sentence made up of two independent clauses that can be joined with a semicolon, a colon, or a dash. Write out all three versions.

---

### Run-on Sentence (Fused Sentence)

The only thing you must *not* choose to do with such a pair of clauses is to omit any punctuation whatever between them: "Summer is over the school year begins." That would create a run-on sentence on the page and an image of you in your readers' minds as either illiterate or extremely careless. Here is a student's sentence:

> DRAFT: I had to be careful not to strike the tent wall otherwise I would get wet from the condensation.

But the word *otherwise* is not a conjunction; it is not equivalent to *or*. For that reason not even a comma would be enough; this spot requires a semicolon (or a period):

> REVISED: I had to be careful not to strike the tent wall; otherwise I would get wet from the condensation.

Don't let yourself be tricked by words like *otherwise*—see the discussion following, on comma splices.

## Comma Splice

The comma splice (or comma fault) is another error that could make your readers think you illiterate. In the examples above, option (c)—joining the two independent clauses with only a comma—is technically a comma splice, which is why it is risky. If you have any reason to think that your readers would frown on it, don't take the risk. But in certain very limited circumstances, joining independent clauses with a comma alone can be effective. If you know what you're doing—that is, if you make the choice consciously and test its stylistic effect (and would be able to defend your choice if criticized, say by an instructor)—then use a comma alone if

a. the clauses are short, as in the example above, and
b. especially if they are also parallel in structure, and,
c. even more especially, if they have the same subject.

For example, commas work well in a sentence like Caesar's "I came, I saw, I conquered," or in "The peak loomed, it dominated." Think of it this way: if you're sure your readers' eyes and minds can take in the entire sentence in a single glance, understanding the separate clauses almost simultaneously, then you can probably get away with only a comma. Clearly such instantaneous comprehension is possible only when the clauses are short, and just as clearly it is aided by both parallel structure and identity of subject.

And of course if the independent clauses are in a series of three or more, commas are enough to join them, as in the following sentence:

> I didn't mind the lecture, I liked the swimming and the exercises, and I did quite well on the tests, but when the day came that the teacher said it was time for us to be able to dive off the high board I was far from enthusiastic.

The first half of the sentence consists of a parallel series of three independent clauses. In the following sentence, however, discussing a character in a short story, another student thought he was dealing with a series when he was not:

> DRAFT: But this is not all, he feels that he is even luckier, he was able to save most of his belongings from the flood.

Both of the commas here are joining clauses in a way that suggests they are in a series, but since they aren't a real series the result is a sentence that is awkward and difficult to read. Here are two possible ways to revise its punctuation to make the connection between the clauses clearer:

> REVISED: But this is not all: he feels that he is even luckier, for he was able to save most of his belongings from the flood.
>
> REVISED: But this is not all; he feels that he is even luckier: he was able to save most of his belongings from the flood.

In the first of these, the added word *for* defines the relations between the two clauses; in the second version, the colon does that job all by itself.

Examine your draft particularly carefully for places where you've joined independent clauses with one of the following terms:

| | | |
|---|---|---|
| accordingly | however | on the other hand |
| afterward | in addition | otherwise |
| also | indeed | particularly |
| as a result | in fact | second |
| besides | instead | similarly |
| consequently | later | still |
| conversely | likewise | subsequently |
| finally | meanwhile | that is |
| for example | moreover | then |
| furthermore | namely | therefore |
| hence | nevertheless | thus |

The list is not complete, but these are the most common ones. Be particularly careful with these and others like them. They are connectors, to be sure, but they are not conjunctions; rather they are "conjunctive" adverbs and common transitional phrases (see the list on pp. 187-188). When you use one of them to join independent clauses, you must precede it with a semicolon. Here there is no choice: to precede one of these with only a comma is to commit the worst kind of comma splice. Here's an example:

> DRAFT: My teddy bear is covered with a layer of white fur, however, in some places the fur is worn away.

The comma before *however* must be changed to a semicolon:

> REVISED: My teddy bear is covered with a layer of white fur; however, in some places the fur is worn away.

But a comma is enough to join independent clauses that are connected with one of the *coordinating conjunctions*. There are only seven of these. Memorize them:

| | | | | | | |
|---|---|---|---|---|---|---|
| and | but | or | nor | for | yet | so |

*Note:* The conjunction *so* is seldom used except in colloquial writing; avoid it in anything at all formal. If you feel inclined to use it, try instead subordinating the first clause with a *since*; it usually works:

DRAFT: Punctuation can affect meaning, so it pays to be careful with it.
REVISED: Since punctuation can affect meaning, it pays to be careful with it.

When you join independent clauses with one of the coordinators, it is customary to put a comma before it:

Few people consider music to be a real career, and even fewer realize the importance of music in education.

When you use the conjunction *for*, it is essential that you precede it with a comma so that your readers won't think it is the preposition *for*:

DRAFT: I decided to take two courses in the summer for the extra credits would look good on my record.
REVISED: I decided to take two courses in the summer, for the extra credits would look good on my record.

And the conjunctions *yet* and *but* between clauses, since they mark a contrast or other sharp turn in thought, usually need a comma.

Not everyone is athletic or able to get straight A's in chemistry, but every student should be given the chance to excel in at least one subject.

But with the others a comma is not always necessary, especially if you don't want to emphasize the second clause over the first. If the clauses are short a comma probably won't be needed:

He went one way and she went the other.

Even longer clauses can sometimes get along without a comma if their subjects are the same:

During the coming year food prices may go up or they may go down.

He did not protest the decision at the time nor did he complain about it later.

(Note that when *nor* begins a clause the subject is delayed.)

Another exception requires you to go in the other direction and use a semicolon instead of a comma:

In attempting to explain why religious cults are gaining in vogue, we must consider our increasing inability to accept ourselves as consequential individuals, due largely to the impersonal nature of urban society; for is it not, ultimately, the individual who must bear the herculean burden of existence in a dispassionate universe?

The student who wrote that sentence could have chosen to start a new sentence with *For*. But she decided it would be better to connect the two long clauses. (*For* at the beginning of a sentence sometimes sounds a little awkward; and the obviously formal stance indicates that the context will support the unusually long sentence.) But since both clauses already have commas in them, to use only a comma before *for* could make the sentence more difficult to read; therefore she used a semicolon instead.

Occasionally, if you want a heavier pause than a comma would give, you can use a semicolon along with a coordinating conjunction even if there is no other punctuation within the clause, as we chose to do in the sentence in parentheses just above. And of course you can use a colon or, more likely, a dash instead of a comma—but you wouldn't want to do that often.

*Warning:* Usually, avoid using a comma with one of these conjunctions when it connects only elements within a clause rather than two clauses. Note the awkward rhythm of the following sentence:

> DRAFT: Grinding the valve seats in the block, and adjusting the carburetor both require special equipment.

The comma must come out. The sentence then reads smoothly and clearly:

> REVISED: Grinding the valve seats in the block and adjusting the carburetor both require special equipment.

Here is a diagram to help you see the way independent clauses are joined. Fix the pattern in your mind; memorize it if necessary. Think of the independent clauses as bricks and of the items between the dotted lines as mortar. A comma alone is (normally) not enough mortar to hold the bricks together; the comma splice will cause them to fall apart and the wall you are building will fall down.

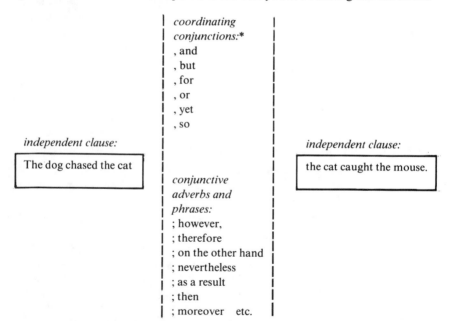

*We have omitted the coordinating conjunction *nor* since it would not work in the example sentence.

Note that the conjunctions can be placed only between the two clauses, whereas the adverbs and phrases can be placed not only there but also after the word *cat* and at the end of the sentence. This movability of the adverbs and phrases may help you distinguish them from the coordinating conjunctions, which cannot be moved. Indeed you can often improve the rhythm of a sentence by taking such adverbs and transitional phrases away from the beginning of a clause (or a sentence) and inserting them a few words later; here, after *cat* would be the best place. The adverb *however*, especially, is almost always stiff and awkward at the beginning of a clause; putting it first is equivalent to underlining it. Unless you want such a heavy emphasis, always try the effect of delaying it:

> The cat, however, caught the mouse.

Note that when the word *however* is inserted in a clause it must be set off by a pair of commas. Most of the others should also be set off by a pair of commas, though *therefore* would not need to be, in this example; and if *then* were so set off it would change in meaning (and not make sense in the sample sentence).

And if you do move your conjunctive adverbs into your clauses, they won't trap you into committing comma splices.

---

### Exercise 11E

(a)  Compose three sentences using a comma and a coordinating conjunction to join two independent clauses.
(b)  Compose three sentences using a semicolon and a conjunctive adverb to join two independent clauses.

---

## 2. Punctuating Openers of Sentences and Clauses

### a. Connectors

In the discussion of the comma splice we used the following example:

> My teddy bear is covered with a layer of white fur; however, in some places the fur is worn away.

Note that *however* is followed by a comma. When *however* means "yet" or "nevertheless" it must be followed by a comma:

> The weather looked threatening. However, we decided to go anyway.

Otherwise it could easily be mistaken for *however* meaning "by whatever means" or "to whatever degree," which is not followed by a comma:

> However threatening the weather, we decided to go anyway.

The word has two different meanings; only the comma's presence or absence tells readers which one you intend. (But see the preceding section regarding *however* as an opener.)

Similarly, such other openers as *nevertheless, moreover, furthermore, that is, besides,* and *similarly* are almost always followed by a comma. If you read the preceding sentence aloud, you'll sense the slight pause that naturally follows its first word. But don't make the mistake of thinking that *all* such opening words and phrases need a comma after them: they often don't. Here are a few examples where such openers are left without commas; read them aloud and you'll hear that they flow smoothly and clearly:

> It began to rain; therefore we decided to stay home.
> Finally the answer came to him.
> Accordingly she put tab A in slot B.
> They were well trained; indeed they performed like professionals.

To put commas after the openers in such sentences as these might unnecessarily, even awkwardly, slow down the sentences. In addition, modern punctuation, compared to that of the past, tends to be lighter, more "open," less cluttered. If you find that in your draft you have slavishly put a comma after every opening *yet* and *therefore* and *conversely* and *hence* and so on, consider revising at least some of them out. The best test is to read aloud: if rhythm or emphasis tells you to pause, leave the comma in; if when reading in a natural tone you don't pause, take the comma out.

Especially (do you want a comma here?) don't put a comma after an opening *But*. If *But* is followed by a parenthetical interrupter that needs to be set off by *two* commas, all right. But never put a single comma after an opening *But*. The same goes for an opening *Perhaps*. (But perhaps you already knew that.)

### b. Prepositional Phrases

Short opening prepositional phrases seldom need commas after them:

> In a year he was back at work.
> From there they moved to Halifax.

Commas after *year* and *there* would force unnecessary pauses and make the sentences awkwardly heavy. Even longer phrases often don't need commas:

> At the beginning of the novel the author sets up several symbolic patterns.

But the longer the phrase the more likely it is that a comma will be needed to keep readers posted on just where they are:

> In a period of higher prices and lower real income, financial security becomes difficult to maintain.

The best test, as usual, is to read such sentences aloud. Then punctuate them the way you want your readers to hear them in their minds.

### c. Subordinate Clauses

The same principle generally applies to opening subordinate clauses. A long one will usually need a comma:

> When the heroine returns from Europe with a foreign husband in tow, her family is at first flabbergasted.

Short ones often don't need commas:

> When they left I went back to what I had been doing.

But even after relatively short clauses a comma sometimes helps achieve a desirable rhythm and emphasis. Read aloud the two following sentences:

When you sit down to write you need first to consider your reader.

When you sit down to write, you need first to consider your reader.

Either would do. With such a sentence choose according to how you want your readers to hear it.

If you can't decide whether or not a comma would be best, you'll usually be safer to put one in. Be especially careful not to omit a comma from a sentence like the following:

DRAFT: Although sales are increasing profits in many businesses are declining.

Readers would at first take *profits* to be the object of *are increasing* rather than the subject of a new clause. Then when they got to the second *are* they would, with a jolt, realize their mistake—but they would have to go back and start the sentence all over again, and they would be annoyed; they might well simply stop reading. Putting in the comma after the introductory clause makes the sentences flow smoothly and clearly:

REVISED: Although sales are increasing, profits in many businesses are declining.

**Closing Clauses:**  Only occasionally will subordinate clauses that follow the main clause need to be set off by a comma—for example those beginning with *though* or *although*, or those beginning with *because* after a negative statement. For example:

The minister had no authority to do what he did, though he was not aware of it.

They were not given jobs, because they were inexperienced.

Without the comma, the last example would seem to say that they *were* given jobs, but for some other reason than their lack of experience; the comma prevents the possible ambiguity by in effect separating the two clauses: "They were not given jobs. Why? Because they were inexperienced." Note that changing the negative verb *were not given* to the positive *were denied* removes the possible ambiguity and the need for the comma. (See pp. 227-228.)

### d. Participial Phrases

With opening (or closing) participial phrases that modify the subject, you have no choice; they must be set off by commas. Otherwise they sound at best awkward; at worst they invite misreading.

DRAFT: Tumbling down the stairs I bruised myself badly.
DRAFT: Altering the proportions in the formula I began to think the experiment might work after all.
DRAFT: Depressed by the results we headed home.

Put the commas in:

REVISED: Tumbling down the stairs, I bruised myself badly.
REVISED: Altering the proportions in the formula, I began to think the experiment might work after all.
REVISED: Depressed by the results, we headed home.

The same principles apply to *absolute phrases;* see Sentence-Combining 10.

## 3. Punctuating Series

### a. Comma before "and"

There is little to check for in the punctuation of series. You probably punctuate them automatically. But what you perhaps do not do automatically is put a comma between the *last two* elements of a series as well as between the others. If you don't you should. Look at this sentence:

> DRAFT: The Indus script contains approximately three hundred and ninety-six hieroglyphic or picto-graphic symbols which were discovered on baked clay tablets, stone seals and pottery fragments.

Did you find yourself speeding up slightly as you read the last five words? The lack of a comma after *seals* invites readers to do so and thus throws off the rhythm of the sentence. Had the sentence continued beyond that point, it would be almost impossible to avoid misreading it at least briefly:

> DRAFT: The Indus script contains approximately three hundred and ninety-six hieroglyphic or picto-graphic symbols which were discovered on baked clay tablets, stone seals and pottery fragments and came into being during the same period as the better-known scripts of ancient Egypt and Mesopotamia.

A comma after *fragments* might help—but there shouldn't be a comma after *fragments* (between two parts of a compound predicate). But there should be one after *seals*; put one there, in both versions, and again try reading them. You should find it much easier.

Many people consider such a comma optional. But if you get in the habit of using a comma before the *and* in a series, you will be less likely to mislead or confuse your readers and your sentences will have smoother rhythm.

### b. Semicolons

When one or more elements in a series already contain commas, it is necessary to use semicolons rather than commas to separate them, as in the following example:

> The firm has branches in Lethbridge, Alberta; Brandon, Manitoba; and Hull, Quebec.

You can occasionally also use semicolons simply because the elements in a series are unusually long or because you want the emphasis gained by the heavier pause, as in this sentence by a student:

> Honesty; trust; patience; love—these are the qualities of an ideal marriage.

### c. Other Devices

In a description of a first sky-diving experience, a student wrote the following passage, having led up to it with relatively calm prose:

> I jump. Then: the count—check—open—tangle—panic—grasp the risers—pull frantically. Untangled. Floating; glorious floating. All the world is below, the canopy above silhouetted against the sky which surrounds me in shades of pale blue wisped with grey and white.

It works. Only dashes could help convey the movement and mental agitation. The opening two-word sentence starts it off; the "Then:" with its unorthodox colon sets up the series; the single-word sentence "Untangled" expresses sudden relief; the weight of the unorthodox semicolon helps express the now slow movement in "Floating; glorious floating"; and the long final sentence, with its single comma, imitates the slow, graceful movement being experienced. The creative punctuation works superbly with the minor sentences and other stylistic devices to evoke the desired effect. (See also how dashes work effectively in the first descriptive paragraph in Exercise 4I.)

Here are two sentences (from "The Motive for Metaphor," by Northrop Frye) that show another way to handle a series:

> Suppose you're shipwrecked on an uninhabited island in the South Seas. The first thing you do is to take a long look at the world around you, a world of sky and sea and earth and stars and trees and hills.

The series of general and flat nouns is dramatically heightened by being connected with *and*'s instead of separated by commas. On rare occasions no punctuation at all works better than conventional punctuation—as again in this last example, in which a student is describing part of what happened at a baseball game:

> Objects hurtled down from the crowd. Beer-bottles hot-dog wrappers hot-dogs ice-cream sticks BOOS.

They all come hurtling together, unseparated by punctuation.

## 4. Enclosing Interrupters

Parenthetical sentence-interrupters must be set off *at both ends* by a pair of punctuation marks. You will usually enclose interrupters in a pair of commas. But you will sometimes want to use a pair of dashes. And occasionally you will use a pair of parentheses. The difference is simple: commas are normal, neutral; dashes emphasize; parentheses de-emphasize. Consider the following sentence from George Whalley's *The Legend of John Hornby*:

> As long as he travelled alone, which he almost invariably did from choice, his eccentricities were harmless enough.

> As long as he travelled alone—which he almost invariably did from choice—his eccentricities were harmless enough.

> As long as he travelled alone (which he almost invariably did from choice) his eccentricities were harmless enough.

Whalley could have chosen any one of the three ways to set off the interrupting clause. A pair of commas maintains a neutral, level tone. A pair of dashes calls attention to the clause; aloud, one would read it—especially the word *invariably*—a little more loudly than the rest of the sentence. The parentheses mark off the clause as incidental to the meaning of the sentence; aloud, one would lower one's voice slightly while reading the clause. (But note that the parentheses, by so strongly separating the clause, also call attention to it and thus, in an oblique way, also emphasize it a little.) Whalley chose to use dashes: he wanted the straightforward emphasis on the clause's point.

### a. Short Interrupters

You will usually want to set off short interrupters:

> There are many, no doubt, who would disagree with me.
>
> Robertson Davies's *Fifth Business*, for example, is both a first-rate and a highly popular novel.
>
> The results of the survey will of course be, at best, tentative.

But not always. This last example would be absurdly choppy if commas were put around "of course" as well as "at best." The writer could also have decided to put commas around "of course" and not around "at best," producing a different emphasis. Or all the commas could be omitted, producing a more streamlined sentence. And in the first example, a changed word order would remove the need for the commas:

> There are no doubt many who would disagree with me.

But if you wanted the kind of slower rhythm and greater emphasis they give, you could still enclose the phrase in commas:

> ~~There are, no doubt, many who would disagree with me.~~

If you feel that such an interrupter is strongly parenthetical, enclose it in commas; if you feel that it is only slightly parenthetical or not parenthetical at all, omit the commas.

> Here is a sentence that got past a student on his first draft:

> DRAFT: The teachers' training in music is extremely limited and as a result, the courses are weak and in many cases, nonexistent.

But on rereading it, aloud, he felt the awkward rhythm and finished enclosing the two short interrupters.

> REVISED: The teacher's training in music is extremely limited and, as a result, the courses are weak and, in many cases, nonexistent.

(The sentence still needs three or four more things done to it before it can be considered fully revised. Practise on it.)

### b. Nonrestrictive Clauses

Relative clauses, mainly those adjective clauses which begin with *who, which,* or *that,* can be either restrictive or nonrestrictive. Consider the difference in meaning between the two following sentences:

> RESTRICTIVE: The order which you have already paid for will be delivered on Friday.
>
> NONRESTRICTIVE: The order, which you have already paid for, will be delivered on Friday.

In the first sentence, the *which* clause, not set off by commas, restricts the meaning of "the order" to "that particular order which you have already paid for." In the second sentence, the *which* clause, enclosed in commas, is thus designated as incidental, parenthetical, as if the sentence said, "The order will be delivered on Friday. (Oh, by the way, you have already paid for it.)" In the first sentence, the restrictive clause distinguishes the particular order that has been paid for from one or more other orders that have not been paid for and that will presumably not be delivered on Friday. In the second sentence, there is only one order involved.

One way you can test a clause you aren't sure about is to try substituting the pronoun *that* for the pronoun *which or who* . Try it on the examples:

> The order that you have already paid for will be delivered on Friday.
>
> The order, that you have already paid for, will be delivered on Friday.

The second one won't work. Readers would be puzzled by a *that* in a nonrestrictive clause. Try substituting *that* in George Whalley's sentence at the beginning of this section; it won't work: the clause is clearly nonrestrictive and has to be set off by punctuation. Many writers keep this distinction clear in their writing by using *which* only in nonrestrictive clauses, never in restrictive ones. Since *that* cannot be used in nonrestrictive clauses, only in restrictive ones, there is then little chance for confusion in a reader's mind.

Another way to check a relative clause that you aren't sure about is to try omitting the relative pronoun; if the sentence then makes the kind of sense that you want it to, you know the clause is restrictive and should not be punctuated. Both *that*'s in the preceding sentence could be omitted; therefore both the clauses (that) they introduce are restrictive. Here is a sentence from a student's draft:

> DRAFT: Further irony is present in that the peace, to which the narrator refers, turns out to be far from permanent.

In revising, the writer felt uneasy about the relative clause enclosed in commas. First he tried substituting *that* for *which* and removing the commas (and also changing the word order):

> DRAFT: Further irony is present in that the peace that the narrator refers to turns out to be far from permanent.

That sounded better. But to make sure, he tried dropping the word *that*; he then knew he had the meaning he originally intended (and by omitting the second *that* he avoided its awkward repetition):

> REVISED: Further irony is present in that the peace the narrator refers to turns out to be far from permanent.

Here is one more example, this time with the pronoun *who*:

> RESTRICTIVE: The teacher who came from a small town was very kind to me.
> NONRESTRICTIVE: The teacher, who came from a small town, was very kind to me.

In the first sentence the *who* clause serves to separate this teacher from other teachers (the ones not from small towns) and is therefore restrictive. (As in the earlier examples, the *who* of this restrictive clause could be changed to a *that*: "The teacher that came from a small town was very kind to me." The pronoun *that* can refer to either people or things, though it is usually best to use *who* for people; the pronoun *which* cannot refer to people.) In the second sentence the *who* clause is nonrestrictive because it is set off by commas, meaning that it adds only incidental information; it does not serve to identify or restrict. Even though it adds possible useful clarifying information, it could be omitted without destroying the main meaning of the sentence: "The teacher was very kind to me." Such a parenthetical clause, then, must be enclosed, usually by a pair of commas. But remember the sentence near the beginning of this section: by using dashes, Whalley made even the incidental and parenthetical clause into something emphatic.

### c. Appositives

You also need to make sure that you've put an enclosing pair of punctuation marks around nonrestrictive appositives. An appositive is a noun or pronoun—often in a phrase—that further identifies another noun or pronoun, usually one just preceding. In the following sentence, for example, the words "my grade-ten teacher" constitute an appositive further identifying "Mrs. McGillivray":

> Mrs. McGillivray, my grade-ten teacher, had been an actress.

Note that you could consider such an appositive an abbreviated non-restrictive clause, here one from which "who was" has been omitted.

> Mrs. McGillivray, who was my grade-ten teacher, had been an actress.

Note also that appositives can often be reversed; it's worth trying, for sometimes it's an improvement:

> My grade-ten teacher, Mrs. McGillivray, had been an actress.

Appositives aren't always short. Here's an extended one—still set off by a pair of commas—from a sentence by Hugh Hood:

> Never in the age of the Romantic movement, that tremendous complex of revolution and reaction and revolution again in every aspect of human life and thought, did a single Canadian arise to make his voice heard among the chorus of prophets.
>
> ("Where the Promise Comes From")

But most will be relatively short:

> My favourite car, an old rebuilt MG, carted me around in style for years.

*Warning:* Note that at the beginning of this section we said that non-restrictive appositives *further* identify a preceding noun or pronoun. In the examples above, the original nouns were already identified: "Mrs. McGillivray" (or in the reversed version, "My tenth-grade teacher"), "the Romantic movement," "My favourite car." The appositives, like nonrestrictive clauses, merely add extra information. Occasionally, however, an appositive will be restrictive and thus *not* set off with commas:

> The great English poet Chaucer died in 1400.

"The great English poet" is not sufficient identification; there are other great English poets. The name *Chaucer* is essential to the meaning. Using the indefinite article *a* rather than the definite article *the* would make the name nonrestrictive.

> A great English poet, Chaucer, died in 1400.

Reversing the order would make the new second part a nonrestrictive appositive.

> Chaucer, the great English poet, died in 1400.

Appositives can be tricky. Be carefully with them. For example stop and think when you're referring to such things as literary works:

> DRAFT: Conrad's long novel, *Nostromo*, is set in South America.

The commas around the title wrongly imply that *Nostromo* was Conrad's only "long novel"; the title should be considered a restrictive appositive:

> REVISED: Conrad's long novel *Nostromo* is set in South America.

But if that sounds a trifle awkward, try revising the sentence another way, for example by reversing the order and adding a clarifying word or two:

> REVISED: *Nostromo*, one of Conrad's longer novels, is set in South America.

Nonrestrictive appositives are usually set off with commas, but if you want to emphasize one, use dashes:

> *The Watch that Ends the Night*—in my opinion Hugh MacLennan's best novel—was published in 1959.

And if an appositive consists of more than one noun, set if off with dashes in order to avoid confusing your readers. Look for example at this sentence:

> DRAFT: Three students, Alice, Nicole, and Bruce, raised their hands.

The comma after *Bruce* should make it clear, but at least up to that point a reader couldn't be sure whether Alice, Nicole, and Bruce were the "three students" or three other people who were present and also raised their hands. Using dashes avoids the ambiguity:

> REVISED: Three students—Alice, Nicole, and Bruce—raised their hands.

You can also of course use a pair of parentheses to set off an appositive if you want to de-emphasize it; parentheses are often used, for example, to enclose a brief definition in order to minimize its interruption of the sentence (see p. 70).

One final note about interrupters: if one of these words or phrases or clauses comes at the beginning or, more likely the end of a sentence, then it would not truly be an "interrupter" and would of course need only one comma or dash to set it off from the rest of the sentence, as with the long concluding appositive in this sentence by Hugh MacLennan, discussing the Group of Seven painters:

> They not only revealed, they made tolerable and beautiful, one of the chief sources of the Canadian neurosis—the stark, sombre, cold, and empty land in which our ancestors had to make a living in stark, sombre, and lonely ways.

> (from a speech printed in
> *The Price of Being Canadian*, ed. D.B.L. Hamlin)

## Exercise 11F

Here is the way the student punctuated the paragraph we quoted—without punctuation—at the beginning of the chapter. Compare it with your version. Which one do you think better?

> The human voice is music itself. It rises and falls, it pauses, it gets louder and softer. If this music were not present in our voices, we would all speak in monotones, and conversation would soon become very tedious. Our speech pattern is song, and it reflects our emotions: happiness, anger, sorrow, fatigue, and nonchalance all show up in our voices. Thus we can see that music is man's chief way of expressing his inner emotions—whether he realizes it or not.

## Exercise 11G

Here are some poorly punctuated sentences from students' drafts for you to practise your revising techniques on. If you think anything else besides punctuation needs revising, go ahead and do it.

1. Therefore, it is much more beneficial to the reader, because they can better understand the story.
2. Some say that *Jane Eyre* is an autobiographical work, Brontë, however, used to deny that claim.
3. Every mature adult possesses a vocabulary of several thousand words; but, how many of us really know the meaning of each of these words?
4. No matter how well perfectionists do something they always ask themselves "Could I have done better."
5. It would seem that for politicians the issues aren't what's really important, it's the argument that counts.
6. How such a nice colour as green ever came to symbolize such nasty human tendencies as envy, greed and deceit, is a mystery to me.
7. When you are unable to see your senses become highly tuned and your imagination will react to any message received by these senses.
8. It has been hypothesized that the new brain, or cerebral cortex controls reason and intuition, and allows cognitive thought processes.
9. But, I decided to go ahead with the project.
10. The weather is a force we will never control and it is a good thing.
11. Her character, throughout the early part of the novel is most definitely flat.
12. The plain omelette is a simple quick meal of eggs mixed with water, salt, pepper and herbs such as dill, chives or marjoram.
13. Harmony, as opposed to melody, is the vertical structure of a musical composition; the melody being the horizontal structure.
14. The old cliché, which says that a dog is a man's best friend, acquired a new meaning for me last summer.
15. By the early 70's the author observes, people's habits had changed.

## Exercise 11H

Here are two more paragraphs printed without punctuation. Practise your skills by punctuating them. Wherever possible, try alternatives until you decide which is best. You can do it without changing any of the wording, but you may want to add one or two small function-words.

## Abroadening

travel can be broadening as almost everyone who has travelled much will agree experiencing a foreign culture stretches the mind it can so to speak enrich one's soul further we need to learn about other people how they live and think foreign countries being increasingly important to us in today's rapidly shrinking world and how better to learn about foreign countries than by actually visiting them what one can learn from books won't stick so well in the mind it tends to evaporate soon after but the sensation of eating foreign food of hearing foreign voices of seeing foreign buildings of walking about in foreign streets these experiences will last in one's memory become a vital part of one's real inner self even though many details may be forgotten the essence will remain one can perhaps get along without travelling nevertheless one would then be missing the considerable enrichment that it can bring

## The Information Gap

magazines and newspapers the print media they are no longer people's major sources of news as they used to be although they continue to thrive or at least some do others have fallen victim to the great popularity of television the tube seems to have conquered the minds of the masses many of whom spend increasing numbers of hours each week staring at the glowing box some would argue that people's brains are therefore turning to jelly figuratively speaking they claim that television even in news programming offers little to challenge a viewer's mind but many viewers would disagree they find television a sufficient source of information and some go on to point out that whether as a result of television's influence or of some other cause many newspapers and magazines are turning away from their old formats and packed contents that they are turning instead to popular features and shallow coverage like the vacuous boob-tube they seem to be emulating if the process continues where will one be able to turn for news for information the kind of in-depth information one needs in order to understand and perhaps try to improve our increasingly complex and troubled world no one seems to have an answer we'll just have to wait and see

---

# Unwanted Punctuation

If you find "no p" in the margin of a paper, you may have made one of the following errors:

1. No single comma or dash should come between subject and verb:

    WRONG: Many people in Europe and North America, are being forced to lower their expectations.

There should be no pause there. If the sentence were changed so that an interrupter came between subject and verb, then the interrupter would be set off with a pair of commas:

Many people, especially those in industrialized countries, are being forced to lower their expectations.

There are two exceptions to this rule, but they occur infrequently. One is that an unusually long subject, especially one consisting of a series, often needs to be set off simply for clarity; readers naturally pause for breath before going on to the predicate:

> Increased fuel costs, increased transportation costs, increased labour costs, increased costs of materials, increased traffic congestion, increased pressure on budgets from other directions—all these are prompting many people to turn to smaller cars.

But note that in such a sentence clarity also often requires that the long subject be repeated or summed up, as here in the words "all these," before the sentence can comfortably continue. The other exception occurs when a comma is necessary to prevent mis-reading:

> Whether there is anything more important than human happiness, is thought by some to be debatable.

Without the comma, readers would at first take *is* to be the verb for the single word *happiness* rather than for the entire preceding clause. But it might be worth recasting the sentence to avoid having to use such a comma. Try it.

2. Similarly, no single comma or dash should come between a verb and its object or complement:

> WRONG: After carefully considering all his arguments I decided, that the courses my adviser recommended were best for me.

Since the word *that* introduces a noun clause which is the object of the verb *decided*, there should be no comma between them. But perhaps the writer felt the need for a pause: a comma after *arguments* would do the trick; in fact, there should be one there.

3. No single comma should come between the last adjective of a series and the noun it modifies:

> WRONG: It turned out to be an inexpensive, relaxing, enjoyable, and educational, holiday for all of us.

The last comma is wrong. Don't let the rhythm of a series of adjectives trap you into wanting another pause after the final adjective.

### Punctuation Review Exercise

Punctuate the following sentences as you think necessary or best. Some may need no punctuation.

1. The flowers in the garden were predominantly roses daffodils and camellias.
2. Having received his bachelor's degree after four long hard years Sean felt that society owed him a decent job.
3. The salesman was no doubt eager for the sale was an important one.
4. The salesman carefully explained to me that no interest would be charged.
5. The next day however I changed my mind.

6. There are three things wrong with that hotel the rooms are too small the food is terrible and the price is too high.
7. She was born in Halifax Nova Scotia in 1910.
8. The mayor made a long statement describing the problem then the council began to debate it.
9. While parking the car he suddenly remembered that he had left his wallet at home.
10. Winding the clock she thought once again of the work awaiting her the next morning.
11. It promised to be an unusually warm day but we decided to go on the hike anyway.
12. High winds are forecast for this afternoon therefore the regatta has been postponed.
13. She started for the door as soon as the whistle sounded.
14. His favourite Canadian authors are Atwood Davies and Laurence.
15. The book that they sent me interesting as it was was not the one that I had ordered.
16. In the introduction to her book the author says that a proper diet is essential to good health.
17. Three years have passed since they moved to the country and they no longer miss city life at all.
18. She was assured it would not be a difficult task however she still did not look forward to it.
19. According to the reviewer this novel is one that "everyone who calls himself educated should read."
20. Disturbed by the event he tried very hard to remember how it had all begun.
21. "I absolutely refuse to be intimidated" said Magda quietly but forcefully.
22. Jonathan slept until almost noon and then fixed himself a large and leisurely breakfast it being a holiday that he was determined to enjoy in his own way.
23. The gardener told me that my roses my lilacs my hydrangeas and my geraniums all needed a good dose of fertilizer.
24. It was time to get on the phone and call Mr. Johnson our plumber.
25. Diana didn't like the looks of the house at all in fact she couldn't imagine why her friends had bought it.

## Exercise 11 I

Sloppy punctuation can also spoil the rhythm or movement of otherwise good sentences, as in this example:

> Often, when we come upon a scene in which a person is either injured or in danger, we do nothing. We might feel that we can't just stand there, and let the person suffer or die, but on the other hand, we feel that we don't have enough expertise to deal with the problem. Confronted, then, with an emergency we rationalize away our lack of action by saying to ourselves that we might do more harm than good.

Revise the punctuation to make the sentences flow the way they should. You may want to change a word or two in the process. (Maybe you can also get rid of the word *person*.)

### Exploration 11A

William Blake wrote a series of short poems called *Songs of Innocence*, and later a series called *Songs of Experience*. Each poem in the first series is matched and contrasted by a poem in the second. Write your own short "song of innocence" and follow it with a matched and contrasting "song of experience." This is intended as an assignment for two short pieces of autobiographical prose; but if that doesn't grab you, feel free to write about someone else, or some imaginary person; and do write in verse, if you feel so inclined.

### Exploration 11B

In a paragraph—a long one if necessary—describe your room, or one of your rooms. Take your notes, and perhaps even write your first draft, while actually observing the room. Have a dominant impression in mind, but leave it implicit; make your selection and ordering of details convey the desired impression. Use some kind of spatial order: for example left to right, up to down, far to near, or some combination. Use no more than three or four adjectives; find instead concrete verbs and nouns. And do not use *there is* or *there are*.

### Essay 11A

Imagine yourself in the seat of power. If you were an absolute monarch or a dictator, how would you redesign society—and why? Explain as much of it as you can in an essay of around 1000-1200 words.

  OR

Suppose you could go back five, ten, or twenty years and change one political decision, or the outcome of one public event. What would you change, and why?

### Essay 11B

Describe and analyze one painting or sculpture in a current exhibit in a local gallery. Or compare two works in the exhibit. Make your primary purpose simply to inform, but indulge in a little evaluation along the way.

### Sentence-Combining 11:  Colons and Dashes

Several earlier exercises, both sentence-combining and other kinds, give you practice with punctuation marks, mostly commas and semicolons. The final patterned sentence-combining exercise focusses on the colon and the dash, punctuation marks often either underused or misused because not understood. The two patterns that follow don't exhaust the possibilities of these two marks, but they do suggest the character of each.

### Pattern 11A

a.  Money is important to all of us.
b.  We need it to get along from day to day.
Result of combining *a* and *b*:
  Money is important to all of us: we need it to get along from day to day.

COPY the pattern sentence carefully, inserting the colon.

COMBINE each of the following pairs into a sentence modelled on the pattern sentence:
a.  Science-fiction movies are getting boring.
b.  They use the same tricks over and over again.

a.  Television is a useful tool for families with children.
b.  It makes a good babysitter.

a.  Two things are undeniable.
b.  The brakes were unreliable, and the driver had been drinking.

COMPOSE at least two more sentences modelled on Pattern 11A.

In this exercise you are using a colon to join two base sentences. The colon is appropriate when the second sentence explains or elaborates on the first in a particularly close way.

## Pattern 11B

a.  The trumpeter swan is a beautiful bird.
b.  It is also a rare one.

RESULT:  The trumpeter swan is a beautiful bird—and also a rare one.

Copy the pattern sentence, noting that a dash and the word *and* replace the *It is* of sentence *b*.

Combine each of the following pairs into a sentence modelled on the pattern sentence:
a.  Television is a prime source of home entertainment.
b.  It is also a good babysitter.

a.  Home-made wine is often as good as commercially produced wine.
b.  It is also much less expensive.

a.  Stars of stage and screen sometimes lead a romantic kind of life.
b.  It is also a hectic one.

Compose at least two more sentences modelled on Pattern 11B.

In this exercise, as in Pattern 1I and 1J, you are making two simple sentences into a single sentence by turning the second into part of a compound complement or object and joining the two parts with *and*. In these sentences, however, instead of using no punctuation before the and, you use a dash, which points to an intended slight twist or unexpected irony in the second part. If you want a similar effect but without so much emphasis, try using a comma. Does it work with the above sentences and the ones you composed? Then try keeping the dash but omitting *also*. How does that change the effect?

---

## Playing with Language 11A

Have some fun with punctuation marks. Write a little narrative in which they figure as characters; or perhaps a short poem made up entirely or mostly of them. Do something imaginative and amusing with them.

### Playing with Language 11B

Compose a sentence that will let you vary punctuation to produce different meanings. Vary the punctuation in as many ways as you can in order to change the sentence's meaning—which of course includes its emphases and rhythms, its full effect. See if you can find a way to use all the available punctuation marks (even the exclamation point) in one sentence.

### Playing with Language 11C

Write an advertisement for some new-fangled product of your own invention. The copy is to appear in a national wide-circulation magazine and will mostly if not entirely be on the bottom half of one page; you are allowed 150 words, maximum; the top half of the page will contain a picture or drawing, if you want it, and a few words could go up there. Try to convince prospective buyers that they can't possibly get along without your new widget, whatever it is. Remember, your job at the agency is on the line. You've got to come up with a winner.

### Playing with Language 11D

Write a letter about 300-500 words long according to one of the following descriptions:

1. A thank-you note to an older relative for a gift you didn't want or need.
2. A letter to a high-school or university friend you haven't heard from for twenty years but who has suddenly written to ask about staying with you for two weeks in July.
3. A letter to a manufacturer, returning a defective product and asking for a refund. The product did not carry a guarantee.
4. A letter to a finance company explaining why you can't make the payment this month—or next.
5. A note to the principal of your high school complaining that the school failed to prepare you for university English courses.

# STAGE FOUR:
# Presenting

*You shall see them on a beautiful quarto page, where a neat rivulet of text shall meander through a meadow of margin.*

(Richard Brinsley Sheridan)

CHAPTER XII

# Step 8: Preparing the Final Draft

## FINAL SCREENING

You probably do some preliminary screening before you begin revising. That is, you get one or two friends to read through your first draft and give you their impressions. And you may talk with others about various details as you revise, trying out a paragraph or a sentence on them. But probably the most important screening occurs when you think you are through revising, just before you prepare your final draft.

As at the rough-draft stage, it may be possible to arrange some formalized screening session with others, either within a class or outside of class time—perhaps an exchange of papers. And, again, your instructor may want to offer some criticisms and suggestions. You may even want your helpers to again use the evaluation form we suggested earlier, or one similar to it (see p. 148). Or, since you now want a wider range of reactions and more consideration of details, you may want to use a different form, perhaps something more like the one on the facing page (you can also use such a form as a checklist for revising and proofreading).

Feedback at this stage can be valuable, especially if you haven't time to put a piece of writing aside for a while after working so closely with it during revision. Others can be objective where you cannot. Unlike you, they can spot places where you've over-revised, made complicated what should be simple, got carried away with a stylistic device to the point where it overshadows your meaning—such things can easily happen during revision, and it's not easy for writers to see them in their own prose.

Get some help that you can trust, and trust it. You may not yet be quite through revising.

| SCREENING CHART | | | | |
|---|---|---|---|---|
| | good | fair | poor | Comments |
| Title | | | | |
| Beginning (length, tone, occasion, reader's role) | | | | |
| Thesis (clarity, placement) | | | | |
| Proofreading (spelling, grammar, mechanics, etc.) | | | | |
| Paragraphing (unity, topic sentences, development, length, variety) | | | | |
| Coherence in and between paragraphs | | | | |
| Organization | | | | |
| Unity | | | | |
| Development; support of generalizations | | | | |
| Emphasis; proportions | | | | |
| Logic | | | | |
| Sentences (clarity, economy, variety) | | | | |
| Diction (level, usage, concreteness, verbs) | | | | |
| Punctuation | | | | |
| Consistency of stance | | | | |
| Ending (length, thesis) | | | | |
| Scope (topic narrowed?) | | | | |

Major strengths:

What single thing did you like best?

Major weaknesses:

What single thing most needs revising?

Other comments:

## FORMS AND FORMATS

The *occasion* for a particular piece of writing has a good deal to do with the *form* in which you present it.

Want-ads, telegrams, letters (bread-and-butter, personal, business), memos, academic essays, applications, resumés, article or book manuscripts, short notes to roommates or spouses (on a small scrap of paper: "Gone downtown. Back by 3. J."), lab reports—all these and others have their own forms, and each form has its own restrictions and demands.

Whenever you present a piece of writing, you present it *to someone*, and that someone will then do something with it—or not. Have you ever been handed a flyer on a street-corner and thrown it away without reading it? Have you ever seen an ad stuck on a bulletin board, offering for sale something you are interested in—and then been unable to make out the scrawled phone number? No sale. Have you seen notices taped to doors or walls, announcing a lecture or a poetry reading or a rally or other meeting, but whose perpetrators had done a bad job of photo-copying, or had run off so many copies on a duplicating machine that the purple ink was almost invisible? Result: a poor turn-out. Have you ever tried to fill out a form that didn't allow enough space to write what it asked for—perhaps even your name? If you wrote a short note to your prof recently, did you make the mistake of signing off with a "Sincerely," something inappropriate for that form? What someone does or does not do with a piece of writing often depends a great deal on how it is presented. The medium, at least partly, is indeed the message.

To repeat: The *occasion* for a particular piece of writing has a good deal to do with the *form* in which you present it. If you are a student, your occasion for writing is often that of fulfilling an assignment. You present pieces of writing to your instructors and your instructors then do something with them. Usually what they do is mark them and return them to you for revision and correction. And this procedure in part determines the form you should use. For example, you leave margins on all four sides of each page partly for aesthetic purposes; it makes for an attractive page. But there's also a practical reason: there must be white space around your work so that your instructors have room to put marking symbols and to write brief comments and suggestions. Similarly, you double-space your work not only because it is easier to read than if it were single-spaced, but also because sometimes your instructors, but more often yourself when you are revising and correcting according to their suggestions, need the spaces between lines to insert new or different words. In fact the format for academic writing is almost the same as that for work submitted for publication: both you and your editors need the margins and the spaces between lines for emendations, proofreading symbols, and brief instructions to the printer.

When you write essays for your classes you can usually assume that your instructors will read them: it is their job. They are a captive audience. But instructors have been known to return essays unread when they consider them unreadable for one reason or another: no margins, failure to skip lines, messy or otherwise illegible writing, coloured ink, ink or typing so dim as to be difficult to read, italic or other fancy type-face. Or they may read through the first paragraph, find in it ten spelling errors and a comma splice, and decide that it is pointless to go on. Instructors don't enjoy doing this; they don't get some sort of masochistic pleasure out of it; they do suffer on such occasions. But it is the student who suffers most, whether from getting a low grade or—at best—from having to spend the time and energy to re-do the paper; even then it may get a reduced grade because it is late. Presentation is important. (See also "Making Your Reader Your Accomplice," p. 35.)

## Manuscript Conventions

When you are through revising you are ready to prepare your final draft, the finished product. If you care about your work, you will present it in a way that shows that you care about it. Only then can you expect your readers to care about it.

Follow the standard conventions unless you have specific reasons to depart from them—for example if an instructor tells you to do something in a different way, or if you're submitting a manuscript to a publication whose guidelines specify different practices. The following principles and details apply primarily to writing done for class but most of them apply to other kinds of writing as well. (*Note:* This is not an exhaustive list. For more information, consult a comprehensive handbook, the back of a good college dictionary, a style guide, or some other authority.)

1. *Neatness*   Neatness is essential. Nothing puts readers off faster than a sloppy or illegible piece of writing. Sloppy copy spoils your chances even before readers start reading your words.

   Type if possible, or have your work typed for you. Otherwise write legibly. Use a good black ribbon if you type; use dark ink if you write by hand.

   Make any corrections or other changes in ink only, and if you make more than two or three on a page, re-do the page.

   Use standard size white paper of good quality, plain for typed work, ruled for handwritten work. Do not use paper torn from a spiral notebook.

2. *Margins*   Leave generous margins on all four sides of the page. The white space should look like a frame around your prose. Leave approximately 3.5-4 cm (1½ inches) at the left, 2.5-3 cm (1 inch) on the other sides.

3. *Spacing*   If you type, double space. If you write by hand, write only on every other line. Use only one side of each sheet.

4. *First Page*   Centre your title about a quarter of the way down the first page, and quadruple space below it. Don't underline or put quotation marks around your own title, or write it all in capital letters. Don't number the first page, unless at bottom centre; number subsequent pages, with Arabic numerals, either at top right or top centre.

5. *Indention*   Indent each paragraph five spaces. Don't leave extra space between paragraphs except where you want to indicate a major break between sections of an essay.

6. *Punctuation*   Don't begin a new line with a punctuation mark (except the first of a pair of parentheses). Always leave two spaces after any terminal punctuation. Some people put two spaces after colons (except in titles and footnotes), but it is simpler to use only one space after all colons (and semicolons). Type two unspaced hyphens to make a dash. A parenthesis is

the only punctuation mark that can occur next to another mark (except for quotation marks, the period of an abbreviation, or where a dash and a period are used to indicate the abrupt breaking off of a piece of dialogue). Never put a comma in front of a pair of parentheses.

7.  *Word Division*   As much as possible, avoid dividing words at the end of a line; an uneven right-hand margin is preferable to having many divided words. When you must divide a word, divide it only between syllables; and don't guess: use your dictionary to check where a word's syllable breaks occur. Try to avoid breaking off syllables of only two letters (and never break off *-ed*); never break off only one letter. Indicate the break with a hyphen at the end of a line, and try to divide so that the next line begins with a consonant rather than a vowel—for example *con-tinuation* or *continuation* rather than *contin-uation* or *continu-ation*.

8.  *Abbreviations*   Avoid abbreviations when possible, unless they are appropriate, as for example in a technical report. In formal writing, write out "that is" and "for example" rather than use *i.e.* and *e.g.* Otherwise, use only standard abbreviations: Mr., Mrs., Ms., Jr., M.D., B.A., A.D., a.m., Ltd., etc. (Avoid *etc.* in your writing.) Some abbreviations are not followed by periods: RCMP, NASA, CBC, and so on.

9.  *Capitalization*   Capitalize the beginnings of sentences, the pronoun *I*, proper nouns and their abbreviations, titles when part of a name, months and days (but not seasons), languages (English, French), derivations of proper names (Shakespearean, Haligonian), the first and last and all important words of titles of written works (not prepositions and conjunctions unless five or more letters long).

10. *Titles*   When referring to a work by its title, enclose in quotation marks those of short works or parts of works (stories, essays, short poems, chapters, songs); italicize (underline) those of long works or works published as units (books, plays, long poems, operas, movies, magazines, newspapers, paintings, sculptures).

11. *Italics*   Use italics (underlining in typed or handwritten work) for titles of long works (see 10 above); names of ships, planes, and the like; words, letters, or numerals referred to as such ("The word *italics* refers to slanted type"); for emphasis (but this should be minimized, just like exclamation points—see pp. 217, 285-286).

12. *Numerals*   Except in technical reports and the like, use numerals sparingly. Use numerals only in the following instances: when it would take more than two words to spell out a number; when you are citing two or more numbers for comparison or statistics; for time of day with *a.m.* and *p.m.*; for dates; for addresses; for page numbers and the like. Don't begin a sentence with a numeral.

13. *Quotations and quotation marks*   Put quotation marks around the titles of short works (see 10 above), around pieces of dialogue or other rendering of direct speech, and around verbatim quotation from any printed or other source.

    Use double quotation marks ("…") except around a quotation within a quotation ("… '…' …").

    If a quotation from another source takes four or more lines, indent it at least three extra spaces beyond the normal five for a paragraph, single-space it, and leave an extra line before and after it. Such indented or "block" quotation is intended to make your work look the way it would if it were printed. (Some instructors will ask you to double-space even block quotations. If you submit a manuscript to a publication, so that it would be set in type, such long quotations should be double-spaced, and not indented; you instruct the printer to indent and single-space by drawing a vertical line in the left margin beside the quotation.) *Note:* Indenting and single-spacing a long quotation *is* quoting; don't add any quotation marks of your own. If you're quoting a long passage of dialogue, reproduce only the quotation marks you find in the original.

You can put quotation marks around a term you want to qualify or use in a special sense or to which you want to call attention in a certain way, as we did with the word *block* just above. But do not put quotation marks around slang terms and clichés; that practice annoys readers because it insults their intelligence.

If you omit something from a quotation, replace it with three *spaced* periods (called an *ellipsis*). If the omitted material includes the end of a sentence, use four dots: the fourth is the period.

If you add a clarifying word or phrase to quoted material, enclose it in brackets—square brackets, that is, not parentheses.

Put periods and commas inside closing quotation marks; put semicolons and colons outside them. Question marks and exclamation points go either inside or outside, depending on whether they belong to the quotation or to a larger sentence of which the quotation is a part.

14. *Apostrophes*   Apostrophes and hyphens are properly matters of spelling, but since most people think of them as matters of mechanical convention, we include them here. See Chapter XIII for the rest of spelling.

   a.   Apostrophes are used to indicate the possessive case of nouns:

   > Ralph's car, Einstein's theory, women's rights, a week's wages, a day's work

   That is, you add an apostrophe and an *s* to show possession. If the noun is a *plural* that already ends in *s*, add only the apostrophe:

   > boys' club, the Joneses' house, the provinces' wealth, churches' attitudes, two days' work

   Note that often only the position of the apostrophe tells readers whether a word is singular or plural (boy's, boys'; province's, provinces'); a second's carelessness would seriously mislead them.

   When a *singular* noun—usually a proper noun—ends in *s* or an *s*-sound, it is usually best to add both the apostrophe and another *s* to form the possessive, for we usually pronounce such words with an extra syllable:

   > Yeats's poetry, Dickens's novels, Tom Jones's voice, the bus's brakes, the notice's language

   But when this practice could produce an awkward pronunciation (as it often will, even for someone reading silently), avoid the problem by substituting an *of* phrase:

Moses's leadership—the leadership of Moses
Camus's philosophy—the philosophy of Camus
carelessness's consequences—the consequences of carelessness

*Warning:* Apostrophes are *not* used to form the possessive of *pronouns*: *it's* means *it is*, not *of it*. Write *hers*, not *her's*, and *theirs*, not *their's*.

b. Apostrophes are used to form contractions, where they stand for omitted letters:

isn't (is not), aren't (are not), don't (do not), they're (they are), it's (it is), she's (she is)

c. Apostrophes are often used to form the plurals of numerals, symbols, and words referred to as words:

the ABC's, p's and q's, three 9's, too many *is*'s

This is the *only* way apostrophes can be used to form plurals.

15. *Hyphens*   Hyphens can be a problem. Whenever you aren't sure whether to use a hyphen, consult a good up-to-date dictionary; it will often solve the problem. Some uses of the hyphen, however, are clear:

a. In compound numbers from twenty-one to ninety-nine, with fractions used as adjectives (a two-thirds majority), with compounds indicating time (eight-fifteen), and to indicate a range of numbers (pages 12-17).

b. With prefixes before proper nouns:

pre-Cambrian, pan-Slavic, all-Canadian, un-American

and with compounds beginning with the prefix *self*:

self-sufficient, self-made, self-esteem

and usually with the prefixes *vice* and *by*:

vice-president, vice-consul, by-election (but *viceroy, bylaw, bygone*)

c. With *great-* and *-in-law* in words for relatives:

great-grandmother, great-uncle, brother-in-law

d. To prevent a word's being mistaken for another:

re-cover (recover), re-count (recount), re-dress (redress)

e. In compound adjectives preceding a noun:

well-done steak (but "The steak was well done.")

—but never join a *-ly* adverb to an adjective:

cleverly contrived plan, fully accomplished goal

f. When two or more prefixes are used with a single root, use what is called a "suspension hyphen," as in this sentence from Donald Creighton's *The Story of Canada:*

> Montcalm signalled the advance, and the whole array of white- and blue-clad soldiers surged forward.

Otherwise, use a dictionary to find out whether to hyphenate compound modifiers, nouns, and verbs.

## Titles

You should provide a title for everything of any substance you write—except of course a letter. Even a business memo will usually need some sort of heading: "Security Precautions," or "Better inter-office communication." Essays and Explorations, whether of one paragraph or longer, should be titled. Titles can be simply descriptive, or curiosity-arousing, or otherwise provocative. Good titles are often all three. The kind of title you use will also depend partly on your audience and purpose and on your tone. A solemn or otherwise serious piece shouldn't have a flippant title. But if the occasion permits, try to get a little liveliness into your titles. (A little alliteration or rhyme can sometimes help, but don't overdo it.) The one thing no title should be is dull. And most good titles will also at least suggest or hint at your thesis.

But note: Don't think of a title as part of the text; the text must be clear by itself. For example, if your title reads "Disarmament," you should not begin with something like "This is a major problem in the modern world." Rather the beginning itself must state the subject: "Among the major problems facing the world today, clearly the most pressing is disarmament."

---

### *Exercise 12A*

Here are some titles from student essays. Evaluate them. Which ones do you find best? Why? Which are least effective? Why? Does length matter? Is there more freedom for choosing a title for a narrative than, say, for an argument? (When it's not self-evident, we have briefly indicated the kind of essay. Are good titles always self-evident?)

1. What Is Language? (definition)
2. A Case in Favour of a Government-Controlled Dental Plan
3. My Home Town: Growing Up
4. You Never Get a Second Chance to Make a First Impression
5. The Value of Music
6. Just Punishment (argument in favour of capital punishment)
7. A World of Contradictions
8. Fear and Paranoia (definition and comparison)
9. Time (on how time-conscious people are)
10. The First Step: A History of Ballet
11. Run for Your Life (on jogging; see pp. 122-123)
12. Self-Discipline and the Student
13. The Credit Trap (argument warning of dangers of credit cards)

14. The Video Phenomenon: Boom for Business or Bust for Society?
15. What a Lovely Voice! (on the qualities, kinds, and importance of the human voice)
16. The Right to Be Normal (argument favouring mainstreaming of handicapped children)
17. Gold Panning: A Revived Art
18. Rock and Roll
19. One of Those Days (narrative of personal experience)
20. Hurrah for Hiking
21. Banning Sports (an ironic "modest proposal"; see p. 406)
22. Terrific Terror (on a horror movie)
23. A Life-Changing Experience
24. Tennis, Anyone? (narrative of personal experience of playing in a tournament)
25. My First Experience Camping

Now revise all those you think less good than they could be. The writer of "A World of Contradictions," for example, decided to change his title to "On the Contrary." Is that an improvement?

---

## Exploration 12A

Choose one of the proverbs or familiar quotations from the list on pp. 170-171 and write a strongly vivid narrative paragraph (preferably from personal experience) to explain and support it. Incorporate the proverb or quotation (in quotation marks) into either your opening or your closing sentence.

---

## Essay 12A

Write an essay on the topic "My Favourite Canadian Politician" (do not use that as your title). Make conscious use of definition (What is a politician?), example and illustration (perhaps an opening anecdote), and comparison and contrast (Who or what is he or she like or unlike?). You may also find classification useful (if only for defining or comparing and contrasting), or even cause and effect. Use the invention questions in Chapter III freely in order to generate ideas. Draw up a detailed tentative plan before you begin writing your first draft, and on it state your purpose and describe your intended audience.

---

## Sentence-Combining 12: Variety and Experiment

The sentence-combining patterns provided earlier in this book represent only a fraction of the possible kinds of sentences you might want to write. They demonstrate—and give you practice in—some of the basic forms and variations, but your own experience and experimenting will reveal many more. The way you put any given sentence together will depend first, perhaps, on your instinct, or your "ear," and then on your careful consideration of what you want to say and how you want to say it—and the "how" may depend largely on whom you want to say it to, and for what purpose.

While working on the preceding sentence-combining exercises, you will have noticed that we often used the same or similar pairs of base sentences several times—not to bore you, but to illustrate that often the same basic idea can be expressed in a variety of ways. A particular independent clause can remain one in a compound sentence, or it can become, in other patterns, one or another kind of subordinate clause or one or another kind of phrase, or even just a word. The point is that you almost always have a choice, often several choices, of how to say something. Choose according to your rhetorical context; decide what you want to emphasize, what relations between parts you want to point up, and what kind of sentence or sentences you want at any given place.

A. Below are several pairs and some larger groups of base sentences that want combining. But before you start working on them, review all the preceding sentence-combining exercises to refresh your memory of the variety of available ways to put sentences together. Then tackle these new groups of sentences. You will find that some of them seem to invite a particular kind of combination; but even with these relatively restrictive groups, try to come up with at least two possibly useful versions. For some groups you may find that you want to try out a dozen or more possible combinations.

Further, this final exercise is intended to be relatively unstructured. Don't feel so bound to certain mechanical patterns as you were in the earlier exercises. Instead, feel free to move elements around, to add or change a word when you want to, and of course to delete words and phrases that seem unnecessary or in the way. As you work on each sentence, think about a possible context, a possible audience and purpose for it. (In this and the following exercises you may occasionally, if you wish, end up with more than one sentence—for example if you want to include a short snappy sentence, perhaps even a minor sentence, for its effect.)

1. The truck rattled to a stop.
   Its grill and right fender were hopelessly crumpled.
2. Joe Fitzgerald is our most effective union representative.
   He organized the plant in Winnipeg.
   He arrived here on the morning plane.
3. There is nothing inherently funny about locker rooms.
   Locker rooms have a reputation for producing a certain kind of humour.
4. Wolverines are seldom encountered by tourists.
   A wolverine is an animal respected for its ferocity.
5. Some children are disabled.
   Disabled children deserve special attention.
   School systems have room for disabled children.
   Disabled children benefit from their peers' attention.
   Regular teachers can be trained to deal with disabled children.
6. George Bernard Shaw had a low opinion of politicians.
   He called Parliament a talking-shop.
7. Many people may not like the metric system.
   Younger people are more likely to favour it.
   It seems to be here to stay.
8. Conventional broadcasting is becoming less profitable.
   It may have to change its strategies.
   Competition from cable operators is increasing.

9. The Day Care Centre is understaffed.
   Two of the children suffered minor accidents.
10. Junk food is usually low in nutritional value.
    It is often expensive.
    People buy a lot of it anyway.
11. The library shelves are overcrowded.
    The new wing won't be ready for another six months.
    The head librarian is accustomed to crises.
12. Many recent graduates have trouble finding employment.
    Some are willing to accept work outside their major fields.
13. People sometimes smoke from nervousness.
    They seem to need something to occupy their hands.
    I intend to learn how to knit.
14. The satire functions on two levels.
    There is moral satire and there is political satire.
    The writer implicitly questions the relationship of politics to morality.
15. The bricklayers came early in the morning.
    They are fast workers.
    By mid-afternoon they had finished our new fireplace.
16. Provincial politics don't interest me very much.
    I do not subscribe to a local newspaper.
17. Jack Sprat can eat no fat.
    His wife can eat no lean.
    Dietary problems can plague the ordinary household.
    Marketing is a problem.
    Meal-planning is a problem.
    Cooking is a problem.
18. Poets use literary techniques.
    They use rhyme, rhythm, and imagery.
19. I need a holiday.
    I usually enjoy my job.
    I'm bored with my job.
20. Over a hundred people waited in line all night.
    They wanted to be sure to get tickets to the concert.
21. Peanut butter is a nourishing food.
    Parents sometimes feel guilty when they hurriedly slap together a peanut-butter sandwich.
    Kids love peanut butter.
22. One thing is clear.
    Everyone has an off day now and then.
    Even the best athletes can't be entirely consistent.
23. My rent seems to go up faster than my income.
    I am thinking about take a course in economics.
24. Bill Andrewski has gone to Chile.
    He wants to train in the Andes.
    He is probably the strongest skier on the team.
25. England and America are two nations separated by a common language.
    Canadian English sometimes tilts towards British usage.
    Sometimes it tilts towards American usage.

26. Some people think one thing is more important than anything else.
    That thing is money.
27. Ordinary teas and coffees can be boring.
    Herbal teas can provide a pleasant change.
    They include a wide range of flavours.
    Some have a single flavour.
    Some are blends of flavours.
28. The board announced the new regulations.
    It acted as if there had been no protests.
    Almost everyone is against the regulations.
29. Cheese is high in protein.
    It is also high in cholesterol.
30. The history assignment was longer than usual.
    The teacher had threatened to give us a quiz.
    I missed the TV show that everybody was talking about the next day.

B. Here is another way to practise sentence-combining:

Write at least five short sentences (no more than five words each) about each of the following subjects. Then combine each group into a single sentence with only one independent clause; everything else must be subordinated to it. Try at least two combinations for each set. Feel free to change the forms of expression, but not the basic facts you recorded in the short sentences.

Example: *my car*

My car is green.
It was orange.
It is ten years old.
It was rusting.
I got it fixed.
I got it repainted.
I looks like new.

(a) My rusting, ten-year-old orange car looks like new now that I've had it fixed and repainted green.
(b) De-rusted, green, and looking like new, my formerly orange heap hides its ten years well.

1. my parents
2. my favourite game
3. what I eat
4. books in my life
5. school days

C. Here, from students' drafts, are some passages whose sentences require combining in order to be effective. Change whatever else you think needs changing, as if you were revising your own draft.

1. I had only one reason for keeping on digging trail. I did not quit this hard work because I was helping to protect my fellow firefighters. If the fire was to jump the trail, we all would have been in the path of the oncoming inferno.
2. Many people think inflation is caused by higher wages. This is erroneous. Inflation is not primarily caused by higher wages.
3. I would very much like to avoid sexually specific language. Avoiding sexually specific language can create problems. I never saw a *chair*—straight, rocking, or easy—conduct a meeting.

4. There are a number of options. The President can choose one of those options.

5. A good ventilation system in the tent is also necessary. The average camper will produce much moisture from breathing and perspiring. This will happen even in winter.

6. Some countries have little or no choice about what energy source they can use. In Canada we are fortunate to possess many energy options. All have advantages and disadvantages unique to each.

7. My lab partner ruined our experiment. Both homicide and suicide crossed my mind.

8. Along the west coast there is a very great tendency for large numbers of storms. These storms produce rough seas, poor visibility, and generally poor boating conditions. The chance of an oil spill is immeasurably increased by this fact.

9. Pitt was sent by King George III to form a cabinet in 1766. This was when he took the title of the Earl of Chatham and the post of Lord Privy Seal. The Lord Privy Seal is a post where no active duties were attached.

D. *Sentence-Imitating*   In addition to the many patterns of sentences that you have been learning about in the sentence-combining exercises, there are many other sentence strategies worth knowing about and practising. Some of these overlap one or another pattern you already know, but in this exercise the emphasis is less on syntax than on other features of sentences, such as balance and repetition and rhythm.

An excellent way to learn about and get a feel for such sentences is to imitate successful sentences by other writers. Below is a small collection of sentences (those not attributed—which is to say most of them—were written by students). Write out each one, slowly and carefully; examine it to see what features it uses; then write a sentence of your own imitating the *form* as closely as possible. Among the features to look for, and to use in your own sentences, are the following:

Alliteration (and perhaps other sound patterns).

Rhythm—whether simply that of discernible beats, as in Thomas Paine's "These are the times that try men's souls," or that of patterned poetic metre, as in this final sentence from a piece by Bharati Mukherjee: "Force alone still carries the greatest respect."

Repetition of various kinds—sometimes for emphasis, sometimes for a witty or ironic effect.

Balance—whether of parallel or reversed elements.

Parallelism—whether in a balanced two-part structure or in a series.

Series—parallel elements lined up in groups of three or more.

The omission of *and* before the last member of a series (*asyndeton* ), or the inclusion of *and*'s or *or*'s between all the parts of a series (*polysyndeton*).

Figurative language—simile, metaphor, personification.

Effective short sentences of only two or three words.

Inversion of normal order (subject-verb, adjective-noun).

Periodicity (a "periodic" sentence, in contrast to the more common "loose" sentence, opens with subordinate elements and thus delays its main point until at or near the end).

Frequently a sentence will contain two or more of these features. Especially at stylistically heightened points, one such feature seems to attract others. Even a short sentence can contain several:

But the lasting memory is of footprints, footprints etched in the wet sea sand.

In this example, repetition, alliteration, metaphor, and even some metrical rhythm all work together to create a highly effective sentence—one perhaps that could serve to end a paragraph or a short essay.

We're not suggesting that you should try to load your sentences with such devices; if you did you'd soon be charged with over-writing or "fine" writing, of pushing purple prose. Rather we believe that you'll find it advantageous, as well as enjoyable, to be able to call on them when you want them.

Here then are some sentences to use as models for practice:

1. Style matters.
2. Patient, cold, and callous, our hands wrapped in socks, we waited to snowball the cats. (Dylan Thomas)
3. As we quietly entered the Old Norman church, we were met by silence: silent bells, silent organ, silent tombs, silent beauty.
4. I realize that it's no shame to be poor, but it's no great honour either.
5. She ran to the Colonel's, her face anxious, her company arriving, and her dinner burnt.
6. The whisky took him firmly by the hand and whisked him into a waiting gutter.
7. The blood-red bloom of the rose graced the garden like a jewel.
8. War is disgusting.
9. Outside the walls are the accouterments of Ballygunge life: hawkers, beggars, loiterers, squatters, sleepers, cows and pariahs, cars, taxis, buses, mini-buses, cycles, rickshaws, bullock carts, and heedless pedestrians. Inside there is greenery, flowers, a studied calm. (Bharati Mukherjee)
10. Snoopy is a writer, a fighter, a pawputeer, a poet, a hockey player, a shortstop, a buddy, a dog.
11. If anger can erase a smile, a smile can also erase anger.
12. Cats, monkeys, raccoons—all were crowded together in the smelly cages.
13. The sun was like a hot-water bottle on my back.
14. The human hand, the hand is the story. (Loren Eiseley)
15. The shoe was long and narrow and high, the leather smooth and supple and sleek.
16. There is no new transit system, and when all the politicians and planners have had their say there will be no new transit system.
17. The silent one-clouded heavens drifted on to the sea. (Dylan Thomas)
18. My sleep was tormented with dreams, horrifying dreams.
19. The traditionally elegant Minton china and Waterford crystal are truly incredible: incredibly breakable, incredibly expensive, and incredibly unnecessary.
20. The Romans were defeated; they were defeated because they had become weak; and they had become weak because they had lost their moral integrity and their internal unity.
21. In the daytime, in the hot mornings, these motors made a petulant, irritable sound; at night, in the still evening when the afterglow lit the water, they whined about one's ears like mosquitoes. (E.B. White)

22. The ball he smashed through the window; the bat he flung down as he leaped over the fence.
23. The eyes, the dull, cold, lifeless eyes, betrayed him.
24. Apparently she appreciated his appearance.
25. The shallowest waters sometimes hold the greatest danger.
26. For the writer who craves an atmosphere of peace and solitude in which to work, there is always some sort of intrusion: the telephone's periodic ring is an intrusion, the paperboy's piercing whistle is an intrusion, the untimely visit of a well-meaning friend is an intrusion, and the clock in the hall which ticks away the minutes, the hours, the years, is perhaps the most unwelcome intrusion.
27. On our safari into the city we saw many things: under the concrete canopy thousands of people scurried in and out of their immense anthills, while around them giant corporations stalked their prey and businesses were locked in a silent battle for the survival of the fittest; and in the midst of this turmoil, at the waterhole, a sacred alliance was kept and all came together to bask in the sun.
28. Out of sight may be out of mind, but everything has to go somewhere—or so says an ancient law of ecology—and the wastes (human, animal, agricultural, and industrial) flow into the sewers, the sewers flow into the rivers, rivers flow into the ocean, ocean water is evaporated and later condenses as rain, rain becomes acidic, and the acid eats at buildings and monuments, at plants and soils; slowly, inevitably, the world we have created crumbles and dissolves out of sight.

Increase your stylistic repertoire. Copy other interesting sentences as you find them in your reading and practise imitating them as well. Soon you will have a scrapbook of sentence styles to draw on. And the more you work with them, the faster your instinctive sense of style will improve.

---

### *Playing with Language 12A*

Writers sometimes, some writers, try to heighten their style by injecting into it impressive-sounding foreign terms, many of which have themselves—because of such habits—become clichés. Sometimes a foreign phrase is justifiable, if not indispensable, because it says something that essentially can't be translated into equivalent English. But it is not *de rigueur* to use foreign terms just to sound sophisticated. From your current reading, collect whatever foreign terms you come upon (any good dictionary will define most of them), and write sentences using them in ways you consider legitimate. Then compose a paragraph making fun of some of them, playing with them and punning on them for all you're worth. A *casus belli*, for example, might be a severe stomach-ache, or *lapsus linguae* a plate of overturned spaghetti. We leave you to conjure with *in loco parentis, lèse majesté, hors de combat, Weltschmerz, felo de se*, and hundreds of others. Your finished paragraph will, of course, be taken *cum grano salis*.

### *Playing with Language 12B*

Find five or ten dead or moribund metaphors—some may be recognizably clichés—and compose sentences that put new life into them. Here are a few samples to get you started thinking: toe the line, the die is cast, fringe benefit, from stem to stern, soaring costs, the last straw, put the bite on someone, give someone a leg up, boxed in, shoot the works, wade in, take the plunge, sour grapes, last-ditch defense, wheels within wheels, float a loan, gild the lily, shadow someone, wooden expression, a skeleton in the closet, pretty as a picture, cross that bridge when you come to it, apple-pie order, knee-jerk reaction. Do not try to reinvigorate one by labelling it or implicitly apologizing for it ("I got up on the wrong side of the bed, so to speak"; "You could have knocked me over with a feather—to coin a phrase"; "We'll have to toe the proverbial line")—that only makes it worse. But do sometimes try throwing in a modifier to enliven a dead or cliché metaphor; for example: He's a Corinthian pillar of his community"; "she has a peaches and sour cream complexion."

## Playing with Language 12C

A "justified" or perfectly even right-hand margin isn't essential in typed work, of course. But trying for one can be fun. Here is one student's response to the challenge:

```
                    Onward to Chemistry


    Although it may seem silly to write a passage like
    this with no other purpose than to keep within the
    margins without any hyphens or unused spaces where
    the lines end, and no other audience than an essay
    and composition professor, don't be fooled--simple
    exercises often result in profound learning!  Many
    highly complex skills require practice which, at a
    glance, does not look to be even distantly related
    to the ultimate talent.  By writing this paragraph
    in this manner, however, all my abilities of essay
    writing are being exercised:  word choice, using a
    thesaurus, sentence construction, and maybe even a
    little style.  I realize that.  But I also realize
    that I have a lot of organic chemistry studying to
    do in the next few days.  So have I exercised long
    enough for today?  I'm going to guess that I have.
```

Try writing a paragraph of this sort yourself. You're not allowed to put extra spaces between words or to syllabicate a word just to make the line come out right: each line must end with a full word. (After a colon, either one or two spaces is permissible, but be consistent.)

## Playing with Language 12D

Write a verbal "political cartoon" of some prominent figure.

*So ofte a day I moot thy werk renewe,*
*It to correct, and eek to rubbe and scrape:*
*And al is thurgh thy necligence and rape.*
(Geoffrey Chaucer, "To His Scribe Adam")

## CHAPTER XIII
# Step 9: Proofreading

The last step before you turn your manuscript over to your audience is called "proofreading." A "proof" is a preliminary typeset copy that a publisher gives to a writer so that the writer can check it one last time for accuracy before it is sent off for final printing. Even if your work is headed not for the printer but for a teacher's desk, you should still proofread it scrupulously. Don't skimp on this final step, for in its way it is the most important of all just because it *is* final: it's your last chance to correct any embarrassing and damaging errors, of whatever kind—your last chance to exercise any control over the effect a piece of writing is going to have on your readers.

As you go through the various sweeps of revising you also correct any errors you find, of course—ungrammatical sentence structure, incorrect diction, bad punctuation, and so on. This chapter provides you with a brief guide to catching one other possible kind of error—spelling—and then with a brief list of errors discussed elsewhere in this book. Use the list as a reminder of the various things you need to be on guard against as you write, revise, and prepare your final copy. And when your instructor returns a marked paper to you, use this list as an index to point you to the sections of the book that you need to study in order both to understand your errors and to correct them as necessary.

The brief list following the discussion of spelling covers only those matters that can be considered *errors* rather than stylistic or strategic weaknesses. Use the correction symbols and cross-references it includes to help you check your finished work for correctness. These correction symbols are also included (in red) in the list of marking symbols inside the back cover; use this complete list as a checklist as you revise.

As you prepare and get back successive assignments, you should make a list of whatever errors and weaknesses are marked so that you can see at a glance what you need to review and practise on. Make a chart of your progress in getting rid of weaknesses and errors in your writing. And use it as a checklist to help you focus on weak spots as you work on subsequent assignments: if something you do gets marked on one assignment, the same error or weakness should not occur in the next assignment.

As you proofread your final copy, remember that any corrections you make should be in ink. And if you make more than two or three small changes on a page, that page will begin to look messy; recopy it, and then of course proofread the new page to make sure you haven't introduced any new errors.

One final practical hint: If you change something, don't blot it out entirely; rather, draw only a single firm line through it to cross it out, and write the emendation above it. Not only does this look neater than a big black blot, but also your instructor will often want to know what the original said. For example, if you decide at the last minute to change a word, your instructor may be able to help you understand a principle of diction if your original choice of word is still legible. It may even be that your first choice was after all the better one—but your instructor won't be able to tell you that if you've blotted it out.

## SPELLING

Never take spelling lightly. Poor spelling is one of the first things readers notice when they start through a piece of writing. If you misspell words, your readers will immediately form a low opinion of you. They are also likely to conclude that if you're careless with your spelling, you are probably careless with other matters as well—such as your ideas. Your readers will not respect your writing if you show little respect for it yourself: take as much care with your spelling as you do with any other part of your writing.

Two practical hints to help you improve your spelling:

1. Keep a list of words that you have misspelled or that you know you have trouble with. Work on the list regularly, practising the correct spellings until you know them. Have a friend test you on it periodically. You can also use it as a checklist when you are proofreading.
2. Whenever you are not SURE of the correct spelling of a word, LOOK IT UP.

Here are three good desk or college dictionaries for Canadian students to use:

*The Houghton Mifflin Canadian Dictionary of the English Language* (Markham, Ontario: Houghton Mifflin Canada, 1980).
*Funk & Wagnalls Standard College Dictionary*, Canadian Edition (Toronto: Fitzhenry & Whiteside, 1982).
*The Gage Canadian Dictionary*. (Toronto: Gage, 1983)

There is no substitute for memorizing your trouble-words and using a dictionary. But reviewing a few basic rules will help you avoid some of the more common errors, and being aware of a few other common trouble spots will alert you to the need to be careful and to consult your dictionary.

1. *ie/ei:* Use *i* before *e* except after *c*, or when sounded like *a* as in *neighbour* and *weigh*. Errors of this kind almost always occur after *c*; just remember to use *ei: receive, perceive, conceive*. But there are several oddities and exceptions to this rule; therefore if you aren't sure, LOOK IT UP.

2. *-cede, -ceed, -sede:* Memorize *supersede*, the only word using the ending *-sede*. And the *-ceed* ending occurs in only three: *exceed, proceed, succeed*. All the rest with this sound use *-cede*.

3. Final *e* before suffixes: If the suffix begins with a consonant, keep the *e* (*merely, tasteful, hopeless, awesome*). If the suffix begins with a vowel, drop the *e* (*arguing, desirable*). But there are some important exceptions, such as *argument, truly,* and *outrageous*. Whenever you're not sure, LOOK IT UP.

4. Final *y*, after a consonant, before suffixes: Before *-ing,* keep the *y* (*trying, carrying*); otherwise change it to *i* (*trial, happiness, angrily*). But again there are exceptions, such as *shyly* and *shyness*; if you aren't sure, LOOK IT UP.

5. Final consonants before a suffix: Double the final consonant if
   (a) It is preceded by a single vowel,
   (b) the root is either one syllable or has the accent on its last syllable, and
   (c) the suffix begins with a vowel.
   Hence *shopping, admitted, allotted, occurred, hitter, referred, referring*. But if adding the suffix shifts the accent, don't double the final consonant: *reference*.

6. *-able/-ible:* The *-able* ending is most often right, but *-ible* ends many common words: *audible, eligible, irresistible*. Don't guess; whenever you aren't sure, LOOK IT UP: for this and other problems for which there are no rules, your dictionary is indispensable.

7. *-ent, -ence/-ant, -ance:* Again, there's no rule. Since the two endings often sound the same, you have to LOOK IT UP if you're not positive which is right.

8. Plurals of nouns ending in *y*: If the *y* is preceded by a consonant, change the *y* to *i* and add *-es* ( *cities, tries*); otherwise just add *s* (*bays, valleys*). Plurals of most nouns are formed by adding either *-s* or *-es;* add *-es* if forming the plural adds a syllable (*church-churches, box-boxes*), only *-s* if it does not (*girls, cedars*), or if the noun already ends in *-ce, -ge, -se,* or *-ze,* when there'll be an extra syllable anyway (*fireplaces, sages, bases, mazes*). But whenever you're uncertain about a plural, LOOK IT UP. Quite a few nouns have irregular plurals, which your dictionary should list. If the dictionary doesn't list one, you can assume the plural is formed regularly. (The same goes for verbs with irregular parts of speech.)

9. Homophones: Many spelling errors are caused by a writer's confusing words which sound alike but are spelled differently. Such an error could distract readers even more than some other kind of spelling error, since they may see it as a diction error as well (see pp. 245-246). Here are some of the common ones to be careful with; if you're unsure about any of these, add them to your own spelling list:

| | |
|---|---|
| boarder—border | counsel—council |
| born—borne | coarse—course |
| capital—capitol | discreet—discrete |
| compliment—complement | fair—fare |

forgo—forego

holy—wholly

incidence—incidents

its—it's

led—lead

passed—past

pedal—peddle

phase—faze

principal—principle

ring—wring

sight—site—cite

sole—soul

stationary—stationery

vein—vain—vane

If you are unaware of or not certain about the meanings of any of these words, LOOK THEM UP.

10. Other often-confused words: Some pairs of words are easily confused even though they aren't pronounced exactly alike. If you are careful with your pronunciation, you won't be troubled by words like these.

accept—except

access—excess

adapt—adopt

advice—advise

allude—elude

allusion—illusion

bizarre—bazaar

choose—chose

climactic—climatic

device—devise

diffuse—defuse

elicit—illicit

insight—incite

loose—lose

persecute—prosecute

quite—quiet

then—than

whine—wine

If you are unsure of either the meanings or the pronunciations of any of these words, LOOK THEM UP.

*Caution:* Educated readers will consider you illiterate if you confuse the *possessives* of pronouns (no apostrophes) with *contractions* (which use apostrophes); for example:

its (possessive)—it's (contraction of *it is*)

your (possessive)—you're (contraction of *you are*)

their (possessive)—they're (contraction of *they are*)

whose (possessive)—who's (contraction of *who is*)

Be careful with these and the others like them. Be especially careful that you spell *it's* only when you mean *it is*.

11. Separate words: The following should always be spelled as separate words; don't put your readers off by carelessly running them together—or if you do, during the rapid writing of a draft, be sure you separate them again:

a lot

all right

at least

even though

every time

in between

in fact

in front

in order to

in other words

in spite of

up to

12. Finally, here are some terms whose meanings differ, depending on whether they are spelled as one word or two. Be careful to distinguish between them or you will confuse your readers.

altogether—all together
anybody—any body
anyone—any one
anyway—any way
apart—a part

awhile—a while
everyday—every day
maybe—may be
someday—some day
sometime—some time

## Chronic Misspellings

The following list of often-misspelled words is all too brief: there are small books consisting entirely of lists of often-misspelled words. (If you're a poor speller, some such spelling dictionary would be a useful addition to your personal library.) We include here words which we have found misspelled particularly often—not only by students, but by professional writers as well. Almost any composition handbook or other book on writing will give you other such lists—and the best list of all, of course, is the one you make for yourself.

If you learn to spell all of these words correctly (there aren't so many), you will not only please yourself and your instructors, but even impress your friends. Have someone test you by reading them out to you. If you misspell any, add them to your private spelling list and practise them until you can spell them correctly without hesitation.

| | | | |
|---|---|---|---|
| accessible | convenience | fulfill | minuscule |
| accommodate | create | further | mischievous |
| adorable | cries | gauge | myriad |
| affidavit | criticism | genealogy | mementos |
| aging | customs | germane | miniature |
| a lot | decrepit | goddess | necessary |
| among | definitely | guard | negotiations |
| apparent | descendants | harass | obstacle |
| argument | description | height | occasion |
| article | develop | homogeneous | occurred |
| authoritative | dilemma | hypocrisy | opinion |
| auxiliary | dining | hypocrite | optimistic |
| beneficial | dissatisfied | imagery | opulent |
| bulwark | divide | incidentally | parliament |
| calendar | drunkenness | inconsistent | perceive |
| category | ecstasy | indefinite | perseverance |
| cemetery | elegiac | independent | persuade |
| challenge | embarrass | indispensable | playwright |
| changeable | equipment | inevitable | preceded |
| coherent | exalt | inoculate | predominantly |
| coincide | excerpt | intimate | prejudice |
| committee | existence | lackadaisical | profession |
| commitment | exorbitant | leisure | pronunciation |
| competitive | expatriate | luxury | psychology |
| congratulation | feasible | majestic | putrefy |
| conqueror | forgettable | mandatory | receive |
| consensus | forty | medieval | religious |

| | | | |
|---|---|---|---|
| remembrance | shining | symbolic | until |
| reminisce | significance | synonymous | usage |
| resurrection | similar | temperament | variegated |
| rhythm | simile | tendency | vicious |
| ridiculous | skiing | tragedy | vilified |
| sacrifice | solely | transcendent | villain |
| sacrilegious | soliloquy | tries | warrant |
| separate | speech | tyranny | whether |
| servant | sponsor | undoubtedly | whisk |
| shepherd | strategy | unkempt | wondrous |
| sheriff | stupefying | unnoticeable | writing |

*Practical Hint: Proofreading for Spelling* Don't try to check your draft for spelling and typographical errors while you're checking for other things as well. If you see an error early on, of course correct it; but save for one final sweep the job of looking for nothing but misspelled or mistyped words. And make this sweep by *reading backwards*, looking at *one word at a time*. Otherwise it's easy to get so caught up in the flow of sentences and ideas that you will overlook mistakes in individual words.

And finally, the best of all advice about spelling: If you are not CERTAIN about the spelling of a word, LOOK IT UP!

## CORRECTION SYMBOLS FOR COMMON ERRORS

Study this list of errors. Familiarize yourself with them so that you will learn to avoid them. If there are particular errors that you aren't confident that you understand and can recognize and avoid, you should study the sections indicated by the cross-references. If you self-consciously use this as a checklist when you proofread, you should have a good chance to catch not only spelling and typographical errors but mistakes of the other kinds as well. These are, as we said above, not matters of taste or style but matters of right or wrong, of correct and incorrect, of acceptable and unacceptable. They are of course based on convention, not absolute moral or legal *rules* of any kind; but if you care about your writing and about the effect it has on your readers, you will treat them as rules. (Some of these, of course, such as parallelism and punctuation, are sometimes matters of style and sometimes matters of correct or incorrect.)

| | | |
|---|---|---|
| *agr* | Agreement | See pages 213-214. |
| *al* | Illogical or incongruous alignment | See pages 209-210. |
| *apos* | Apostrophe | See pages 319-320. |
| *cap* | Capitalization | See page 318. |
| *CS* | Comma splice | See pages 293-294, 296. |
| *d* | Diction (Consult your dictionary.) | See Chapter X. |
| *dm* | Dangling modifier | See page 211. |
| *doc* | Documentation | See Chapter XIV. |
| *//* | Parallelism | See pages 233-236. |
| *Frag* | Fragment | See pages 206-208. |

| | | |
|---|---|---|
| *id* | Idiom | See pages 13-14, 100, 246-247. |
| *ital* | Italics | See page 318. |
| *mm* | Misplaced modifier | See pages 210-211. |
| *ms* | Manuscript conventions | See Chapter XII. |
| *nsw* | No such word | See page 265. |
| *p* | Punctuation | See Chapter XI. |
| *ref* | Reference of pronoun | See pages 212, 214-215. |
| *Run-on* | Run-on or fused sentence | See page 292. |
| *sp* | Spelling | See the preceding section. |
| *ss* | Sentence structure or sense | See Chapter IX. |
| *syl* | Syllabication | See page 318. |
| *ww* | Wrong word | See pages 245-246. |

Finally, here are some other symbols used by proofreaders and sometimes by instructors marking papers:

| | |
|---|---|
| *stet* | Let it stand; leave it as it was. |
| ℐ | Delete. |
| *lc* | Lower case (not capitalized). |
| ¶ | Paragraph. |
| ✕ | Obvious error. |
| ∧ | Insert something here. |
| =/ | Insert a hyphen. |
| ? | Something questionable or unclear. |
| ∼ | Transpose. |
| ⌒ | Close up. |
| # | Insert a space. |
| ✓ | Something particularly good. |

---

## Exercise 13A

Here is a passage from a letter written in the 1820's by John Clare, a self-educated English farmer whose poetry and writing about nature were for a time popular. This passage is just as he wrote it—without punctuation, and with errors in spelling and grammar. Pretend that you are including it in a collection of pieces to be read by grade-twelve students. You don't want to spoil its distinctive flavour, but since you want it to be accessible to your readers, neither do you want to distract them with its oddities and errors. Edit it as you think necessary.

I forgot to say in my last that the Nightingale sung as common by day as night & as often tho its a fact that is not generaly known your Londoners are very fond of talking about the bird & I believe fancy every bird they hear after sunset a Nightingale I remember while I was there last while walking with a friend in the fields of Shacklwell we saw a gentleman & lady listening very attentive by the side of a shrubbery & when we came up we heard them lavishing praises on the beautiful song of the nightingale which happend to be a thrush but it did for them & they listend & repeated their praise with heartfelt satisfaction while the bird seemed to know the grand distinction that its song had gaind for it & strove exultingly to keep up the deception by attempting a varied & more louder song the dews was ready to fall but the lady was heedless of the wet grass tho the setting sun as a traveller glad to rest was leaning his enlarged rim on the earth like a table of fire & lessening by degrees out of sight leaving night & a few gilt clouds behind him such is the ignorance of Nature in large Citys that are nothing less than overgrown prisons that shut out the world and all its beautys

## Exploration 13A

Examine some poster currently on display in your vicinity. Write a paragraph analyzing the techniques it uses to appeal to those who see it, OR a paragraph describing it satirically.

## Essay 13A

Income tax as we know it is a relatively recent phenomenon. Temporary levies have occurred all through history, but not until 1874 did Great Britain adopt a permanent income tax, and other countries followed, some much later. Now even provinces and states have it. If society got along without a permanent tax before, why can't it do so again? Write an essay on the probable and possible effects of doing away with income tax. Do you find yourself writing an argument, whether you intended to or not? (You may want to do a little preliminary research on this topic. Or you may want to consider this or a similar topic an opportunity for a "modest proposal"—see Playing with Language 14C, p. 406.)

## Essay 13B

Write an essay summing up the school year. Treat it at least partly as a process, one you have gone through, but try to generalize sufficiently to make other students recognize their experience of the year as well. Of course you will have to be selective in order to emphasize the high points, but don't omit the low points entirely, for they can provide illuminating contrasts. Perhaps the school news-paper would be interested in publishing the piece in its last issue of the year. You could begin it with something like "When the year began, I thought..., but now...," and perhaps close with something to complete the frame.

OR

Write an essay of about 1000 words to be placed in a time-capsule and buried on your campus, to be dug up and opened exactly 25 or 50 years from now. Think carefully about your audience.

## Playing with Language 13A

(a) George Bernard Shaw once ridiculed standard English spelling by point-ing out that the word *fish* could be spelled *ghoti* (*gh* as in *tough, o* as in *women, ti* as in *motion*). Make up five more examples illustrating these and other peculiarities of English spelling and pronunciation.

(b) Look up some of the simplified spelling and alphabet systems various people (including Shaw) have proposed. Write a brief report on one of them; end your report with a paragraph that begins by using conventional spelling and gradually shifts, so that its final sentence is entirely in the "reformed" system.

## Playing with Language 13B

Writers customarily use *allusions*. That is, they refer to a person, event, or other phenomenon indirectly or briefly, in the expectation that their readers will recognize the reference and bring to the surface of their minds all the associations necessary to convey the full meaning. Allusions are often expressions of collective proverbial wisdom. For example if we say that someone is as *rich as Croesus*, we expect our readers to understand that the person in question is absurdly, even obscenely wealthy. If we say that something is as *sturdy as the Rock of Gibraltar*, we expect our readers to summon up visions of the fortress guarding the entrance to the Mediterranean, one of the pillars of Hercules (another allusion). If we've miscalculated, if our readers don't recognize the allusion, then we've wasted our breath—unless we can expect them to look it up in a reference book in order to understand what we're saying. But most educated readers will catch most common allusions. Such allusions are part of the furniture of our minds, and writers depend upon such knowledge to help them make their points more clearly, economically, and effectively.

Practise the art of allusion.

Here is a selected miscellany of proper nouns, derivatives of proper nouns, and some other terms often used allusively—including some proper nouns and derivatives therefrom which have become so familiar a part of the language that they are no longer capitalized. Look up any that you aren't familiar with (a standard dictionary will include almost all of them), and if the information isn't fully satisfying do some deeper research; perhaps read about the person or place in its original context—or a translation. You will notice that many of the terms are from classical or biblical sources; knowing the Bible and the Greek and Roman classics, and of course the plays of Shakespeare, can be very useful to a writer—or a reader. You may want to add a couple of good reference books to your library; there are several inexpensive paperbound ones available.

When you have gone through these, select ten or twenty or more of them and compose sentences or short paragraphs using them allusively—perhaps in a metaphor or simile or analogy, or just directly, as when you might say that a certain person had a *Gargantuan* appetite. Perhaps you can devise a way to use two or three of them in one paragraph.

| | | |
|---|---|---|
| Achilles' heel | Armageddon | billingsgate |
| Adonis | Arthurian | Black Hole of Calcutta |
| Aladdin | Atlantis | Bluebeard |
| alchemy | Atlas | Boswell |
| Alice | Augean stables | bowdlerize |
| amazon | Augustan | Brave New World |
| Ancient Mariner | babel | Byronic |
| Apollo | Babbitt | Camelot |
| Arabian Nights | Baedeker | Candide |
| Arcadia | Bastille | Canute |

| | | |
|---|---|---|
| Casanova | Homeric | Perils of Pauline |
| Catch-22 | Houdini | Peter Pan |
| Cerberus | Icarus | phoenix |
| Charon | incubus | Pilate |
| Cheshire cat | inferno, infernal | Pilgrim's Progress |
| chimera | Jekyll and Hyde | pillar of salt |
| Cinderella | Jeremiah, jeremiad | Plato's cave |
| Cupid | Job | Pollyanna |
| cyclopean | Judas | Popeye |
| Dagwood | King Kong | procrustean |
| Delphic | Lazarus | prodigal son |
| Diaspora | Lethe | Prometheus |
| Dionysian | leviathan | protean |
| Draconian | Lilliputian | Pyrrhic victory |
| Edenic | Machiavellian | quisling |
| El Dorado | Malthusian | quixotic |
| Elizabethan | Mammon | Rabelaisian |
| Elysian Fields | manna | Rubicon |
| Emperor's New Clothes | Mata Hari | Samson |
| Eureka! | McCarthyism | Sargasso Sea |
| an eye for an eye | mecca | Scylla and Charybdis |
| Falstaff | medusa | Shangri-la |
| the Fates | Mephistophelean | Sherlock |
| Faustian | Methuselah | sibylline |
| Frankenstein | Mickey Mouse | Slough of Despond |
| the Furies | Midas touch | sphinx |
| Gabriel | Mrs. Grundy | stygian |
| Galahad | Narcissus | Superman |
| Gethsemane | Neanderthal | Sword of Damocles |
| golden age | Nimrod | Tantalus |
| golden calf | 1984 | thirty pieces of silver |
| Golden Fleece | Niobe | Trojan horse |
| Goliath | nirvana | utopian |
| Gordian knot | Noah's ark | Valhalla |
| gorgon | odyssey | Victorian |
| Gradgrind | Olympus, Olympic, Olympian | Waterloo |
| Guy Fawkes | | whited sepulchre |
| harpy | Orpheus | widow's mite |
| Hawkshaw | pander | writing on the wall |
| hegira | Pandora's box | yahoo |
| Helen | Parnassus | Zeus, Jupiter |
| Herod | Pelion on Ossa | Zorro |

*My library*
*Was dukedom large enough.*
*(The Tempest)*

## CHAPTER XIV
# The Library Research Paper

Writing the library research paper follows much the same process we discuss throughout this book. It goes through the same steps, from planning and writing the draft through the several stages of revising, culminating in the presentation of the final draft. The main differences are that a research paper usually has a broader scope, is often written for a wider range of readers, and—most important—employs a broad range of external sources at the stage of invention and requires careful attention to the handling and documentation of sources at the stage of revision.

For other essays you may have used one or two magazine articles or parts of a book or two for examples to support an argument or for facts to help your readers understand an explanation. For a research paper, you need to make systematic use of these and other external sources: bibliographies, indexes, dictionaries and encyclopedias, journal articles, collections of essays, and perhaps government publications or reports. But before you hurry off to begin thumbing through catalogues or indexes or bibliographies, you should systematically go through the earlier stages of the planning process, including choosing and narrowing your topic, specifying your purpose, and identifying your readers and their purposes. That way, when you do get to the library, you will already know a good deal about what to look for.

## STEPS 1 AND 2: FINDING A SUBJECT AND NARROWING IT TO A TOPIC

Instructors usually assign a range of topics for research papers, allowing you an opportunity to explore in more depth one or more of the issues raised in courses. But whether the general subject is political science or history, sociology or literature, science or philosophy, the planning techniques are similar. You need to select a subject and narrow it to a topic that interests you and about which you think you can find enough information. If you have been working right along through a course, it's likely that the reading, lectures, and discussion have left you curious about several issues that haven't been fully resolved in class. The most helpful attitude to foster from the beginning is a genuine curiosity that will sustain your interest over a period of several weeks.

A similar curiosity will help you work up a topic that has not been explicitly assigned by your instructor. If you are free to choose your own topic for a research paper, you can proceed pretty much as we suggest in Chapters II and III, assessing what you know and taking various possibilities through the several methods of invention. But since, by definition, a topic for a library research paper needs to be researchable, your choice is limited by at least three considerations.

First, you are restricted by the amount and quality of material that your library offers. You might find yourself fascinated, for example, by a particular historical figure, but discover that only one not-very-good book and a couple of small magazine articles have been written on him or her. Or you might discover that although a large number of items have been published, your library has only one or two. Even the largest libraries can't afford to acquire all the books and magazines published in North America, let alone the rest of the world.

Second, stay away from a subject that may enjoy a brief popularity that doesn't last, a nine-days' wonder that newspapers and television panelists are currently discussing, like a fad in music or fashion, or a recent flood or volcanic eruption, or the supposed "Hitler diaries" of early 1983. For such subjects you will probably be able to find material only in current newspapers and popular magazines. Recent and widely publicized events like these can provide excellent hooks for beginnings, but for an overall topic choose something treated over a longer time and in a variety of sources: reference works, articles, books. If you have a large number and variety of sources to choose from, you can be selective, and have a better chance of formulating a thesis that will interest both you and your intended reader.

Third, you need to select a subject you can handle, one you can understand without special training. If you try to work on some highly specialized or technical subject, you probably won't be able to assimilate the material and still complete your project in the time you have. For example, if you choose some interesting-looking and seemingly simple subject like "the meaning of the Bible" or "modern trends in economics," but soon find yourself in an impenetrable thicket of incomprehensible language about scriptural hermeneutics or the abstract calculus of micro-economics, get out while you can. Don't throw good time after bad; cut your losses, and find another path to pursue.

You are also limited by the scope of your research project. Ten or fifteen pages can scarcely encompass the full sweep of World War I, World War II, or the Napoleonic wars. But you could well assemble and present material on the battle of Trafalgar or Gallipoli or Dieppe. And the material available for biographical research on Michelangelo or Elizabeth I is immense, overwhelming except for specialists. But, again, you might well work up an excellent paper on Käthe Kollwitz or Jomo Kenyatta. The most important criterion for choosing a subject, though, remains your own interest and curiosity.

If you are uncertain about choosing too narrow a topic too early, you might begin by selecting and then narrowing a subject area such as one in the following list. These are only examples of the enormous variety of possible subjects:

| | |
|---|---|
| advertising | Latin American history |
| amateur sports | modern drama |
| astrology | natural disasters |
| biblical archaeology | nutrition |
| biogenetics | OPEC |
| business ethics | organized labour |
| Canadian agriculture | parapsychology |
| Canadian aviation | popular fiction |
| computers and society | Prince Edward Island |
| cottage industries | public transit |
| dance | satellite communication |
| documentary film | sea power in the ancient world |
| endangered species | sentencing and parole |
| government and education | space exploration |
| guerilla warfare | transpacific trade |

One way to decide if you're genuinely interested in a subject is to try to frame specific questions about it. Stating such questions as specifically as possible will also help you decide whether you are likely to find enough material in your library, and whether you can narrow that topic to a manageable size. Take for example a subject for a course in modern European history, say science and technology. That is of course an enormous subject, but you can explore it for what interests you by thinking up such specifying questions as these:

What were the principal scientific discoveries of the nineteenth century?
When did the terms "science" and "technology" appear? Are these ideas entirely "modern"?
What scientific methods were dominant in the 17th and 18th centuries?
What were the major inventions in the 1600's?
Who were the major French scientists from 1550 to 1650?

Or suppose that in an English course you've been offered as a topic one of the minor characters in Shakespeare's *Hamlet*. Here the topic has already been considerably narrowed. But you can still go on to test it for your own interest by framing questions like these:

On what grounds can Horatio be compared with Hamlet?
Is Polonius any more than a foolish old man?
What is the purpose of old Hamlet's ghost?
Is Claudius a "minor" character?

Try writing ten or twelve such questions, ones that truly interest you; then select one or two to help you focus your research efforts. If you're genuinely interested in finding the answers, when you get to the library you will already have a pretty good idea of where to start looking.

# STEP 3: IDENTIFYING YOUR AUDIENCE
# AND ESTABLISHING YOUR PURPOSE

## Audience

Even though your instructor may be the one who assigned the paper and may well be the only one to read it, you should not think of yourself as writing for that reader alone. Think of a library research paper as a public document, one addressed to a variety of readers in a college or university community who may well have a variety of interests. You may have been told to write for an audience of your peers, and perhaps other members of your class have read some of your earlier compositions. But for a research paper, try to think of your potential audience as consisting of all those currently taking the course, including those who have taken it in the last few years and those who will be taking it in the next few. If you make such an assumption, you can count on a certain amount of shared knowledge: the material studied in the course as well as some of the approaches to and theories about that material. For a course in modern European history, you will not want to patronize your readers by informing them smugly that the English defeated the French and Spanish at the Battle of Trafalgar. And if you are writing for a literary survey course from Chaucer to T.S. Eliot, it would be patronizing to remind your readers that Shakespeare was a well-known Elizabethan playwright or that *Paradise Lost* was written by John Milton.

If you consider that you are writing for this larger audience, you can see that different readers will have different reasons for reading what you write. Some will need only to skim through your paper to see what kinds of information you provide, just as you do when you look at the potential secondary sources for your research paper. Others—including your instructor—will want to read it more carefully, to see how you reach your conclusions and to evaluate the nature and adequacy of the evidence you use to support them.

## Purpose

We discuss throughout this text how writing differs not only for various sorts of readers but also for various purposes. A library research paper will most often have as its aim either providing information or evaluating the claims and conclusions of others who have written on a particular topic.

Even though the range of possible purposes for a research paper is narrower than for other kinds of writing—you will not, for example, be writing primarily to express your feelings or to amuse your readers—you will still need to choose from that narrower range. At one end of this spectrum of purposes is that of reporting facts: you may need only to inform your readers about what others (your sources) have written about the topic. At the other end of the spectrum is exploring a topic and arriving at your own conclusions about it; you may need to evaluate what others have written and thus persuade your readers that one position or one interpretation of the evidence in your sources is better than others. The methods of development and the organizational strategies you use will be different for a paper that evaluates than for one that simply reports.

Where the purpose for your essay falls on this spectrum will often be clear from the way your instructor has worded the assignment. For example, if an assignment reads, "Compare and contrast the main proposals for dealing with the problem of acid rain in Canada," you can see that the words *compare* and *contrast* direct you to evaluate the principal methods that science and government have proposed for handling this contentious issue. Another assignment might instruct you only to report, to provide a representative sampling of the published opinion about a topic. For example, a paper for a commerce course may ask you to explain the sorts of bonds, public and private, that are currently available to investors, and the ways in which they are discounted. At other times it will not be clear what your instructor expects from a research paper. Suppose one of the topics for an anthropology course invites you to "discuss the kinship structure of the Micmac people in the nineteenth century." Here the wording of the assignment does not make it clear whether you are expected to evaluate or report. Presumably you have a choice—but check with your instructor to make sure.

This distinction between reporting on what has been written on a topic and presenting a reasoned conclusion from the published evidence also suggests a difference in your relationship with your readers. If you report, you are most often writing for one of two kinds of readers: (1) those who are unfamiliar with the topic and want information about it, or (2) those who are already familiar with the topic but who are mainly interested in the perspectives you provide in your development and organization. If you argue in support of a thesis (whether for the purpose of evaluating contending proposals or theories or for the purpose of yourself proposing some solution to a problem), you may have to assume that some of your readers will be hostile, or at least skeptical.

## STEP 4: INVENTING

By definition, the library research paper depends heavily upon material you gather from external sources, sources outside your own head. However, before you go to the library and begin looking in encyclopedias or card catalogues or indexes, do what inventing you can on your own. By using the questions from Chapter III, perhaps you can even frame a tentative thesis question to help focus your topic and your research.

Try a bout of brainstorming. Write down quickly, without forcing them into a particular direction or organization, whatever facts or theories you already have about the topic. (You presumably didn't choose a topic that you know absolutely nothing about.) Include any ideas or associations that come to mind. It might surprise you how much you already know about the topic or the contexts in which you might discuss it. At the very least, some of your random associations might help you frame a question or two that will help you direct your research when you do get to the library.

Suppose that for a history course, a student has selected the subject "Science and Technology before the Industrial Revolution." She has chosen her subject, first of all, because it interests her, and also because she feels that the library will have more than enough material on it. But she's already aware that she will need to narrow her topic further. One of the reasons she chose the topic in the first place is that in high school she wrote a report on Sir Issac Newton, and she's still curious about what else was going on in European science at that time. If she remains motivated by her own curiosity and interest, she can maintain her momentum through the necessary weeks of research.

## Invention Questions

The questions in Chapter III might help you focus your thinking. For example, it might help you to think about a topic like "education in Victorian England" if you try out such questions as "How was it caused or brought about? "How did it work?" "Did it change or was it constant?" It might, for instance, help to consider education not as a thing or an institution, but as a part of a process.

Or suppose you have selected a topic and have decided to probe it with the questions about *who, what, where, when, why,* and *how.* If for example you've decided to write on the ghost in *Hamlet,* you could frame such specific questions as these, both to help limit the topic and to discover useful perspectives on it:

1. **Who**

    Who is the ghost?

    Does it exist?

    Is the ghost an *it* or a *he*?

    Who has sent the ghost?

    Who believes (in) the ghost?

    Is the ghost a hallucination?

    To whom can the ghost appear?

    Who sees or hears the ghost?

    Who is frightened by the ghost?

    Whom does the ghost convince?

2. **What**

    What can (or can't) the ghost do?

    Does the ghost behave as a ghost should?

    What does the ghost do?

    What does the ghost say?

    Does the ghost convince Hamlet?

3. **Where**

    Where does the ghost appear?

    Where *can* the ghost appear?

    Where does the ghost go when it disappears?

    Where does the ghost come from?

4. **When**

    When does the ghost appear?

    When does the ghost leave?

    When can (can't) the ghost appear?

    Why does the ghost not appear after the closet scene?

5. **How**

    How does the ghost appear?

    How does the ghost look?

    How does the ghost talk?

    How does the ghost disappear?

    How do the others react to the ghost?

6. **Why**

> Why must the ghost appear?
> Why does Hamlet respond as he does?
> Why do the others react as they do?
> Why does the ghost appear only to Hamlet, later?
> Why can't Gertrude see the ghost?

Your goal is to formulate a specific question that will help you focus your activity as you find out what your library offers on your topic. If you find the right questions to ask, they can provide an initial goal for your research, and the final paper becomes, in part, a record of how you went about answering that question. Once you have formulated a thesis question or a small set of questions that you genuinely want to answer, you can begin exploring external sources.

> *Knowledge is of two kinds. We know a subject ourselves, or we know where we can find information upon it.*
> (Samuel Johnson)

## Search Strategy for External Sources

At first the library may seem intimidating, but your research can be a good deal easier and more effective with the help of experienced librarians and a systematic strategy for your search. The typical search strategy for a topic comprises four stages: locate, evaluate, eliminate, and assimilate. You first of all *locate* the most promising sources; then you *evaluate* them to determine which ones can genuinely help you focus and answer your questions; then you *eliminate* those that are out of date, unreliable, or likely to lead you off on a false scent; and finally you *assimilate* the material from the remaining sources, making sure that you use those sources to serve your purpose, rather than letting your purpose be dominated by them.

The advantage of a systematic strategy for research is that it can save you time and frustration. Draw up an extensive list of books and articles before you begin looking for them. It's discouraging and time-wasting to find a reference to a book, and go through the procedures for locating it in your library, only to discover that it is not on the shelf. You then have to go back to the beginning and start again looking for another source. With an accurate list of several sources in hand, you can locate some of the others and work with them until the missing book has found its way back onto the shelves.

But even before you start your list of books and articles, take a little time to get to know your library. Most libraries put out pamphlets and guides to help you find your way around. Many libraries put on conducted tours to help students and visitors. Some libraries even provide staff to come into classrooms and give lectures and handouts for the particular research needs of a course. Ask your instructor or your reference librarian what kinds of assistance are available.

The more you know about the organization of your library before you start hunting down books and maps and magazines, the easier your search will be.

Librarians will usually suggest that you begin locating sources for your project in one of two places: either the subject catalogue or the reference section. If you already have a good idea of the background or context for your topic, you can begin right away consulting the subject catalogue. But for other topics, especially when you need to explore the background or establish a context for your topic, it's better to begin in the reference section, which offers two basic kinds of information: (1) sources of facts and (2) suggestions for further reading. For a history topic, to take an example, you might need to find out some significant dates and information about what else was going on in the period you want to investigate. If you start in the reference section, you will find such useful resources as encyclopedias, dictionaries, bibliographies, and indexes. Your goal at this point is to collect a number of titles that look as though they will help you start focussing and answering your thesis question.

A reliable encyclopedia article is only a beginning, but it will help develop some background for your topic, and many encyclopedia articles append a short bibliography that you can use to find likely sources. Here for example is a portion of the bibliography that the *Academic American Encyclopedia* lists at the end of its entry on Shakespeare:

> Gurr, Andrew, *The Shakespearean Stage, 1574-1642* (1970); Muir, Kenneth, and Schoenbaum, Samuel, eds., *A New Companion to Shakespeare Studies* (1971); Schoenbaum, Samuel, *William Shakespeare: A Documentary Life* (1975).

You can see that even the most recent of these books was published several years ago. If your topic is a fairly current one, encyclopedias will not be very helpful, partly because the very nature of encyclopedias means that nearly all the information they contain will be somewhat dated, and partly because the most recent information in most fields appears first in magazine or journal articles. It generally takes three or four years for a book to be written, edited, printed and distributed. Journals, however, are usually published monthly or quarterly; the information in them can be more current. To locate journals, you can consult various indexes and bibliographies which are designed to provide access to current journal articles. For example, you may have been introduced to *The Readers' Guide to Periodical Literature*, an index which is published every month and provides listings by subject, title, and author for articles in a variety of general and specialized periodicals such as *Time, Business Week, Science*, and *The Technical Review*. A similar index for specifically Canadian topics and journals is *The Canadian Periodical Index*. Let's say you are trying to find material on pay television in Canada. An entry from the January 1982 issue lists under the heading "TELEVISION broadcasting, subscription" about a dozen magazine articles that appeared in late 1981 about that subject. The fourth item under that heading looks like this:

> Cable firms set for big pay-TV sale. M. Mehr. port Fin Post 75:12 N 7 '81

You can decipher it as follows: in the issue of *The Financial Post* for November 7, 1981, appeared an article written by M. Mehr, entitled, "Cable Firms Set for Big Pay-TV Sale." The numbers 75:12 mean that the article appeared in the seventy-fifth volume on page 12, and the abbreviation *port* means that someone's picture (portrait) appears with the article. To find Mehr's article on pay-TV, you then go to your library's list of periodicals to discover whether it has back issues of *The Financial Post* (most Canadian libraries do) and where they are kept.

You can use a similar procedure to find out whether more specialized journals have published articles on topics like Arctic pollution, elections in Nova Scotia, or labour relations in Nigeria. Many specialized fields index their articles each year. For example, the journal *Victorian Studies* puts out a bibliography of the books and articles on literature and culture of the period from about 1840 to 1890. Such lists, however, are usually three or four years behind, so that if you want to find out what was written on the Victorian poet Robert Browning in 1984, you might not find a particular source indexed until 1987. Some indexes and bibliographies, with the aid of computers, are becoming more up-to-date. Ask your reference librarian about them.

The following is a selection of some of the resources available in most libraries to help you locate sources for your research paper. This list is of course only partial, but we hope that it will give you an idea of the variety of places you can check.

### Encyclopedias

General: *Encyclopaedia Britannica.* 15th ed. 1979.
*Encyclopedia Canadiana.* 10 vols. 1970-77.
*Academic American Encyclopedia.* 1981.

Special: *McGraw-Hill Encyclopedia of Science and Technology.* 5th ed. 15 vols. plus index and yearbooks. 1982.
Langer, William Leonard. *An Encyclopedia of World History.* 5th ed. 1972.
Sills, David L., ed. *International Encyclopedia of the Social Sciences.* 8 vols. 1977 (Supplement, 1979.)

### Dictionaries

General: *Oxford English Dictionary.* 13 vols., plus supplements. 1933-82.
*Webster's Third New International Dictionary of the English Language.* 1976.

Special: *Dictionary of Canadianisms.* 1967. (Lists those words and special senses of words that have originated in Canada.)
*Roget's II: The New Thesaurus.* 1980.
Sloan, Herold S., and Arnold Zurcher. *A Dictionary of Economics.* 5th ed. 1970.
Wentworth, Harold, and Stuart Berg Flexner. *Dictionary of American Slang.* 1975.

### Bibliographies

General: Winchell, Constance. *Guide to Reference Books.* Rev. Eugene Paul Sheehy. 9th edition. 1976. (plus supplements)
*Bibliographic Index: A Cumulative Bibliography of Bibliographies.* 1937-.

Special: *MLA International Bibliography of Books and Articles on the Modern Languages and Literatures.* (Published annually since 1922.)
*Arctic Bibliography.* 1953-71.

## Indexes and Abstracts

An index lists works in a particular field, such as art or management consulting. An abstract also provides a list of what has been published in a given field over a specific period of time, but it provides as well brief summaries of articles, telling what a work is about, its method of proceeding, the sorts of evidence used, and a general summary of the conclusions. Reading the abstract will often help you decide whether it's worth your time to hunt up the actual article.

### Indexes

*Book Review Index.* 1965-.
*Reader's Guide to Periodical Literature.* 1890-.
*Essay and General Literature Index.* 1900-.
   (Contains information on where to find articles that have been collected in books.)
*The New York Times Index.* 1851-. (In many libraries, available on microforms.)
*Art Index.* 1929-.
*Biological and Agricultural Index.* 1963-. (From 1916 to 1963 called *Agricultural Index.*)
*Canadian Periodical Index.* 1929-.

### Abstracts

*Abstracts in Anthropology.* 1970-.
*Book Review Digest.* 1905-. (Collects and abstracts book reviews from selected periodicals in the humanities, social sciences, and general science from the United States, Great Britain, and Canada; the periodicals range from *Ms.* to *English Historical Review* to *Bulletin of Atomic Scientists.*)
*International Political Science Abstracts.* 1951-.
*Language and Language Behavior Abstracts.* 1967-.

## Government Publications

Many governments—national, provincial, and regional—issue publications on a wide range of topics.
*Monthly Catalog of United States Government Publications.* (A subject index to a variety of material.)
*Government of Canada Publications.* (Issued annually with index.)
*Alberta: Bureau of Public Affairs Publication Catalogue.* 1973-. (Issued annually.)
(You can also find in the subject and title catalogues many other publications issued by governments.)

## Sources of Facts

*Facts on File.* 1941-. (A weekly world news digest with a cumulative index.)
*Canadian News Facts.* 1967-. (An indexed digest of Canadian current events. It summarizes and indexes developments in Ottawa and the provincial capitals, news of business and labour, science and the arts, mining and agriculture, religion and education, including Canada's international relations.)
*World Almanac and Book of Facts.* 1868-.
*The Times Atlas of the World.* 1977.
*Columbia Lippincott Gazetteer of the World.* 1962. (A gazetteer is a geographical

dictionary, listing such features as countries, provinces, regions, cities, lakes, rivers, and mountains, and such other information as altitudes and natural resources.)

## Biographical References

*Dictionary of National Biography* (British).
*Dictionary of American Biography.*
*Dictionary of Canadian Biography: 1000-1890.*
Gillispie, C.C., ed. *Dictionary of Scientific Biography.* 16 vols. 1970-80.

When you have checked such resources as encyclopedias, indexes, and specialized dictionaries, you will have a better idea of the backgrounds and contexts for your topic. The reference librarian might then suggest that you go to your library's card catalogue or microfilm catalogue, a catalogue that lists all of the library's holdings — not only books and periodicals, but also other useful sources: microfilms, pamphlets, and so on.

A good place to start is the subject catalogue, where you can look under such subject headings as "Science, history of," "Shakespeare," or "Television—government control." To find out what you need, however, you might need to try several key words, or "descriptors," as some librarians call them. You may not find much under the first heading or two that you consult, for some library catalogues adopt a different terminology. For example, you may have thought about a topic like "Pond ecology," but have found nothing under that heading in the catalogue. Libraries that use the Library of Congress cataloguing system will have available two large volumes that provide an extensive list of subject headings that you can check. If you look up "Pond ecology" in the *Library of Congress Subject Headings,* it will direct you to look under "Fresh-water ecology," where you can find a number of sources relating to the ecology of ponds. If you have decided to investigate the topic "mental telepathy," you will find nothing in the card catalogue itself under that particular heading, but the *Library of Congress Subject Headings* will direct you to "Thought-transference," a heading that might not have occurred to you. When you check under that heading, you will find several other headings that might help you with your topic:

| | |
|---|---|
| Clairvoyance | Second sight |
| Crystal-gazing | Mental telepathy |
| Hypnotism | Psychical research |
| Mental suggestion | Subconscious |
| Mind reading | |

## The Catalogues

Once you have a good idea of some of the headings you can look up in pursuing your topic, your next step is to go to the library's catalogue, which will be either a card catalogue or a microcatalogue, or a combination of both. Usually such catalogues are arranged in two parts: (1) the subject file, which lists books and other material according to the subjects as listed in the *Library of Congress Subject Headings,* and (2) an author-title catalogue, which lists books and other material alphabetically by both the last name of the author and by the title.

Here are examples of the three kinds of cards and microcatalogue entries
—by author, by title, and by subject:

```
HE    Troyer, Warner
8689.6    The sound and the fury: an anecdotal history of
C3
T7    HE
      8689.9    The sound and the fury: an anecdotal history of
      C
      T    HE                                                           A
           8689.9  TELEVISION BROADCASTING-CANADA-HISTORY               B
           C3      Troyer, Warner, 1932                                 C
           T76        The sound and the fury: an anecdotal history of   D
                   Canadian broadcasting/ Warner Troyer-Toronto: J.     E
                   Wiley. 1980.
                      224p.: ill.; 26cm.                                F
                      Bibliography: p. 215-217.                         G
                      Includes index.
                      ISBN 0-471-99872-9: $15.95.                       H

                   1. Radio broadcasting-Canada-History. 2. Television  I
                   broadcasting-Canada-History. I. Title.
```

The subject card provides the following information:
A.  Call number (upper left)
B.  Subject heading
C.  Author's name and date of birth
D.  Title
E.  Publication information (city, publisher's name, and date)
F.  Number of pages, illustrations (if any), size
G.  The fact that the book has a bibliography and index
H.  The International Standard Book Number (ISBN) and price
 I.  Cross references for other subject headings

---

### Exercise 14A

Look over once again the broad subject areas listed on p. 342. All of course need
considerable narrowing in order to become possible topics for research papers.
Select the two or three that most interest you (or come up with one or more
others, of similar scope, that these suggest to you) and consult your library's
catalogues and reference sections to see what narrowing you could do to make
them suitable for further exploration, and also to find out what resources your
library has to help you. Try to formulate two or three provocative thesis questions
for each narrowed topic you come up with.

---

## The Working Bibliography

When you have narrowed your topic to something that both interests you and is researchable, and have followed a systematic search strategy to guide you through bibliographies, dictionaries, indexes, and other lists, you can start to assemble your working bibliography. This preliminary bibliography is not the same as the list of references that will appear at the end of the final draft of your paper. Rather, it is your initial list of possibly useful sources about your topic.

As a rough rule, try to locate at least two reference sources for each page of the length of paper you expect to write. For a twenty-five-page paper, then, you might want to start out with fifty sources; but for a six-page paper (about 1500 words) you might be satisfied with twelve. After you have evaluated the items on your preliminary list, you might decide to eliminate as many as half of them, either because the information they offer is out of date or not clearly relevant or because it duplicates other sources. From an initial list of a dozen sources for a six-page paper, you might end up with only six or seven that are truly worth considering in greater depth, though you may find and add other equally useful sources later.

When you have located a possible source, you need evaluate it only briefly at this point; don't try to read it in depth or start taking notes. Begin by looking it over, trying to decide whether it will merit further serious attention as your topic becomes more sharply focussed. When you are simply trying to determine what a given article or book is about, you can skim through it rapidly, trying to get a sense of its organization, its principal vocabulary, and its main points of argument. Your purpose is to sample in order to decide what or whether to read more carefully. If you are looking for some specific piece of information, you can glance over the pages to see if the information is there, or whether a particular discussion really applies to your topic. As you look over the items in your initial list, trying to decide which to pursue, you will be learning more and more about your topic, a process that will allow you to sharpen your thesis question while at the same time getting a better sense of where you might find the answers.

When you have finished evaluating the items on your list and have eliminated the unpromising sources, prepare a bibliography card for each source that's left. Here is an example:

Most researchers use cards 7.5 by 12.5 cm (3 by 5 inches). On the card carefully copy out the author's name (last name first) as it appears on the title page or at the head of the article, then the title (underlined) exactly as it's printed on the title page, followed by what is called "publication data": for a book give the place of publication (usually a city), the publisher, and the year of publication.

For an article, carefully copy down the author's name (last name first), the full title of the article as printed at its head, the full name of the periodical (underlined), the volume number and the date of the issue in which the article appears, and the inclusive page numbers. Here is an example of a bibliography card for a journal article:

| |
|---|
| MacLulich, T.D. |
| "Colloquial Style and the Tory Mode" |
| Canadian Literature, 89 (Summer 1981), pp. 7-21 |
| |
| PR 8900     [uses Davies as |
| C 27         example of "Tory |
|                 style"] |

As you are scanning the sources you have decided to use, it's a good idea to write brief notes to yourself at the bottom of the card. For instance, at the bottom of the sample cards above, the researchers wrote their impressions of what the works were about. Also include on each card the full call number for the periodical or book in your library. That way, if you need to go back and check your source, you won't have to go to the trouble of consulting the catalogue all over again. Prepare a separate card for each source you decide to use; then you can later sort them out in any order you wish, and you can easily alphabetize them for your list of references at the end of your finished paper.

> *To be apt in quotation is a splendid and dangerous gift. Splendid because it ornaments a man's speech with other men's jewels; dangerous for the same reason.* (Robertson Davies)

## Taking Notes

When you have selected the most promising sources, assembled your working bibliography, and perhaps narrowed your thesis question in the process, you can begin taking notes for direct use in your paper. Now begins the fourth phase of invention: assimilation of the material in your sources.

Before you begin taking notes, here are two major principles that you must keep constantly in mind as you work through the process of writing a research paper:

## 1. TAKE EVERY PRECAUTION TO AVOID PLAGIARISM.

Every word, phrase, or idea that you get from a source must be fully and accurately acknowledged and documented. For a full discussion of this important matter, see pp. 360-363.

## 2. STAY IN CONTROL OF YOUR SOURCES: DON'T LET THEM CONTROL YOU.

The tendency, especially for inexperienced researchers, is to copy a series of quotations from sources and then try to stitch them together with a few stilted bits of their own prose. The result of such patchwork is that the writer nearly always remains under the control of the sources. Therefore make this a special point to keep in mind from the time you begin taking notes until the time you finish revising: you are the boss; *your* purpose and thesis should determine all the decisions about how much of what source to use and where to use it. Keep thinking about and refining your thesis question so that you can take notes selectively; if you allow yourself to become merely a passive recorder, an unselective accumulator of information, you will be controlled by your sources. Take only the notes you need. Stay in the saddle: don't let your sources ride you.

*Use Cards*   Take your notes on cards, either the same size you use for your bibliography cards or the 10 by 15 cm (4 by 6 inch) size.

*One Note per Card*   Record only one point on each card; then you can easily arrange all your points according to your own needs rather than according to the order of your source. For example, you may get several points from one paragraph of a source, but you may want to use them in widely different parts of your paper; with separate cards for each point, organizing is easy.

In the upper left corner, identify each note card with the author's name and the page number, for instance "Bevis, p. 63"; you will later need to provide the exact page numbers in your paper. In the upper right corner you can label the note, or indicate what part of your plan it pertains to.

*Be Brief*   Try to keep your notes short. If you must record a long one, continue it on the back of the card, and be sure to remind yourself that you have done so with the word [*over*] or a symbol [ ↵➤ ].

*Minimize Quotation: Use Paraphrase and Summary*   The ideal is to produce a research paper with a minimum of direct quotations. The less quotation you use in your notes, the less you are merely passively recording data and the more you are *assimilating* the material from your sources. As much as possible, make the material your own, now, at the note-taking stage, for that will make it much easier to work with later, at the writing and revising stages. As much as possible, take your notes *in your own words*. Rather than quote directly, paraphrase and summarize; as you do so, you'll have to assimilate the ideas, making them your own. You will be in control.

To *paraphrase* something, you restate it in your own words *and your own syntax*; merely trying to substitute synonyms here and there does not constitute paraphrase. Paraphrases are sometimes about the same length as the original, though usually a little shorter.

To *summarize* something, you again use your own words, but you boil down the essential points of the original to a much shorter version—perhaps only a sentence or two for a whole chapter or article.

If an article or chapter is interesting or relevant, but not *central* to your argument, you might decide that you need to provide only a short summary of its contents, without using any direct quotations at all. Your goal is to capture the author's main point, his thesis, in your own words. Suppose, for example, that a student wanted to use only the main idea of an article on the productivity of workers in Japanese industry and wrote a short summary of it:

> Kermov, 23-26    Innovation of J. workers
>
> Japan is best known for its productive and innovative workers who, though they appear to be more submissive and rule-bound because less individually oriented than Western workers, in fact do more original thinking.

Here the writer has summarized the main point of the article, but does not need to put in any quotation marks, because the note does not quote anything directly. Of course words like *Japan* and *workers* and *thinking* almost surely occur in the original; the point is that the student is using them in a context he has made his own. It would be silly to try to avoid such use of ordinary words by substituting *Nippon, labourers* and *cogitating,* for example. But if you want to use a particularly significant or striking word from the original, put it in quotation marks. And be sure to record the page numbers: even for a paraphrase, you must still document the source in your paper.

For other kinds of notes, for example those dealing with issues that are more central to your own argument, you might want to record more of your source in a longer note. But remember, the more you can assimilate the data and use paraphrase rather than quotation, the less you will be at the mercy of the language and the perspective of your source. Here for example is a passage from a popularizing work about some of the findings of linguistics in the 1970's:

> Since children are not born to speak baby talk, what could possibly be the explanation for its prevalence around the world? Most of the adults in the six cultures claimed that baby talk made it easier for children to learn to speak. It is indeed true

that in most cases baby talk words have simpler consonant arrangements and fewer vowels than adult language. On the other hand, some baby talk, such as that of Arabic, employs difficult sounds which children do not ordinarily master until they have had considerable experience in speaking the adult language. And is it really easier for an English-speaking child to say *itsy-bitsy* than *tiny*? Despite such exceptions, folk wisdom about baby talk apparently is correct: it does give children practice in speaking. Baby talk presents the child with a stock of simpler utterances, and reduplication increases practice in their use. These utterances can gradually be discarded when adult words begin to be used, by which time they have served their purpose.

> (Peter Farb, *Word Play: What Happens When People Talk*
> [New York: Bantam Books, 1975], p. 274.)

And here is a paraphrase of it that retains the note-taker's independence yet still makes some detailed use of the source by mixing in some direct quotation:

> The study explains why baby talk is so widespread in different countries even though babies don't automatically start speaking that way. Most parents said that baby talk "made it easier for children to learn to speak." Most baby talk uses relatively simple sound patterns. But Farb wonders if it is "really easier" to say "*itsy-bitsy*" rather than "*tiny*." Even so, the parents are probably right when they say that baby talk allows children to practise their language. It provides a vocabulary of easy phrases, and "reduplication increases practice" in using them. Children can drop these phrases when they begin to talk more like adults.

This note summarizes parts of Farb's original and directly quotes others. Note the quotation marks around the phrases that come directly from the source.

Another time you might want to quote directly rather than summarize is when a source cites specific figures or statistics, or is particularly striking or well expressed:

> According to Lewis Thomas, running is not only beneficial in itself but also "has acquired the medicinal value formerly attributed to rare herbs from Indonesia."

If, for whatever reason, you decide that you must quote something—whether a word, a phrase, a sentence, or a whole paragraph—enclose it in prominent, clearly visible quotation marks. If you are careful to put quotation marks around ANYTHING you copy verbatim onto a note card, you will always know what you must enclose in quotation marks in your paper. To fail to acknowledge direct quotation *as quotation* is to be guilty of one form of plagiarism.

## STEP 5: ORGANIZING; PLANNING DEVELOPMENT

When you have completed your research and note-taking, sort your note cards into groups. If you have been careful and systematic, you may find that a fairly clear organization emerges from those groups. If it does, then you can proceed to write a provisional outline to guide you in writing the first draft. But don't stop at the first arrangement that suggests itself; a better one may occur to you as you try different arrangements, which could, in turn, suggest different, and perhaps better, methods of development.

It will help you keep control of your material if you consider several different methods of development. Remember that a good research paper is much more than a mere summary of the sources you have consulted. If all of your sources use a chronological method of development, for example, that does not mean that you must do likewise. You might instead decide to begin with an effect, describing it in some detail, and then turn to a consideration of the causes, one by one. Presumably each of your sources has its own purpose, but don't let that force you into making one of them your purpose, as well. Be independent and tough-minded; let your own thinking and thesis guide you.

Review the various methods of development we discuss in Chapter IV, and try to decide which will best organize your note cards so as to serve your thesis. Since a research paper will probably be longer than other papers you write, you may want to develop different parts in different ways.

The best way to stay in command of your development and organization is to keep refining your thesis question as you go through the various steps of planning, including your reading and note-taking. Then formulate from that question a thesis statement that reflects your decisions about what you have read and recorded. One student, for example, wrote the first form of her thesis question as follows:

> How did the education of women in early Victorian England compare with that of men?

When she came to reformulating it as a guide for organizing her notes, she was tempted to take the easy way and formulate a thesis sentence like this:

> There were many reasons why women in mid-Victorian England received poorer education than men.

Such a statement, though, did little to help her organize her notes or develop her thinking. But as she began to arrange and rearrange her groups of note cards, she began to see that a better form for her thesis statement could be something like this:

> In Victorian England, women's education was inferior to that of men because [she went from here to state three chief points].

Such a formulation helped her because it reflected her own thinking, not that of her sources: she had found evidence for one point in one source, evidence for her second point in three other sources, and evidence for her final point in two others.

## The Preliminary Outline

When you have sorted your note cards into groups and arranged those groups into a likely order, you are about ready to write a first draft. But before you begin writing, draw up a *preliminary* or *working outline,* complete with tentative thesis statement or thesis question. You may find that this longer and more complex paper will require a more elaborate and detailed outline than the rough sorts of plans you use for other writing assignments.

The preliminary outline serves two purposes: First, it guides you as you write the draft. By using it as a sort of road map, you can see at a glance where you've been, where you are, and where you're going. Since you should seldom need to pause to wonder what to say next, you can maintain a good momentum during the writing of a first draft. The outline's second function is to let you see your project more clearly. With all your materials laid out schematically in front of you, you can begin assessing their relationships and order. You can more easily decide whether your material is complete and whether the organization is coherent and effective.

Here for example is the preliminary outline the student drew up for her paper on eighteenth-century science. Note that the act of writing it all down prompted several questions; she jotted them down too, in order to keep them in mind as she wrote her draft:

Preliminary Outline

## Newton and His Contemporaries

*Thesis Question:* What was going on in science around 1700?
*Possible beginning:* Look at science field by field. Newton was not alone: many scientists were busy. Mention some names (surely familiar to most people): Newton, Boyle, Halley, Fahrenheit, Newcomen.

   I. Astronomy
        observatories (why?)
        Flamsteed
        Newton and Halley and his comet
        Halley and Ptolemy's star chart
  II. Mathematics
        Newton again
        Newton vs. Leibnitz
 III. Physics
        Newton yet again; "the greatest" (use as transition?)
        *Opticks, Principia,* and "Queries"
        Fahrenheit (what about Celsius?)
  IV. Chemistry
        the phlogiston caper
   V. Medicine (try to order my grab-bag of data)
  VI. Biology
        Linnaeus's taxonomy (too late?); on to Darwin (off my chronological map?)
        (try reversing V and VI — can biology lead into medicine?)
 VII. The steam engine — Savery or Newcomen?
VIII. Science vs. Religion
        Darwin and evolution
        Voltaire on Newton

*Ending:* Much in present-day science was prepared for earlier: Newton and others set the stage for later discoveries and advances. (Sounds rather lame.)

(*Queries:* Too many parts? Can VIII be a sub-part of VI, via Darwin? Can IV be made part of III? See if Newton works as a frame.)

But obviously such an outline is preliminary, tentative. Be prepared, even eager, to change it; don't let yourself be trapped into sticking with a plan just because you've written it down. As you write the draft, and even more so as you work through the several sweeps of revising, you should find yourself revising and refining your outline as you discover new ideas, different relations among the parts, and better arrangements. Eventually you will have a polished outline that conforms completely to your finished paper. (We recommend that you make this a *sentence* outline, for both its clarity and its formality.) This final outline, as it takes shape, will serve as your guide and your safeguard throughout the writing and revising stages; when submitted along with the finished paper, it will serve as a guide for your reader, a sort of combination abstract and table of contents.

If you compare the sample preliminary outline above with the final sentence outline for the paper (see pp. 385-386), you will see that during writing and revising, the student not only answered her own Queries but also changed her mind about several other points. For example she managed to reduce the overall number of parts to six by finding a smaller and better place for the steam engine and by using Biology as a lead-in to Science and Religion, which also both gave her a context for introducing Darwin and enabled her to build toward an effective ending. She moved Chemistry to take advantage of the transitional link provided by Stahl, who also appears at the end of Medicine. She found a way to organize the material under Medicine. And she changed her thesis and title to reflect her decision to deemphasize Newton and broaden the focus of interest of her paper.

## STEP 6: WRITING THE FIRST DRAFT

With a good set of note cards and a preliminary outline that reflects your decisions about development and arrangement, you are ready to write the first draft. As we suggest in Chapter VI, it is usually better to write the first draft quickly in order to maintain the flow of your writing. If you plan your time so as to leave several hours for careful revising, you won't have to worry about polished sentences or minor matters of grammar and spelling in this draft. And don't hold yourself back by planning an elaborate introduction; the best time to write your introduction is when you have finished your draft and can see where it wants to take you.

### Integrating Quotations

Start with the note cards you have divided into groups and subgroups: weave them into paragraphs, providing any necessary transitions. But remember that writing an effective research paper is a good deal more than combining patches of quotations and paraphrase with a few hasty stitchings of transitional prose. All the material from your sources—especially the verbatim quotations—must be carefully woven into the warp of your decisions about your purpose, your audience, and your thesis. The most alluring temptation when you write a research paper is to let your sources do all the work. Remember, however, that your purpose is to present or explain a set of facts or to pursue an argument, and that all the other elements, including the quotations or paraphrases or summaries that you have in your notes, must be subordinated to that purpose. You choose your own voice and tone, your own rhetorical stance; one of your goals is to keep it consistent throughout. Don't let your sources—especially one major source—dictate how your writing is going to sound.

To avoid sounding like your sources, try to blend quotations into the flow of your own writing, for example as the student does with a quotation of part of a sentence in the sample research paper at the end of this chapter:

> ...but unfortunately Haulksbee was not able "to grasp the connection between electricity and the luminous phenomena observed."

If you decide to use a longer quotation, the temptation will be even stronger to let yourself be dominated by the language of your source. Therefore always think twice before using a long quotation: try to substitute a paraphrase that you can weave more smoothly into your own prose.

Most of the time use summary or paraphrase. Occasionally combine these with a phrase or two of direct quotation. Less often, quote a whole sentence or two, still blending the quotation smoothly into your own syntax. Least often, use longer block quotations; reserve them for when they will be most effective for your own purpose or when their language is especially memorable—as in Newton's striking statement of scientific modesty that the student sets off as a short block quotation in her paper—the only block quotation in her fourteen pages of text. Like other devices in writing (the short sentence, for instance, or the long word), block quotations will be most effective when you use them sparingly. Don't let your anxiety about filling up a page tempt you into using long quotations for their own sakes. As a rule of thumb, your comments on any quotation should be at least as long as what you have quoted or paraphrased.

## Acknowledging Your Sources: Avoiding Plagiarism

When you finish a first draft, you are ready to begin revising. But when you are working on a research paper, it is essential that you prepare for that major step by reemphasizing for yourself the all-important principle of acknowledging and documenting sources. If you fail to keep this principle in mind as you revise, you will likely finish with some sources unacknowledged or inadequately acknowledged. If you leave them that way, you will be guilty of plagiarism and face probable failure. But if you try to correct matters at that late stage, you will at best have to do a great deal of extra work, going back over nearly everything you've done—or at worst still miss a few and leave yourself open to the charge of plagiarism. Therefore during the several sweeps of revising, keep your eyes open for possible instances of inadequate acknowledgment or documentation. And at the end of revising, thoroughly double-check all your documentation.

### What to Acknowledge and Document

When told that they must document everything that comes from somewhere other than their own heads, some students feel that they have to footnote almost every sentence. But if you have used the invention strategies suggested in this chapter and in Chapter III, you're aware that you began with a good deal of information of your own. You do not have to document what is called "common knowledge"—for instance the fact that Charles Dickens wrote *Great Expectations*, that Bern is the capital of Switzerland, that Newton formulated the law of gravity, or that Daniel is a character in the Old Testament. But other kinds of facts and ideas are often more difficult to assess, and you need to ask yourself, "Common to whom?" Many facts in a journal on nuclear physics are common knowledge to nuclear physicists, and many facts in a specalized book on linguistics will be common knowledge to most linguists. It all depends on your assessment of your readers.

English teachers know that "Let me not to the marriage of true minds / Admit impediments" comes from one of Shakespeare's sonnets, but that would not be common knowledge for most students in grade twelve: they would need a footnote. But for a group of readers that had just been studying that and several other Elizabethan sonnets, such a footnote would probably be unnecessary. If you write to an audience of the students and instructors of the course for which you're preparing the research paper, you will have a better idea of what to document. If you're not certain whether a piece of information is common knowledge, be on the safe side: acknowledge your source. And if something is new to you, don't immediately decide that everyone else must know all about it; it's probably safer to assume that it will be equally new to your readers.

> pla'giary   *A thief in literature; one who*
> *steals the thought or writing of another.*
> (Samuel Johnson, *A Dictionary of*
> *the English Language*)

## Quoting, Paraphrasing, and Plagiarism

*Plagiarism* is literary burglary. This is no idle metaphor. A plagiarist is a writer who filches something that belongs to somebody else and presents it to readers as if it were his own. In the world of professional writing, plagiarism is a crime. Don't be a plagiarist, either intentionally or unintentionally.

Except for something that is clearly "common knowledge," then, be scrupulous in your adherence to the following principles: If you use *anything at all* from one of your sources, acknowledge it; otherwise you will be guilty of plagiarism. If you use a phrase consisting of no more than a verb with its modifying adverb or a noun with its adjective, or even a single word that is other than ordinary—a single noun, verb, adjective or adverb—you must not only enclose it in quotation marks but also provide a reference that gives your source credit. Even such a small instance of plagiarism as a forgotten pair of quotation marks could destroy much of the credibility of your paper, and of you as its author. And even if you use not words but ideas, if you carefully paraphrase or summarize a passage without directly quoting anything in it, you still must acknowledge your source; otherwise it's plagiarism. The obligation to keep your reader apprised of your sources is one of the reasons we insist that on your note cards you keep careful track of authors and page numbers and all verbatim copying.

Here is a passage from one of the sources that the student used for her paper:

> By 1700 carbon dioxide, impure carbon monoxide mixtures, intestinal gas (an impure hydrogen-methane mixture), hydrogen and nitric oxide (Boyle) had been generated and described as gases. Boyle's experiments with tubes over mercury and water had led to the first formulation of the gas laws, and it was Boyle who first collected a gas over water by inverting a full flask and allowing the rising gas to displace the water.

A writer who copied out this whole passage word for word without putting quotation marks around it or otherwise acknowledging it—which would be more like armed robbery than burglary—would be committing the grossest kind of plagiarism. But there are three other kinds of unacknowledged borrowing that, though less extreme, still constitute plagiarism. Consider the following passage:

> Scientists had, before 1700, generated and described as gases the following: hydrogen, nitric oxide, carbon dioxide, certain impure carbon mixtures, and intestinal gas. Boyle collected gases by using tubes over water and by inverting a full flask and letting the rising gas displace the fluid.

As you can see, the passage uses many of the words of the original source as well as the same ideas; only a few of the facts have been omitted and some of the material rearranged. Even if it were acknowledged with a footnote, this passage would still be plagiarism; to make it legitimate, a writer would have to put quotation marks around those words and phrases taken directly from the source. As a result, the passage would have to look like this:

> As Cecil J. Schneer describes it, scientists had "by 1700...generated and described as gases" the following: "hydrogen" and "nitric oxide," "carbon dioxide," certain "impure carbon...mixtures," and "intestinal gas." Boyle "collected gases" by using "tubes over water" and "by inverting a full flask and" letting "the rising gas...displace" the fluid.[5]

But rather than concoct such a hash of quoted words and phrases, a student would do better either to quote most of Schneer's original passage or to paraphrase it with little or no quotation.

A second plagiarized use of the passage, which may be less dishonest but still constitutes plagiarism, occurs when the student uses largely his own words but still borrows, without acknowledging them, some of the significant phrases from the source, as follows:

> By the turn of the century, a number of gases had been identified by Boyle and others, for example carbon dioxide, some impure carbon monoxide mixtures, and even intestinal gas, which is an impure hydrogen-methane mixture. Out of their experiments grew the first formulation of the laws of gases.

Here, as you can see, the greater part of the matter is still Schneer's, and should be so acknowledged, for example as follows:

> By the turn of the century, according to Cecil J. Schneer, a number of gases had been identified by Boyle and others, for example "carbon dioxide," some "impure

carbon monoxide mixtures," and even "intestinal gas," which is "an impure hydrogen-methane mixture." Out of their experiments grew the "first formulation" of the laws of gases.

Again, acknowledging indebtedness by identifying the author and showing exactly what has been borrowed absolves the writer of plagiarism, but such a passage still borders on the illegitimate, for it adheres too closely to the patterns of the original. The writer has still not taken control of the material.

The third kind of plagiarism is that consisting of pure paraphrase—no quotation—but without any acknowledgment of the source. Here is such a paraphrase of the passage from Schneer:

> Before the end of the seventeenth century, Robert Boyle had shown how to collect gases in flasks inverted over liquids, and he and other scientists had isolated and identified several gases, including some of the basic carbon combinations and mixtures of hydrogen, nitrogen, and oxygen, resulting in the first versions of the now-familiar laws governing the behaviour of gases.

Providing a footnote legitimizes such a paraphrase. But consider making your reader feel more comfortable by weaving into the paraphrase a nod to your source:

> Before the end of the seventeenth century, according to Cecil J. Schneer, Robert Boyle had....[5]

Note that in such a paraphrase the writer has assimilated the material, taken control of it. It no longer sounds like even a partial echo of Schneer's original, either in overall order and syntax or in small details of phrasing. In such a context, then, there is nothing wrong with repeating such ordinary and unavoidable words as *Boyle, gases, mixtures, carbon, hydrogen, first,* and *laws*; nor do the near-repetitions in such words as *flask, collect,* and *inverted* sound like feeble attempts to avoid copying too closely. They all sound, and are, quite legitimate, simply because the writer is clearly in command of the context.

## STEP 7: REVISING THE RESEARCH PAPER

As we emphasize in chapters VII through XI, the best writing results from careful and systematic revision. Because of the greater length and complexity of a research paper, it is even more important than usual to proceed through four or five sweeps of revising. Further, these sweeps of revising are your last chance to make sure the paper is one you can call your own.

Because so much of a research paper depends on the sources you use, it's nearly inevitable that at least some of their orientation has crept in, and perhaps some of their language as well. In revising, you can reclaim your writing. During each sweep of revision keep in mind that you are not only making the writing clearer, more coherent, more forceful, more graceful, and so on, you are also taking command of the arrangement, the paragraphs, the sentences and the words. You are making sure the whole is guided by your own purpose, that the single ruling principle is your own thesis.

## The First Sweep:  Revising Large Matters

Begin your revising by restating that thesis for yourself—and for your readers—in a revised thesis sentence. Suppose that you began your first draft with this narrowed thesis:

> The purpose of the ghost is to tell Hamlet of the murder and to keep him on the path of revenge.

After working through your draft, arranging the evidence and drawing it all together into a clarified whole, you can now write a more focussed thesis sentence:

> Old Hamlet's ghost serves not only to reveal the murder and urge his son to revenge, but also to provide a continuing reminder of the order and virtue that have departed from Denmark.

Until you had worked it all out in your draft, you probably hadn't really appreciated that the last part of this revised thesis sentence was what most of the evidence and your thinking about it had led to. When you have composed such a revised sentence, you can use it as your guide during the subsequent sweeps of revising.

You can now write your opening paragraph because you now know where the whole thing is going. One of the main functions of the opening paragraph is to orient your readers, to let them know where you're starting from and where you're going to take them. As we suggest in Chapter VII, the beginning or introductory paragraph is like a contract between you and your readers: in it you set out the terms of what you are offering them, and they in turn tacitly agree to read your paper under the terms you have set out. If you don't deliver what you have contracted for, you will puzzle or annoy or anger them. Use your opening paragraph to prepare your readers: provide any necessary background, and indicate the purpose and scope of your paper, and indicate at least the main lines you will develop.

You can now turn your attention in this first sweep to revising other matters of development and arrangement. Use the following questions and suggestions to help you make decisions:

1. Are all the points you have developed genuinely relevant to *your own* purpose and not that of one or more of your sources?
2. Can you significantly condense the first third or the first half of your draft? (Often, in getting going, writers include too much in the early paragraphs, perhaps by giving more background or history or other facts and quotations than purpose and thesis require.)
3. Have you left anything out? Ask yourself what your reader needs to know for each section. Have you made your assumptions clear?
4. Are the various sections and sub-sections in the best order? If your purpose is even partly to persuade, have you kept your strongest arguments for near the end? Does your newly focussed thesis suggest a better order than the one you used in your draft?
5. Are the main ideas sufficiently emphasized? In writing the draft, you may have been so engrossed in facts, quotations, or paraphrase that you let some of your main points become obscured.

6. Check the introductory paragraph to make sure that it accords with how you now see your thesis and purpose and that it establishes your own rhetorical stance and tone, not that of your sources.
7. Go back and rewrite your concluding paragraph. Does it both reflect and reemphasize your thesis? Does it harmonize with the rhetorical stance of your new opening paragraph?

## The Second Sweep: Revising Paragraphs

The first stage of revising ends when you are satisfied that you have provided a strong thesis to make your material clear and available to your readers, that the sections and sub-sections of your paper are arranged in the best way to support that thesis, and that you have drafted a beginning and an ending that are right for your purpose, thesis, and readers. In the second stage of revising, examine the individual paragraphs in your draft to make sure that they do what you want them to.

Consider the following draft paragraphs; note the strong stylistic contrast between the student's own material and what she has taken over from her sources:

> Outbursts of anger are common in Auntie Martha. Before, she always preferred to be rational and discuss problems, her voice rarely raised above a normal speaking tone. But now she is incapable of discussing problems and resorts to violent outbursts to express her frustration. Often I have heard her lash out at Lillian — "You hate me!" As a child and young teenager, I remember a bright and vibrant Auntie Martha. As a young adult, I see a helpless, forgetful woman who at the age of sixty-five can't always remember my name.
>
> In February of '83, Auntie Martha was diagnosed as having Alzheimer's disease. A disease that is little known about and that few people are aware of.
>
> The fact that many people have never heard of the name *Alzheimer* does not mean that it is a rare problem. "Alzheimer makes up five percent of all dementias."[1] The disease affects five to ten percent of the population over the age of sixty-five. Or, in other words "one out of every six persons over the age of 65 — about 1 million people."[2] However, Alzheimer's disease will also often strike those between the ages of fifty and sixty-five. It is estimated that Alzheimer's is the fourth most common disease in Canada.[3]
>
> Alzheimer's disease is a disease in which the brain gradually wastes over a period of months or years. There are three stages of Alzheimer's disease. The first stage shows subtle changes....

The passage shifts abruptly from a kind of informal narrative to the more formal tone of technical explanation. It moves from the first person (I) and the familiar (Auntie) to a more formal and impersonal style with its medical terminology, its passive voice, and its objective statistics; and the multiple footnotes are symptomatic of the stiffness and choppiness of such a source-controlled paragraph. Another symptom of the discomfort the writer felt in moving from one stance to another is the sentence fragment at the end of the short transitional second paragraph. In revising, the first paragraph can be made a little more formal. And in the next paragraph, where she begins to depend on one of her sources, she can refer directly to the source so that her reader can understand why some of the language changes. She also needs to incorporate a little of the informality of her earlier narration into this paragraph. Here is a revised version of the passage, which is easier to read because of its greater coherence and more uniform tone:

> Outbursts of anger are common in Aunt Martha. She had always preferred to discuss problems calmly and rationally, her voice rarely raised above a normal speaking tone. But now she seems incapable of discussing problems and resorts to violent outbursts to express her frustration. Often I have heard her lash out at Lillian: "You hate me!" As a child and young teenager, I remember a bright, vibrant Aunt Martha; as a young adult, I see a helpless, forgetful, irritable woman who at the age of sixty-five can't always remember my name.
>
> In February of this year, Aunt Martha's problem was diagnosed as a disease that few people are aware of: Alzheimer's disease.
>
> I had never heard of it, either, but the fact that most of us have never heard of the name *Alzheimer* doesn't mean that the disease is rare. As Hilda Johnson explains in *The Canadian Nurse*, "Alzheimer makes up five percent of all dementias."[1] The disease affects five to ten percent of those who, like Aunt Martha, are over the age of sixty-five—in Johnson's words, "one out of every six persons over the age of 65— about 1 million people." But the disease also often strikes those between fifty and sixty-five. According to Johnson, Alzheimer's is the fourth most common cause of death in Canada.
>
> The brain of someone like Aunt Martha who suffers from Alzheimer's disease gradually wastes away over a period of months or years, usually in three stages. The first stage shows some subtle changes....

In addition to its improved smoothness and coherence, the revised version refers specifically to the source before quoting it, so that readers can understand the difference in tone. And by referring to the source twice more, she in effect notifies her readers that she is still relying only on that one source; consequently she needs only one footnote. If she feels that some of her readers will require a definition of the psychiatric term *dementia*, she can incorporate that definition into the same note. As much as possible, then, integrate smoothly into your own paragraphs everything you have derived from your sources.

Here are some further questions and suggestions to keep in mind as you pass your draft through this second sweep of revision:

1. Do you end any paragraphs with a quotation—especially a long one? If so, add a brief comment or observation that indicates to your readers how you want them to take what you have quoted; keep the paragraph in your control right to its end.
2. Can you divide some longer paragraphs into shorter ones for sharper emphasis?
3. Can you visualize how the paragraphs will look to your reader when they are typed? A series of short paragraphs may distract readers from the progress of your explanation or argument.
4. Consider using a brief transitional paragraph between major sections of your paper; such a paragraph can also help to emphasize important ideas.
5. Consider rearranging a complex batch of data into point form or a chart so that your reader can grasp it more easily.

6. Is each paragraph unified and coherent, with a clear beginning, middle, and end?
7. Have you made the most of such strategies for achieving emphasis as parallelism, repetition, and using explicit pronouns?
8. Check the opening sentence of each paragraph to see that it
   a. refers in some way to your guiding purpose.
   b. provides a smooth transition from the preceding paragraph;
   c. clearly introduces the topic of the paragraph.
9. Does each paragraph end with sufficient emphasis?

## The Third Sweep: Revising Sentences

When you revise paragraphs, you probably change some sentences to help the paragraphs go right and to maintain a consistent tone. In this third sweep, focus on the sentences themselves. In addition to other matters (see Chapter IX), when working with a research paper you will here, again, be looking for opportunities to improve your control of your material, for even if you have paraphrased your sources as you were taking notes, it's almost inevitable that some of their language, especially their syntax, will find its way into your first draft.

In the following example from a student's draft about the psychological state known as depression, the first two sentences of a paragraph reveal too much reliance on one of his sources:

> Depression may also show a lack of appetite and a subsequent weight loss. This anorexia may reach a point where the patient would have to be fed intravenously to prevent death.

These sentences are so similar to the source that they amount to plagiarism; and the lack of a note would compound the error. In revising, the student decided to acknowledge his indebtedness by referring back to the source, one that he had already mentioned, which also helped him, at least partly, to account for the technical term:

> A further sign of depression is that the patient has no appetite and has lost a significant amount of weight. According to Mendels, this *anorexia* may even become severe enough for the patient to need intravenous feeding to prevent death.[7]

The student has won back his style from the somewhat clinical tone of his source, while at the same time acknowledging that source.

As you try to maintain your tone, your rhetorical stance, by going through the sentences of your draft, be sure to check that every sentence you have produced is a full sentence, especially if you have incorporated in it a direct quotation from one of your sources. Consider the following sentence from the draft of a paper on Elizabethan astrology:

> Another often-printed treatise entitled *The Most Excellent, Profitable and pleasant booke of the famous Doctour and expert Astrologien Arcandam or Aleandrin, to fynd the fatal desteny, constellation, complexion, and naturall inclination of every man and childe by his byrth: with an addition of Phisiognomie very delectable to reade.*

As he was writing and copying this sentence (or rather fragment), the student was apparently so struck by the title he found in his source that he neglected to provide a verb for his own sentence. In revising, he needed only to substitute the phrase "bore the title" for the participle *entitled*.

Whenever you can, work the language of your source into the syntax of your own sentence. One way to ensure this kind of integration is to quote only parts of sentences from a source, rather than whole sentences. Note how in the following sentence the historian Jacob Opper (in *Science and The Arts*) manages to incorporate two separate parts of a letter into his own sentence:

> It is no wonder that Cézanne desired to "make of Impressionism something hard and durable," and wrote that the painter ought to "treat nature by the cylinder, the sphere, [and] the cone."[1]

Note that in order to make the quotation work smoothly, Opper has interpolated the conjunction *and* into Cézanne's phrase and indicated that he has done so by enclosing it in square brackets.

As you are going through this sweep of revision, use the following questions and suggestions to help you make your sentences more effective (for more details consult Chapter IX):

1. Have you cut as much deadwood as you can from the sentences?
2. If you have written a series of long or complicated sentences, can you break some of them into shorter sentences for contrast and clarity?
3. If you have begun a sentence with *There is* or *There are*, see if you can eliminate the phrase by finding an effective verb for the sentence.
4. When necessary, provide explicit transitions between sentences to help your readers keep track of where you're taking them. (Try not to rely on the word *also* or such often vague transitions as the pronoun *This* and phrases such as *Another factor was*.)
5. Try to improve the emphasis of sentences by using parallelism and by repeating key words and phrases.
6. Put the main ideas of sentences into independent clauses—and as much as possible see to it that these independent clauses are parts of *your* syntax rather than that of your sources. Only then can you maintain control of your style.
7. Try to end your sentences strongly, avoiding particularly *etc.* and *and so forth*, and other weak terms like *sometimes* and *in a way*.

## The Fourth Sweep:  Revising Diction

Still keeping in mind that one of your principal aims is to maintain a clear and consistent rhetorical stance, use the next sweep to look closely at the words in your draft. If the temptation is strong to retain sentence and phrase patterns from your sources, it's probably just as strong to retain vocabulary from those sources, especially if it sounds impressive. Though it is true that research papers are relatively formal, you are still writing to persuade or inform your readers, and that is rarely accomplished by trying to sound impressive. Writing that is more formal than conversational does not have to sound pompous.

It's particularly important to reconsider your diction after you have gone through your draft revising sentences, for if you change the syntax at one place in a sentence, you may need to change one or more words at another place. Consider, for example, how the diction in the following sentence reveals that the writer has not assimilated her source material:

> The schools enabled paupers the opportunity to acquire skills necessary to work in an industry.

In this draft sentence, the phrase "enabled ... the opportunity" is not idiomatic. In addition, the word *paupers* suggests adults, though the context makes it clear that the student is discussing children. A third problem is the article *an* before the word *industry*: she has not been discussing any particular industry and thus needs the idea of industry in general. Finding better words to remedy these problems led her to the following revision:

> The schools gave children from poor families the opportunity to learn the skills needed to work in industry.

The temptation to retain the diction of a source led to similar problems in idiom in the following draft sentence:

> Phrenologists had an optimistic approach to develop good in criminals which started the attitude of today's rehabilitation programs.

Here the unidiomatic expressions are "approach to develop" and "started the attitude." The word *optimistic* occurs in the writer's source; it should, then, have appeared in quotation marks. And then, in order to avoid such near-plagiarism, he clumsily substituted the word *good* for the source's *benevolence*, introducing further awkwardness. Finding his own words to make the point enabled the student to improve the clarity and tone in his revision:

> Phrenologists hoped to develop the good side of criminals' nature, an attitude that underlies today's rehabilitation programs.

Note how the revised sentence also gets rid of the uncertain reference of the pronoun *which* in the draft sentence.

Consider another example of writing that has not resisted the temptation to use the diction of its source. The student has just quoted a source that lists four "abilities" or "response patterns" that are characteristic of someone who can be considered "assertive." The student goes on to try to paraphrase from the same source:

> The use of assertiveness deficient in any of these components can be the cause of undesirable reactions, Lazarus writes.

Such a sentence, with its heavy diction (*deficient, components*), suggests that the student has not really assimilated the material from his source. It looks as though he had merely neglected to supply quotation marks—which would be plagiarism. Its relative formality also contrasts with the less stilted tone the writer was trying to catch and finally caught in his revision:

Those who try to act assertively without all four of these abilities, Lazarus warns, often fail to elicit the reactions they want from others.

Although this sentence is a little longer than the draft, it's better because it better suits the student's own rhetorical stance. Note in addition how the writer added a little vigour by replacing the nouns *use* and *cause* with the verbs *try to act* and *fail*. The result is that the sentence now suits the student's tone, not the source's. (See the complete research report in Chapter XV.)

As you go through this sweep, look at the individual words; try to establish and maintain a consistent rhetorical stance and tone. It may help to ask the following questions (and see Chapter X):

1. *Clarity:*

   Have you looked up in your dictionary any words you don't feel comfortable using?

   Have you double-checked words that are frequently confused (*imply* and *infer, comprise* and *compose,* etc.)?

> *"I am a Bear of Very Little Brain,*
> *and long words Bother me."*
> (A. A. Milne, *Winnie-the-Pooh*)

2. *Economy:*

   Have you preferred the shorter word (not *utilize* but *use*; not *eventuate* but *occur* or *happen,* not *purchased* but *bought*)?

   Have you avoided such deadwood phrases as these:

   | *not* | *but* |
   | --- | --- |
   | at that point in time | then |
   | for the purpose of | for |
   | in the event that | if |
   | by the use of | by |
   | on a daily basis | daily |

   Can you substitute concrete for abstract terms (not *youth* but *young people,* not *transportation* but *cars, ships, airplanes*)?

   Can you substitute the specific for the general (not *scientific experts* but *marine biologists*)?

   Have you avoided technical jargon, especially if your audience is different from that of your sources?

3. *Vigour:*

   Can you substitute active verbs for abstract nouns (not "Morton's decision to surrender" but "Morton decided to surrender")?

   Can you change into a phrase a series of nouns that serve to modify other nouns, especially abstract nouns (not "member income protection proposal" but "proposal to protect the members' incomes"; not "voter distribution reorganization" but "reorganizing the distribution of voters")?

## The Fifth Sweep:  Revising Punctuation

Chapter XI covers the main matters of punctuation; review those as necessary. In working with research papers, you need also to check the way you punctuate quotations.

### Quotations Run into Your Own Text

The main principle is simple: to enable your reader to see what is yours and what comes from elsewhere, enclose in quotation marks anything you quote directly, anything that is verbatim, word for word from a source. In this matter you have no choice; the alternative is plagiarism.

Other strategies for using quotations offer you some choice. As we have suggested, it's best to save longer quotations for material from your sources that is particularly important for your thesis or especially well expressed—or both. Most of the direct quotations you use would thus be fairly short and as much as possible integrated into your own sentences.

Generally, use a *comma* before or after a quotation with a verb of speaking or writing:

Cinderella whispered, "It's nearly midnight."
"Nothing is more frightful than ignorance in action," wrote Goethe.

Use a *colon* to introduce longer or more formal quotations, especially those consisting of one or two complete sentences:

In his essay "Teaching the Humanities Today," Northrop Frye writes: "Everything we know is formed out of words and numbers, and literature and mathematics are the only subjects of knowledge which are also a means of knowing."[1]

[1] *Divisions on a Ground: Essays on Canadian Culture,* ed. James Polk (Toronto: Anansi, 1982), p. 99.

Note that the closing quotation mark follows the period, and that the footnote numeral follows the quotation mark. Periods and commas always go *inside* quotation marks, colons and semicolons *outside* them:

Margaret Laurence provides a similar contrast in "Merchant of Heaven":

But when you insert a parenthetical page reference rather than a footnote numeral, as you can do if you are using a large number of quotations for a clearly indicated source, you put the quotation mark *before* the parentheses, and the period or other mark *after* the parentheses:

These studies are at the same time "subjects of knowledge" and "a means of knowing" (p. 99).

After a *block* quotation, however, a parenthetical reference follows the period. If you run part of a quotation into the syntax of your own sentence, you do not need to use a comma or a colon to introduce it:

Frye claims that these two studies are at the same time "subjects of knowledge" and "a means of knowing."[2]

If your own sentence doesn't need a comma or other mark, it won't need one when you insert the quotation.

## Using Square Brackets

Occasionally you will need to alter the syntax of a source slightly so that it will fit smoothly into the syntax of your own sentence. If you insert or change a word or a phrase in a quotation, indicate that you have done so by using square brackets. (If your typewriter does not have square brackets, you must put them in with a pen.) Here is an example:

> Mathematics is not only one of the "subjects of knowledge," Frye points out, but one "which [is] also a means of knowing."

The resulting sentence can thus retain the emphasis you want and at the same time accurately acknowledge the language you have used from your source. You can also use square brackets when you want to identify someone or something in a quotation, while at the same time keeping the rest of the quotation intact, as in the following:

> Guildenstern reports to the King: "Nor do we find him [Hamlet] forward to be sounded" (III.i.6).

Here the writer prevented any confusion about the reference of the pronoun *him* in the quotation from *Hamlet*.

You can also use square brackets to indicate that you are quoting a source accurately, but that it contains an error. Simply put the Latin word *sic* (which means "thus") in square brackets after the error:

> Keats again reveals this mixed strain of skepticism and belief when he writes to his brother in March, 1819: "May there not be superior beings amused with any graceful, though instinctive attitude my mind my [sic] fall into, as I am entertained with the alertness of a Stoat or the anxiety of a Deer?" (p. 268).

Or the writer could have chosen simply to correct the obvious slip by changing *my* to *m[a]y*. Note that in the example above a period still follows the parenthetical reference even though the quotation itself ends in a question mark.

## Indicating Omissions in Quotations

If you quote only a part of a sentence from a source, indicate the omission, or *ellipsis,* with three *spaced* periods (. . .):

> Northrop Frye makes a similar point when he observes that ". . . literature and mathematics . . . are also a means of knowing."[3]

Readers can tell immediately that you have left out the beginning of Frye's sentence as well as something in the middle of it. You need to indicate an ellipsis at the beginning of a quotation only if it could be mistaken for the beginning of a sentence, as could the word *literature* here. Similarly, only if the words you quote could be mistakenly read as a complete sentence need you indicate an ellipsis at the end. And if the ellipsis coincides with the end of your own sentence, then you must use *four* periods (the three ellipsis periods followed by your own sentence period). Suppose for example that you want to make use of the following sentence (from "Enzyme," in the *Encyclopaedia Britannica*):

> The extracts of yeast convert sugar to alcohol, just as living yeast does, and in a similar manner extracts of muscle can convert sugar to lactic acid, just as living muscle does.

If you want to quote only the first half of the sentence, you indicate the ellipsis together with your own period at the end of the sentence:

> For this process, you do not need to use live yeast, because, as Vennesland suggests, "The extracts of yeast convert sugar to alcohol, just as living yeast does . . . ."[2]

If you end the sentence with a citation in parentheses, you put your own period *after* the closing parenthesis, as follows:

> For this process, you do not have to use live yeast, because, as Vennesland suggests, "The extracts of yeast convert sugar to alcohol, just as living yeast does . . ." (1967, p. 621).

Note the space *before* the first period, indicating that the omission is from the end of the sentence. If you omit something from the *beginning* of, say, the second of two quoted sentences, the first dot, *without* a space, is the sentence period, and the next three dots mark the ellipsis:

> Remember Northrop Frye's admonition in "The Motive for Metaphor": "In descriptive writing you have to be careful of associative language. . . . analogy, or likeness to something else, is very tricky to handle in description, because the differences are as important as the resemblances."

Use a similar four periods to indicate that you have omitted a whole sentence or more. Use a full line of spaced periods to indicate that you have omitted a paragraph or more of prose, or a line or more of poetry.

### Quotations Within Quotations

If what you quote contains something in quotation marks, use single quotation marks around the inner quotation:

> In 1972 David Suzuki wrote that "In the past 20 years, the science of 'molecular genetics' has dazzled the world with its insights into living organisms."

And if your source has itself used quotations within quotations, then you go back to double quotation marks to indicate the innermost quoted material:

> As Gallant describes Jeanie's alarm at first hearing the old record: "...the Thomsons screamed with laughter and Vern smiled. The dwarf sang on: 'And each little bird in the treetop high/Sang "O you kid!" and winked his eye.'"[3]

The dwarf quotes the bird's song; the story writer, Mavis Gallant, quotes the dwarf; and the student quotes Gallant.

**Block Quotations**

As we suggest earlier, you should use long quotations sparingly. But when you decide to quote a passage that will take up four or more lines, set it off from the rest of your text by indenting it eight or ten spaces and by triple-spacing above and below it. Since they are already set off in this way, *do not use quotation marks to indicate block quotations.* (But do reproduce any that are already in your source, for example as there would be with dialogue.)

Usually, introduce a block quotation with a colon, or sometimes a comma; if you weave it into your own syntax—for example by leading into it with an *and* or a *that*—you won't need a punctuation mark.

# Documenting Your Sources

Another of the features that make a research paper different from other sorts of writing is the elaborate system it uses to acknowledge sources: the system of documentation. The system has three fundamental purposes: (1) it lets you acknowledge your debts to particular sources; (2) it helps you support your statements or arguments with the weight of authority; and (3) it enables your readers to follow up on your discussion—just as you have been doing during your research. For these reasons you need to make your acknowledgments complete and accurate.

## The Mechanics of Documentation

Writers of research papers can choose between two basic methods of documenting sources: the "note" method or the "name and date" method. The first is most widely used in the humanities; the second is more widely used in the sciences and social sciences. The purpose of both methods is to provide a clear, complete, and convenient form for documenting sources.

### THE NOTE METHOD

In this method, you insert a raised (superscript) numeral immediately after the material you have summarized, paraphrased, or quoted, or otherwise referred to. The numeral directs your reader to a numbered note identifying the source. These notes may appear either at the foot of that same page ("footnotes") or in a list at the end of the paper ("endnotes"). The note form we recommend here is that of the Modern Language Association (MLA), the form most widely used in North American books and journals (and the one illustrated in the sample research paper at the end of this chapter). Below we provide examples of the most common kinds of notes in both formats. For further information and examples, consult an up-to-date comprehensive handbook of English, or a guide like the *MLA Handbook for Writers of Research Papers, Theses, and Dissertations* (New York, 1977). For more information about the name-date method, see the *Publication Manual of the American Psychological Association,* 2nd edition (Washington, D.C., 1974). Here are the note forms for the most common kinds of sources:

## A Book:

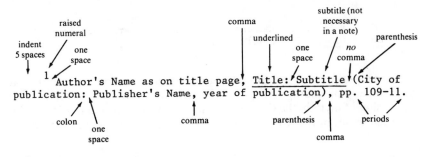

### Example:

<sup></sup>¹ Northrop Frye, <u>The Great Code: The Bible and Literature</u> (Toronto: Academic Press Canada, 1982), pp. 109–11.

## An Article in a Monthly Magazine:

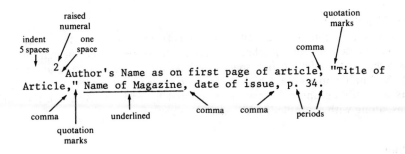

### Example:

² Edward G. Owen, "Inflation Adjustment for Corporate Profits," <u>CGA Magazine</u>, March 1981, p. 34.

## An Article in a Journal with Continuous Pagination Throughout a Volume:

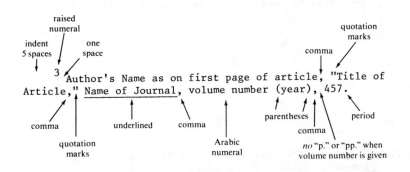

*Example:*

> 3
> Ruby Cohn, "Modest Proposals of Modern Socialists,"
> <u>Modern Drama</u>, 25 (1982), 457.

If you have given the author's name in your text, you need not repeat it in your note. For example, if you have written a sentence as follows: "In his discussion of myth in the Old Testament, Northrop Frye is careful to distinguish between senses of the word *myth*."[1]—then your note would read like this:

> 1
> <u>The Great Code: The Bible and Literature</u> (Toronto:
> Academic Press Canada, 1982), pp. 112-15.

But if you give both the author's name and the title in your text, you should still provide the title in your note, as a courtesy to your reader.

---

### Bibliographical Entries:

The form for a bibliographical citation differs from that for a note. Authors are listed last name first, for alphabetizing; each entry begins at the left margin, with subsequent lines indented five spaces, so that authors' last names are easy to find. And unlike in a note, which is meant to be read like a sentence, the major parts of a bibliographical entry are separated by periods. Here are the basic forms, along with examples for the same three works:

### A Book:

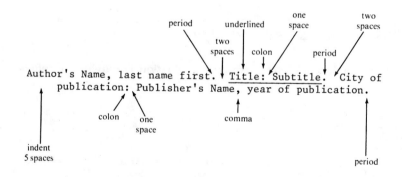

*Example:*

> Frye, Northrop.  <u>The Great Code: The Bible and Literature</u>.
> Toronto: Academic Press Canada, 1982.

## An Article in a Monthly Magazine:

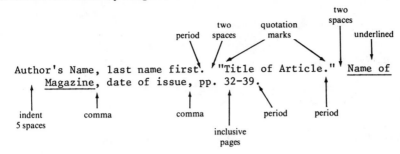

*Example:*

```
Owen, Edward G.  "Inflation Adjustment for Corporate Profits."
     CGA Magazine, March 1981, pp. 32-39.
```

## An Article in a Journal with Continuous Pagination Throughout a Volume:

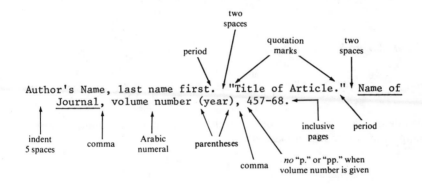

*Example:*

```
Cohn, Ruby.  "Modest Proposals of Modern Socialists."  Modern
     Drama, 25 (1982), 457-68.
```

The following examples illustrate the form of a first note, a subsequent note to the same work, and a bibliography entry for most of the other kinds of sources you will need to use:

## A Translation:

*first reference:*

```
    4 Carlos Fuentes, Where the Air Is Clear, trans. Sam
Hileman (New York: Oblonsky, 1960), p. 117.
```

*subsequent reference:*

> 5 Fuentes, pp. 223-24.

*entry in bibliography:*

> Fuentes, Carlos. <u>Where the Air Is Clear</u>. Trans. Sam Hileman.
> New York: Oblonsky, 1960.

## A Piece Reprinted in a Collection of Works by Several Authors:

> 6 Alice Munro, "Thanks for the Ride," in <u>Modern Stories</u>
> <u>in English</u>, ed. W. H. New and H. J. Rosengarten (Toronto:
> Copp Clark Pitman, 1977), pp. 273-74.

> 7 Munro, p. 282.

> Munro, Alice. "Thanks for the Ride." In <u>Modern Stories in</u>
> <u>English</u>. Ed. W. H. New and H. J. Rosengarten. Toronto:
> Copp Clark Pitman, 1977, pp. 273-84.

## A Reprint of an Earlier Edition:

> 8 Hugh MacLennan, <u>Barometer Rising</u> (New York, 1941; rpt.
> Toronto: McClelland and Stewart, 1958), p. 151.

[Include the place of original publication only when it is in a country other than that in which the reprint appeared.]

> 9 MacLennan, p. 164.

> MacLennan, Hugh. <u>Barometer Rising</u>. New York, 1941; rpt.
> Toronto: McClelland and Stewart, 1958.

## An Unsigned Newspaper Article:

> 10 "Indonesia Reopens an Ancient Temple," <u>New York Times</u>,
> West Coast Ed., 27 Feb. 1983, Sec. A, p. 11.

> 11 "Indonesia Reopens an Ancient Temple."

[The entire article appeared on the same page.]

> "Indonesia Reopens an Ancient Temple." <u>New York Times</u>, West
> Coast Ed., Sec. A, p. 11.

**A Signed Encyclopedia Article:**

> [12] Wilfred Eggleston, "Woodsworth, James Shaver,"
> Encyclopedia Canadiana, 1975 ed.

> [13] Eggleston, "Woodsworth."

> Eggleston, Wilfred. "Woodsworth, James Shaver." Encyclopedia
>     Canadiana. 1975 ed.

[No volume or page number is necessary for works that are arranged alphabetically.]

**A Work with a Corporate or Group Author:**

> [14] MLA Handbook for Writers of Research Papers, Theses,
> and Dissertations (New York: Modern Language Association,
> 1977), p. 60.

> [15] MLA Handbook, p. 103.

[Note the shortened but clearly recognizable version of the long title.]

> MLA Handbook for Writers of Research Papers, Theses, and
>     Dissertations. New York: Modern Language Association.

**The Bible:**

You do not need a note if you're citing the Authorized (King James) Version of the Bible. Note also that you do not enclose in quotation marks or underline the name of the Bible itself or of its books. Cite individual books, chapters, and verses of the Bible in parentheses in your own text:

> (Isaiah 42:1).

---

## Exercise 14B

Each of the following items describes a source that requires documentation. For each one, write the footnote for the first reference; then the footnote for a subsequent reference; and then write the bibliographical entry.

1. A reference to page 357 of a book written by Lionel Casson, published in 1971 by Princeton University Press (which is in Princeton, New Jersey) and entitled *Ships and Seamanship in the Ancient World.*
2. An article that appears in *Maclean's*, on pages 50 and 51 of the issue that came out May 9, 1983; the article is entitled "The War on Strokes," and was written by Brian D. Johnson; the issue of the magazine is number 19 of volume 96.
3. A passage from a book entitled *Speaking Canadian English,* by Mark Orkin; it was published in 1970 by General Publishing Company Limited in Toronto; the

passage is on page 213, and the book has a subtitle: An Informal Account of the English Language in Canada.

4. An article that was published in the Summer, 1967, issue of the quarterly journal *The American Scholar*; the article is called "Medical Education and Psychoanalysis" and was written by Richard W. Noland and is printed on pages 417 through 427. The journal has continuous pagination throughout the year.

5. A poem called "An Unsolved Enigma," printed in a collection of poems edited by Carolyn Wells and entitled *A Whimsey Anthology*; it was reprinted in 1963 by Dover Publications, Inc. in New York, but was first published by Charles Scribner's Sons (also in New York) in 1906; the poem appears on pages 68 and 69 and was written by Anna Seward.

Now write the two footnotes and the bibliographical entry for this page in this book.

---

## THE NAME-DATE METHOD

The main difference between the note system and the name-date system is that in the first a raised numeral directs your readers to a note, whereas in the second the necessary information appears right in the text, enclosed by parentheses, as in the following example:

> "Dominant" subjects, for example, "liked the submissive characters more than the assertive characters" (Battistich, 1980, pp. 7-8).

Such a reference includes the author's name (unless it has just been mentioned), the year of publication (unless mentioned in your text), and the page numbers (unless the reference is to an entire work):

> Wilder Penfield (1975, pp. 40-43) summarizes these surprising results from the experiments that he and his staff conducted at the Montreal Neurological Institute in the late 1940's (Penfield and Rasmussen, 1950).

Some writers prefer the note method because they feel that it is less distracting for the reader to see only a number to indicate a reference. Others prefer the name-date method because it allows the reader to see the reference immediately, without having to look at the bottom of the page or turn to the back.

The entries in the bibliographical list of references at the end of a paper are a little different from those in the note method. The first line begins at the margin, and subsequent lines are indented five spaces, as in the other form; but capitalize only the first word of the title (and a subtitle) and proper nouns; and provide only the initial[s] of an author's first name[s]. Here is the form for a book:

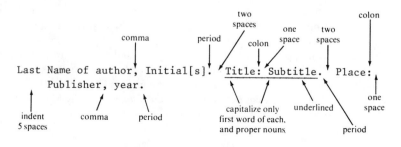

**Example:**

> Frye, N.   The great code: The Bible and literature.   Toronto:
> Academic Press Canada, 1982.

## For an article in a monthly magazine:

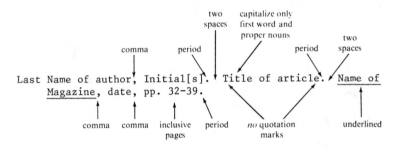

> Owen, E. G.   Inflation adjustment for corporate profits.   CGA
> Magazine, March 1981, pp. 32-39.

## For an article in a journal with continuous pagination throughout a volume:

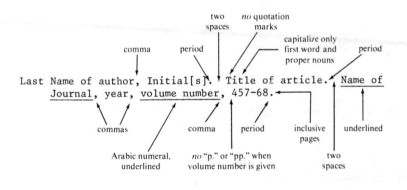

> Cohn, R.   Modest proposals of modern socialists.   Modern Drama,
> 1982, 25, 457-68.

Here are some other examples of the parenthetical and reference-list forms in the name-date method:

## A Translation:

parenthetical reference in text:

> (Fuentes, 1960, p. 233)

entry in list of references:

> Fuentes, C.  [Where the air is clear]   (S. Hileman, Trans.).
> New York: Oblonsky, 1960.

## A Piece Reprinted in a Collection of Works by Several Authors:

> (Munro, in New & Rosengarten, 1977, p. 282)

> Munro, A.  Thanks for the ride.  In W. H. New and H. J.
> Rosengarten (Eds.), Modern stories in English.  Toronto:
> Copp Clark Pitman, 1977.

## A Reprint of an Earlier Edition:

> (MacLennan, 1941/1958, p. 151)

> MacLennan, H.  Barometer rising.  Toronto: McClelland and
> Stewart, 1958.  (Originally published: New York: Duell,
> Sloan & Pearce, 1941.)

## An Unsigned Newspaper Article:

> (Indonesia reopens an ancient temple, 1983, p. A-11)

> Indonesia reopens an ancient temple.  New York Times, West Coast
> Ed., 27 Feb. 1983, Sec. A, p. 11.

## A Signed Encyclopedia Article:

> (Eggleston, 1975)

> Eggleston, W.  Woodsworth, James Shaver.  Encyclopedia
> Canadiana, 1975.

## A Work with a Corporate or Group Author:

> (MLA Handbook, 1977, p. 60)

The shortened version of the title is sufficient; the full title must appear in the list of references:

```
Modern Language Association.  MLA handbook for writers of research
    papers, theses, and dissertations.  New York: Author, 1977.
```

---

### Exercise 14C

For each of the items in Exercise 14B (pp. 379-380), using the name-date method, write the note form you would use in your text and the form you would write for your list of references.

---

### BIBLIOGRAPHIES

A full-scale "bibliography" lists just about all applicable works a writer has seen. Its purpose is to give readers an idea of the scope of available information. As you probably do in your own research, other readers use bibliographies to help them locate information on a topic.

But for academic papers it has become much more common to provide only a list of the sources specifically cited in the text. (For a relatively short paper with only a few notes, the notes themselves will sometimes be considered a sufficient bibliography.) In the name-date method, the list of references automatically includes only the works cited in the text.

If you list all the sources you have looked at, whether or not you have referred to them in your text or notes, you can use the word "Bibliography" as a heading; or you might divide your list into "Works Cited" and "Works Consulted." But if you make it a practice to list only "Works Cited," you won't be tempted to pad a bibliography with sources that you may only have skimmed through, or worse yet, not even seen, but taken from someone else's bibliography—an offence almost as dishonest as plagiarism. If you use the name-date method, label your final list simply "References."

Whichever form you use, start your list on an unnumbered page at the end of your paper. Alphabetize the entries according to the authors' last names. If a work's author is not given, use the first major word of the title to determine its place in the list—see for example the entry "Science" in the bibliography of the sample paper. For an example of a list of references using the name-date method, see the report "On Appropriate Assertiveness" in Chapter XV.

## STEP 8: PREPARING THE FINAL DRAFT

The next step is to prepare the finished copy for presentation. More than other academic papers you submit, a formal research paper approaches being a public document. Try to make it look like one. Consider your reader.

Consult the reminders about manuscript conventions in Chapter XII; here we add or repeat only a few that are especially important for research papers.

## Manuscript Conventions

### Typing

Always type your research paper, or have it typed. More and more, people are using word processors; if your typist is using one, secure a copy of your paper for proofreading before you O.K. it for final copying. If you are typing it yourself, make sure that the type is clean and that you use a good (preferably new) black ribbon. Avoid the small portable typewriters with their minute type, and use a standard typeface; no fancy italic, all capitals, or other sorts.

### Paper

Use only standard white typing paper, 21 by 28 cm (8½ by 11 inches). Do not use thin copy paper or the easy-erase paper that smudges so easily.

### Format

Type on only one side of each sheet. Double-space between lines (not 1½ spaces). Unless directed to do otherwise, single-space block quotations; triple-space before and after block quotations. If you're using footnotes, quadruple-space between your text and the notes (rule or type a line one third or more of the way across the page between the end of your text and a note continued from the preceding page). Unless directed otherwise, single-space within notes and bibliography entries; double-space between entries. If you use endnotes rather than footnotes, begin them on an unnumbered page following your text, and use the word *Notes* to head the page.

Indent the first line of each paragraph five spaces. Indent all lines of block quotations eight or ten spaces.

### Title Page

If you use a title page, don't repeat the title on the first page of your text; but begin your text about one quarter of the way down the page so readers can see that they're beginning at the beginning. Compose your title page so that it appears balanced and attractive. For example, centre the title (NOT underlined or enclosed in quotation marks or all in capital letters or with a period after it) and centre your name below it. Near the bottom, centre your instructor's name, below it the course and number, and below that the date.

If you don't use a title page, centre your title on the first page of your text, about a quarter of the way down the page. Quadruple-space between the title and the first line of your text. With no title page, you will of course have to endorse your paper elsewhere—on a folder or a cover sheet or in the upper right-hand corner of the first page.

### Pagination

Number the pages consecutively, beginning with "2" on the second page of your text. (Do not number the title page; number the outline or other prefatory material with lower-case Roman numerals: i, ii, iii, etc.—number the first such page, if at all, at the bottom centre.) If you begin your essay about a quarter of the way down the first page, it will be obvious to readers that they are beginning at the beginning; but if you want to number it, do so at bottom centre.

Use Arabic numerals at top centre or in the upper right corner, and use only the numeral: no period or circle or dashes to set it off—it's already set off by being placed where it is. If you want to number your first endnotes or bibliography page, do so only at bottom centre.

## Binding

Generally, no binding or folder is necessary. Most instructors prefer the pages of your paper to be fastened only with a paper clip. (Do not use a staple or a pin or torn corners.) If your instructor requires a binder, use a light cardboard one. Avoid the clear plastic binders that generate static electricity and make pages stick to them. And avoid simple file folders: you don't want a page to be lost before anyone begins reading your paper.

## The Final Outline

We mention earlier the usefulness of an outline as a continuing guide during writing and revising. When you are through revising the paper you should also be through revising the outline. If you submit a finished outline with the paper, prepare it as carefully as any other part. You will probably want to use a formal sentence outline; to illustrate the appropriate format, here is the final outline for the sample paper below.

*Sentence Outline*

### Scientific Endeavour
### in the
### Early Eighteenth Century

*Thesis Statement (Beginning):* It is not only interesting but also instructive to see how much happened in the world of science before our own time, for example in the pivotal period of the early eighteenth century.

I. Largely because of the increasing importance of navigation, interest in astronomy was growing.
    A. Observatories were being built throughout Europe.
    B. Flamsteed and Halley worked on the first modern star catalogues.
    C. Newtonian theory was bolstered by the return of Halley's comet.

II. Mathematics was an active field in the early eighteenth century.
    A. Newton refined his earlier work on calculus, and won out in his dispute with Leibnitz.
    B. Other mathematical discoveries were also important.
        1. William Jones introduced the concept of $\pi$.
        2. Jacob van 'sGravesande did influential work on geometrical perspective.

III. Newton and others made progress in both theoretical and practical physics.
    A. Newton left physics a double heritage.
        1. He made significant discoveries in dynamics and in theories of light and colour.
        2. His "Queries" stimulated further investigation.

    B.  Fahrenheit established his temperature scale.

    C.  Haulksbee worked on luminescence in rarefied gases.

    D.  Savery and Newcomen invented the steam engine, which was useful in mines and virtually began the industrial revolution.

IV.  In medicine, work was being done on combatting diseases and on understanding physiology.

    A.  Several discoveries helped fight common diseases.

       1.  Citrus juices were used against scurvy.

       2.  Various epidemics were for the first time studied systematically.

       3.  Successful inoculation against smallpox was developed.

    B.  In physiology, there were disputing theories about how the brain controls the body.

       1.  Boerhaave and Hoffmann favoured a "mechanistic" theory.

       2.  Stahl's "spiritual" theories, however wrong, led to later studies in neurology.

V.  Chemistry was held back by the mistaken theory of "Phlogiston" (the name was Stahl's).

VI.  Advances in biology led to disputes about the claims of science and religion.

    A.  Basic identification of plants and animals led to Linnaean taxonomy and eventually to Darwin's theory of evolution, which aroused great controversy.

    B.  Early scientists believed that their findings supported Christian teachings.

       1.  Newton studied theological questions and biblical chronology.

       2.  Voltaire later claimed that Newton's work "undermined" scriptural authority.

*Ending:* The dispute between science and religion is still with us. But in general the achievements of early eighteenth-century science provided many beginnings for the world of science as we know it today.

> *...the accuracy of the report being*
> *always tried by the most severe and*
> *detailed tests possible.* (Thucydides)

# STEP 9: PROOFREADING THE RESEARCH PAPER

The last step before submitting a paper is that of careful proofreading. Even if you have corrected many errors in the process of revising, many may remain undetected; you can almost count on finding at least one on every page. Careful proofreading will allow you to catch not only typographical errors, but also previously undetected errors in spelling, punctuation, or even grammar.

    Don't hurry through this final stage; do your proofreading with exaggerated care. Examine each sentence, including its punctuation, and check the spelling of each word. Proofread for spelling by going through the final draft backwards, word by word. And check each item in your notes and bibliography: examine them scrupulously, for it would be almost miraculous if no error has crept in.

Double-check all spellings of names and all page numbers and dates against your bibliography cards and note cards; if you were careful to be accurate when you made them out, you won't have to return to your sources to check for accuracy.

## Corrections and Interpolations

You can correct errors with dark ink. But remember that in presenting your paper you should consider your reader's convenience, not your own. Cross out each wrong mark or letter or word with a small, neat stroke—no big blots—and print the correction neatly above it. If you have to make more than two corrections on a page, you should seriously consider retyping it.

### Checklist for Research Papers

Use this checklist when you are revising and proofreading.

- As much as possible, avoid direct quotation; instead, assimilate source material into your own prose with paraphrase and summary.
- As much as possible, work quotations into your own syntax, keep long and set-off quotations to a minimum.
- Double-check each quotation, whether long or short, to ensure that it is absolutely accurate and faithful to the original.
- Avoid unfairly quoting out of context or otherwise distorting the meaning and intention of your sources.
- Make sure you have provided a footnote for *everything* you have used from *any* other source (except for "common knowledge"); be especially careful not to overlook places where you have summarized or paraphrased rather than quoted directly.
- Carefully check each footnote and bibliographical entry to make sure it follows the right form in spacing, punctuation, indenting, and underlining (italicizing) of book titles and the like. For example, does each of your footnotes and bibliographical entries end with a period?
- Strive to keep the number of footnotes to a minimum—for example by consolidating footnotes and using parenthetical references where possible.
- Manage your footnotes so that your reader can easily see exactly where each item, each detail, each sentence or phrase comes from—whether it's from you or from one of your sources.
- Proofread with great care, more than once.

## SAMPLE LIBRARY RESEARCH PAPER

The following research paper, written by a first-year university student, is intended less as a model than as an illustration of various techniques discussed in this chapter. Note for example how the writer handles quotations and how she keeps the number of footnotes down by incorporating references to her two major sources into her text. The paper also provides you with further examples of the forms for various kinds of footnotes and bibliographical entries. And note the carefully handled details of format.

Scientific Endeavour in the Early Eighteenth Century

Most of us think of the twentieth century as the great age
of science, of astonishing discoveries and dazzling technological
advances.  There is no denying the achievements of our age, but
there is a danger that we will be so impressed by them that we
will tend to forget about how much was done, or at least begun,
long before.  For example look at what was going on in scientific
fields during the early eighteenth century.  Not only are some of
the scientific activities during this short period interesting in
themselves, but more important, a brief look at them should help
us see our own age in a clearer perspective.

By the early eighteenth century in Europe, the religious
revolution of the seventeenth century had only recently begun to
recede, and the thoughts of many Europeans were turning to
science.  In Dartmouth, England, Thomas Newcomen and Thomas
Savery were working--quite separately--on the steam engine;
Edmund Halley was beginning to study the stars and planets
visible from the northern hemisphere; Bartolomeo Christofori was
working on his new invention, the piano; and Isaac Newton was
busy revising some of his earlier works.  Several different

2

sectors of the scientific world were undergoing change, and all
were beginning to realize the advantages of the modern approach
to science as set out by Sir Francis Bacon and as practised by
such important seventeenth-century figures as Robert Boyle.

Because of the rising interest in astronomy, mainly as an
aid to navigation, new observatories were popping up all over
Europe: in 1706 an observatory was built on the Great Gate at
Trinity College, Cambridge; between 1706 and 1711 a larger one
was built at Berlin; and in 1712 a third major observatory was
constructed on top of the University building in Bologna.[1]
In 1709, John Flamsteed, England's first Astronomer Royal, was
hard at the laborious task of compiling a star catalogue. He
published his partial results in 1712, at Newton's insistence,
but his main work, the Historia Coelestis Britannica, was not
published until 1725, several years after his death. According
to a French historian, it was the first modern star catalogue and
showed "the right ascensions and polar distances, as well as the
longitudes and latitudes, of nearly 3,000 stars . . . ."[2] Edmund
Halley, during the same period, was studying Ptolemy's catalogue

----

[1] M. C. Donnelly, Astronomical Observatories in the 17th and
18th Centuries (Brussels: Académie Royale de Belgique, 1964),
pp. 19, 21.

[2] Jacques Lévy, "Star Catalogues," in The Beginnings of
Modern Science, Vol. II of History of Science, ed. René Taton,
trans. A. J. Pomerans (New York: Basic Books, 1964), p. 451.
Subsequent references to this volume will appear in parentheses
in my text.

3

of the stars.  After many careful observations of approximately three hundred stars that had been mentioned by Ptolemy, Halley inferred that the stars must have individual movements, for several of these stars had significantly changed position since Ptolemy had written his catalogue in A.D. 150, while others seemed not to have moved at all.  Halley decided that different stars were at different distances from the earth, and that those that appeared to have remained in the same places must be so far away that it would be impossible to detect their movements over 1,500 years.[3]

By the beginning of the eighteenth century, the Copernican revolution was virtually won, and astronomy was beginning to be based securely on Newtonian physics.[4]  One of Newton's theories has to do with the attraction of objects to one another (his well-known law of gravity).  Using this theory, he made several calculations that led him to predict that the orbit of a comet has the shape of a flattened ellipse, but he had not yet proved his hypothesis.  Then, in 1705, Halley published in the Philosophical Transactions of the Royal Society his deduction

[3] Colin Ronan, "Edmond Halley," Dictionary of Scientific Biography, ed. Charles Coulston Gillispie, VI (New York: Scribner's, 1974), p. 70.  Subsequent references to this work will appear in parentheses in my text, identified as DSB.

[4] For this fact and for part of the phrasing, I am indebted to Professor H. J. Metcalf, in his lecture in History 155, University of British Columbia, 11 Feb. 1982.

4

that the three comets observed in 1507, 1631, and 1682 were one
and the same (Ronan, DSB, VI, p. 69).  He held that this comet
had a period of revolution of seventy-six years and went so far
as to predict its return in 1758.  Newton was proved right when
the comet actually "did return in 1759--having been delayed by
the pull of Jupiter and Saturn--[and] the Newtonian theory scored
one of its greatest triumphs" (Lévy, in Taton, p. 444).  The work
of these men was crucial to the future of astronomy: present-day
studies of the movements of the planets, the sun, and the stars
depend heavily upon star catalogues such as Flamsteed's and upon
Newton's theory and Halley's proof of it.

 In the early years of the century, mathematicians were consolidating old ideas and introducing new ones.  Newton was
revising several of his earlier works on differential and
integral calculus.  He had by this time realized the importance
of accuracy in studying convergence and stated firmly that "the
very smallest Errors in mathematical Matters are not to be
neglected" (I. B. Cohen, "Isaac Newton," DSB, X, p. 51).  Two
Swiss brothers, Jacques and Johann (Jean) Bernoulli, as well as
Gottfried Wilhelm von Leibnitz, the eminent German philosopher
and mathematician, had also developed theories of calculus and
practical uses for it.  A. Rupert Hall tells how in 1710 one of
Newton's pupils, John Keill, accused Leibnitz of plagiarizing
Newton's work on fluxions, the calculus of velocities.  A similar
accusation had been made at least twice before, but this time the

5

quarrel was so bitter that the influential Royal Society, of
which Newton was president, was asked to arbitrate. The Society
concluded that Leibnitz was in the wrong, and from then on
Leibnitz and Newton were set against each other.[5]

In 1706 William Jones, a teacher of mathematics who briefly
collaborated with Newton, introduced a new symbol, $\pi$, and
contributed to work on proving its value as an algebraic
notation. A Dutch professor, Jacob van 'sGravesande, in 1711
published a book on geometrical perspective, a book whose
importance was not to be realized until almost a hundred years
later (M. E. Baron, "William Jones," DSB, VII, p. 163, and in
Taton, p. 419).

Isaac Newton was undoubtedly "the greatest figure of the
period,"[6] the most influential scientist active during the late
seventeenth and early eighteenth centuries. He made major
contributions to mathematics and astronomy, but by far his
greatest discoveries dealt with physics: Newton defined the
three basic laws of motion, wrote a book on the nature of light
and colours (Opticks, 1704), and discussed dynamics in his

[5] Philosophers at War: The Quarrel Between Newton and
Leibnitz (Cambridge: Cambridge Univ. Press, 1980), p. 145.
Subsequent scholarship, according to Hall, has shown that Newton
and Leibnitz arrived at their theories independently.

[6] "Science," The New Columbia Encyclopedia, ed. William H.
Harris and Judith S. Levey (New York and London: Columbia Univ.
Press, 1975).

6

<u>Principia</u>, the second edition of which appeared in 1713.  Yet he
was a modest man when it came to his own achievements.  Shortly
before his death, he wrote:

> I do not know what I may appear to the world, but to
> myself, I seem to have been only like a boy playing on
> the seashore, and diverting myself in now and then
> finding a smoother pebble or a prettier shell than
> ordinary, whilst the great ocean of truth lay all
> undiscovered before me.[7]

By 1710, Newton was busy working on the set of sixteen
"Queries" that he planned to add to his <u>Opticks</u>; these consisted
of questions that had occurred to him throughout his career but
that he himself did not wish to research (Cohen, <u>DSB</u>, X, p. 59).
As Newtonian ideology spread through Britain and the continent in
the first quarter of the eighteenth century, his queries proved
to be important, for they spurred other scientists to further
investigation.  Newton therefore left science a double heritage:
the benefits of his own discoveries, and ideas to stimulate
further studies.

But Newton was not the only eminent physicist of these
years.  In his historical survey, Edmond Bauer tells of how
Gabriel Daniel Fahrenheit was experimenting with heat and ways to
measure it, and of how he defined his temperature scale in 1719;

---

[7] Quoted in I. Bernard Cohen, "Isaac Newton," <u>World Book
Encyclopedia</u>, 1964 ed.

7

and Georges Allard tells of how Francis Haulksbee was making
observations on electrical discharges in rarefied gases. Even
though his studies were not conclusive, they approached the
discovery of electrostatic induction, but unfortunately he was
not able "to grasp the connection between electricity and the
luminous phenomena he had observed" (in Taton, pp. 467, 472).

Science in the early eighteenth century was not only
theoretical, but practical as well. Probably the most important
practical application of physics at the time was the steam
engine. Thomas Newcomen has officially been credited with its
invention in 1712, but another Englishman, Thomas Savery, had
designed a simpler engine ten years before. According to Robert
Henry Thurston, Savery's engine was "the first really practicable
and commercially viable steam engine," and therefore "Savery is
entitled to the credit of having been the first to introduce a
machine in which the power of heat, acting through the medium of
steam, was rendered generally useful."[8] Unfortunately, Savery's
engine could not stand high pressures and his machine once blew
up, with fatal results to an attendant. Thurston points out that
Newcomen remedied this problem by proposing an engine that would
incorporate a steam cylinder with a safety valve. This new
device was successful enough for Newcomen and John Galley, his

[8] *A History of the Growth of the Steam Engine* (1939; rpt.
New York: Kennikat, 1972), p. 38. The succeeding points in this
paragraph are also from Thurston, especially pp. 39 and 58.

8

assistant, to take out a patent for it in 1705 and to begin
adapting it for use in pumping water out of the mines.  By a
lucky accident, they discovered that cold water condensed the
steam much more efficiently when applied directly to the inside
of the cylinder than when sprayed on the outside.  This
modification made Newcomen's steam engine especially useful in
mine work and is the development that earned him his reputation
as the inventor of the steam engine.

In the field of medicine in the early eighteenth century,
progress was less spectacular than in physics, but interesting
things were going on even so, as shown by an almost random
dipping into what various contributors to René Taton's <u>The
Beginnings of Modern Science</u> describe.  For example,
eighteenth-century rationalism went to work: ". . . the
considerable body of anatomical knowledge handed down by the
Renaissance and the 17th century was put into some sort of order"
(Louis Dulieu, in Taton, p. 540).  But individuals were active as
well.  For example in 1720 an obscure Austrian doctor named
Kramer suggested using lime or orange juice to treat scurvy
(Dulieu, p. 547).  Kramer's small discovery must have been
particularly important, because it enabled ships' crews (the
"Limeys") to remain healthy on long voyages and thus contributed
to the long voyages of exploration later in the century, such as
those of Cook and Vancouver.

A Viennese surgeon named Planciz "suggested that all

9

diseases are caused by micro-organisms"--but he "provided no evidence" (Dulieu, p. 541); perhaps he was too far ahead of his time. But specific diseases were causing concern, not least bubonic plague, which was still a serious threat in Europe. This period saw the beginnings of the systematic study of epidemics, and as Dulieu tells us, such diseases as malaria, diphtheria, typhoid, rabies, influenza, and yellow fever--"the new scourge"--were the subjects of epidemiologists' attention; they even studied whooping cough (p. 547). And experiments with vaccination were giving preventive medicine greater credibility. In a crude form, known as "variolation," inoculation against smallpox, for example, was performed by "prick[ing] the skin in three places with a needle that had previously been pushed into a fresh smallpox pustule." In 1717 Lady Mary Wortley Montagu had her son inoculated (I suppose successfully)--a courageous act which along with others helped gain wide approval for the new technique (Dulieu, p. 548). Only recently has smallpox been virtually eradicated from the earth; we can only guess how much we owe to the early experimenters and people like Lady Mary, who pioneered so many things that we now take for granted.

In physiology, less dramatically perhaps, but nonetheless interestingly, contending theories were surfacing. The Dutch professor Hermann Boerhaave and others were beginning to make connections between specific bodily movements and different parts of the brain. But toward the end of the first decade of the

10

century, a German scientist, Georg Ernst Stahl, published three
books arguing particularly against the theories of Boerhaave and
Friedrich Hoffmann (Dulieu, pp. 542, 544).  They believed that
"Biology could be reduced to simple mathematical, chemical or
mechanical laws," and that it was blood and nerves within the
muscles that produced muscular activity; but Stahl held out for a
spiritual component in which "the soul's action" played a part.
Ironically, by their attempts to combat mechanistic explanations
of the movements of the muscles, Stahl and others opened the door
to such later studies as Galvani's on the electrical characteristics of the nervous system and Lavoisier's proof of the chemical
nature of respiration (Georges Canguilhem, in Taton, pp. 534-
36).  It seems clear that the early eighteenth century was a
period not only of some exciting advances and discoveries but
also of considerable systematizing of previous and current
discoveries, all refining the scientific method in ways that
would eventually make it possible for medicine to become a true
science.

Chemistry, which in the seventeenth century was only just
emerging from the centuries-old domination of alchemy,
accelerated more slowly than physics because it was retarded by
the erroneous theory of "phlogiston."  Stahl had given that name
to a substance first hypothesized by Johann J. Becher, who had
argued that fire can be explained by the idea that "all
combustibles contain a subtle material that is given off from

11

them when they burn."[9]  The notion of a combustible substance
within the burning material was eagerly taken up by most of the
advanced scientists in Europe, and the strength of its apparent
simplicity and explanatory power set chemistry back for nearly a
century.  The theory of phlogiston seemed to be confirmed by the
common observation that many combustible materials, like wood,
lose weight when they are burned; the weight loss was explained
by the hypothesis that the original material contained phlogiston
which it lost during the process of combustion.  The observed
fact, however, that several metals actually gain weight when they
are burned was explained by an ingenious--but totally wrong--
notion that "phlogiston had negative weight, or levity rather
than gravity."[10]  Despite the skepticism of some well-known
scientists, like Boerhaave, who wrote the most important
chemistry textbook to appear in the first half of the century,
most of the English chemists, especially Henry Cavendish and
Joseph Priestley, took up the theory because it seemed to explain
so much.  It was not until nearly the end of the eighteenth
century that the Frenchman Antoine Laurent Lavoisier (who
provided chemistry with a new terminology that included such

[9] J. H. White, The History of the Phlogiston Theory (London:
Arnold, 1932), p. 31.

[10] Cecil J. Schneer, Mind and Matter: Man's Changing
Concepts of the Material World (New York: Grove Press, 1969), p.
85.

12

words as <u>oxygen</u> and <u>hydrogen</u>) finally discredited the phlogiston theory by exposing its confusions and contradictions.[11]

Finally we turn to biology and the growing conflict between science and religion. Most educated people today know of the Linnaean classification for plants and animals. Its inventor, the Swedish botanist and taxonomist Carl von Linné (Latinized as <u>Carolus Linnaeus</u>), was not born until 1707, but much of the work of basic identification was accomplished in the early years of the eighteenth century, preparing the way for him. Sir Hans Sloane studied Caribbean flora and made drawings of eight hundred plants (Adrien Davy de Virville, in Taton, pp. 554, 562). In 1709 Johann Jacob Scheuchzer of Switzerland published the <u>Herbarium diluvianum</u>, in which he described many European fossils. His work also convinced him "that the Flood must have taken place in the month of May!" Such an idea sounds odd now, but it was not unusual in the early 1700's, when science was still trying to support the authority of the Bible. In 1716 Scheuchzer published a catalogue of fifteen hundred fossils (Raymond Furon, in Taton, pp. 566-67). These and other studies were the beginning of a collection of data that helped Linnaeus with his classification and helped lead Charles Darwin to the theory of evolution almost a century and a half later.

[11] Trevor I. Williams, "Hermann Boerhaave, 1688-1738," <u>Endeavour</u>, 28, No. 103 (1969), 2; and White, p. 117.

13

Of course Darwin's theory caused great controversy between those who accepted the idea of evolution and those who believed in the biblical story of creation. But in the early years of the eighteenth century, the majority of scientists still felt that their discoveries strongly supported scripture. For instance, according to his recent biographer, Newton spent a great deal of his time on questions of theology and biblical chronology,[12] and most of his contemporaries saw no conflict between science and religion. As early as 1750, however, "Voltaire held that Newton's discoveries undermined much orthodox Christian dogma and the authority of the scriptures."[13] Voltaire was responding to P. L. M. de Maupertuis' statement in 1744 that it "cannot be doubted that all things are governed by a supreme Being who has impressed on matter forces that reflect His power, and has destined them to produce effects that reveal His wisdom." Maupertuis had come to this conclusion by trying to prove that nature does not follow the shortest path, but the path requiring the least energy. He believed that this principle of the "economy of energy" was the final proof of the existence of God (René Dugas and Pierre Costabel, in Taton, p. 428).

The early eighteenth century, then, witnessed the beginning

[12] Richard S. Westfall, Never at Rest: A Biography of Isaac Newton (Cambridge: Cambridge Univ. Press, 1980), pp. 589-94.

[13] Leonard W. Cowie, Eighteenth-Century Europe (London: Bell, 1963), p. 33.

14

of the struggle to find a harmonic co-existence between science
and religion, a struggle that is in part still with us today.
Newton's discoveries in mathematics, dynamics, celestial mechanics, and natural philosophy spurred younger scientists to
investigate the complexities of the material world.  His
"Queries" have been seen by some as his greatest contribution to
the furthering of scientific discovery (Cohen, DSB, X, p. 59).
When Halley's predictions of his comet's return were fulfilled in
1759, the science of astronomy gained greatly in both progress
and prestige.  Halley's and Flamsteed's studies of the stars then
got much more notice than when they were first published.
Although the preoccupation with the theory of phlogiston retarded
the development of chemistry, its refutation showed how closely
scientific theory and experimental method must work together.
Botany was advanced by the several plant catalogues compiled in
the first quarter of the century.  Further, scientists of that
period were among the first to unite theoretical science with
technology: Newcomen's steam engine greatly eased the
difficulties of mine work and has become the identifying symbol
of the industrial revolution.  The methods of early eighteenth-
century scientists and their sometimes ingenious approaches to
the problems they faced have set high standards for the
scientists of today.

WORKS CITED

Cohen, I. Bernard. "Isaac Newton." World Book Encyclopedia. 1964 ed.

Cowie, Leonard W. Eighteenth-Century Europe. London: Bell, 1963.

Donnelly, M. C. Astronomical Observatories in the 17th and 18th Centuries. Brussels: Académie Royale de Belgique, 1964.

Gillispie, Charles Coulston, ed. Dictionary of Scientific Biography. New York: Scribner's, 1973.

Hall, A. Rupert. Philosophers at War: The Quarrel Between Newton and Leibnitz. Cambridge: Cambridge Univ. Press, 1980.

Jenkins, Rhys. "The Heat Engine Idea in the Seventeenth Century." Transactions of the Newcomen Society, 17 (1936-37), 1-11.

Metcalf, H. J. Lecture in History 155. University of British Columbia, 11 Feb. 1982.

Schneer, Cecil J. Mind and Matter: Man's Changing Concepts of the Material World. New York: Grove Press, 1969.

"Science." The New Columbia Encyclopedia. Ed. William H. Harris and Judith S. Levey. New York and London: Columbia Univ. Press, 1975.

Taton, René, ed. The Beginnings of Modern Science: From 1450 to 1800. Volume II of History of Science. Trans. A. J. Pomerans. New York: Basic Books, 1964.

Thurston, Robert Henry. A History of the Growth of the Steam Engine. 1939; rpt. New York: Kennikat, 1972.

Westfall, Richard S. Never at Rest: A Biography of Isaac Newton. Cambridge: Cambridge Univ. Press, 1980.

White, J. H. The History of the Phlogiston Theory. London: Arnold, 1932.

Williams, Trevor I. "Hermann Boerhaave, 1688-1738," Endeavour, 28, No. 103 (1969), 2-6.

## Exercise 14D

Evaluate the following sentence outline, prepared by a student. What are its strengths and weaknesses? Do you detect any possible trouble arising from overlapping between main sections? If so, what can be done about it?

> T.S. Construction of canals and railways before 1867 had great economic, social, and political effects on Canada.
>
> I. Construction of canals and railways brought a large increase in Canada's economy by easily transferring people and goods throughout Canada, by enabling new industries to start, and by opening trade with the western American settlements.
>
> II. With the large networks of canals and railways, Canada's society flourished because communication was easier, a new breed of working middle-class arose, and a feeling of nationalism evolved.
>
> III. The Canadian political system was affected by the building of the canals and railways because it reinforced the idea of political unity and led to greater democratization of provincial politics by enabling people and ideas to move about more easily.

## Exercise 14E

By consulting reference books only, come up with five potentially useful facts about a number of the following. Cast each fact in the form of a sentence, in your own words.

| | | |
|---|---|---|
| Babylon | Paul Bunyan | Tamerlaine |
| Socrates | Walt Whitman | the Galapagos |
| Rembrandt | Cecil Rhodes | Sir John A. MacDonald |
| Akhenaten | Giordano Bruno | Helen Keller |
| The War of 1812 | Mars | Alexander Graham Bell |
| Emmeline Pankhurst | Rocket Richard | Garibaldi |
| Wimbledon | Galileo | the Yukon |
| Charlemagne | Sarah Bernhardt | alchemy |
| Swedenborg | Erasmus | Henry VIII |
| Louis Riel | Rasputin | Joan of Arc |
| Sitting Bull | Lucretius | Vivaldi |
| Margaret Laurence | the Gulf Stream | Krakatoa |
| Jim Thorpe | Pisarro | the Pyramids |
| Marie Curie | Beau Brummel | Charles Dickens |

## Exploration 14A

After consulting two or three dictionaries and some other books about writing (handbooks, rhetorics, books on writing research papers), define, in one or two paragraphs, the word *summary*. Do so partly by distinguishing it from *paraphrase* and *précis*. Document all sources you use. In writing this definition, or in taking notes for it, did you yourself use the techniques of summary, paraphrase, or précis?

## *Exploration 14B*

The "character" as a literary genre has a long history, from at least as far back as Theophrastus and down through Sir Thomas Overbury and John Earle and others into modern times, when a "character" is more likely to be part of a story or novel than a set-piece by itself. Compose a one- or two-paragraph "character" defining a recognizable "type." The overall piece must be general, since you are supposedly not describing any real person; but make it sound as specific as you can, for example by detailing certain characteristics and traits of behaviour as concretely as you can without naming names. Below are some suggestions; but consult your own experience for the kinds of characters you know best. Perhaps you can construct a character peculiar to your own time or even your own setting—but one still recognizable to your readers. Clearly there is opportunity for wit and satire in this topic, if you find yourself that way inclined.

| | | |
|---|---|---|
| the hypocrite | the flirt | the smoker |
| the pedant | the jogger | the computer whiz |
| the practical joker | the romantic | the road-hog |
| the teacher's pet | the loser | the dieter |
| the Canadian | the gourmet | the hockey fan |

## *Essay 14A*

You may find that you want to write a longer "character" than the preceding Exploration permits—for example if the subject you decide on contains varieties of "types" that you want to classify and discuss separately, within the larger class. If so, do so.

## *Essay 14B*

One way to approach a large research project is to do a relatively quick survey of the subject and draw up a concise report setting out basic facts, relationships, chronologies, structures, and so on—whatever is appropriate to the topic. That is, you explore the large subject in order to determine what it's all about. And be sure to use the questions from the planning stage to help you get at the subject efficiently. The resulting report can then be a big help to you in planning the larger project: it reveals the bare bones of the whole, it enables you to narrow the subject and draw up a preliminary bibliography, and it helps you focus and organize both your research and the final essay.

Here is a list of historical events of various times, kinds, scope, and complexity. Choose one of them that interests you, and do enough preliminary research on it to enable you to present a summary report. Aim for between 750 and 1000 words. You'll have to be selective and economical. And even for this preliminary report, you'll probably want to go beyond general reference books. In any event, include full documentation of your sources. And use at least five.

| | |
|---|---|
| the first conquest of Mt. Everest | founding the Red River Settlement |
| the Alaska boundary dispute | the raid on Dieppe |
| the Boxer Rebellion | Scott in the Antarctic |
| the South Sea Bubble | the end of the British Raj |
| the Plains of Abraham | the expulsion of the Acadians |

| | |
|---|---|
| putting the first men on the moon | the Boer War |
| the Charge of the Light Brigade | the Industrial Revolution |
| the coming to power of the P.Q. | the defeat of the Spanish Armada |
| the mutiny on the *Bounty* | the Lisbon earthquake |
| the discovery of insulin | the 1837 rebellion |
| cleaning up Lake Erie | the battle of El Alamein |
| building the Aswan Dam | the Vikings in North America |
| deciphering the Rosetta Stone | Newfoundland joins confederation |

*Note:* These are large subjects. Most of them have had whole books written about them. In your report, you will have to either

(a) present a broad overview of the whole subject, or
(b) sketch in the whole event, but focus on a small segment of it.

Decide upon which of these two tacks you're going to take by first deciding upon your audience and your purpose. Are you going to enlighten a new generation about something important that happened in the past, or are you going to analyze part of something that happened in order to make a point about it to readers who already know the general outline?

## Essay 14C

Choose a three-year period from 1750 to 1900 and prepare a report on what was happening in one of the following areas of interest or activity (length, about five pages or 1200 words):

| | | |
|---|---|---|
| advertising | fashion | penology |
| agriculture | geography | philosophy |
| architecture | law | police work |
| banking/finance | literature | psychology |
| commerce | marriage | religion |
| dentistry | mathematics | science |
| drama | medicine | social work |
| exploration/travel | music | technology |
| education | painting | transportation |

Of course you will need to narrow all of these subjects, some more substantially than others. Only a list would result if, for example, you were to choose the subject of technology from 1873 to 1876. But you could provide an adequate report on, say, telegraphy or shipbuilding in those years. After exploring the area generally, try to focus your research efforts with a specific thesis question.

Use at least five sources, with at least one from each of the following kinds: a reference work, a general book, a journal article, and an essay in a collection.

## Essay 14D

(a) Choose a year from recent history, but before your own time—perhaps the year of your parents' or your grandparents' marriage, or the year one of them was born, or the year of an ancestor's arrival in this country. Research that year thoroughly, and then write up a "portrait" of it. You may decide to focus on one or two kinds of events—for example those in politics, the arts, science—but even then try also to give a sense of the year as a whole.

(b) Do the same thing for the *day* of your own birth. How does your research differ from what you did for (a)? Is it harder, or easier?

## Essay 14E

Write a report on the origin and meaning of the name *Canada*.

## Essay 14F

When you have studied the process and the principles discussed in this chapter, select an appropriate subject and compose a full-scale research paper of between 10 and 20 pages (2500-5000 words). You may want to use one of the topics you arrived at for Exercise 14A (p. 351).

---

## Playing with Language 14A

Write a short research essay, or perhaps a short story, explaining the meaning of your own name (surname, or given name, or both). Provide proper documentation for all the sources you use. There are many books about names and naming.

## Playing with Language 14B

Said W.C. Fields in one of his films: "I'll bend every effort. I come from a long line of effort benders." Select five or ten metaphorical clichés from your ever-growing list and use them in sentences that treat them literally. Try to write sentences that are not only funny in themselves but that make fun of the cliché as well. For example, have you ever heard of a town named "Dire Straits"? What might you do with a phrase like *the road to recovery*?

## Playing with Language 14C

Find and read Jonathan Swift's "A Modest Proposal"—probably the best and best-known piece of irony in English. Study its techniques, and then write a "modest proposal" of your own. You'll probably do best to choose a less drastic subject than Swift's—perhaps something of local interest. Even topics so simple as parking regulations on campus, or the nature of residence cafeteria food, can make good modest-proposal topics.

Like Swift, create a *persona* for yourself; wear a mask; create a character as your speaker, and keep that character and its point of view consistent throughout. Propose some action or plan that is just the opposite of what you really think should be done—but, like Swift, find some way to smuggle your real, non-ironic recommendations into the piece. It need not be a long essay; indeed, small "modest proposals" turn up quite often in Letters to the Editor.

---

*Reading maketh a full man,
conference a ready man, and
writing an exact man.*
(Francis Bacon)

## CHAPTER XV
# Samples of Writing

The pieces that follow are intended to illustrate several different kinds of writing done for different kinds of occasions, including standard forms for business letters and memos. All except the letters and memos were written by students. Number 1 is a short piece of personal, expressive writing. The three paragraphs of number 2 are a response to Exploration 4H and Playing with Language 7A (pp. 85 and 177). Numbers 3 and 4 are descriptive and narrative pieces working partly through contrast. Number 5 is the process paper whose early stages we refer to late in Chapter III and early in Chapter IV. Number 6 uses a personal experience to lend weight to a piece whose purpose is persuasion. Numbers 7 and 8 are on literary topics, one a paper on two poems (included) that uses comparison as an organizing principle, the other a tightly controlled analysis of the main character in a short story. Number 9 illustrates the basic principles of a research report (conciseness, clarity, and objectivity) and the name-date method of documentation. The rest are self-explanatory: 10 is a letter applying for a job; 11 and 12 are formal letters of protest and complaint; 13 and 14 are memos, the first highly informal, the second more formal.

These, along with the other pieces and excerpts in the book, constitute a variety of illustrative examples to focus on for a variety of purposes. Analyze and evaluate them, criticize and discuss them, use them as models insofar as they merit imitation; learn from them in all the ways you can.

**No. 1**

### Morning Lament

Mornings have never been my best time of day. In fact, if I want to get to a class or an appointment by nine-thirty, I have to take a flying leap at it from as far back as seven o'clock. No matter how well organized I think I'll be, no matter how well I've laid out clothes, breakfast, books the night before, something always seems to stop me before I can get out the door. If my plants don't need to be talked to, my landlady does; if I can find enough food for breakfast, there's nothing in the house for lunch. Or, if I manage to avoid all the usual pitfalls, then just as I scramble into my coat, the telephone rings. Sometimes I really believe my apartment conspires with the clock to make me late, especially toward the end of the week. Then it assumes the characteristics of an obstacle course. Everything sits on the floor in piles arranged chronologically from Monday to Thursday, each day being represented by a collection of discarded clothing, scrap paper, and empty lunch containers. As I hop, step, and jump from this pile to that, the back door recedes, mocking my efforts to escape, and I begin to make up apologies for being late again.

## No. 2

### Wineskin

Three basic parts—a sack, a nozzle, and a carrying cord—make up the wineskin. The sack is simply two pieces of deep-brown calf-skin sewn together in such a way that, when inflated, they form a curved bag: narrow at the neck but bulbous at the bottom. From the red carrying cord the sack hangs with its narrow neck pointing upward and the large portion arching downward and outward into a horizontal position. The cord itself is cyclical, the ends of its five-foot length being joined to form a loop that cradles rather than suspends the sack in place by means of six small leather loops sewn right into the sack's seam. Into the neck is screwed the black plastic nozzle that allows the wine to be squirted out in a fine stream. A black plastic cap dangling from a piece of red string tied around the neck of the bag can be screwed onto the nozzle to close it.

\* \* \*

Inflated, the wine sack's calf-skin walls taper in a rapid curve from a wide, bloated body up into a slender neck topped with a rigid nozzle. Stained a deep, blotchy brown, the suede-textured container rests, cradled, in the life-line loop of an endless red rope. For each of the many stains pocking its surface, I try to picture a setting in which the mark may have been made. The grey greasy area: I remember putting it down on the grimy platform at San Sebastian Central Station. And the rich red blotches spattered over the skin: the time we drank so much of its *vino tinto* contents, became slightly exuberant, and our spastic laughter caused us to splash wine, in sticky showers, over everything. And the round black spots from the hot fat that dripped off the sausage we'd roasted over a fire; and the chewing gum from the sidewalk; and the purple streak dripping down from the nozzle's nose—smeared with sweet, dribbling wine like the wino's chin.

### One Wineless Wineskin Waiting

Narration: what a laugh! I don't belong in a narrative—nothing's happened to me for months. I just hang here all day cradled in the rope he's slung over the wall-lamp at the end of the room. Nothing's happened for months; nothing will. I hang in front of this wooden cupboard door, directly under the lamp, and await my twice-daily "excitement." Two times a day—morning and evening—he comes over to the cupboard door, swings it back, and reaches in to pull out a large towel, a bar of soap, and a toothbrush. He then leaves the room, but returns in about ten minutes and puts the articles back on their shelves. The door is closed and I swing back into place, rocking in a pendulum motion, slowing to a gentle brushing of the grained wood, then stopping completely, to hang in stillness, left to my own reminiscences. Nothing else to do but think of old times. The times I'd be full and fat with his raunchy wine, bouncing off his swivelling hip, swinging from his bony shoulders... But now I'm filled with air while hanging in storage, and can only dream. I hope he comes soon, for it's been a long night and cold. I heard his alarm ring; he should be getting up for his shower any minute now...

## No. 3

### A Forgotten Home

The old vacant house had lost its sturdiness over the years. The wood panels were loose, and the staircase was weak and eroded. Age had had its effect on everything. Only the skeleton of the house remained. Every room was empty and ramshackle. Odd fragments of worthless scrap lay scattered on the cold floor. Broken light bulbs, crumpled pieces of newspaper, and useless strips of wire were left behind. Debris that had loosened from the cracks in the tall ceilings also added to the small piles of rubble, and traces of dust and cobwebs clogged the corners. Time had yellowed the wallpaper and faded its roses, releasing a stagnant smell of mustiness that hung in the damp air. The windows, some broken with stones, were clouded with city dirt. The only light came through the windows, but the greyness of the wet afternoon offered little to brighten the gloom. Everything was half-hidden by the dinginess. A deadly silence lingered throughout the deserted rooms. Nothing moved and nothing could be heard in the stillness. The voices that once filled the house had now died.

## No. 4

### The Gift

Growing up in an isolated area, I spent much of my childhood alone, exploring wooded hillsides and shady creeks. My course never varied much: down the same trails, across the creek on the same log, or into the same secret hide-out, concealed by tall grasses and weeds. But for me, the terrain was as varied and exciting as if I were constantly exploring new ground. Sometimes I was a pioneer striking out for another land; sometimes, a pirate digging holes to bury fabulous treasure and making maps complete with false clues or code writing; and sometimes I was a cowgirl rounding up wild stallions that only I would ever ride. But in my favourite game I was an Indian, moving stealthily through the undergrowth beside shining waters, and pausing to rest in secret places that were all named with secret Indian names. Often, I crept silently across patches of moss and smooth pine needles into a sacred grove that always smelled of wet earth and decaying plant life. This was the burial ground of my ancestors, whose stories had been handed down by word of mouth, and whose legends were carved in totem poles—the trees I now stood under. I felt myself grow strong and Indian-proud as I told myself tales of brave deeds and happy celebrations. It seemed as though I had inherited this place from my people, the Indians; and in my reverence for them, I found a kind of silence, like soft breathing, that permeated the air and gently crept into my soul. I called it medicine and carried it away with me as a gift.

As children do when they grow up, I stopped playing those games, and forgot the names I gave to all my secret places. My imaginary world is only a memory now. But the gift: I still have it, and the medicine still works.

## No. 5

### How to Remain Sane While Writing Exams

Well, that time of year has rolled around again. You're still struggling over your term papers, and already Christmas exams are looming. You wonder how you can possibly find the time to do everything—let alone do everything well. Unfortunately, it's all too common for students to feel frustrated and oppressed at this time of year. But it doesn't have to be that way. Careful planning, along with a bit of pampering, can alleviate any pre-exam and exam-period jitters you may be feeling.

The most important step in preparing for the exam period is making a schedule. Decide what hours of the day you are going to study, and what courses you will study in these hours. Decide ahead of time which exams you have to study for most, and which least, and budget your time accordingly. And don't make the common mistake of putting off your least enjoyable course till last, for then it might get crowded out of your schedule altogether—and it may well be the one you need to work on hardest. Instead, put it high on your list, perhaps even first. Get it over with. Then you can enjoy the later stages of studying even more, and be in a better frame of mind when the exam period arrives. And be realistic! Don't plan to study fourteen hours a day if you know you will fall asleep after nine. And don't hesitate to reevaluate and change your schedule as you see your needs and expectations changing. But once you come up with what seems a suitable schedule, post it over your desk—and stick to it.

There are certain other necessities you must include in your schedule besides studying: sleep, food, and exercise. In general, it is wiser to rise at seven and go to bed at eleven than to get up at noon and go to bed in the middle of the night. Because exams are often scheduled for the morning, it is a good idea to get used to being awake early in the day. But if you're one of those strange creatures who study best at night, go ahead. Just make sure you allow yourself adequate sleep—but be prepared to readjust your schedule before exams begin, so that you can be up bright (you hope) and early, if you need to be.

It is also important to eat well. For example, try not to succumb to exam-pressure bingeing. It might make you feel better at the moment, but in the long run you'll feel worse for it. On the other hand, absolutely do not skip meals in order to study: mental activity consumes a lot of energy, and you'll soon fizzle out if your body runs out of fuel.

And be sure you allocate time for physical activity, preferably out of doors. "Fresh air and plenty of exercise" may sound like an old cliché, but there's good sense in it. Not only will you give your body a good stretch, but you will also clear your tired mind and vent any pent-up frustrations.

Finally, it may not be essential, but I think it is decidedly worthwhile to pamper yourself a little during your long weeks and even your hard final days of studying. A little self-administered TLC never hurt anyone. Take a break. Take frequent breaks. It is kinder to your body, and your mind, to break ten minutes every hour than thirty minutes every three hours. And treat yourself by planning at least one bright spot for each day. Arrange to meet a friend for coffee or tea, or soak in a bath full of bubbles. These interludes don't have to last more than fifteen minutes, and I guarantee you will feel happier and more relaxed as a result of them. Even go to a movie the night before an exam; that will do you more good than trying to cram all night.

By following these suggestions, and conscientiously applying yourself to your studies, you should be able to walk into any examination room feeling calm and confident. Good luck. And remember, you're not the only one in this position: an exam is always more pleasant—or less unpleasant—if you don't regard it as your own personal plague.

## No. 6

### Blood Line

"Victim: one who suffers from a harmful agency; one who is cheated and duped." Now, read this definition once more and ask who this victim could be. Could it be you? It was almost me. Last summer I came close to being cheated of my life by something that can make victims of us all—bleeding. Bleeding is a universal killer: it can strike down anyone at any time. No one can be promised that disease or accident won't claim the life in his veins, because every human body is a potential bleeder and can bleed to death if other people do not offer their help.

I did not die from last summer's automobile accident: there was enough blood available to replace what I had lost. But what if there had been no blood supply? How likely is it that someone will die because of a blood shortage? No one can answer this question definitely, but I do know that there is seldom more than a two-or three-day blood reserve available to the eighty-some hospitals in B.C. and the Yukon. And who can know if this will be enough to provide for all unexpected emergencies? One statutory holiday alone drains this reserve to nearly nothing because of the increase in accidents. Canadian hospitals depend on the Red Cross Society for blood, and the Red Cross depends entirely on volunteer donors. But a mere five percent of the population struggles to keep this small reserve on hand. More people need to be aware of the importance of donating blood. It is not a painful procedure. The Red Cross assistants are professional people and make donors feel as comfortable as possible. It is not a lengthy procedure. It requires only thirty minutes every three months. Maybe if those who do not donate blood were to meet a few bleeders they might recognize the seriousness of donating—the seriousness of saving people.

Meet Joey. He's five years old and has no cavities. That's right, no cavities. But after his visit to the dentist today three pints of blood had to be pumped into him. Oh, the dentist was a nice man, but his metal pick missed Joey's tooth and cut his gum. Joey is a hemophiliac—a bleeder. Two hundred or more hemophiliacs reside in B.C. alone. These frequent bleeders are in continual need of large amounts of blood. Because their blood lacks a clotting substance called cryoprecipitate, even a small cut could cause death. But cryoprecipitate is easily separated from fresh blood and administered to people like Joey who live in constant fear of hemorrhaging. The slightest bump or fall can bruise their bodies and cause internal bleeding. Joey's first big lesson was not how to use the toilet seat, but rather how to tell his parents when and where he feels pain. These victims must always be alert to signs of pain and swelling so that they can get treatment before it is too late. Such bleeders are given their lives back again and again by people who accept the responsibility of sharing blood. If Joey falls out of bed tonight, blood donors will save his life.

Meet Cindy. She's three years old and might not live to be as old as Joey. Her fragile veins could literally spring leaks at any time. She wasn't born with lympho-blastic leukemia but was diagnosed last month as being infested with this acute cancer. Cancer is the number two killer of kids. It is second only to accidents. Though medical researchers have discovered a few treatments for Cindy, they have found no cures. She, and all other cancer kids, will die if blood is not provided. Platelets can be taken from normal, healthy blood to patch the holes in Cindy's veins.

But children are not the only ones susceptible to cancer. Chronic leukemia attacks the elderly while non-lymphoblastic leukemia steals the prime of life from young adults. Anyone is a candidate for this monster who creeps into your veins. Your grandma, your mom, or even you yourself could wake up tomorrow dependent on the Red Cross's volunteer blood service for life.

The next person I would like to introduce is me—the accident victim. More lives are threatened by this cause of bleeding than by anything else. Poor road conditions, poor weather conditions, and poor drivers are just a few hazards that can cause the smashing and crushing of machine against machine. But it is not just automobile accidents that will spill enough blood to kill: the flesh will open to any hard or sharp object. No specific age group or nationality is more prone than another to this cause of bleeding. It's not hereditary or linked to one sex. Any body can bleed.

To meet these and increasing blood needs, the Red Cross must depend on an increase in blood donations. Two thousand eight hundred units of blood are already needed each week for the bleeders who fill B.C and Yukon hospitals—who knows how much more will be needed if the number of emergencies climbs past what is expected? Blood cannot be quickly manufactured if calculations are slightly wrong and our small reserve runs dry. But no one can be forced to put away a spare pint for emergencies either. We can only hope that each day there will be enough donors keeping the lifeline out to bleeding victims by keeping the blood line strong.

**No. 7**                     **Nurse's Song**

When the voices of children are heard on the green
And laughing is heard on the hill,
My heart is at rest within my breast
And every thing else is still.

"Then come home, my children, the sun is gone down
And the dews of night arise;
Come, come, leave off play, and let us away
Till the morning appears in the skies."

"No no let us play, for it is yet day
And we cannot go to sleep;
Besides, in the sky the little birds fly
And the hills are all cover'd with sheep."

"Well well go & play till the light fades away
And then go home to bed."
The little ones leaped & shouted & laugh'd
And all the hills ecchoed.

*(Songs of Innocence)*

## NURSE'S Song

When the voices of children are heard on the green
And whisprings are in the dale:
The days of my youth rise fresh in my mind,
My face turns green and pale.

Then come home my children, the sun is gone down
And the dews of night arise.
Your spring & your day are wasted in play
And your winter and night in disguise.

(*Songs of Experience*)

## The Two Worlds of the Nurse's Songs

The complementary, paired poems in William Blake's *Songs of Innocence* and *Songs of Experience* offer contrasting visions of similar events. The contrasts are evident even in what might be thought of as minor elements. Take for example the two poems entitled "Nurse's Song." The settings of the two poems seem at first glance to be the same. In each there is an action, children playing on a green; and there is an onlooker and speaker, a nursemaid. But Blake refers to the children only indirectly, saying that their voices "are heard." He offers little if any visual picture. The passive voice suggests that the main action is not the children playing but a viewer perceiving. The settings, therefore, are different: they are in the perceptions of the two completely different viewers—or the same viewer overheard at two quite different times.

In Innocence, the action of perceiving dissolves the separate entity of the nurse and absorbs her into the scene. When her "heart is at rest" she seems almost to fade out of the picture. It is the laughter and shouting of the children that we are left with at the end. In Experience, we are faced with a double world from the beginning. Instead of disappearing, the perceiver grows larger. Her lost youth and her green, pale face rise into the poem in the first stanza. In the second and final stanza, this frightened, jealous being pours malice over the initial scene.

Throughout the two poems, Blake's imagery and description consistently set up two opposed worlds. In the second lines "laughing" and "whisprings," respectively, provide the overtones for each poem. Laughter, especially children's laughter, implies unrestrained joy. Whispering suggests repression, the restraining of the natural voice. Also, the "laughing" of Innocence clearly originates with the children. The "whisprings," however, are left disembodied, emanating mysteriously from the dale. The expansive and embracing world of spring, with its sheep and birds, creatures appropriate to Innocence and joy, gives way to the barren winter of Experience, its cramped and excluding character suggested by the second poem's being only half the length of the first. Even the contrasting use of a hill in one poem and a dale in the other, especially a secretive, less than visible dale, has its implications.

The peace and tranquillity induced in the nurse of Innocence, and the stillness of "every thing else," are contrasted in Experience with the rise of a world from the past that causes unpleasant physiological changes (line 4). The unity and harmony of Innocence is contrasted with the duality, the self-consciousness, and the fear and jealousy of Experience.

**414**  *Elements of Writing*

Different senses of time are also contrasted in these poems. In Innocence, the moment seems eternal. There are hints of a night to come, but in the children's world "it is yet day," even though "the sun is gone down / And the dews of night arise"; day and night are entirely different and mutually exclusive worlds. The children will evidently go "away" to "sleep" "Till the morning appears in the skies," thus avoiding the night world altogether. But unlike in Innocence, where the night is kept offstage, in Experience night is given equal billing with day and coupled with winter to give it an ominous, harsh character; "winter and night" even seem to subsume "spring" and "day." In Experience, "days" from the past arise, clouding the present with jealousy and fear: the two poems contrast the endless day of Innocence with a day that knows other days and knows of a bitter night to come.

## No. 8

### The Metamorphosis of Brian Halligan

In "The Religion of the Country," Jack Hodgins has cleverly traced the metamorphosis of the main character, Brian Halligan. At the beginning of the story, Halligan is a typical British immigrant who has come out to the colonies to make his fortune while dispensing suitable amounts of culture to the natives of Vancouver Island, where he opens a bookstore. His character at this point in the story is all sensitivity and sensibility as he scorns the boorish behaviour and crass materialism of those around him in an effort to fend off "vulgarianism."[1] He is highly critical of the townspeople around him, complaining that

> "They waste their lives accumulating things, grabbing and hoarding, fighting over bits of land and stabbing each other in the back to get ahead. And if they have any spare time you'd never catch them reading a book, they're off somewhere in the mountains shooting animals or killing fish." (p. 99)

All this is particularly painful for him because it affects his revenue from book sales. Because of his penchant for culture, which is his bulwark against "the logger and coalminer mentality of the island" (p. 98), at the age of thirty-six he still has a great deal to learn about earning a living. According to Halligan, "...the only reason he was not a financial success was that he refused to embrace the values of the people he lived amongst" (p. 100). One might call these "values" he refuses to embrace survival skills.

Although his aptitude for survival, Vancouver Island style, leaves much to be desired, he does display a commitment to his mother, whom he visits in Ireland shortly after she informs him of his father's death. Otherwise, his relations with women are at about the same stage of development as his business acumen. "He was thirty-six and still poor, and still very much alone..." (p. 100). Eventually he is wooed and, rather to his surprise, won by a determined hotel owner named Babe, and it is at this point that Halligan begins to emerge from his cultured cocoon. His marriage to the rough-and-ready Babe is the turning point in his way of thinking. Because Babe shows a distinct talent for making money and is a competent teacher,

---

[1] Jack Hodgins, *Spit Delaney's Island* (1976), Laurentian Library edition (Toronto: Macmillan of Canada, 1977), p. 98. Subsequent references will appear in parentheses in the text.

Halligan's book store and newly added record shop become profitable and he begins to dabble successfully in real estate. While developing his entrepreneurial skills, however, Halligan loses most of his previous sensitivity and becomes quite cold-hearted—as we see from his refusal to go to Ireland to attend his mother's funeral. The story's final sentence puts it succinctly: "Land development was a cut-throat business, he said, and there was no room in it for sentiment" (p. 114). Halligan has become a different person. Previously, he "never failed to make the proper expected gesture" (p. 98); now, he could scarcely be bothered.

Generally, a reader questions the credibility of a character whose whole way of thinking undergoes such a complete metamorphosis within a short space of time. But the question doesn't arise as we follow the changing character of Brian Halligan in "The Religion of the Country." Halligan, who changes from a passive bookstore owner into an aggressive land developer, is at all times an easily identifiable and completely believable character.

## No. 9

### On Appropriate Assertiveness
### Introduction

Assertiveness is a means to effective communication. Originated in 1949 by Salter and developed in the 1960's by Wolpe and Lazarus, assertiveness training has since become highly popular with teachers, administrators, and people in business—with people who want not only to improve their relations with others, but to increase their ability to influence others. But behavioural scientists, in their research on what assertiveness is and what its effects are, have identified—along with the benefits—several problems either induced by or related to its use.

### Defining Assertiveness

Most of the literature agrees on the theoretical principles of assertiveness. Unlike the dictionary definition, it not only distinguishes between assertion and aggression, but also contrasts them with non-assertiveness: aggressive people fight while non-assertive people take flight—but assertive people stand their ground (Lange and Jakubowski, 1977).

Assertiveness has been more particularly defined according to various systems developed by researchers, for example the Galassi et al (1974) "College Self-expression Scale" and the Rathus (1973) "30-Item Schedule for Assessing Assertive Behaviour." Eisler, Hersen, and Miller (1973) use eight criteria to evaluate behaviour for assertive content: duration of looking and of reply, latency of response, loudness and intonation of speech, content requesting new behaviour or compliance, and overall assertiveness. Elsewhere they explain that assertive people "respond to the interpersonal problems quickly and in a strongly audible voice with marked intonation" and that they "are more likely [than non-assertive people] to request that the interpersonal partner change his behaviour" (Eisler, Miller, and Hersen, 1973, p. 299). This would seem to mean that they are impatient, loud, and domineering—but appropriate assertiveness is not so harsh as all that.

### Why Assertiveness?

Nivens contends that "a primary purpose of assertiveness is to increase and encourage further dialog," a goal not achievable, she claims, with either aggressive or non-assertive behaviour (1978, p. 5). Others use assertiveness to combat, or at least to modify, undesirable behaviour in another person. Canter and 20,000 teachers trained by him (1979a) use components of assertiveness to form what he calls "a competency-based approach to discipline" (1979b, p. 11).

Encouraging dialogue, establishing discipline, modifying behaviour—all these functions are summed up by Lazarus. He divides assertive behaviour into four abilities, "four separate and specific response patterns":

...the ability to say no;
the ability to ask for favors and make requests;
the ability to express positive and negative feelings;
the ability to initiate, continue, and terminate
   general conversations. (1973, p. 697)

Those who try to act assertively without all four of these abilities, Lazarus warns, often fail to elicit the reactions they want from others. Imbalanced assertiveness is inappropriate, and inappropriate assertiveness exacerbates problems and precludes effective communication.

## Problems with Assertiveness

I here list and explain the problems without reference to possible solutions, since I address these collectively in the next section.

### The complementary-personality phenomenon:

In mating and dating, it has been said, opposites attract. Battistich reports that this kind of behaviour was observable in the subjects of his study, who were required to rate assertive people according to predetermined criteria. The results confirmed the expected reaction: In general, the subjects rated those people highest who "appeared to have a complementary personality...." "Dominant" subjects, for example, "liked the submissive characters more than the assertive characters" (1980, pp. 7, 8).

### Abuses of assertiveness:

There is little question about the power of assertiveness; that is well documented. But this power can easily be abused, as Lazarus noted nearly a decade ago: "People are being programmed to mete out punishment, to deal with their intimates as adversaries, to ignore the needs of others, and to make a fetish of gaining the upper hand" (1973, p. 698). And later, in the preface to an assertiveness-training text, he writes that "Some compulsively 'assertive' individuals go through life busily chalking up interpersonal 'victories' while remaining puzzled by their consequent lack of emotional intimacy." He concludes that "There are many circumstances when wisdom decrees that *unassertive* behaviors are more adaptive than assertive responses" (in Lange and Jakubowski, 1977, p. xvii).

The most common abuse is not intentional, but rather occurs through ignorance. Of Lazarus's four "abilities," many training courses teach only one. "Assertiveness" as often taught, then, is not "assertiveness" as researchers define it in the literature. Lazarus's study shows that "the degree of generalization... from one assertive area to another is very slight" (1973, p. 697). Someone may become quite capable with "combat" assertiveness, for example, but will jeopardize any beginnings of a good relationship by failing to assert reinforcing, loving, or caring messages.

## Prepackaged methods:

Lange and Jakubowski criticize certain packaged, ready-to-use "pseudo-assertive" methods. "Fogging," a technique labelled by Smith (1975), is a way of undercutting an aggressor's offensiveness by unexpectedly agreeing that the agressor is "probably right." Fogging is based on the valid assumption that aggressiveness cannot thrive in the absence of a challenge or rebuttal. But fogging lacks many of the components of true assertive behaviour; and though its efficacy is not in question, its effects are. Lange and Jakubowski warn that it is not an honest, forthright response, that—although sometimes successful—it can often be "countermanipulative" (1977, p 38).

They also warn the prospective trainee about the "broken record" technique (Smith, 1975)—a tactic which an assertor can use when a stubborn subject fails to react as desired. The assertor, barely acknowleding any opposing arguments, simply repeats his assertion over and over, refusing to be distracted, until either he is successful or good timing dictates that he stop; he in effect forces the misbehaving subject to choose between complying and suffering some negative consequences. Their warning is that "improperly carried out, broken record can easily become an aggressive manipulation in which the person using it fails to respond to the other person's legitimate points and steamrollers the other person" (1977, p. 34).

## Side effects:

Rathus, in pointing out that assertiveness is sometimes perverted to the point of being a "gratuitous expression of nastiness," concludes that "The social desirability of assertiveness is brought into question" (1973, p. 404). And Schnidman and Layne found that assertiveness training "may exert a deleterious effect upon personality structure" (1980, p. 19). These side effects exemplify the results of improper—or incomplete—methods of assertiveness training.

## The efficacy-satisfaction trade-off:

Hull and Schroeder give clear evidence that assertive people trade off respondents' satisfaction for their own efficacy. They report that assertiveness works better overall than either aggressive behaviour or non-assertiveness: (1) aggressive behaviour accomplishes goals, but causes poor relationship; (2) non-assertiveness is ineffective, but maintains good relationship; and (3) assertiveness achieves goals and causes a better relationship than does aggressiveness. Paradoxically, however, their subjects evaluated assertiveness both as "fair, assertive, non-revengeful, and friendly" and as "dominant, unsympathetic, and aggressive" (1979, p. 27). The research of Woolfolk and Dever (1979) produced similar results.

## Proven and Proposed Solutions

But Woolfolk and Dever also tested a new kind of behaviour: assertiveness applied with politeness, kindness, and empathy. This modification proved successful in achieving efficacy without compromising respondents' satisfaction. It appears that when mastered, and used properly, assertiveness is calm and simple, sincere and forthright; it generates an atmosphere of naturalness and common sense. Appropriate assertiveness promotes effective and satisfying communication in which "resentment and suspicion" are "decreased" (Galassi and Galassi, 1975, p. 353).

Perhaps understanding contributes the most to appropriateness. One must understand the other's needs before asserting one's own. One needs also to anticipate the effect of one's assertiveness, as Hull and Schroeder suggest (1979).

Lazarus claims that success results from "adaptive assertive response" (1973, p. 698). He recounts his experience with a "surly, brusque" shirt salesman. Instead of using "combat" assertiveness, he responded empathically: "You seem to be having a hell of a bad day. Is something wrong?" Since Lazarus was willing to participate in the salesman's emotions, the man was able to confide his concern about his wife's hospitalization, making reassurance possible. Lazarus succeeded in satisfying his own wants (assistance in his shirt-buying), and says the salesman "appeared immensely relieved and his entire demeanor changed" (1973, p. 698). For Lazarus, "*style* is all-important" (in Lange and Jakubowski, 1977, p. xvii).

For assertiveness to be appropriate, the assertor should be proficient in Lazarus's four abilities, the necessary components of assertiveness—a sort of flexibility in different circumstances, but always accentuating the positive. As the research of Woolfolk and Dever shows, the "negative effects of assertion were not present when an empathy and consideration component accompanied the effort..." (1979, p. 410). Also, Hull and Schroeder point out that "assertions which suggest compromise are frequently the most appropriate..." (1979, p. 28), an idea similar to Gordon's "no-lose" method of resolving conflicts (Gordon, 1974).

In summary, appropriate assertiveness is anticipative (Hull and Schroeder, 1979), adaptive (Lazarus, 1973), empathic and considerate (Woolfolk and Dever, 1979), and suggestive of compromise (Hull and Schroeder, 1979).

## Conclusion

Although it may seem largely a matter of simple common sense, appropriate assertiveness seldom, if ever, comes naturally. It is a way of communicating that involves values, concepts, and modes of behaviour which must be learned and practised—not as techniques of individual behaviour modification, discipline, or dialogue, but as parts of an integral approach to all interactions. And one can be appropriately assertive only by not trampling on the needs and wishes of others. Indeed, a properly assertive person will use his strengths more as prophylaxis than as remedy.

## References

Battistich, V.A. Personality and person perception: A person-situation analysis. Paper presented at the meeting of the American Psychological Association, Montreal, September 1980.

Canter, L. Assertive discipline: A competency based approach to discipline that works. Paper presented at the meeting of the Association for Supervision and Curriculum Development, March 1979. (a)

Canter, L. Competency-based approach to discipline—it's assertive. *Thrust for Educational Leadership*, 1979, *8* (3), 11-13. (b)

Eisler, R.M., Hersen, M., & Miller, P.M. Effects of modelling on components of assertive behavior. *Journal of Behavior Therapy and Experimental Psychiatry*, 1973, *4*, 1-6.

Eisler, R.M., Miller, P.M., & Herson, M. Components of assertive behavior. *Journal of Clinical Psychology*, 1973, *29*, 295-299.

Galassi, J.P., Delo, J.S., Galassi, M.D., & Bastein, S. The college self-expression scale: A measure of assertiveness. *Behavior Therapy*, 1974, *5*, 165-171.

Galassi, J.P., & Galassi, M.D. Relationship between assertiveness and aggressiveness. *Psychological Reports*, 1975, *36*, 352-354.

Gordon, T. *Teacher effectiveness training.* New York: Peter H. Wyden, 1974.

Hull, D.B., & Schroeder, H.E. Some interpersonal effects of assertion, nonassertion, and aggression. *Behavior Therapy,* 1979, *10,* 20-28.

Lange, A.J., & Jakubowski, P. *Responsible assertive behavior: Cognitive/behavioral procedures for trainers.* Champaign, Ill.: Research Press, 1977.

Lazarus, A.A. On assertive behavior: A brief note. *Behavior Therapy,* 1973, *4,* 697-699.

Nivens, M.K. Parent power: Assertive training as a tool for obtaining services for exceptional children. Paper presented at the meeting of the Alabama Association for Children with Learning Disabilities, Montgomery, Jan. 1978.

Rathus, S.A. A 30-item schedule for assessing assertive behavior. *Behavior Therapy,* 1973, *4,* 398-406.

Salter, A. *Conditioned reflex therapy.* New York: Putnam's, 1961. (Originally published, 1949.)

Schnidman, R.E., & Layne, C. A multi-modal assessment of didactic versus rehearsal group assertion training. Paper presented at the meeting of the Southeastern Psychological Association, Washington, March 1980.

Smith, M.J. *When I say no, I feel guilty.* New York: Dial Press, 1975.

Wolpe, J., & Lazarus, A.A. *Behavior therapy techniques: A guide to the treatment of neuroses.* New York: Pergamon Press, 1966.

Woolfolk, R.L., & Dever, S. Perceptions of assertion: An empirical analysis. *Behavior Therapy,* 1979, *10,* 404-411.

## No. 10

1164 N. Kitchener
Windsor, Ontario
February 24, 1984.

Mrs. A. Bonforte
Personnel Department
Moore and Bohnen, Ltd.
77 Industrial Way
Hamilton, Ontario

Dear Mrs. Bonforte:

Your February 20 advertisement in the *Globe and Mail* for a Junior Accountant caught my eye. I believe that my training and experience qualify me for the position.

Since July 1983 I have been working in the accounting department of a large industrial supply firm in Windsor. In the course of my work I have become familiar with several of the firm's accounting operations, for I have had the opportunity to work with several supervisors. Details are included in my résumé.

In addition, I am at present enrolled in the second year of the diploma program in accounting at Peninsula College, and I would appreciate having the opportunity to work for a diversified national organization like yours. I believe that my varied experience in accounting and computers would be useful to you.

My present salary is in the range of $1200/month, and I would like to improve it somewhat, but I realize that depends upon proof of my abilities.

. I enclose my résumé. If you would like to see me for an interview, I can arrange to come to your office almost any afternoon in March. I can be reached at 224-5341, or 271-7735 in the evenings.

Yours very truly,

Carl Emig

**No. 11**

336 Pearson Hall<br>10 July, 1983

Mrs. Ruth Marcus, Registrar
Administration Building
Northern Line College

Dear Mrs. Marcus:

I would like to protest the way your office processes receipts for the summer session.

When I registered for Economics 23 and paid my fee on June 12, the clerk did not give me an official receipt, but only a mimeographed slip with my name and the date, without any indication of the course and without a signature of any kind.

When I came to the first class on July 7, the instructor, Dr. Rhys (who has been teaching at Northern for eight years), explained that I can be enrolled in the class only when my name appears on the official list or when I present an official receipt. I do not know why my name was left off the list, nor why I have not received your official receipt.

I am anxious about my status in the course because the class is nearly full, and as far as Dr. Rhys can see, I am not registered, even though I signed up and paid my fees before the June 15 deadline. Four others in the class have received the same treatment, as we discovered on the first day of class.

I would like to protest your policy and to suggest that students be given an official form that is both dated and signed and that includes the name and number of the course they are enrolling in.

Dr. Rhys told me that he would be writing you as well. I hope you can implement such a change. It will save instructors unnecessary trouble and students unnecessary anxiety.

Yours truly,<br><br>Dale Schroeder<br>Student Number:<br>47 SCH 814

Copy to Dr. D.E. Rhys
Department of Economics

**No. 12**

1268 Duncan Avenue
Fredericton, N.B.
12 February, 1984

Sales Manager
Conlin's Stereo Studio
733 River Street
St. John, N.B.

Dear Sir or Madam:

I've been having trouble with the Mishi tape deck I bought from Conlin's.

Last March I purchased a Mishi MRC-7 stereo receiver with tape deck from Conlin's here in Fredericton. The receiver works fine, but the tape deck tends to run slow. Under your one-year warranty for all parts and labour, I have twice returned the set to the shop, hoping each time that the motor would be repaired. Both times, the tape seemed to work well for a couple of weeks, but then it started to slow down again.

Each time I was at the repair counter, I spoke to a different serviceman, the second time (the third week in January) to a man named Ted. When I telephoned the store yesterday, I was told that Ted no longer works there but that I should bring it in to see what could be done. I am reluctant to do so because of the two previous disappointments.

But I do want it fixed right. I will be in St. John for three days beginning March 3, and I would like to bring the set into your repair department at that time.

I would also like your written assurance that if I do, the set will be repaired to work the way it should, even if it takes until after March 16, when the warranty expires.

I originally purchased the Mishi set at Conlin's because of your strong reputation for quality and service. I am confident that this is a reputation you want to retain.

Yours truly,

Martin Leblanc

**No. 13**

## MEMO

TO: Mike Irwin                    FROM: Anna Donnelli
      Service Manager                    Sales Manager
                                                21 Feb. 1983

### White-glove repair job

I got a blast from a customer in Fredericton—unhappy about the tape drive on his MRC-7. Another of Tom's foul-ups.

Let's fix it, even if we have to send to Halifax for the drive.

He's coming in on March 3. Please leave a slot for MARTIN LEBLANC in your W/O schedule for that day. I've sent him a note saying we'll be happy to take care of it for him.

And no charge, even if he has to bring it in again here or in Fred. after the warranty, OK? Charge Sales for any extra parts.

Let's try to keep him happy.

Thanks<br>A

**No. 14**

MEMORANDUM

TO:   C.L. Thomas, President,           FROM:   Janet Prater
and the Executive
University Sailing Club                    September 22, 1983

Rules for the boat shed

I would like to see put on the agenda for the October meeting an item about implementing new rules for the boat shed.

Don Preisser and I went to the boat shed last Sunday afternoon at 3:00 to sail the R-17. We were surprised and annoyed to find the following:
- damp life jackets left in a pile in the corner,
- R-17 sails not properly stowed, but just stuffed into the sail locker,
- a half-eaten and smelly lunch under the bench, despite the notice about rats.

Up to now we've been able to get along on a general agreement, but since the club has grown so large that most of us don't know all the members, I'm afraid we need explicit rules that we all must follow or be kept out of the boat shed.

I look forward to (1) hearing that you and the executive have put this item on the agenda.
(2) a well-ordered boat shed.

# Glossary: A Selected Vocabulary of Writing

Here are some simplified definitions of the main terms of style and syntax, including most of those used in this book. Check the cross-references provided. (For punctuation marks, not included here, see Chapter XI.) For further details and other terms, consult a comprehensive handbook and a good dictionary.

**absolute**—a modifying phrase with no syntactical connection to the rest of the sentence: *Tail between its legs*, the dog slunk away. *It being Sunday*, they all slept in. *All things considered*, your health isn't bad. See Sentence-Combining 10.

**abstract**—not material, not perceptible by the physical senses, as ideas or qualities. Compare *concrete*, and see pp. 254-258.

**active voice**—see *voice*.

**adjective**—a "part of speech." Adjectives modify nouns and pronouns, usually answering the questions What? What kind of? How many? (*that* man, *large* meal, *abstract* noun, *three blind* mice, *fast* car; He was *ill*). See also *participle*.

**adverb**—a "part of speech." Adverbs modify verbs, adjectives, or other adverbs, usually answering the questions How? When? Where? Why? To what degree? (drive *slowly*, *stubbornly* persist, live *well*, go *now*, *mortally* ill, *very* quickly).

**agreement**—grammatical correspondence between verbs and their subjects or between pronouns and their antecedents. See pp. 213-214.

**alliteration**—the same beginning sound for adjacent words: **A**ll the **a**ardvarks **a**dvanced with **a**lacrity; **phr**enology is **f**oolish. See pp. 231-232 and Playing with Language 9C, pp. 243-244.

**antecedent**—"coming before": the word or phrase a pronoun refers (usually back) to.

**appositive**—a noun or noun phrase repeating the meaning of another: Anna, *the lawyer*; the watchman, *George Smith*; the meal, *a sumptuous repast*. See Sentence-Combining 5.

**article**—sometimes considered a "part of speech." The definite article *the* and the indefinite articles *a* and *an* are "markers" or "determiners" always followed by nouns: *a* boat, *an* athlete, *the* idea, *the* present government.

**assonance**—the same or similar vowel sounds in adjacent words, especially in stressed syllables: **a** b**u**nch of f**u**nny p**u**mped-**u**p companies.

**auxiliary**—a "helping" verb used with other verbs to form different tenses: *is* going, *will* go, *will be* going, *can* go, *should* go, *has* gone, *did* go, *must have* gone.

**case**—designating the forms of pronouns or nouns according to their function: subjective (or nominative) *he, they*; objective *him, them*; possessive *his, their, Susan's*.

**clause**—a group of words including a subject and a verb. A clause may be *independent*, capable of standing by itself as a simple sentence (*Dogs have fleas*), or *subordinate* (*dependent*). Subordinate clauses function as elements in complex sentences (Dogs have fleas, *which they scratch. When I itch,* I scratch).

**coherence**—the *sticking together*, the cohesion, the logical or mechanical connection between the parts of a piece of writing: words, sentences, paragraphs, sections.

**complement**—something that *completes* the meaning of a verb. Strictly, a complement is a noun, pronoun, or adjective that follows a linking verb: Sandra is a *consultant* (predicate noun); Jasper's report is *excellent* (predicate adjective). More broadly, complements also include objects which complete the meanings of verbs: We sent *him* (indirect object) a *copy* (direct object) of the book.

**complex sentence**—a sentence consisting of one independent clause and one or more subordinate clauses: *I know that she knows. She knows that I know that she knows.* See also p. 206.

**compound**—two or more like elements joined to function as a unit in a sentence: *Apollo* and *Hermes* were Greek gods (compound subject); people *feared* and *worshipped* them (compound predicate); they brought both *fortune* and *misfortune* (compound objects).

**compound sentence**—a sentence consisting of two or more independent clauses: *He commanded, and they obeyed. He came, he saw, he conquered.* See also p. 206.

**compound-complex sentence**—a sentence consisting of two or more independent clauses and one or more subordinate clauses: *He felt terrible, but the doctor assured him that he would soon be well.* See also p. 206.

**concrete**—perceptible by the physical senses. Compare *abstract*, and see pp. 245-248.

**conjunction**—a "part of speech." A *coordinating* conjunction (*and, but, or, nor, for, yet, so*) joins equal elements; a *subordinating* conjunction (*because, when, though, since*, etc.) joins unequal parts; *correlative* conjunctions (*not only ...but also, both...and, neither...nor*, etc.) link parallel pairs of sentence elements. See Sentence-Combining 1 and 2, and pp. 218-219, 235, 294-296.

**conjunctive adverb**—an adverb (*therefore, however, nevertheless*, etc.) used to connect independent clauses, but not equivalent to a coordinating conjunction. See pp. 294, 296-297.

**connotation**—the associative or suggestive meaning of a word. Compare *denotation*, and see pp. 247-248.

**consonance**—the same or similar consonant sounds within adjacent words, especially in stressed syllables: Intrepid had masterly control; what past imposters expressed; fussing over easily resolved issues. (When the repeated sound is that of *s*, the result is called *sibilance*.)

**contraction**—an informal or colloquial combining of two words, spelled with an apostrophe to mark the omitted letter: *there's* (there is), *isn't* (is not), *they're* (they are), *it's* (it is).

**coordination**—combining syntactical elements of equal weight or importance into a compound construction. See *compound, conjunction,* and Sentence-Combining 1.

**correlative**—see *conjunction.*

**dangling modifier**—a modifying phrase, usually participial (but sometimes a gerund, infinitive, prepositional, or appositive phrase), that has no proper word in the sentence to connect to logically and grammatically. See p. 211.

**demonstrative**—a word that in effect points: *That* is the man I saw; *this* is the car he stole; *these* are the bruises I received (demonstrative *pronouns*). *That* man is guilty; *this* car is rightfully mine; *these* bruises are evidence of his brutality (demonstrative *adjectives*).

**denotation**—the specific, direct meaning of a word. Compare *connotation*, and see pp. 247-248.

**dependent clause**—see *clause.*

**diction**—the choice and use of words; see Chapter X.

**direct object**—see *object.*

**ellipsis**—the spaced periods representing material omitted from a quotation. See pp. 372-373.

**etymology**—the origin and history of a word's form and meaning. The word *helicopter*, for example, was formed from the Greek roots *helix, helicos* (spiral) and *pteron* (wing). See Exercise 3D, p. 50, and Playing with Language 3B, p. 60.

**euphemism**—from the Greek *eu* (well) plus *phemizein, phanai* (to speak): the use of a mild or roundabout expression to avoid another felt to be too harsh or unpleasant. See pp. 274-275.

**gerund**—an *-ing* form of a verb, used as a noun: *Hiking* is good exercise. He tried *malingering.* See Sentence-Combining 9.

**grammar**—the systematic study and description of how the elements of a language operate in themselves and in relation to each other. (See *syntax.*)

**idiom**—an expression peculiar to a language, not always comprehensible from its construction and thus frequently not literally translatable, for example *put across* (an argument), *put up with.* See pp. 13-14, 100, 246-247.

**independent clause**—see *clause.*

**infinitive**—a verb form usually consisting of *to* and the basic form of the verb: *to go, to listen, to run.* Infinitives and infinitive phrases can function as nouns, adjectives, or adverbs. See Sentence-Combining 8.

**interjection**—a "part of speech" having no syntactical properties, but merely interjected into a sentence (It was, *well*, not so easy as I expected) or used by itself, often with an exclamation point (*Heavens! Ouch!*).

**intransitive verb**—see *verb.*

**irony**—a way of saying one thing while meaning something else, often just the opposite. For example a speaker might begin, "I don't wish to alarm anyone, but...," and then proceed to divulge some alarming statistics. Or consider the famous opening sentence of Jane Austen's *Pride and Prejudice*: "It is a truth universally acknowledged, that a single man in possession of a good fortune, must be in want of a wife." That is verbal irony. There can also be situational irony, as when expectations are aroused but unfulfilled, or when something happens at precisely the wrong moment.

**jargon**—strictly, the specialized technical vocabulary of a particular profession (legal *jargon*); broadly, unintelligible or confusing language, often familiarly referred to as gobbledygook, bafflegab, or—more specifically—bureaucratese, sociologese, educationese, etc.

**linking verb**—see *verb*.

**modifier**—a word, phrase, or subordinate clause that in some way describes, qualifies, or restricts another word or group of words. Adjectives modify nouns; adverbs modify verbs, adjectives, or other adverbs. An absolute construction can be thought of as modifying the rest of the sentence (a "sentence modifier"), as can occasionally a phrase or even a single adverb: *Ironically*, the equipment arrived just as we finished doing the job by hand.

**nonrestrictive modifier**—a word, a phrase, or (often) a relative clause that does not limit the meaning of the noun or pronoun it modifies; such a modifier is not essential to the meaning of the sentence and is therefore set off with commas. Compare *restrictive modifier*, and see Sentence-Combining 4 and 5, and pp. 302-305.

**noun**—a "part of speech." A noun names or stands for a person, place, thing, idea, quality, action, or the like. *Proper nouns* refer to particular persons, places, or things and are capitalized: *Ingrid, Halifax*, the *Panama Canal*, the *Challenger*. *Common nouns* refer to one or more members of a class of things or ideas: *woman, city, canal, spacecraft*.

**noun clause**—a subordinate clause used as a noun. See Sentence-Combining 6.

**number**—refers to either *singular* or *plural* as the form of a noun, pronoun, or verb.

**object**—a noun (whether word, phrase, or clause) or pronoun that receives the action of a transitive verb or completes a prepositional phrase. Objects of transitive verbs can be *direct* (Samantha snubbed *Roger*) or *indirect* (She gave *him* the air). The object of a preposition usually follows it (*on* the *table, under* a *cloud*), except sometimes in questions (*What* are you talking *about?*).

**participle**—a verb form ending in *-ing* (present participle) or, for regular verbs, *-ed* (past participle), used either as part of a verb with an auxiliary (*was running*) or, without an auxiliary, as an adjective (the *growing* crisis, the *engraved* invitation). See Sentence-Combining 7.

**parts of speech**—the eight categories into which traditional grammar divides words according to their function: noun, pronoun, verb, adjective, adverb, conjunction, preposition, interjection.

**passive voice**—see *voice*.

**person**—designates the form of a pronoun as referring to the speaker or speakers (first person: *I* write; *we* write), the one or ones spoken to (second person: *you* write), or the one or ones spoken about (third person: *she* writes; *he* writes; *they* write; *it* doesn't write). See pp. 213-215.

**phrase**—a group of words lacking a subject-verb combination; compare *clause*. Any group of words can loosely be called a phrase, but in discussions of writing the term usually refers to a group of words that functions as a syntactical unit, as a particular part of speech: a noun phrase, a verb phrase, an adjective phrase, an adverbial phrase.

**predicate**—the part of a sentence or clause that asserts something about the subject. The complete predicate consists of the verb and any complements, along with any modifiers of either.

**preposition**—a "part of speech." Prepositions are words like *into, of, on, among, about, under.* They are usually *pre-positioned*, put before the nouns or pronouns which are their objects.

**prepositional phrase**—a group of words consisting of a preposition and its object or objects, along with any modifiers. A prepositional phrase functions either adjectivally (The man *in the brown suit* spoke first) or adverbially (Algernon was sent *to the big house*). See Sentence-Combining 3.

**pronoun**—a "part of speech." A pronoun stands for or refers to a noun or another pronoun, its antecedent. Pronouns are personal (*I, me, my, you, she, her, his, they*, etc.), interrogative (*who, whom, which, what, whose*), relative (*who, whom, which, that, whose*), demonstrative (*this, these, that, those*), indefinite (*any, some, all, one*, etc.), reflexive or intensive (*myself, himself, themselves*, etc.), or reciprocal (*each other, one another*). See *agreement, antecedent, case, number, person.*

**relative clause**—an adjective clause usually introduced by a relative pronoun. See Sentence-Combining 4, and pp. 302-304.

**restrictive modifier**—a word, phrase, or (often) relative clause that, because it limits or identifies the meaning of the noun or pronoun it modifies, is essential to the meaning of the sentence and is therefore not set off with commas. Compare *nonrestrictive modifier*, and see Sentence-Combining 4 and 5, and pp. 302-305.

**sarcasm**—from the Greek *sarkazein* (to tear flesh): a cutting and obvious kind of irony whose purpose is to hurt, or at least cause discomfort, as when you might say to someone who has just spilled hot coffee in your lap: "My, you do have elegant serving techniques!" (See *irony.*)

**sentence**—a group of words constituting a satisfyingly complete utterance. Most sentences are *major* sentences, with one or more subject-verb combinations. But some sentences are *minor* sentences, lacking a subject-verb combination yet still expressing a complete thought. See also pp. 205-208.

**simple sentence**—a sentence consisting of a single independent clause: *Pollution kills.* Another: *Much radio and television advertising, by trying to make us want something unnecessary, or make us envious of our neighbours, or make us desire our neighbours to be envious of us, not only treats us as unintelligent bumpkins but also appeals to some of our basest instincts.* Long and complicated, but no subordinate clauses; therefore technically only a simple sentence. See also p. 206.

**subject**—the noun or pronoun, with modifiers, that constitutes the topic of a sentence and about which the predicate makes a statement or asks a question. A noun clause can function as a subject. See *predicate.*

**subordination**—combining syntactical elements of unequal weight or importance in a single sentence. See *conjunction* and Sentence-Combining 2.

**syntax**—the arrangement of words in sentences and the grammatical and other relations among them.

**tense**—the quality of a verb that indicates time; for example; Yesterday I *misunderstood* (past tense); Today I *understand* (present tense); Tomorrow I *will understand* even better (future tense).

**tone**—the attitude toward subject matter and audience that a writer's style and sentiments reveal. See *rhetorical stance*, pp. 5, 151-157.

**transitive verb**—see *verb*.

**unity**—the desired quality of oneness of a piece of writing that is about a single topic, with everything directed toward that topic, and without digressions.

**usage**—the customary way of using words and combinations of words in a given language; the conventions.

**verb**—a "part of speech." Verbs are those words in sentences that indicate action or assert existence or condition. Verbs may be *transitive*, taking a direct object (Melanie *hates* mathematics; Richard *lifts* weights), *intransitive*, requiring no object (Mark *relaxed* in the sun; Annette *snores*), or *linking*, requiring either a predicate noun or a predicate adjective as a complement (René *was* a journalist; Sally *is* ambidextrous). By far the most common linking verb is *be*.

**verbal**—a word formed from a verb but acting syntactically as another part of speech. See *gerund, infinitive,* and *participle*.

**voice**—the quality of a verb's being either *active* or *passive* in form. With a verb in the active voice, the subject of the sentence is performing the action (I *wrote* this sentence); with a verb in the passive voice, the subject of the sentence is being acted upon (This sentence *was written* by me). Active voice is almost always preferable to passive voice; see pp. 223-225.

# Index

coherence, 424
  of essays, 191-92
  between paragraphs, 183, 185, 191
  in paragraphs, 185-91 (*ex*, 190-91, 196-98)
  in sentences, 210-16 (*ex*, 216)
coined words, 265
colloquial style, 151-57
colloquialisms, 264 (*ex*, 264, 276-77)
colons, 289-90 (*ex*, 289, 310-11)
  in formal letters, 290
  misuse of, 290
  with quotations, 371
  spacing after, 317
combining sentences, 222 (*ex*, 222-23).
    *See also* sentence-combining.
comma fault. *See* comma splice.
commas, 287-89
  before *and* in a series, 300
  in dates, 288
  with direct address, 288
  before *for*, 295
  between independent clauses, 287, 292-97
  around interrupters, 301-305
  in letters, 288
  not between adjective and noun, 308
  not between subject and verb, 307-08
  not between verb and object, 308
  to show omissions, 289
  to set off parenthetical elements, 288
  in place-names, 288
  with quotations, 289
  in a series, 287-88, 300-01, 308
comma splice, 293-94, 296
"common knowledge," 361-62
common nouns, 426
common sense, in argument, 113-14
comparison and contrast, 75-81 (*ex*, 39, 77-78, 172, 173, 199, 277)
  in argument, 111
comparisons, faulty, 215, 216
complements, 424
  compound, 18-19
complex sentences, 39-41, 100-04, 206, 424
  as thesis statements, 93
compound adjectives, hyphens in, 320

compound complements, 18-19
compound numbers, hyphens in, 320
compound objects, 19, 424
compound predicates, 17-18, 424
compounds, 424
compound sentences, 15-17, 200, 424
  as thesis statements, 93
compound subjects, 424
  agreement of verb with, 213
compound-complex sentences, 206, 424
*comprise*, 250
conclusions, logical, as ending, 167-68
  in argument, 107-10
  *See also* endings.
concrete. *See* abstract and concrete.
conjunctions, 424
  coordinating, 15, 16-17, 17-19, 218-19, 294-96, 424
  correlative, 17, 235
conjunctive adverbs, 294, 296-97, 424
  punctuation with, 294, 296-97
connectors, 77, 186-88
  opening, punctuation with, 297-98
  *See also* transitional signals.
connotation, 247-48, 424, (*ex*, 248)
consonance, 424
context, defining by, 70
contractions, 152-57, 424
  spelling of, 320, 333
contrast, in beginnings, 164. *See also*
    comparison and contrast.
cooling-off period, 10, 147-48
coordinating conjunctions, 15, 16-17, 17-19, 218-19, 294-96, 424
  punctuation with, 294-96
coordination, 15-19, 424
  faulty or loose, 218-219
  *See also* subordination.
correction symbols for errors, 335-36
correlative conjunctions, 17, 424
  parallelism with, 235
cross-fertilizing (inventing), 52-53 (*ex*, 55, 58)

**D**

dangling modifiers, 211, 425
  with passive voice, 224-25

of paragraphs, 184-85
proportion of, to whole, 157-59
strategies for, 168-69
things to avoid in, 169-70
endnotes, 374. *See also* footnotes.
*enormity*, 249
*equally... as*, 249
errors, correction symbols for, 335-36
essays
broken-backed, 76-77
number of parts of, 65, 88
sample, 407-22, and *passim*
etymology, 425
inventing with, 47, 49 (*ex*, 50, 60-61)
euphemisms, 274-75, 425
evidence, in argument, 113
example and illustration, 66-68 (*ex*, 50,
68, 99, 172, 277)
in argument, 110
exclamation points, 285-86
for emphasis, 217
experience, personal, 67-68
expressive writing, 13 (*ex*, 13, 38, 57,
100)

**F**
fact, in argument, 112-13 (*ex*, 113)
*factor*, 273
fallacies, *See* logical fallacies.
faulty coordination, 218-19
faulty parallelism, 235-36
figurative language, 232-33, 326. *See also*
metaphors; personification.
final consonants before suffixes, 332
final draft, 12, 314-22
of research paper, 383-86
final *e* before suffixes, 332
final *y* before suffixes, 332
first draft, 6, 132-37 (*ex*, 139)
mechanics of, 137
of research paper, 359-63
flow charts, 8, 96
footnotes, 374-79
*for*, comma before, 295
foreign terms (*ex*, 329)
formal style, 151-57 (*ex*, 276-77)
forms and formats, 316-19
of research paper, 384-85

fragments, 206-08, 280
free-writing, 135
*fulsome*, 249
fused sentences. *See* run-on sentences.

**G**
gender, agreement in, 214
general and specific, 67 (*ex*, 50, 67, 277)
nouns, 153-57, 258
verbs, 258, 260-61 (*ex*, 261)
words, 254-58 (*ex*, 255, 257-58)
generalization, 66-67
genus and differentiae, defining by, 70-71
gerund phrases, 240-42
gerunds, 240-42, 425
possessives with, 242
glossary of terms, 423-28
grace
in diction, 264-67, 268-75
in sentences, 205, 228-33, 236-37
grammar, 425

**H**
hasty generalization, 115
*have*, 226 (*ex*, 239)
*he or she, he/she*, 214, 267-68
*him or her, him/her*, 214, 267-68
homophones, 332-33
*hopefully*, 251
*however*, 230-31, 297
punctuation with, 297
humour
in argument, 119-20
in beginnings, 164
in endings, 169
hyphens, 320-21
in compound adjectives, 320
in compound numbers, 320
suspension, 320-21
to prevent misreading, 320
in words for relatives, 320

**I**
idioms, 13-14, 100, 246-47, 421 (*ex*, see
inside front cover)
*ie/ei* (spelling), 332
illustration. *See* example and
illustration.